Curious Pursuits

ALSO BY MARGARET ATWOOD

FICTION
The Edible Woman (1969)
Surfacing (1972)
Lady Oracle (1976)
Dancing Girls (1977)
Life Before Man (1979)
Bodily Harm (1981)
Murder in the Dark (1983)
Bluebeard's Egg (1983)
The Handmaid's Tale (1985)
Cat's Eye (1988)
Wilderness Tips (1991)
Good Bones (1992)
The Robber Bride (1993)
Bones & Murder (1995)
Alias Grace (1996)
The Blind Assassin (2000)
Oryx and Crake (2003)

FOR CHILDREN
Up in the Tree (1978)
Anna's Pet [with Joyce Barkhouse] (1980)
For the Birds (1990)
Princess Prunella and the Purple Peanut (1995)

NON-FICTION
Survival: A Thematic Guide to Canadian Literature (1972)
Days of the Rebels 1815–1840 (1977)
Second Words (1982)
Strange Things: The Malevolent North in Canadian Literature (1996)
Two Solicitudes: Conversations [with Victor-Lévy Beaulieu] (1998)
Negotiating with the Dead: A Writer on Writing (2002)

POETRY
Double Persephone (1961)
The Circle Game (1966)
The Animals in That Country (1968)
The Journals of Susanna Moodie (1970)
Procedures for Underground (1970)
Power Politics (1971)
You Are Happy (1974)
Selected Poems (1976)
Two-Headed Poems (1978)
True Stories (1981)
Interlunar (1984)
Selected Poems II: Poems Selected and New 1976–1986 (1986)
Morning in the Burned House (1995)
Eating Fire: Selected Poetry 1965–1995 (1998)

Curious Pursuits

OCCASIONAL WRITING

1970–2005

MARGARET ATWOOD

Virago

VIRAGO

First published in Great Britain in May 2005 by Virago Press
Reprinted 2005

A CIP catalogue record for this book is available from the
British Library

ISBN 1 84408 149 4

Typeset in Spectrum by M Rules
Printed and bound in Great Britain by
Clays Ltd, St Ives plc

Virago Press
An imprint of
Time Warner Book Group UK
Brettenham House
Lancaster Place
London WC2E 7EN

www.virago.co.uk

For my family

Contents

General Introduction   xi

PART ONE: 1970–1989

Introduction 1970–1989   3
1   Travels Back   7
2   Review of *Diving into the Wreck: Poems 1971–1972*
     by Adrienne Rich   15
3   Review of *Anne Sexton: A Self-Portrait in Letters*   19
4   The Curse of Eve – Or, What I Learned in School   23
5   Northrop Frye Observed   37
6   Writing the Male Character   47
7   Wondering What It's Like to Be a Woman.
     Review of *The Witches of Eastwick* by John Updike   65
8   Introduction to *Roughing It in the Bush* by
     Susanna Moodie   71
9   Haunted by Their Nightmares. Review of *Beloved*
     by Toni Morrison   79
10   Writing Utopia   85
11   Great Aunts. From *Family Portraits: Remembrances by
     Twenty Distinguished Writers*   95
12   Introduction: Reading Blind. Introduction to
     The Best American Short Stories   109
13   The Public Woman as Honorary Man. Review of
     The Warrior Queens by Antonia Fraser   123

PART TWO: 1990–1999

Introduction 1990–1999   129

14   A Double-Bladed Knife: Subversive Laughter in Two Stories by Thomas King   131

15   Nine Beginnings. From *The Writer on Her Work, Volume 1*   143

16   A Slave to His Own Liberation. Review of *The General in His Labyrinth* by Gabriel García Márquez   151

17   Angela Carter: 1940–1992   155

18   Afterword to *Anne of Green Gables* by Lucy Maud Montgomery   159

19   Introduction: The Early Years. Introduction to *The Poetry of Gwendolyn MacEwen: The Early Years*   165

20   Spotty-Handed Villainesses: Problems of Female Bad Behaviour in the Creation of Literature   171

21   The Grunge Look. From *Writing Away: The PEN Canada Travel Anthology*   187

22   Not So Grimm: The Staying Power of Fairy Tales. Review of *From the Beast to the Blonde: On Fairy Tales and Their Tellers* by Marina Warner   197

23   'Little Chappies with Breasts.' Review of *An Experiment in Love* by Hilary Mantel   203

24   In Search of *Alias Grace*: On Writing Canadian Historical Fiction   209

25   Why I Love *The Night of the Hunter*   231

PART THREE: 2000–2005

Introduction 2000–2005   237

26   Pinteresque   241

27   Mordecai Richler: 1931–2001: Diogenes of Montreal   243

28   When Afghanistan Was at Peace   245

29   Introduction to *She* by H. Rider Haggard   249

30   Introduction to *Doctor Glas* by Hjalmar Söderberg   257

Contents   ix

31 Mystery Man: *Some clues to Dashiell Hammett*   263

32 Of Myths and Men. Review of *Atanarjuat: The Fast Runner*   277

33 Cops and Robbers. Review of *Tishomingo Blues* by
    Elmore Leonard   281

34 The Indelible Woman   293

35 The Queen of Quinkdom. Review of *The Birthday of the
    World and Other Stories* by Ursula K. Le Guin   297

36 Victory Gardens. Foreword to *A Breath of Fresh Air:
    Celebrating Nature and School Gardens* by Elise Houghton   309

37 Mortification. From *Mortifications: Writers' Stories of
    Their Public Shame*   317

38 Writing *Oryx and Crake*   321

39 Letter to America   325

40 Edinburgh and Its Festival   329

41 George Orwell: Some Personal Connections   333

42 Carol Shields, Who Died Last Week, Wrote Books
    That Were Full of Delights   341

43 He Springs Eternal. Review of *Hope Dies Last:
    Keeping the Faith in Difficult Times* by Studs Terkel   345

44 To Beechey Island. From *Solo: Writers on Pilgrimage*   359

45 Uncovered: An American *Iliad*. Review of *A Story
    as Sharp as a Knife: The Classical Haida Mythtellers and
    Their World* by Robert Bringhurst   369

46 Headscarves to Die For. Review of *Snow* by Orhan
    Pamuk   377

47 Ten Ways of Looking at *The Island of Doctor Moreau*   383

    Bibliography   397
    Acknowledgements   401
    Index   403

General Introduction

Curious Pursuits is a grab-bag of occasional pieces – that is, pieces written for specific occasions. Some of the occasions have been books written by other people, resulting in reviews and articles; some of them have been political in nature, resulting in journalism of various kinds; some of them – increasingly, as time has moved on – have been deaths, so I've often been asked to write obituaries at short notice and in odd locations. (The article on Carol Shields, for instance, was written on a moving train.)

Looking back over the decades, I find I've averaged about twenty of these pieces a year. I've spared the reader the political ephemera having to do with such things as mayoralty elections in Toronto, and the shame-on-you environmentalist pieces – most of them – and the Gilbert-and-Sullivan style parodies done for people's retirement celebrations, and the mangled pop songs performed by myself and whatever other stooges I could corral in order to raise money for such organizations as PEN. Canadians have a long tradition of making idiots of themselves in public for worthy causes, a tradition I stand firmly behind.

I began writing occasional pieces in the 1950s, when I was sixteen: I was the designated reporter for my school's Home and School Association meetings, and my accounts of these sometimes fraught events appeared in the mimeographed newsletter that was sent around to the parents to keep them informed on such topics as the proper length of girls' skirts. By this age I had decided to be a dedicated novelist – a very dedicated one, with the resulting lung illnesses, unhappy affairs, alcoholism, and early death that would surely follow – but I knew I would have to have a day job in order to afford the squalid flat and the absinthe, and this was my first foray into the humiliating world of turning out Grub Street hack work. Did I learn anything from this experience? I ought to have learned that for every tale there is a teller but also a listener, and that some jokes are not suitable for all occasions, but that particular lesson took a while to sink in.

Once at university, I took to producing book reviews and articles for the literary magazine – some of them under other names, since we liked to pretend, back then, that there were more people interested in the arts than there actually were. Like many young people I was demanding and intolerant, but I didn't let that show too much in the reviews, which are inclined to be amiably condescending, and to have too many long words and qualifying clauses in them. I continued with my reviewing after I'd graduated, and while I was attending the Harvard Graduate School in the 1960s, and while I was holding down various low-paying jobs and beginning to publish poetry and fiction in small magazines.

This collection does not begin at the beginning. The reader has been spared the mimeographed masterpieces and the lofty undergraduate pronouncements. The starting point is 1970, by which time I'd published two collections of poetry and a novel and could be described as 'award-winning' on the backs of books. The Women's Movement, in its later twentieth-century phase, had kicked off in 1968 and was now at full gallop, at least in North America, and any woman who'd ever set pen to paper was being viewed in a fresh light, the red-eyed hue of rabid feminism. Proponents adopted them, opponents attacked them; there was no neutral ground. Into this whirling vortex I was sucked, discovering many intriguing new worlds along the way.

And so it has continued. Eventually I found myself appearing in larger places such as *The New York Times*, and *The Washington Post*, and *The Times*, and *The New York Review of Books*, and the *Guardian*, but that took a while.

Looking back over this gathering of pages I see that my interests have remained fairly constant over the decades, although I like to believe their scope has broadened somewhat. Some of my earlier concerns – my environmental fretting, for example – were considered lunatic-fringe when I first voiced them, but have since moved to the centre of the stage. I dislike advocacy writing – it's not fun, because the issues that generate it are not fun – but I still feel compelled to do a certain amount of it anyway. The effects are not always pleasant, since what may be simple common sense to one person is annoying polemic to another.

Some of these pieces were originally lectures and speeches. I made my first speech at the age of ten; it was bad for me. I still have the stage fright in advance, during the writing of the speech. I'm haunted by a metaphor from Edith Wharton's story 'The Pelican,' in which a public lecturer's talk is compared to the trick by which a magician produces reams and reams of blank white paper out of his mouth. I still find book reviewing a problem: it's so much like homework, and it forces me to have opinions, instead of the Negative Capability that is so much more soothing to the digestion. I review anyway, because those who are reviewed must review in their turn, or the principle of reciprocity fails.

There's another reason, however: reviewing the work of others forces you to examine your own ethical and aesthetic tastes. What do we mean by 'good', in a book? What qualities do we consider 'bad', and why? Aren't there in fact two kinds of reviews, derived from two different ancestries? There's the newspaper review, which descends from gossip around the village well (loved her, hated him, and did you get a load of the shoes?). And then there's the 'academic' review, which descends from biblical exegesis and other traditions that involved the minute examination of sacred texts. This kind of analysis secretly believes that some texts are more sacred than others, and that the application of a magnifying glass or lemon juice will reveal hidden meanings. I've written both.

I don't review books I don't like, although to do so would doubtless be amusing for the Ms Hyde side of me and entertaining for the more malicious class of reader. But either the book is really bad, in which case no one should review it, or it's good but not my cup of tea, in which case someone else should review it. It's a great luxury not to be a professional full-time reviewer: I'm at liberty to close books that don't seize hold of me, without having to savage them in print. Over the years, history – military history included – has become more interesting to me; so has biography. As for fiction, some of my less high-falutin reading preferences (crime writing, science fiction) have come out of the closet.

Speaking of these, it's as well to mention a pattern that recurs in these pages. As one reader of this manuscript has pointed out, I have a habit of kicking off my discussion of a book or author or group of books by saying that I read it (or him, or her, or them) in the cellar when I was growing up; or that I came across them in the bookcase at home; or that I found them at the cottage; or that I took them out from the library. If these statements were metaphors I'd excise all of them except one, but they are simply snippets of my reading history. My justification for mentioning where and when I first read a book is that – as many other readers have observed – the impression a book makes on you is often tied to your age and circumstances at the time you read it, and your fondness for books you loved when young continues with you through your life.

I've divided *Curious Pursuits* into three sections. Part One covers the seventies and eighties, during which I wrote and published a number of volumes of poetry and several novels, including *The Handmaid's Tale*, the book of mine that's most likely to turn up on college reading lists. This was the period during which I graduated from being world-famous in Canada – as Mordecai Richler used to say – to being world-famous, sort of, in the way that writers are. (We're not talking The Rolling Stones here.) It ends with 1989, the year the Berlin Wall came down, thus ending the Cold War and causing all the men on the world's political chessboard to be set in rapid motion. Part Two collects pieces from the nineties – a sort of lull, during which some folk proclaimed the end of history, a bit prematurely – culminating in the year 1999, when the twentieth century ended. Part Three runs from 2000, year of the millennium when nothing exploded as expected, through 2001, when the unexpected 9/11 explosion rocked the world, and thus to the present time. Not surprisingly I found myself writing more about political issues during this last period than I had done for some time.

Why is this book called *Curious Pursuits*? 'Curious' describes both my habitual state of mind – a less kind word would be 'nosy' – as well as the subject matter of some of these writings. Like Alice, I've become curiouser and curiouser myself, and the world has done the same. Another way of putting it: if something doesn't arouse my curiosity, I'm not likely to write about it. Though perhaps 'curious' as a word carries too light a weight: my curiosities are (I hope) not idle ones. 'Passionate' might have been more accurate; however, it would have given a wrong impression, and disappointed a few men in raincoats.

As for 'pursuits', it's a noun that contains a verb. What can you ever do with reality but chase it around? You can't expect to capture it in any final way, because the thing keeps moving. Picture me then, butterfly net or popgun in hand, flapping over the fields with the elusive subject flitting away into the distance, or crouched behind the bushes in hopes of catching a glimpse.

A glimpse of what?

That's just it. You never know.

Part One

1970–1989

1970–1989

At the beginning of the 1970s I was living in London, in an area called Parson's Green – now gentrified, then in transition, which meant that the water froze in the kitchen when it was cold. Maxi-coats worn with long boots and crushed velvet miniskirts were the fashion; you could get these on the King's Road, which was still in full swing. That was a year that saw both an electricity strike and a garbage strike; both of which the Londoners seemed to enjoy.

It was here that I finished a book of poems called *Power Politics* and began a novel called *Surfacing*, using a typewriter with a German keyboard. Right after that I was in France (a sublet, in a town near St Tropez), where I wrote on a rented French key-board typewriter and conspired with the director Tony Richardson on a screenplay of my first novel, *The Edible Woman*. Shortly thereafter, I was in Italy – another sublet – where I fin-ished *Surfacing* on a typewriter with an Italian keyboard. There are some advantages to not really knowing how to type: the tran-sitions are easier.

I then returned to Toronto for two years on staff at universities – York and Toronto – and worked with a small literary publisher called House of Anansi Press. For them I edited the poetry list; I also put together *Survival*, a book on Canadian writing –

the first on this subject for a popular audience. The book was an immediate and huge success in the Canada of its day, as well as being 'controversial.' The combination of these factors, mixed with the ongoing Feminism furore, caused me to be attacked a lot.

Soon after that, I was to be found living on a farm with fellow-writer Graeme Gibson. We stayed there for nine years, working the farm in an energetic but not very financially rewarding way. We had a large kitchen garden and did a lot of canning. We even went so far as to make sauerkraut, a thing you should not do anywhere near your house. We had cows, chickens, geese, sheep, ducks, horses, cats, dogs, and peacocks, to name a few. Many of these we ate, our jolly meals punctuated by the sound of our bottles of home-made beer exploding in the cellar and Graeme's children asking if this was Susan on the plate.

In 1976 we had a baby, and when it came time for school and we realized that the child would have to spend two hours on a school bus every day, we moved into the city. During this period we lived in Edinburgh for a year, as Graeme was the Canadian half of the Scottish-Canadian writers' exchange. Edinburgh outdid London by having a truckers' strike, a collapse of the train tunnel to London, and a gritters' strike. We ate a lot of Brussels sprouts, salmon, and wool.

At this time I did my first book tour in Germany. We also went around the world on our way to the Adelaide Festival in Australia, taking our eighteen-month-old baby and stopping in Iran (the Shah would fall eight months later), Afghanistan (the civil war would start six weeks after our departure), and India, where our child learned to climb stairs at a hotel in Agra while we were visiting the Taj Mahal.

The years of the 1980s were energetic ones for me, and proved to be momentous for the world. At their beginning, the Soviet Union seemed firmly in place, due to last for a long while yet. But it had already been sucked into a costly and debilitating war in Afghanistan, and in 1989 the Berlin Wall would come tumbling down. It's amazing how quickly certain kinds of power structures crumble once the cornerstone falls out. But in 1980 nobody foresaw this outcome.

I began the period quietly enough. I was trying, unsuccessfully and for the second time, to write the book that was later to become *Cat's Eye*, and I was ruminating about *The Handmaid's Tale*, although I was avoiding this second book as much as possible: it seemed too hopeless a task, and too weird a concept.

Our family was now living in Toronto's Chinatown, in a row house that had been modernized by the removal of many of its inner doors. I couldn't write there because it was too noisy, so I would bicycle westward to the Portuguese district, where I wrote on the third floor of another row house. I'd just finished editing *The Oxford Book of Canadian Poetry in English*, which had been spread out all over the same third floor.

In the autumn of 1983 we went to England, where we rented a Norfolk manse said to be haunted by nuns in the parlour, a jolly cavalier in the dining room, and a headless woman in the kitchen. None of these were seen by us, though a jolly cavalier did stray in from the neighbouring pub, looking for the washroom. The phone was a pay phone outside the house, in a booth also used for storing potatoes, and I would clamber over and through these vegetables to deal with the editing of – for instance – the Updike review that appears here.

I wrote in a fisherman's cottage turned vacation home, where I struggled with the Aga heater as well as with the novel I'd started. I got my first case of chilblains doing this, but had to give up the novel when I found myself snarled up in the time sequence, with no way out.

Right after that we went to West Berlin, where, in the spring of 1984, I began *The Handmaid's Tale*. We made some side visits, to Poland, East Germany, and Czechoslovakia, which contributed to the atmosphere of the book: totalitarian dictatorships, however different the costumes, share the same climate of fear and silence.

I finished the book in the spring of 1985, when I was a Visiting Chair at the University of Alabama in Tuscaloosa. It was the last book I wrote on an electric typewriter. I faxed the chapters as they were finished to my typist in Toronto, to be re-typed properly, and I recall being amazed by the magic of instant transmission. *The Handmaid's Tale* came out in Canada in 1985 and in England and the United States in 1986, and was shortlisted for the Booker Prize, among other forms of uproar.

We spent part of 1987 in Australia, where I was finally able to come to grips with *Cat's Eye,* a novel I'd been struggling with for years. The snowiest scenes in the book were written during balmy spring days in Sydney, with cuckaburras yelling for hamburger on the back porch. The book was published in 1988 in Canada and the United States and in England in 1989, where it too was shortlisted for the Booker Prize. It was at this time that the fatwa was proclaimed against Salman Rushdie. Who knew that this was the first straw in what was to become not only a wind, but a hurricane?

All this time *The Handmaid's Tale* had been making its progress through the intestinal workings of the film industry. It finally emerged in finished form, scripted by Harold Pinter and directed by Volker Schlorndorff. The film premiered in the two Berlins in 1989, just as the Wall had fallen: you could buy pieces of it, with the coloured ones being more expensive. I went over for the festivities. There were the same kinds of border guards who had been so cold in 1984, but now they were grinning and exchanging cigars with tourists. The East Berlin audience was the more receptive to the film. 'This was our life,' one woman told me quietly.

How euphoric we felt, for a short time, in 1989. How dazed by the spectacle of the impossible made real. How wrong we were about the brave new world we were about to enter.

I

Travels Back

Three hours past midnight, Highway 17 between Ottawa and North Bay, November, I'm looking out the Greyhound bus window at the almost nothing I can see. Coffee taste still with me from the Ottawa station, where I was marooned for four hours because someone in Toronto mixed up the schedules; I sat writing letters and trying not to watch as the waitresses disposed of a tiny wizened drunk. 'I been all over the world, girlie,' he told them as they forced his coat on him, 'I been places you never seen.'

The headlights pick out asphalt, snow-salted road borders, dark trees as we lean round the frequent bends. What I picture is that we'll pass the motel, which they said was on the highway outside Renfrew – but *which* side? – and I'll have to walk, a mile maybe carrying the two suitcases full of my own books I'm lugging around because there may not be any bookstores, who in Toronto knows? A passing truck, Canadian Content squashed all over the road, later the police wondering what I was doing there anyway, as I am myself at this moment. Tomorrow at nine (nine!) I'm supposed to be giving a poetry reading in the Renfrew high school. Have fun in Renfrew, my friends in Toronto said with, I guess, irony before I left.

I'm thinking of summer, a swimming pool in France, an acquaintance of mine floating on his back and explaining why bank managers in Canada shouldn't be allowed to hang Group of Seven pictures on their walls – it's a false image, all nature, no people – while a clutch of assorted Europeans and Americans listen incredulously.

'I mean, *Canada*,' one of them drawls. 'I think they should give it to the United States, then it would be good. All except Quebec, they should give that to France. You should come and live here. I mean, you don't really live *there* any more.'

We get to Renfrew finally and I step off the bus into six inches of early snow. He was wrong, this if anywhere is where I live. Highway 17 was my first highway, I travelled along it six months after I was born, from Ottawa to North Bay and then to Temiskaming, and from there over a one-track dirt road into the bush. After that, twice a year, north when the ice went out, south when the snow came, the time between spent in tents; or in the cabin built by my father on a granite point a mile by water from a Quebec village so remote that the road went in only two years before I was born. The towns I've passed and will pass – Arnprior, Renfrew, Pembroke, Chalk River, Mattawa, the old gingerbread mansions in each of them built on lumber money and the assumption that the forest would never give out – they were landmarks, way stations. That was thirty years ago though and they've improved the highway, now there are motels. To me nothing but the darkness of the trees is familiar.

I didn't spend a full year in school until I was eleven. Americans usually find this account of my childhood – woodsy, isolated, nomadic – less surprising than do Canadians: after all, it's what the glossy magazine ads say Canada is supposed to be like. They're disappointed when they hear I've never lived in an igloo and my father doesn't say 'On, huskies!' like Sergeant Preston on the defunct (American) radio programme, but other than that they find me plausible enough. It's Canadians who raise eyebrows. Or rather the Torontonians. It's as though I'm a part of their own past they find disreputable or fake or just can't believe ever happened.

I've never read at a high school before. At first I'm terrified, I chew
Tums while the teacher introduces me, remembering the kinds of
things we used to do to visiting dignitaries when I was in high
school: rude whispers, noises, elastic bands and paper clips if we
could get away with it. Surely they've never heard of me and won't
be interested: we had no Canadian poetry in high school and not
much of anything else Canadian. In the first four years we studied
the Greeks and Romans and the Ancient Egyptians and the Kings
of England, and in the fifth we got Canada in a dull blue book that
was mostly about wheat. Once a year a frail old man would turn
up and read a poem about a crow; afterward he would sell his own
books (as I'm about to do), autographing them in his thin spidery
handwriting. That was Canadian poetry. I wonder if I look like
him, vulnerable, misplaced and redundant. Isn't the real action –
the *real* action – their football game this afternoon?

Question period: Do you have a message? Is your hair really like
that, or do you get it done? Where do you get the ideas? How long
does it take? What does it *mean*? Does it bother you, reading your
poems out loud like that? It would bother me. What is the
Canadian identity? Where can I send my poems? To get them
published.

They are all questions with answers, some short, some long.
What astonishes me is that they ask them at all, that they want to
talk: at my high school you didn't ask questions. And they *write*,
some of them. Inconceivable. It wasn't like that, I think, feeling
very old, in my day.

In Deep River I stay with my second cousin, a scientist with the
blue inhuman eyes, craggy domed forehead and hawk nose of my
maternal Nova Scotian relatives. He takes me through the Atomic
Research Plant, where he works; we wear white coats and socks to
keep from being contaminated and watch a metal claw moving
innocent-looking lethal items – pencils, a tin can, a Kleenex –
behind a 14-inch leaded glass window. 'Three minutes in there,' he
says, 'will kill you.' The fascination of invisible force.

After that we examine beaver damage on his property and he tells me stories about my grandfather, before there were cars and radios. I like these stories, I collect them from all my relatives, they give me a link, however tenuous, with the past and with a culture made up of people and their relationships and their ancestors rather than objects in a landscape. This trip I learn a new story: my grandfather's disastrous muskrat farm. It consisted of a fence built carefully around a swamp, the idea being that it would be easier to gather in the muskrats that way; though my cousin says he trapped more muskrat outside the fence than my grandfather ever did inside it. The enterprise failed when a farmer dumped out some of his apple spray upstream and the muskrats were extinguished; but the Depression hit and the bottom fell out of the muskrat market anyway. The fence is still there.

Most of the stories about my grandfather are success stories, but I add this one to my collection: when totems are hard to come by, failure stories have their place. 'Do you know,' I say to my cousin, repeating a piece of lore recently gleaned from my grandmother, 'that one of our ancestresses was doused as a witch?' That was in New England; whether she sank and was innocent or swam and was guilty isn't recorded.

Out his living-room window, across the Ottawa River, solid trees, is my place. More or less.

Freezing rain overnight; I make it to the next poetry reading pulling my suitcases on a toboggan two miles over thin ice.

I reach North Bay, an hour late because of the sleet. That evening I read at the Oddfellows' Hall, in the basement. The academics who have organized the reading are nervous, they think no one will come, there's never been a poetry reading in North Bay before. In a town where everyone's seen the movie, I tell them, you don't have to worry, and in fact they spent the first fifteen minutes bringing in extra chairs. These aren't students, there are all kinds of people, old ones, young ones, a friend of my mother's who used to stay with us in Quebec, a man whose uncle ran the fishing camp at the end of the lake . . .

In the afternoon I was interviewed for the local TV station by a stiff-spined man in a tight suit. 'What's this,' he said, dangling one of my books nonchalantly by the corner to show the viewers that poetry isn't his thing, he's virile really, 'a children's book?' I suggested that if he wanted to know what was inside it he might try reading it. He became enraged and said he had never been so insulted, and Jack McClelland hadn't been mean like that when *he* was in North Bay. In place of the interview they ran a feature on green noodles.

Later, thirty poetry readings later. Reading a poem in New York that has an outhouse in it and having to define outhouse (and having the two or three people come up furtively afterwards and say that they, too, once . . .). Meeting a man who has never seen a cow; who has never, in fact, been outside the city of New York. Talking then about whether there is indeed a difference between Canada and the US. (I been places you never seen . . .) Trying to explain, in Detroit, that in Canada for some strange reason it isn't just other poets who come to poetry readings. ('You mean . . . people like *our mothers* read poetry?') Having someone tell me that maybe what accounts for the 'strength' of my work is its fetching 'regional' qualities – 'you know, like Faulkner . . .'

In London, Ontario, the last poetry reading of the year and perhaps, I'm thinking, for ever, I'm beginning to feel like a phonograph. A lady: 'I've never felt less like a Canadian since all this nationalism came along.' Another lady, very old, with astonishing sharp eyes: 'Do you think in metaphor?' Someone else: 'What is the Canadian identity?' That seems to be on people's minds.

How to keep all this together in your head, my head. Because where I live is where everyone lives: it isn't just a place or a region, though it is also that (and I could have put in Vancouver and Montreal, where I lived for a year each, and Edmonton where I lived for two, and Lake Superior and Toronto . . .). It's a space composed of images, experiences, the weather, your own past and your ancestors', what people say and what they look like and how they react to what you're doing, important events and trivial ones, the connections among them not always obvious. The images come from outside, they are *there*, they are the things we live with and must deal with. But the judgements and the connections (what does it *mean*?) have to be made inside your head and they are made with words: good, bad, like, dislike, whether to go, whether to stay, whether to live there any more. For me that's partly what writing is: an exploration of where in reality I live.

I think Canada, more than most countries, is a place you choose to live in. It's easy for us to leave, and many of us have. There's the US and England, we've been taught more about their histories than our own, we can blend in, become permanent tourists. There's been a kind of standing invitation here to refuse authenticity to your actual experience, to think life can be meaningful or important only in 'real' places like New York or London or Paris. And it's a temptation: the swimming pool in France is nothing if not detached. The question is always, Why stay? and you have to answer that over and over.

I don't think Canada is 'better' than any other place, any more than I think Canadian literature is 'better'; I live in one and read the other for a simple reason: they are mine, with all the sense of territory that implies. Refusing to acknowledge where you come from – and that must include the noodle man and his hostilities, the anti-nationalist lady and her doubts – is an act of amputation: you may become free floating, a citizen of the world (and in what other country is that an ambition?) but only at the cost of arms, legs or heart. By discovering your place you discover yourself.

But there's another image, fact, coming from the outside that I have to fit in. This territory, this thing I have called 'mine', may not be mine much longer. Part of the much-sought Canadian identity is that few nationals have done a more enthusiastic job of selling their country than have Canadians. Of course there are buyers willing to exploit, as they say, our resources; there always are. It is our eagerness to sell that needs attention. Exploiting resources and developing potential are two different things: one is done from without by money, the other from within, by something I hesitate only for a moment to call love.

2

Review of *Diving into the Wreck*

This is Adrienne Rich's seventh book of poems, and it is an extraordinary one. When I first heard the author read from it, I felt as though the top of my head was being attacked, sometimes with an ice pick, sometimes with a blunter instrument: a hatchet or a hammer. The predominant emotions seemed to be anger and hatred, and these are certainly present; but when I read the poems later, they evoked a far more subtle reaction. *Diving into the Wreck* is one of those rare books that forces you to decide not just what you think about it; but what you think about yourself. It is a book that takes risks, and it forces the reader to take them also.

If Adrienne Rich were not a good poet, it would be easy to classify her as just another vocal Women's Libber, substituting polemic for poetry, simplistic messages for complex meanings. But she is a good poet, and her book is not a manifesto, though it subsumes manifestos; nor is it a proclamation, though it makes proclamations. It is instead a book of explorations, of travels. The wreck she is diving into, in the very strong title poem, is the wreck of obsolete myths, particularly myths about men and women. She is journeying to something that is already in the past, in order to discover for herself the reality behind the myth, 'the wreck and not the story of the wreck / the thing itself and not the myth'. What she

finds is part treasure and part corpse, and she also finds that she
herself is part of it, a 'half-destroyed instrument'. As explorer she
is detached; she carries a knife to cut her way in, cut structures
apart; a camera to record; and the book of myths itself, a book
which has hitherto had no place for explorers like herself.

This quest – the quest for something beyond myths, for the
truths about men and women, about the I and the You, the He and
the She, or more generally (in the references to wars and persecu-
tions of various kinds) about the powerless and the powerful – is
presented throughout the book through a sharp, clear style and
through metaphors which become their own myths. At their most
successful the poems move like dreams, simultaneously revealing
and alluding, disguising and concealing. The truth, it seems, is not
just what you find when you open a door: it is itself a door, which
the poet is always on the verge of going through.

The landscapes are diverse. The first poem, 'Trying to Talk with
a Man', occurs in a desert, a desert which is not only deprivation
and sterility, the place where everything except the essentials has
been discarded, but the place where bombs are tested. The 'I' and
the 'You' have given up all frivolities of their previous lives, 'suicide
notes' as well as 'love-letters', in order to undertake the risk of
changing the desert; but it becomes clear that the 'scenery' is
already 'condemned', that the bombs are not external threats but
internal ones. The poet realizes they are deceiving themselves,
'talking of the danger / as if it were not ourselves / as if we were test-
ing anything else'.

Like the wreck, the desert is already in the past, beyond salvation
though not beyond understanding, as is the landscape of 'Waking
in the Dark':

> The tragedy of sex
> lies around us, a woodlot
> the axes are sharpened for . . .
> Nothing will save this. I am alone,
>   kicking the last rotting logs

with their strange smell of life,
>   not death
wondering what on earth it all
>   might have become.

Given her view that the wreck, the desert, the woodlot cannot be redeemed, the task of the woman, the She, the powerless, is to concentrate not on fitting into the landscape but on redeeming herself, creating a new landscape, getting herself born:

. . . your mother dead and you
>   unborn
your two hands grasping your head
drawing it against the blade
>   of life
your nerves the nerves of a midwife
>   learning her trade
>   – from 'The Mirror in Which Two Are Seen as One'

The difficulty of doing this (the poet is, after all, still surrounded by the old condemned landscape and 'the evidence of damage' it has caused) is one of the major concerns of the book. Trying to see clearly and to record what has been seen – the rapes, the wars, the murders, the various kinds of violation and mutilation – is half of the poet's effort; for this she requires a third eye, an eye that can see pain with 'clarity'. The other half is to respond, and the response is anger; but it is a 'visionary anger', which hopefully will precede the ability to love.

These poems convince me most often when they are true to themselves as structures of words and images, when they resist the temptation to sloganize, when they don't preach at me. 'The words are purposes / the words are maps', Rich says, and I like them better when they are maps (though Rich would probably say the two depend on each other and I would probably agree). I respond less fully to poems like 'Rape' and references to the

Vietnam war – though their truth is undeniable – than I do to poems such as 'From a Survivor', and 'August' with its terrifying final image:

> His mind is too simple, I cannot go on
> sharing his nightmares
>
> My own are becoming clearer, they
> 　　　open
> into prehistory
> which looks like a village lit with
> 　　　blood
>
> where all the fathers are crying:
> 　　*My son is mine!*

It is not enough to state the truth; it must be imaged, imagined, and when Rich does this she is irresistible. When she does this she is also most characteristically herself. You feel about her best images, her best myths, that nobody else writes quite like this.

3

Review of *Anne Sexton: A Self-Portrait in Letters*

Anne Sexton was one of the most important American poets of her generation. She was both praised and condemned by critics for the intense 'confessional' quality of her poetry. At first, it would have been easy to dismiss her, as the fifties often dismissed budding young female writers as just another stir-crazy neurotic house-wife who wanted to write. But it was not easy to do so for long. She was a housewife and she was also neurotic – she is emphatic, in her letters, about both – but she had energy, talent and ambition. Although she did not start to write seriously until she was twenty-nine, by the end of her eighteen-year poetic career she had published nine books and had whatever worldly success poetry can bestow. She had won a Pulitzer Prize, had appeared at interna-tional poetry festivals, had held down a university teaching position although she had never gone to university, and had attracted a wide readership. In 1974, for no immediate reason, she killed herself at her home in Weston, Mass.

Before doing so, she had willed this book of letters into exis-tence. She had appointed both a literary executor and an official biographer, and for her entire adult life she had been a hoarder, saving everything – pressed flowers, dance cards, postcards and snapshots. She also saved carbon copies of her letters, and the editors of this book had to read their way through 50,000 assorted papers before making this relatively small selection. One's immediate reaction is to rush to the incinerator, not with this book, but with one's own scrap heaps. Do any of us, really, want strangers reading our mash notes to highschool boyfriends, our petty gossip and our private love letters after we are dead? For some reason perhaps not unconnected with her final act, Anne Sexton did. Her carefully preserved correspondence was part of the monument to her dead self she had been building for much of her life. If you can stop time with yourself inside it, no unknown monster from the future can get at you. And Anne Sexton had a profound fear of the future.

The letters of poets are not necessarily any more interesting than the letters of bank managers, but Anne Sexton was an exceptional writer of letters. Although, as her editors make painfully clear, she was often difficult and at times impossible to live with, she kept the best of herself for her relationships-by-mail. It is probable that she found it easier to deal with people at this distance. In any case, her letters – even to people we are told she disliked – are charming, inventive, immediate and alive, though sometimes overly eager to please, even fawning. Of course, many of them are to fellow-writers, and they swarm with literary asides and details of the kind that delight historians, but it is not this that holds the reader's attention. Rather it is the sinuous, mercurial and engaging voice of the letters themselves.

But it is not the voice of Anne Sexton; it is only one of her voices. She herself was in the habit of splitting herself in two – 'good Anne' and 'bad Anne' – and the letters are written by 'good Anne'. A much bleaker voice authored her poems, and yet another was responsible for the rages and episodes of paranoia, breakdown, shameless manipulation and alcoholism that marked her life. She was demanding of her friends, insatiably hungry for attention and especially for approval and love. She was a flamboyant romantic, capable of extreme joy and extreme depression almost in the same minute. But we learn about this side of her from her tough-minded editors – one of them her daughter – who are to be congratulated for resisting the doubtless strong temptation to turn out a pious cosmetic job. In their hands, Sexton emerges as neither a heroine nor a victim but as an angular, complex, often loving and at times rather insufferable human being.

The letters themselves, however, are not exactly a 'self-portrait'. Like the letters of Sylvia Plath, Sexton's letters read like a sort of cover, a blithe mask. Plath's breathless and often glassy epistolatory style seems to have almost nothing to do with the person who wrote her extraordinary poems. Sexton's letters and poems are closer to each other, but there is still an enormous gulf between the two. Even when she is describing her own suicide attempts, Sexton's letters do not read like the letters of someone who wanted to die. They are very much those of a woman who wished, passionately, to live, and who wished to live passionately.

This wish and her eventual suicide were not, to her mind, incompatible. Although she says at one point that suicide is the opposite of poetry, she was also capable of speculating on suicide as a way of acquiring 'a certain power . . . I guess I see it as a way of cheating death'. (It is typical of her that she descends to earth rapidly, adding, 'Killing yourself is merely a way to avoid pain despite all my interesting ideas about it.')

A suicide is both a rebuke to the living and a puzzle that defies them to solve it. Like a poem, suicide is finished and refuses to answer questions as to its final cause. The unfortunate effect of such acts is to obscure the lives of their authors, leaving only the riddle of their deaths.

It would be a shame if this happened in the case of Anne Sexton. These letters should be read, not just for the clues to her suicide which they certainly contain, but for their exuberance and affirmation: not for their death but for their life.

4

The Curse of Eve – Or, What I
Learned in School

Once upon a time, I would have not been invited to speak to you today. That time isn't really very long ago. In 1960, when I was attending university, it was widely known that the University College English department did not hire women, no matter what their qualifications. My own college did hire women, it just didn't promote them very rapidly. One of my teachers was a respected authority on Samuel Taylor Coleridge. She was a respected authority on Coleridge for a great many years before anyone saw fit to raise her from the position of Lecturer.

Luckily, I myself did not want to be an authority on Coleridge. I wanted to be a writer, but writers, as far as I could see, made even less than Lecturers, so I decided to go to graduate school. If I had had any burning academic ambitions, they would have taken a turn for the venomous when I was asked by one of my professors whether I really wanted to go to graduate school . . . wouldn't I rather get married? I've known a couple of men for whom marriage would have been a reasonable alternative to a career. Most, however, by force of circumstance, if not by inclination, have been like a friend of mine who is well known for never finishing anything he started.

'When I'm thirty,' he said to me once, 'I'll have to choose between marriage and a career.'

'What do you mean?' I said.

'Well, if I get married, I'll have to have a career,' he replied.

I, however, was expected to have one or the other, and this is one of the many ways in which I hope times have changed. Back then, no university in its right mind would have run a lecture series entitled 'Women on Women'. If it had done anything at all on the subject, it probably would have invited a distinguished psychologist, male, to talk about innate female masochism. College education for women was justified, if at all, on the grounds that it would make women into more intelligent wives and better-informed mothers. Authorities on women were usually men. They were assumed to possess that knowledge, like all other knowledge, by virtue of gender. The tables have turned and now it's women who are supposed to possess this knowledge, simply by birthright. I can only assume that's the reason I've been invited to speak to you, since I'm not an authority on women, or indeed on anything else.

I escaped from academia and bypassed journalism – which was the other career I considered, until I was told that women journalists usually ended up writing obituaries or wedding announcements for the women's page, in accordance with their ancient roles as goddesses of life and death, deckers of nuptial beds and washers of corpses. Finally I became a professional writer. I've just finished a novel, so it's as a working novelist that I'd like to approach this general area.

I'll begin with a simple question, one which confronts every novelist, male or female, at some point in the proceedings and which certainly confronts every critic.

What are novels for? What function are they supposed to perform? What good, if any, are they supposed to do the reader? Are they supposed to delight or instruct, or both, and if so, is there ever a conflict between what we find delightful and what we find instructive? Should a novel be an exploration of hypothetical possibilities, a statement of truth, or just a good yarn? Should it be about how one ought to live one's life, how one can live one's life (usually more limited), or how most people live their lives? Should it tell us something about our society? Can it avoid doing this? More specifically, suppose I am writing a novel with a woman as the central character; how much attention should I pay to any of the above questions? How much attention will I be *forced* to pay through the preconceptions of the critics? Do I want this character to be likeable, respectable, or believable? Is it possible for her to be all three? What are the assumptions of those who will do the liking, the respecting, or the believing? Does she have to be a good 'role model'?

I dislike the term 'role model' partly because of the context in which I first heard it. It was, of course, at university, a very male-oriented university which had a female college attached. The female college was looking for a Dean. My friend, who was a sociologist, explained that this person would have to be a good role model. 'What's that?' I asked. Well, the future Dean would not just have to have high academic credentials and the ability to get along with students, she would also have to be married, with children, good-looking, well dressed, active in community work and so forth. I decided that I was a terrible role model. But then, I did not want to be a role model, I wanted to be a writer. One obviously would not have time for both.

It may be just barely acceptable for prospective Deans to be judged as role models, but as this is also a favourite technique of critics, especially when evaluating female characters in books and sometimes when evaluating the writers themselves, it has to be looked at quite carefully. Let me cite an example: several years ago, I read a review of Marian Engel's *The Honeyman Festival*, written by a female reviewer. The heroine of this novel is Minn, a very pregnant woman who spends a lot of her time reminiscing about the past and complaining about the present. She doesn't have a job. She doesn't have much self-esteem. She's sloppy and self-indulgent and guilt-ridden and has ambiguous feelings about her children, and also about her husband, who is away most of the time. The reviewer complained about this character's lack of initiative,

apparent laziness and disorganization. She wanted a more positive, more energetic character, one capable of taking her life in
hand, of acting more in accordance with the ideal woman then
beginning to be projected by the women's movement. Minn was
not seen as an acceptable role model, and the book lost points
because of this.

My own feeling is that there are a lot more Minn-like women
than there are ideal women. The reviewer might have agreed, but
might also have claimed that by depicting Minn and only Minn –
by providing no alternative to Minn – the writer was making a
statement about the nature of Woman that would merely
reinforce these undesirable Minnish qualities, already too much in
evidence. She wanted success stories, not failure stories, and this is
indeed a problem for the writer of fiction. When writing about
women, what constitutes success? Is success even plausible? Why,
for instance, did George Eliot, herself a successful female writer,
never compose a story with a successful female writer as the central character? Why did Maggie Tulliver have to drown for her
rebelliousness? Why could Dorothea Brooke find nothing better to
do with her idealism than to invest it in two men, one totally
unworthy of it, the other a bit of a simp? Why did Jane Austen's
characters exercise their wit and intelligence in choosing the
proper man rather than in the composition of comic novels?

One possible answer is that these novelists concerned themselves with the typical, or at least with events that would fall within
the range of credibility for their readers; and they felt themselves,
as women writers, to be so exceptional as to lack credibility. In
those days, a woman writer was a freak, an oddity, a suspicious
character. How much of that sentiment lingers on today, I will
leave you to ask yourselves, while at the same time quoting a
remark made to me several years ago by a distinguished male
writer. 'Women poets,' he said, 'always have a furtive look about
them. They know they're invading male territory.' He followed
this with a statement to the effect that women, including women
writers, were only good for one thing, but since this lecture is

going to be printed, I will not quote this rather unprintable remark.

To return to my problem, the creation of a fictional female character . . . I'll come at it from a different angle. There's no shortage of female characters in the literary tradition, and the novelist gets her or his ideas about women from the same sources everyone else does: from the media, books, films, radios, television and newspapers, from home and school, and from the culture at large, the body of received opinion. Also, luckily, sometimes, through personal experience which contradicts all of these. But my hypothetical character would have a choice of many literary ancestresses. For example, I might say a few words about Old Crones, Delphic Oracles, the Three Fates, Evil Witches, White Witches, White Goddesses, Bitch Goddesses, Medusas with snaky heads who turn men to stone, Mermaids with no souls, Little Mermaids with no tongues, Snow Queens, Sirens with songs, Harpies with wings, Sphinxes with and without secrets, women who turn into dragons, dragons who turn into women, Grendel's mother and why she is worse than Grendel; also about evil stepmothers, comic mothers-in-law, fairy godmothers, unnatural mothers, natural mothers, Mad Mothers, Medea who slew her own children, Lady Macbeth and her spot, Eve the mother of us all, the all-mothering sea, and Mother, what have I to do with thee? Also about Wonder Woman, Superwoman, Batgirl, Mary Marvel, Catwoman and Rider Haggard's She with her supernatural powers and electric organ, who could kill a mere mortal man by her embrace; also about Little Miss Muffet and her relationship with the spider, Little Red Riding Hood and her indiscretions with the wolf, Andromeda chained to her rock, Rapunzel and her tower, Cinderella and her sackcloth and ashes, Beauty and the Beast, the wives of Bluebeard (all but the last), Mrs Radcliffe's persecuted Maidens fleeing seduction and murder, Jane Eyre fleeing impropriety and Mr Rochester, Tess of the D'Urbervilles seduced and abandoned; also about the Angel in the House, Agnes pointing upwards, the redemptive love of a good woman, Little Nell dying to the hypocritical sobs of the

whole century, Little Eva doing likewise, much to the relief of the
reader, Ophelia babbling down her babbling brook, the Lady of
Shalott swan-songing her way towards Camelot, Fielding's Amelia
snivelling her way through hundreds of pages of gloom and peril
and Thackeray's Amelia doing likewise but with less sympathy
from her author. Also about the rape of Europa by the bull, the
rape of Leda by the swan, the rape of Lucretia and her consequent
suicide, miraculous escapes from rape on the parts of several
female saints, rape fantasies and how they differ from rape realities,
men's magazines featuring pictures of blondes and Nazis, sex and
violence from *The Canterbury Tales* to T. S. Eliot . . . and I quote . . . 'I
knew a man once did a girl in. Any man might do a girl in. Any
man has to, needs to, wants to, once in a lifetime do a girl in.' Also
about the Whore of Babylon, the whore with the heart of gold, the
love of a bad woman, the whore without a heart of gold, the
Scarlet Letter, the Scarlet Woman, the Red Shoes, Madame Bovary
and her quest for the zipless fuck, Molly Bloom and her chamber
pot and her eternal yes, Cleopatra and her friend the Asp, an association which casts a new light on Little Orphan Annie. Also about
orphans, also about Salome and the head of John the Baptist, and
Judith and the head of Holofernes. Also about True Romance magazines and their relationship to Calvinism. Unfortunately, I have
neither the time nor the knowledge necessary to discuss all of
these in the depth and breadth they deserve, and they do deserve
it. All, of course, are stereotypes of women drawn from the
Western European literary tradition and its Canadian and
American mutations.

There are a good many more variations than those I've mentioned, and although the Western literary tradition was created
largely by men, by no means all of the female figures I have mentioned were male-invented, male-transmitted or male-consumed.
My point in mentioning them is to indicate not only the multiplicity of female images likely to be encountered by a reader but
especially the range. Depictions of women, even by men, are by no
means limited to the figure of the Solitary Weeper (that creature of

helpless passivity who cannot act but only suffer), which seems to have been encouraged by the dominant philosophy about women up until the nineteenth century. There was more to women, even stereotypical women, even then.

The moral range of female stereotypes seems to me to be wider than that of male characters in literature. Heroes and villains have much in common, after all. Both are strong, both are in control of themselves, both perform actions and face the consequences. Even those supernatural male figures, God and the Devil, share a number of characteristics. Sherlock Holmes and Professor Moriarty are practically twins, and it is very difficult to tell by the costumes and activities alone which of the Marvel Comics' supermen are supposed to be bad and which good. Macbeth, although not very nice, is understandable, and besides, he never would have done it if it hadn't been for the Three Witches and Lady Macbeth. The Three Witches are a case in point. Macbeth's motive is ambition, but what are the witches' motives? They have no motives. Like stones or trees, they simply are: the good ones purely good, the bad ones purely bad. About the closest a male figure can come to this is Iago or Mr Hyde, but Iago is at least partly motivated by envy and the other half of Mr Hyde is the all-too-human Dr Jekyll. Even the Devil wants to win, but the extreme types of female figure do not seem to want anything at all. Sirens eat men because that is what Sirens do. The horrible spider-like old women in D. H. Lawrence's stories — I am thinking especially of the grandmother in 'The Virgin and the Gypsy' — are given no motives for their horribleness other than something Lawrence called 'the female will'. Macbeth murders because he wants to be king, to gain power, whereas the Three Witches are merely acting the way witches act. Witches, like poems, should not mean, but be. One may as well ask why the sun shines.

This quality of natural force, good or bad, this quality of thing-hood, appears most frequently in stories about male heroes, especially the travelling variety such as Odysseus. In such stories, the female figures are events that happen to the hero, adventures in which he is involved. The women are static, the hero dynamic. He experiences the adventure and moves on through a landscape that is a landscape of women as well as one of geographical features. This kind of story is still very much with us, as anyone who has read the James Bond stories, Henry Miller or, closer to home, Robert Kroetsch's *The Studhorse Man* can testify. There are few female literary adventurers of this kind. One might call them adventuresses, and the connotation alone indicates how they differ from the male variety. A man who recites a catalogue of women, such as Don Giovanni, is held to be a rogue, perhaps, but a rather enviable one, whereas female characters, from Moll Flanders to Isadora Wing, of Erica Jong's *Fear of Flying*, are not allowed to do the same without a great deal of explanation, suffering and guilt.

I have mentioned the Solitary Weeper, that passive female victim to whom everything gets done and whose only activity is running away. There are male figures of a similar type but they are usually children, like Dickens's Paul Dombey, Oliver Twist and the suffering pupils of Dotheboys Hall. For the grown-up male to exhibit these characteristics – fearfulness, inability to act, feelings of extreme powerlessness, tearfulness, feelings of being trapped and helpless – he has to be crazy or a member of a minority group. Such feelings are usually viewed as a violation of his male nature, whereas the same feelings in a female character are treated as an expression of hers. Passive helpless men are aberrations; passive women within the range of the norm. But powerful, or at any rate active, heroes and villains are seen as the fulfilment of a *human* ideal; whereas powerful women, and there are many of them in literature, are usually given a supernatural aura. They are witches, Wonder Women or Grendel's mothers. They are monsters. They are not quite human. Grendel's mother is worse than Grendel because she is seen as a greater departure from the norm. Grendel, after all, is just a sort of Beowulf, only bigger and hungrier.

Suppose, however, that I want to create a female character who is not a natural force, whether good or evil; who is not a passive Solitary Weeper; who makes decisions, performs actions, causes as well as endures events, and has perhaps even some ambition, some creative power. What stories does my culture have to tell me about such women? Not very many at the public school level, which is probably the reason why I can remember nothing at all about Dick and Jane, although some vague imprints of Puff and Spot still remain. But, outside school hours, there were the comic books: Batman and Robin, Superman (and Lois Lane, the eternal dumb rescuee), the Human Torch and Zorro and many others, all male. Of course, there was Wonder Woman. Wonder Woman was an Amazon princess who lived on an island with some other Amazons but no men. She had magic bullet-deflecting bracelets, a transparent airplane, a magic lasso and super skills and powers. She fought crime. There was only one catch – she had a boyfriend. But, if he kissed her, her superhuman strength disappeared like Samson's after a clean shave. Wonder Woman could never get married and still remain Wonder Woman.

Then there was *The Red Shoes* – not the Hans Christian Andersen fairy tale but the movie, starring Moira Shearer, with beautiful red hair. A whole generation of little girls were taken to see it as a special treat for their birthday parties. Moira Shearer was a famous dancer but alas, she fell in love with the orchestra conductor, who, for some reason totally obscure to me at the time, forbade her to dance after they got married. This prohibition made her very unhappy. She wanted the man, but she wanted to dance as well, and the conflict drove her to fling herself in front of a train. The message was clear. You could not have both your artistic career and the love of a good man as well, and if you tried, you would end up committing suicide.

Then there were Robert Graves's poetic theories, set forth in many books, especially *The White Goddess*, which I read at the age of nineteen. For Graves, man does, woman simply is. Man is the poet, woman is the Muse, the White Goddess herself, inspiring but ultimately destroying. What about a woman who wants to be a poet? Well, it is possible, but the woman has to somehow *become* the White Goddess, acting as her incarnation and mouthpiece, and presumably behaving just as destructively. Instead of 'create and be destroyed', Graves's pattern for the female artist was 'create and destroy'. A little more attractive than jumping in front of a train, but not much. Of course, you could always forget the whole thing, settle down and have babies. A safer course, it would seem, and that was certainly the message of the entire culture.

The most lurid cautionary tales provided by society, however, were the lives of actual female writers themselves. Women writers could not be ignored by literary history; at least not nineteenth-century ones. Jane Austen, the Brontë sisters, George Eliot, Christina Rossetti, Emily Dickinson, and Elizabeth Barrett Browning were too important for that. But their biographies could certainly emphasize their eccentricities and weirdness, and they did. Jane Austen never got married. Neither did Emily Brontë, who also died young. Charlotte Brontë died in childbirth. George Eliot lived with a man she was not married to and never had any children. Christina Rossetti 'looked at life through the wormholes in a shroud'. Emily Dickinson lived behind closed doors and was probably nuts. Elizabeth Barrett Browning did manage to squeeze out a child but did not bring him up properly and indulged in seances. These women were writers, true, but they were somehow not women, or if they were women, they were not *good* women. They were bad role models, or so their biographies implied.

'I used to have a boyfriend who called me Wonder Woman,' says Broom Hilda, the witch, in a recent comic strip.

'Because you are strong, courageous and true?' asks the Troll.

'No, because he wondered if I was a woman.'

If you want to be good at anything, said the message, you will have to sacrifice your femininity. If you want to be female, you'll have to have your tongue removed, like the Little Mermaid.

It's true that much was made of Poe's alcoholism, Byron's incest, Keats's tuberculosis, and Shelley's immoral behaviour, but somehow these romantic rebellions made male poets not only more interesting, but more male. It was rarely suggested that the two Emilys, Jane, Christina and the rest lived as they did because it was the only way they could get the time and develop the concentration to write. The amazing thing about women writers in the nineteenth century is not that there were so few of them but that there were any at all. If you think this syndrome is dead and buried, take a look at Margaret Laurence's *The Diviners*. The central character is a successful woman writer, but it becomes obvious to her that she cannot write and retain the love of a good man. She chooses the writing and throws an ashtray at the man, and at the end of the book she is living alone. Writers, both male and female, have to be selfish just to get the time to write, but women are not trained to be selfish.

A much more extreme version of the perils of creativity is provided by the suicides of Sylvia Plath and Anne Sexton and the rather ghoulish attention paid to them. Female writers in the twentieth century are seen not just as eccentric and unfeminine, but as doomed. The temptation to act out the role of isolated or doomed female artist, either in one's life or through one's characters, is quite strong. Luckily, there are alternatives. When hard pressed, you can always contemplate the life of Mrs Gaskell, Harriet Beecher Stowe or even, say, Alice Munro or Adele Wiseman or the many other female writers who seem to have been able to combine marriage, motherhood, and writing without becoming more noticeably deformed than anyone else in this culture.

However, there is some truth to the *Red Shoes* syndrome. It *is* more difficult for a woman writer in this society than for a male writer. But not because of any innate mysterious hormonal or spiritual differences: it is more difficult because it has been made more difficult, and the stereotypes still lurk in the wings, ready to spring fully formed from the heads of critics, both male and female, and attach themselves to any unwary character or author that wanders by. Women are still expected to be better than men, morally that is, even by women, even by some branches of the women's movement; and if you are not an angel, if you happen to have human failings, as most of us do, especially if you display any kind of strength or power, creative or otherwise, then you are not merely human, you're worse than human. You are a witch, a Medusa, a destructive, powerful, scary monster. An angel with pimples and flaws is not seen as a human being but as a devil. A character who behaves with the inconsistency that most of us display most of the time is not a believable creation but a slur on the Nature of Woman or a sermon, not on human frailty, but on the special frailer-than-frail shortcomings of all Womankind. There is still a lot of social pressure on a woman to be perfect, and also a lot of resentment of her should she approach this goal in any but the most rigidly prescribed fashion.

I could easily illustrate by reading from my own clipping file: I could tell you about Margaret the Magician, Margaret the Medusa, Margaret the Man-eater, clawing her way to success over the corpses of many hapless men. Margaret the powerhungry Hitler, with her megalomaniac plans to take over the entire field of Canadian Literature. This woman must be stopped! All these mythological creatures are inventions of critics; not all of them male. (No one has yet called me an angel, but Margaret the Martyr will surely not take long to appear, especially if I die young in a car accident.)

It would be amusing to continue with these excerpts, but it would also be rather mean, considering the fact that some of the perpetrators are, if not in the audience, employed by this university. So instead of doing that, I will enter a simple plea; women, both as characters and as people, must be allowed their imperfections. If I create a female character, I would like to be able to show her having the emotions all human beings have – hate, envy, spite, lust, anger and fear, as well as love, compassion, tolerance and joy – without having her pronounced a monster, a slur, or a bad example. I would also like her to be cunning, intelligent and sly, if necessary for the plot, without having her branded as a bitch goddess or a glaring instance of the deviousness of women. For a long time, men in literature have been seen as individuals, women merely as examples of a gender; perhaps it is time to take the capital W off Woman. I myself have never known an angel, a harpy, a witch or an earth mother. I've known a number of real women, not all of whom have been nicer or more noble or more long-suffering or less self-righteous and pompous than men. Increasingly it is becoming possible to write about them, though as always it remains difficult for us to separate what we see from what we have been taught to see. Who knows? Even I may judge women more harshly than I do men; after all, they were responsible for Original Sin, or that is what I learned in school.

I will end with a quote from Agnes Macphail, who was not a writer but who was very familiar with at least one literary stereotype. 'When I hear men talk about women being the angel of the home, I always, mentally at least, shrug my shoulders in doubt. I do not want to be the angel of the home. I want for myself what I want for other women: absolute equality. After that is secured, then men and women can take their turns at being angels.' I myself would rephrase that: 'Then men and women can take their turns at being human, with all the individuality and variety that term implies.'

5

Northrop Frye Observed

This is not Frye objectified, but Frye subjectified, a mini-memoir, if you like, by one of his former students whose ambition it was to become a writer.

And a strange ambition it was, too, at Leaside High School in 1956. It was a sudden one. Up to 1956, I'd thought I was going to be a botanist, or, at the very least, a Home Economist though by then I knew that this latter was unlikely: people with snarls on the insides of their zippers were not so destined. There was nothing at Leaside High School to indicate to me that writing was even a possibility for a young person in Canada in the twentieth century. We did study authors, it's true, but they were neither Canadian nor alive. However, the spirit bloweth where it listeth, and after a short period of looking over my shoulder to see if it really meant to be blowing on somebody else I resigned myself to fate and tried to figure out how to go about the thing. I contemplated journalism school; but women, I was told, were not allowed to write anything but obituaries and the ladies' page; and although some of my critics seem to be under the impression that this is what I ended up writing anyway, I felt that something broader was in order. University, in short, where I might at least learn to spell.

Luckily I had a sympathetic English teacher named Miss Billings.

She did not tell me how awful my poetry was (it did rhyme, how-ever), but instead led me to understand that Victoria College at the University of Toronto was where I ought to be. There was someone there called Northrop Frye, she said. I had never heard of him, but then I had never heard of almost everything. I took her word.

I entered Victoria College in 1957, the year that Frye published *Anatomy of Criticism*, but I didn't know that then. Frye was only a blur on the horizon, something I would have to deal with in third year, when I took Milton. Meanwhile I was agonizing over the fact that I'd spent the summer trying to read *The Waste Land* and hadn't understood a word of it. I wondered if it was too late for Botany after all, and began writing poems that didn't rhyme and had coffee cups in them, which may have had something to do with Eliot or something to do with the fact that I was killing far too much time in the coffee shop, where Frye, incidentally, never went. For under-graduates, Frye was a kind of rumour. You heard things about him, but you rarely saw him. Occasionally you could hear him typing.

In third year, having struggled through Anglo-Saxon and Chaucer, I actually got to take a course from him. In those days you were either in something called the General Course, which lasted three years, or you were in a four-year Honours course, which made you specialize. In Honours English, life was chrono-logical and Milton came in the third year. Northrop Frye taught Milton. 'Taught' isn't exactly the word. Frye said, 'Let there be Milton,' and lo, there was. It was done like this. He stood at the front of the room. He took one step forward, put his left hand on the table, took another step forward, put his right hand on the table, took a step back, removed his left hand, another step back, removed his right hand, and repeated the pattern. While he was doing this, pure prose, in real sentences and paragraphs, issued from his mouth. He didn't say 'um', as most of us did, or leave sen-tences unfinished, or correct himself. I had never heard anyone do this before. It was like seeing a magician producing birds from a hat. You kept wanting to go around behind Frye or look under the table to see how he did it.

Which brings us to the delicate question of 'influence'. There are those who, upon hearing that I was once a student of Northrop Frye's, need to have their fingers pried loose from the hem of my garment. Conversely, there are those who start circling to the left, hoping to catch a glimpse of the Mark of the Vampire which they are sure must lurk somewhere, if not on my neck, at least in my work. Those who have never occupied that blissful position, 'a student of Frye's', assume that he exerted some odd Svengali-like influence on young writers, taking their putty-like minds and running them through the Play-Doh machine of his 'system' until they came out moulded. If such an assumption had any truth to it, Canada ought to have filled up with a lot of zonked-out Trilbys, all 'students of Frye', all warbling Frye's tune. Why didn't it?

Possibly because any genuine writer is 'influenced' only by sources with which he already has some affinity. Writers are pilferers, as Eliot has remarked; the caddis-fly larvae of the literary world. Or possibly because Frye wasn't interested in 'influencing' anyone, especially young writers. His approach to creation was not prescriptive. The last thing he ever would have done to his students would have been to tell them what or how to write, and nothing would embarrass him more than to be credited with producing a sort of poetic backup section. Or possibly because, if Frye is right, and poets are influenced by other poets, novelists by other novelists, the only thing Frye would be able to influence would be other critics. This he has certainly done; but poets? I've read somewhere the expression, 'a Northrop Frye poet', but I'm not sure what it means. A view of poetry so comprehensive as Frye's surely subsumes just about everything. In any case, as he himself has said, poets are ornery, especially in the face of critical systems. Try to confine them in one and they'll react by doing something quite other. The critic's job is not to tell poets what to do, but to tell readers what they have done. The writer's job is to write. This was an arrangement that seemed appropriate to me, and still does.

Back in 1960, Frye came and went, distantly but benevolently enough. Occasionally he would murmur something indicative of

the fact that he had actually read one's tawdry effusion in this or
that campus literary journal, but he offered neither criticism nor
guidance, merely a general attentiveness, a sort of literary pho-
totropism. It was rather like being watched by a sunflower. He was
not what you would call intrusive. At that stage of my life I was a
good deal more upset by Robert Graves than I was by Frye. *The
White Goddess* gave me the cold sweats: I wanted to be a poet, true,
but not at the price of cannibalizing my fellow creatures, as Graves
seemed to think I was honour-bound to do. Women could only be
poets, he said, if they were willing to *be* the White Goddess, a prime
example of whom was Coleridge's Nightmare Life-In-Death. I had
no particular wish to thick men's blood with cold – I preferred a
nice game of bridge, any day – and although some of my work
seems to have had that effect on certain Canadian critics, it was
inadvertent. How reassuring to turn instead to Frye's essay on
Emily Dickinson, which presents her neither as the White Goddess,
despite her manner of dressing, nor as a feeble neurotic, but as a
skilled professional who knew exactly what she was doing. It was,
somehow, a more positive role-model.

So although Frye was not an 'influence' in the sense that people
usually mean the word, that is, a manufacturer of plaster castings,
he was an influence in another and greater respect. He was a counterbalance not only to Mr Graves and his oddly arachnoid theories
of poetic creation, but also to the Canadian milieu of the late fifties.
At this time Toronto was not the multi-restauranted glitter city it
is today, entranced by its own trendy reflection, but Hogtown, the
place Montrealers made jokes about. It had one repertory theatre,
no ballet company, and hardly any decent brie. Canadian authors
were invisible to the general public, ghettoized in the *Canadiana*
section by booksellers, along with the cookbooks on 101 Things To
Do With Maple Sugar, and considered oxymorons by snobbish
young would-be writers like myself, who thought we had to run
away to England in order to let our genius fully flower. On the
average, there were about five novels by Canadians published in
Canada per year, and sales were doing very well if they reached a

thousand copies. There were two advantages to this state of affairs. The first was that if you published anything of a serious literary nature, anything at all, you would get reviewed somewhere, and you would be read by the hard-core Canadian Literature audience, which had a shifting population of about 200. The second was that women were not discriminated against. To announce that you wanted to be a writer did not produce a gender-specific response. Nobody said, 'You can't do that because you're a girl.' They did not tell you you were up against Shakespeare and Melville. Instead they said, 'A what?'

Even at the university level, your fellow seekers after wisdom were likely to think you pretentious or deluded. But then there was Frye, who possessed that most necessary of qualifications for credibility in Canada, an international reputation. Frye appeared to take writing for granted. He seemed to view it not as something done by the emotionally brain-damaged but as an essential human activity. He took our ambitions seriously. In Toronto, in 1959, this was more than encouraging.

The same people who clutch my hem at parties also want to know whether I didn't find being a student of Frye's awfully, well, intimidating. Usually I say Yes or No, as occasion seems to require. A full explanation would take longer. The curious fact remains that it's possible to be very impressed by a mind without necessarily being intimidated by a person. I was more intimidated by the Philosophy professor who lectured with his eyes closed and could always tell when an extra person was in the room. It was hard, though, to be completely intimidated by anyone as easily embarrassed as Frye. It's also hard to be intimidated by someone who's trying so hard not to be intimidating. Frye, when he'd had the bad luck to come face to face with one of his students outside the lecture hall, would lapse from perfectly punctuated prose into a kind of reassuring and inarticulate mumble. 'They're just as frightened of you as you are of them,' my parents used to say about things like bumblebees. The same could be said of Frye. So lacking in intimidation was I, I recall, that I wrote and published a literary parody in which I applied archetypal criticism to the Ajax commercial, the eternal battle of the recurrent figure of the Housewife against the dark and menacing figure of The Dirt. Undergraduate, but then, what's the use of being an undergraduate if you can't be undergraduate? The point is that I did not fear retaliation. I expected Frye to find it almost as funny as I did, which may or may not have happened. Possibly he thought I was just getting it right.

It's quite possible though that my version of Frye is subjectively coloured by the fact that my parents were from Nova Scotia. The things that intimidated other people did not intimidate me. The deadpan delivery, the irony, the monotone, and the concealed jokes, may have seemed odd to those from Ontario, but to me they were more than familiar. In the Maritimes they're the norm. Puritanism takes odd shapes there, some brilliant, most eccentric, and no Maritimer could ever mistake a lack of flamboyance for a lack of commitment, engagement, courage or passion. Light dawned when I found out Frye had originated in New Brunswick. Not quite the same as Nova Scotia, where my relatives all lived, but close enough. A Nova Scotian joke of the 1930s had been that Nova Scotia's main export was brains. Frye was an export.

When I visited Australia, the Australians were constantly asking, 'Why is there no Australian Northrop Frye?', much as Canadians of my generation used to ask why there is no Canadian *Moby Dick* and Americans of 1840 used to ask why there was no American Walter Scott. It's a good question, but there's an even better one: why is there a *Canadian* Northrop Frye? Or, to particularize, how did such a creature ever survive having been born in Moncton, New Brunswick, and having grown up in Sherbrooke, Quebec, in the first part of this century?

To those who do not know these places it's difficult to explain my amazement. Let us say only that a soul waiting to be reincarnated as a major literary critic would have chosen another location and time, on the supposition that there are easier ways of doing it. Canada, from the literary point of view, was a bit of a void. There was a tradition, it's true, but it had the curious habit of vanishing and having to be re-discovered by each successive generation. There's always been a certain amount of dredging involved. Canadian nationalists of the kind whose eyes whirl around a lot (as distinguished from lumpish and stolid ones like me) have, in recent years, accused Frye of all sorts of things vis à vis Canada: continentalism, internationalism, ignoring them, and so forth. But it seems to me that almost every seminal idea in the newly watered fields of Canlit, including the currently fashionable 'regionalism', sprang, if not fully formed, at least in some form, from the forehead of Northrop Frye, back in the days when he was dutifully reviewing Canadian poetry for *The Canadian Forum* and other slender journals, a task which may have contributed to Frye's formulations of the connection between the imagination and the society it finds itself surrounded by. Frye is of course a social thinker whose efforts have always been directed towards the evaluation not only of the writer but of the reader. What better field for an educator than a country in which almost nobody knows how – in the broader sense – to read?

There were, however, poets of considerable range and skill buried down there in the Canlit substrata, and Frye did his best with them, E. J. Pratt in particular. But what about their influence on him, or their shared view of the universe? Parts of Frye read as if they could have been written by A. M. Klein, had he been a critic; there is something of the same Adam-naming-the-beasts motif about both of them. Some have referred to Frye's labelling of literary genera and species as 'dead taxonomy', which only means among other things that they have never seen two taxonomists having an argument. They have never reflected either on the fact that a kangaroo is just as alive whether you call it by its Latin name or by no name. But Frye's push towards *naming*, towards an interconnected system, seems to me a Canadian reaction to a Canadian situation. Stranded in the midst of a vast space which nobody has made sense out of for you, you settle down to map-making, charting the territory, the discovery of where things are in relation to each other, the extraction of meaning. The poets were doing it with their own times and spaces, Frye was doing it with literature as a whole, but the motive – which is that too of Innes and McLuhan, those other megasystem thinkers of the University of Toronto – is *au fond* the same. Frye's central metaphor is spatial and it is very large. An American or English critic of this time would not have even thought of anything like this. The English were doing their usual social classification, handing out the nuances and assigning rungs on the ladder, and the Americans were deep in the motors of their chosen poems, figuring out which little gizmos got pressed to make the thing work. Metonymy and synecdoche are the newest items, I'm told; but the days when I would have had to find out what they meant are long past.

Which brings me back to my starting point. It's twenty-odd years later and tomorrow I have to get on the plane for Winnipeg, where people will ask me about page-turnability and bad images of men. If I were an American I wouldn't have to do this; if I were English I could do it all in London, and the questions would be different; but this is Canada, which was, is and remains a whole different hockey game. That, however, is another story. My next rhetorical question is, What have I to do with Frye, now that I'm no longer a student? Has anything, as it were, rubbed off? And if so, is it of much use to a writer, trapped in the practical, struggling from plot to plot, character to character, book-signing to book-signing, TV station to TV station, and every Fall brought face to face with waving acres of low demotic?

Well, being a former student of Frye's does help out with the answers. When someone asks you, live, on air, how come you're such a pessimist and why you don't have happier endings, you can think to yourself, 'Because I'm writing in the ironic mode, thickhead.' You can't say it too loud, of course – Frye's dream of a language of common literary discourse hasn't made it to the heavy rock stations yet – but at least, in the silence of the night, as you toss and turn in your Holiday Inn bed, having failed to discover how to lower the room temperature, haunted by the smart replies you did not think of at the time – at least you can whisper it to yourself.

And when things are at their nadir and the reasons for which you wrote your book appear to have come completely unbuckled from the result, which seems to be a long line of people wanting you to write things in the fronts of their copies – things such as, 'Happy Birthday with love from Annie' – in vain do you remonstrate that you are not Annie – you can always tell yourself that the pursuit of literature is a significant human activity.

Believing it is sometimes an act of faith. But then, Northrop Frye believes it, and he *knows*.

6

Writing the Male Character

I'm more than delighted that you've invited a token woman to give the Hagey lectures this year, and though you might have chosen one more respectable than myself, I realize that the supply is limited.

My lack of respectability I have on good authority: the authority, in fact, of the male academics at the University of Victoria, in British Columbia, where I was being interviewed on radio not long ago. 'I did a little survey,' said the rather pleasant male interviewer, 'among the professors here. I asked them what they thought of your work. The women were all very positive, but the men said that they weren't sure whether or not you were respectable.' So I'm giving you advance warning that everything you are about to hear is not academically respectable. The point of view I'm presenting is that of a practising novelist, inhabitant of New Grub Street for many years, not that of the Victorianist I spent four years at Harvard learning to be; though the Victorianism does creep in, as you can already see. So I will not even mention metonymy and synecdoche, except right now, just to impress you and let you know that I know they exist.

All of the above, of course, is by way of letting the male members of the audience know that, despite the title of this lecture, they don't need to feel threatened. I believe we have now reached, as a culture, the point at which we need a little positive reinforcement for men. I'm starting my own private project along these lines tonight. I have with me some gold stars, some silver stars and some blue stars, fictional ones, of course. You get a blue star, if you want one, just for being unthreatened enough to have actually turned up tonight. You get a silver star if you are unthreatened enough to laugh at the jokes, and you get a gold star if you don't feel threatened at all. On the other hand, you get a black mark if you say, 'My *wife* just *loves* your books.' You get two black marks if you say, as a male CBC producer said to me not long ago, 'A number of us are upset because we feel women are taking over the Canadian literary scene.'

'Why do men feel threatened by women?' I asked a male friend of mine. (I love that wonderful rhetorical device, 'a male friend of mine'. It's often used by female journalists when they want to say something particularly bitchy but don't want to be held responsible for it themselves. It also lets people know that you *do* have male friends, that you aren't one of those fire-breathing mythical monsters, The Radical Feminists, who walk around with little pairs of scissors and kick men in the shins if they open doors for you. 'A male friend of mine' also gives – let us admit it – a certain weight to the opinions expressed.) So this male friend of mine, who does by the way exist, conveniently entered into the following dialogue. 'I mean,' I said, 'men are bigger, most of the time, they can run faster, strangle better, and they have on the average a lot more money and power.' 'They're afraid women will laugh at them,' he said. 'Undercut their world view.' Then I asked some women students in a quickie poetry seminar I was giving, 'Why do women feel threatened by men?' 'They're afraid of being killed,' they said.

From this I concluded that men and women are indeed different, if only in the range and scope of their threatenability. A man is not just a woman in funny clothes and a jock strap. *They don't think the same*, except about things like higher math. But neither are they an alien or inferior form of life. From the point of view of the novelist, this discovery has wide-ranging implications; and you can see that we are approaching this evening's topic, albeit in a crab-wise, scuttling, devious and feminine manner; nevertheless, approaching. But first, a small digression, partly to demonstrate that when people ask you if you hate men, the proper reply is 'Which ones?' – because, of course, the other big revelation of the evening is that *not all men are the same.* Some of them have beards. Apart from that, I have never been among those who would speak slightingly of men by lumping them all in together; I would never say, for instance – as some have – 'Put a paper bag over their bodies and they're all the same.' I give you Albert Schweitzer in one corner, Hitler in another.

But think of what civilization would be today without the con-tributions of men. No electric floor polishers, no neutron bomb, no Freudian psychology, no heavy metal rock groups, no pornog-raphy, no repatriated Canadian Constitution . . . the list could go on and on. And they're fun to play Scrabble with and handy for eating up the leftovers. I have heard some rather tired women express the opinion that the only good man is a dead man, but this is far from correct. They may be hard to find, but think of it this way: like diamonds, in the rough or not, their rarity makes them all the more appreciated. Treat them like human beings! This may surprise them at first, but sooner or later their good qualities will emerge, most of the time. Well, in view of the statistics . . . some of the time.

That wasn't the digression . . . this is the digression. I grew up in a family of scientists. My father was a forest entomologist and fond of children, and incidentally not threatened by women, and many were the happy hours we spent listening to his explanations of the ways of the wood-boring beetle, or picking forest tent caterpillars out of the soup because he had forgotten to feed them and they had gone crawling all over the house in search of leaves. One of the results of my upbringing was that I had a big advantage in the schoolyard when little boys tried to frighten me with worms, snakes and the like; the other was that I developed, slightly later, an affection for the writings of the great nineteenth-century naturalist and father of modern entomology, Henri Fabre. Fabre was, like Charles Darwin, one of those gifted and obsessive amateur naturalists which the nineteenth century produced in such abundance. He pursued his investigations for the love of the subject, and unlike many biologists today, whose language tends to be composed of numbers rather than words, he was an enthusiastic and delightful writer. I read with pleasure his account of the life of the spider, and of his experiments with ant-lions, by which he tried to prove that they could reason. But it was not only Fabre's subject matter that intrigued me; it was the character of the man himself, so full of energy, so pleased with everything, so resourceful, so willing to follow his line of study wherever it might lead. Received opinion he would take into account, but would believe nothing until he had put it to the test himself. It pleases me to think of him, spade in hand, setting forth to a field full of sheep droppings, in search of the Sacred Dung Beetle and the secrets of her egg-laying ritual. 'I am all eyes,' he exclaimed, as he brought to light a little object, not round like the Sacred Beetle's usual edible dung-ball, but cunningly pear-shaped! 'Oh blessed joys of truth suddenly shining forth,' he wrote. 'What others are there to compare with you!'

And it is in this spirit, it seems to me, that we should approach all subjects. If a dung-beetle is worthy of it, why not that somewhat more complex object, the human male? Admittedly the analogy has certain drawbacks. For instance, one dung-beetle is much like another, whereas, as we've noted, there's quite a range in men. Also, we are supposed to be talking about novels here, and, to belabour the obvious, a novel is not a scientific treatise; that is, it can make no claim to present the kind of factual truth which can be demonstrated by repeatable experiments. Although the novelist presents observations and reaches conclusions, they are not of the same order as the observations of Fabre on the behaviour of the mating practices of the female scorpion, although some critics react as though they are.

Note that we have landed in the middle of a swamp, that is, at the crux of the problem: if a novel is not a scientific treatise, what is it? Our evaluation of the role of the male character within the novel will of course depend on what kind of beast we think we're dealing with. I'm sure you've all heard the one about the four blind philosophers and the elephant. Substitute 'critics' for 'philosophers' and 'novel' for 'elephant' and you'll have the picture. One critic gets hold of the novelist's life and decides that novels are disguised spiritual autobiographies, or disguised personal sexual phobias, or something of the kind. Another gets hold of the *Zeitgeist* (or Spirit of the Times, for those unlucky enough never to have had to pass a PhD language exam in German) and writes about the Restoration Novel or the Novel of Sensibility or The Rise of the Political Novel or The Novel of Twentieth-Century Alienation; another figures out that the limitations of the language have something to do with what can be said, or that certain pieces of writing display similar patterns, and the air fills with mythopoeia, structuralism and similar delights; another goes to Harvard and gets hold of the Human Condition, a favourite of mine, and very handy to fall back on when you can't think of anything else to say. The elephant however remains an elephant, and sooner or later gets tired of having the blind philosophers feeling its parts, whereupon it stretches itself, rises to its feet and ambles away in another direction altogether. This is not to say that critical exercises are futile or trivial. From what I have said about dung-beetles – which also preserve their innermost secrets – you will know that I think the description of elephants is a worthwhile activity. But describing an elephant and giving birth to one are two different things, and the novelist and the critic approach the novel with quite different sets of preconceptions, problems and emotions.

'Whence comest thou?' says a well-known male character in a multi-faceted prose narrative with which I am sure you are all familiar. 'From going to and fro in the earth, and from walking up and down in it,' answers his adversary. Thus the novelist. One would of course not want to continue with this analogy – a critic is not God, contrary to some opinions, and a novelist is not the Devil, although one could remark, with Blake, that creative energies are more likely to emerge from the underworld than from the upper world of rational order. Let us say only that the going to and fro and the walking up and down in the earth are things that all novelists seem to have done in some way or another, and that the novel proper, as distinguished from the romance and its variants, is one of the points in human civilization at which the human world as it is collides with language and imagination. This is not to limit the novel to a Zola-like naturalism (though Zola himself was not a narrow Zola-like naturalist, as anyone who has read the triumphant final passage of *Germinal* will testify); but it is to state that some of the things that get into novels get into them because they are there in the world. There would have been no flogging scene in *Moby Dick* if there had been none on nineteenth-century whaling ships, and its inclusion is not mere sado-masochism on the part of Melville. However, if the book consisted of nothing but, one might have cause to wonder.

Thus one must conclude that the less than commendable behaviour of male characters in certain novels by women is not necessarily due to a warped view of the opposite sex on behalf of the authors. Could it be . . . I say it hesitantly, in a whisper, since like most women I cringe at the very thought of being called – how can I even say it – a *man-hater* . . . could it be that the behaviour of some men in what we are fond of considering real life . . . could it be that not every man always behaves well? Could it be that some emperors have no clothes on?

This may seem to you an obvious point to make. But not so. Among the going to and fro that novelists do these days is the going to and fro across Canada during the McClelland & Stewart Wreck-an-Author tour, talking to media denizens, and some of the walking up and down they do happens after reading the reviews of their books. Let's pretend for the sake of argument that media denizens and newspaper critics bear at least some relation, if not to the average reader, at least to the officially promoted climate of opinion; that is, what it is considered, at the moment, fashionable and therefore safe to state publicly. If so, the officially promoted climate of opinion these days shows a noteworthy shift towards male whining.

Let me take you back a few years, to the days of Kate Millett's *Sexual Politics*, which was preceded ancestrally by Leslie Fiedler's *Love and Death in the American Novel*. Both were criticisms based on an analysis of the relations, within novels, of men and women, and both gave black marks to certain male authors for simplistic and stereotyped negative depictions of women. Well, that was interesting, but the worm has turned. Now we're handing out black marks for what male critics (and, to be fair, some female ones) consider to be unfavourable depictions of men by female authors. I base this conclusion mainly on reviews of my own books, naturally, since that's what I see most of, but I've noted it elsewhere too.

Now, we know there's no such thing as value-free novel writing. Creation does not happen in a vacuum, and a novelist is either depicting or exposing some of the values of the society in which he or she lives. Novelists from Defoe through Dickens and Faulkner have always done that. But it sometimes escapes us that the same is true of criticism. We are all organisms within environments, and we interpret what we read in the light of how we live and how we would like to live, which are almost never the same thing, at least for most novel readers. I think that political interpretations of novels have a place in the body of criticism, as long as we recognize them for what they are; but total polarization can only be a disservice to literature. For instance, a male friend of mine – just to let you know I have more than one – wrote a novel which has a scene in it in which men are depicted urinating outdoors standing up. Now, so far as I know, this is something men have been doing for many years, and they are still doing it, judging from the handwriting in the snow; it is merely one of those things that happens. But a female poet took my friend to task in print. She found this piece of writing not only unforgivably Central Canadian –

you can tell she was from British Columbia – she also found it unforgivably *macho*. I'm not sure what novelistic solution she had in mind. Possibly she wanted my friend to leave out the subject of urination altogether, thus avoiding the upsetting problem of physiological differences; maybe she wanted the men to demonstrate equality of attitude by sitting on toilets to perform this function. Or maybe she wanted them to urinate outdoors standing up but also to feel guilty about it. Or maybe it would have been all right if they had been urinating into the Pacific Ocean, regionalism being what it is today. You may think this kind of criticism is silly, but it happens all the time on New Grub Street, which is where I live.

For the female novelist, it means that certain men will find it objectionable if she depicts men behaving the way they do behave a lot of the time. Not enough that she may avoid making them rapists and murderers, child molesters, warmongers, sadists, power-hungry, callous, domineering, pompous, foolish or immoral, though I'm sure we will all agree that such men do exist. Even if she makes them sensitive and kind she's open to the charge of having depicted them as 'weak'. What this kind of critic wants is Captain Marvel, without the Billy Batson alter ego; nothing less will do.

Excuse me for underlining the obvious, but it seems to me that a good, that is, a successfully-written, character in a novel is not at all the same as a 'good', that is, a morally good, character in real life. In fact, a character in a book who is consistently well-behaved probably spells disaster for the book. There's a lot of public pressure on the novelist to write such characters, however, and it isn't new. I take you back to Samuel Richardson, author of such running-away-from-rape classics as *Pamela* and *Clarissa*. Both contain relatively virtuous women and relatively lecherous and nasty-minded men, who also happen to be English gentlemen. No one accused Richardson of being mean to men, but some English gentlemen felt that dirt had been done to them; in other words, the insecurities were primarily class ones rather than sex ones.

Obligingly, Richardson came up with *Sir Charles Grandison*, a novel in which he set out to do right by the image of the English gentleman. It starts out promisingly enough, with an abduction with intent to rape by a villain after that priceless pot of gold, the heroine's virginity. Unfortunately Sir Charles Grandison enters the picture, saves the heroine from a fate worse than death, and invites her to his country residence; after which most readers kiss the novel goodbye. I however always sit to the end, even of bad movies, and since I'm the only person I've ever met who has actually made it through to page 900 of this novel I can tell you what happens. Sir Charles Grandison displays his virtues; the heroine admires them. That's it. Oh, and then there's a proposal. Feel like reading it? You bet you don't, and neither do all those male critics who complain about the image of men in books by women. A friend of mine – not a male one this time, but a perceptive reader and critic – says that her essential criterion for evaluating literature is, 'Does it live or does it die?' A novel based on other people's needs for having their egos stroked, their images shored up, or their sensitivities pandered to is unlikely to live.

Let us take a brief look at what literature has actually done. Is *Hamlet*, for instance, a slur on men? Is *Macbeth*? Is *Faust*, in any version? How about the behaviour of the men in *Moll Flanders*? Or *Tom Jones*? Is *A Sentimental Journey* about the quintessential wimp? Because Dickens created Orlick, Gradgrind, Dotheboys Hall, Fagin, Uriah Heep, Steerforth, and Bill Sykes, must we conclude that he's a man-hater? Meredith was unrelentingly critical of men and quite admiring of women in such novels as *Richard Feverel* and *The Egoist*. Does that mean he's the equivalent of a class traitor? How about the fascinating Isabel Archer's failure to match herself with a man who's up to her, in James's *Portrait of A Lady*? Then there's *Tess of the D'Urbervilles*, with sweet gentle victimized Tess, and the two male protagonists, one of whom is a cad, the other a prig. I give you *Anna Karenina* and *Madame Bovary*, just to do a little culture-hopping; and while we're at it, we might mention that Captain Ahab, although a forceful literary creation, is hardly anybody's idea of an acceptable role model. Please note that all these characters and novels were the creations of men, not women; but nobody, to my knowledge, has accused these male authors of being mean to men, although they've been accused of all sorts of other things. Possibly the principle involved is the same one involved in the telling of ethnic jokes: it's all right within the group, but coming from the outside it's racism, though the joke may be exactly the same. If a man depicts a male character unfavourably, it's The Human Condition; if a woman does it, she's being mean to men. I think you can to a certain extent reverse this and apply it to women's reactions to books by women. I, for instance, was expecting to be denounced by at least a few feminists for having written my characters Elizabeth and Auntie Muriel in *Life Before Man*, both of whom would be less than desirable as roommates. But not a bit of it. By the time the book appeared, even feminist critics had tired somewhat of their own expectations; they no longer required all female protagonists to be warm but tough, wise and experienced but sensitive and open, competent, earth-motherly and passionate but chock full of dignity and integrity; they were willing to admit that women too might have blemishes, and that universal sisterhood, though desirable, had not yet been fully instituted upon this earth. Nevertheless, women have traditionally been harder on women's image issues in connection with books by women than men have. Maybe it's time to do away with judgement by role model and bring back The Human Condition, this time acknowledging that there may in fact be more than one of them.

Incidentally, you could make a case – if you wanted to – for concluding that women authors have historically been easier on men in their books than male authors have. Nowhere in major English novels by women do we find anything approaching that fallen angel and monster of depravity, Mr Kurtz, of *Heart of Darkness* fame; about the closest you could come, I think, would be the infamous Simon Legree (but I said *major* novels). The norm is more likely to range between Heathcliff and Mr Darcy, both of them flawed but sympathetically depicted; or, to invoke the greatest single English novel of the nineteenth century, George Eliot's *Middlemarch*, between dried-up envious Mr Casaubon and idealistic but misguided Dr Lydgate. The wonder of this book is that George Eliot can make us understand not only how awful it is to be married to Mr Casaubon, but how awful it is to *be* Mr Casaubon. This seems to me a worthy model to emulate. George Orwell said that every man's life viewed from within is a failure. If I said it, would it be sexist?

The Victorians, of course, had certain advantages that we lack. For one thing, they were not as self-conscious about the kind of thing we're discussing this evening as we have been forced to become. Though under constant pressure from the Mr and Mrs Grundies of their world never to write a line that might bring a blush to the cheek of a maiden of eighteen, which would in fact give you quite a lot of latitude today, they were not hesitant about depicting evil and calling it evil, or parading in front of their readers whole menageries of comic and grotesque figures, without worrying that such portraits might be interpreted as a slur upon one sex or the other. Female Victorian novelists had a couple of other advantages. Sex was out, so if they were creating a male character they could get away without trying to depict what sex felt like from a male point of view. Not only that, novels were assumed to be female-oriented, which meant that it took them a while to be viewed as a serious art form. Some of the first English novels were by women, the readership was preponderantly female, and even male novelists slanted their work accordingly. There are of course lots of exceptions, but on the whole we can say that the novel for almost two centuries had a decidedly female bias, which may account for the fact that many more male writers depicted female characters as central protagonists than the other way around. The advantage to the female novelist (as opposed to the Walter Scott romancer) was obvious. If novels were aimed at women, women had inside information.

The novel as a form has changed and expanded a good deal since then. Still, one of the questions people have been asking me most frequently is, 'Do you write women's novels?' You have to watch this question, since, like many other questions, its meaning varies according to who's asking it and of whom. 'Women's novels' can mean pop genre novels, such as the kind with nurses and doctors on the covers or the kind with rolling-eyed heroines in period costumes and windblown hair in front of gothic castles or Southern mansions or other locales where villainy may threaten and Heathcliff is still lurking around in the Spanish moss. Or it may mean novels for whom the main audience is assumed to be women, which would take in quite a lot, since the main audience for novels of all kinds, with the exception of Louis L'Amour western romances and certain kinds of porn, is also women. Or it can mean feminist propaganda novels. Or it can mean novels depicting male–female relationships, which again covers quite a lot of ground. Is *War and Peace* a women's novel? Is *Gone with the Wind*, even though it's got a war in it? Is *Middlemarch*, even though it's got The Human Condition in it? Could it be that women aren't afraid to be caught reading books that might be considered 'men's novels', whereas men still think something they need will fall off them if they look too hard at certain supposedly malevolent combinations of words put together by women? Judging from my recent walking to and fro in the earth and going up and down in bookstores for the purpose of signing my name on a lot of fly-leafs, I can tell you that this attitude is on the fade. More and more men are willing to stand in the line and *be seen*; fewer and fewer of them say, 'It's for my wife's birthday.'

But I almost put the boots to my old friend and cohort, the redoubtable Pierre Berton, when he asked me on television why all the men in my recent book *Bodily Harm* were wimps. Displaying the celebrated female compassion, not to be confused with feeble-mindedness, I merely dribbled aimlessly for a few minutes. 'Pierre,' I should have said, 'who do you think is likely to have had more experience of men in sexual relationships: you, or me?' This is not quite so mean as it sounds, and there's even something to it. Women as people have a relatively large pool of experiences from which to draw. They have their own experiences with men, of course, but they also have their friends', since, yes, girls do discuss men more than men – beyond the dirty anecdote syndrome – discuss women. Women are willing to talk about their weaknesses and fears to other women; men are not willing to talk about theirs to men, since it's still a dog-eat-dog world out there for them and no man wants to reveal his underbelly to a pack of fang-toothed potential rivals. If men are going to talk about their problems with women to anybody, it's usually either to a shrink or – guess what? – to another woman. In both reading and writing, women are likely to know more about how men actually behave with women than men are; so that what a man finds a slur on his self-image, a woman may find merely realistic or indeed unduly soft.

But to go back to Pierre Berton's assertion. I thought quite carefully about my male characters in *Bodily Harm*. There are three of them with whom the heroine actually sleeps, and the fourth main male character with whom she doesn't. A female novelist and critic noted that there is one good man in the book and no good women, and she's quite right. The other men are not 'bad' – in fact they are quite nice and attractive as male characters in literature go, a sight better than Mr Kurtz and Iago – but the *good* man is *black*, which is perhaps why the 'mean-to-menners' overlooked him. When playing the role-model game, you have to read carefully; otherwise you may be caught in an embarrassing position, like that one.

Now, back to the practical concerns of New Grub Street. Let us suppose that I am writing a novel. First: how many points of view will this novel have? If it has only one point of view, will it be that of a man, a woman or a seagull? Let us suppose that my novel will have one point of view and that the eyes through which we see the world of the novel unfolding will be those of a woman. Immediately it follows that the perceptions of all male characters in the book will have to pass through the perceiving apparatus of this central character. Nor will the central character necessarily be accurate or just. It also follows that all the other characters will be, of necessity, secondary. If I'm skilful I will be able to bounce another set of perceptions off those of the central character, through dialogue and between-the-lines innuendo, but there will be a strong bias toward A as truth-teller and we will never get to hear what Characters B and C really think when they're by themselves, urinating outdoors perhaps or doing other male things. However, the picture changes if I use a multiple point of view. Now I can have Characters B and C think for themselves, and what they think won't always be what Character A thinks of *them*. If I like, I can add in yet another point of view, that of the omniscient author (who is of course not 'me', the same me that had bran muffins for breakfast this morning and is right now giving this speech) but yet another voice within the novel. The omniscient author can claim to know things about the characters that even they don't know, thus letting the reader know these things as well.

The next thing I have to decide is what tone I'm taking, what mode I'm writing in. A careful study of *Wuthering Heights* will reveal that Heathcliff is never to be observed picking his nose, or indeed even blowing it, and you can search through Walter Scott in vain for any mention of bathrooms. Leopold Bloom on the other hand is preoccupied with the mundane wants of the body on almost every page, and we find him sympathetic, yes, and comic and also pathetic, but he is not exactly love's young dream. Leopold Bloom climbing in through Cathy's window would probably slip. Which is the more accurate portrayal of Man with a capital M? Or, like Walter Mitty, does each man contain within him both an ordinary, limited and trivial self and a heroic concept, and if so, which should we be writing about? I carry no brief for either, except to remark that serious novelists in the twentieth century usually opt for Leopold, and poor Heathcliff has been relegated to the Gothic romance. If a given serious novelist of the twentieth century is female, she too will probably go for Leopold, with all his habits, daydreams and wants. This doesn't mean she hates men; merely that she's interested in what they look like without the cloak.

All right. Suppose I've chosen to have in my novel at least one male character as a narrator or protagonist (not necessarily the same thing). I do not want to make my male character unnaturally evil, like Mr Hyde; instead I'm trying for Dr Jekyll, an essentially good man with certain flaws. That's a problem right there; because, as Stevenson knew, evil is a lot easier to write about and make interesting than goodness. What, these days, is a believable notion of a good man? Let us suppose that I'm talking about a man who is merely unbad; that is, one who obeys the major laws, pays his bills, helps with the dishes, doesn't beat up his wife or molest his kids, and so forth. Let's suppose that I want him to have some actual good qualities, good in the active, positive sense. What is he to do? And how can I make him – unlike Sir Charles Grandison – interesting in a novel?

This I suspect is the point at which the concerns of the novelist coincide with those of society. Once upon a time, when we defined people – much more than we do now – by how far they lived up or failed to live up to certain pre-defined sexual role models, it was a lot easier to tell what was meant by 'a good man' or 'a good woman'. 'A good woman' was one that fulfilled our notions of what a woman should be and how she should behave. Likewise 'a good man'. There were certain concepts about what constituted manliness and how you got it – most authorities agreed that you weren't just born with it, you somehow had to earn, acquire or be initiated into it; acts of courage and heroism counted for something, ability to endure pain without flinching, or drink a lot without passing out, or whatever. In any case there were rules, and you could cross a line that separated the men from the boys.

It's true that the male sexual role model had a lot of drawbacks, even for men – not everybody could be Superman, many were stuck with Clark Kent – but there were certain positive and, at that time, useful features. What have we replaced this package with? We know that women have been in a state of upheaval and ferment for some time now, and movement generates energy; many things can be said by women now that were once not possible, many things can be thought that were once unthinkable. But what are we offering men? Their territory, though still large, is shrinking. The confusion and desperation and anger and conflicts that we find in male characters in novels don't exist only in novels. They're out there in the real world. 'Be a person, my son', doesn't yet have the same ring to it as 'Be a man', though it is indeed a worthy goal. The novelist *qua* novelist, as opposed to the utopian romancer, takes *what is there* as a point of departure. What is there, when we're talking about men, is a state of change, new attitudes overlapping with old ones, no simple rules any more. Some exciting form of life may emerge from all this.

Meanwhile, I think women have to take the concerns of men as seriously as they expect men to take theirs, both as novelists and as inhabitants of this earth. One encounters, too often, the attitude that only the pain felt by persons of the female sex is real pain, that only female fears are real fears. That for me is the equivalent of the notion that only working-class people are real, that middle-class people are not, and so forth. Of course there's a distinction between earned pain and mere childish self-pity, and yes, women's fear of being killed by men is grounded in authenticity, not to mention statistics, to a greater extent than men's fear of being laughed at. Damage to one's self-image is not quite the same as damage to one's neck, though not to be underestimated: men have been known to murder and kill themselves because of it.

I'm not advocating a return to door-mat status for women, or even to the arrangement whereby women prop up and nurture and stroke and feed the egos of men without having men do at least some of the same for them. To understand is not necessarily to condone; and it could be pointed out that women have been 'understanding' men for centuries, partly because it was necessary for survival. If the other fellow has the heavy artillery, it's best to be able to anticipate his probable moves. Women, like guerrilla fighters, developed infiltration rather than frontal attack as their favoured strategy. But 'understanding' as a manipulative tool – which is really a form of contempt for the thing understood – isn't the kind I would like to see. However, some women are not in the mood to dish out any more understanding, of any kind; they're feeling a lot like René Lévesque: the time for that is over, they want power instead. But one cannot deprive any part of humanity of the definition 'human' without grievous risk to one's own soul. And for women to define themselves as powerless and men as all-powerful is to fall into an ancient trap, to shirk responsibility as well as to warp reality. The opposite also is true; to depict a world in which women are already equal to men, in power, opportunities and freedom of movement, is a similar abdication.

I know I haven't given any specific directions for writing the male character; how can I? They're all different, remember. All I've given are a few warnings, an indication of what you're up against from the real world and from critics. But just because it's difficult is no reason not to try.

When I was young and reading a lot of comic books and fairy tales, I used to wish for two things: the cloak of invisibility, so I could follow people around and listen to what they were saying when I wasn't there, and the ability to teleport my mind into somebody else's mind, still retaining my own perceptions and memory. You can see that I was cut out to be a novelist, because these are the two fantasies novelists act out every time they write a page. Throwing your mind is easier to do if you're throwing it into a character who has a few things in common with you, which may be why I've written more pages from a female character's point of view than from a male's. But male characters are more of a challenge, and now that I'm middle-aged and less lazy I'll undoubtedly try a few more of them. If writing novels – and reading them – have any redeeming social value, it's probably that they force you to imagine what it's like to be somebody else.

Which, increasingly, is something we all need to know.

7

Wondering What It's Like to Be a Woman

The Witches of Eastwick is John Updike's first novel since the much-celebrated *Rabbit Is Rich*, and a strange and marvellous organism it proves to be. Like his third novel, *The Centaur*, it is a departure from baroque realism. This time, too, Mr Updike transposes mythology into the minor keys of small-town America, but this time he pulls it off, possibly because, like Shakespeare and Robert Louis Stevenson before him, he finds wickedness and mischief more engrossing as subjects than goodness and wisdom.

Mr Updike's titles are often quite literal, and *The Witches of Eastwick* is just what it says. It's indeed about witches, real ones, who can fly through the air, levitate, hex people and make love charms that work, and they live in a town called Eastwick. It's Eastwick rather than Westwick, since, as we all know, it's the east wind that blows no good. Eastwick purports to be in Rhode Island because, as the book itself points out, Rhode Island was the place of exile for Anne Hutchinson, the Puritan foremother who was kicked out of the Massachusetts Bay colony by the forefathers for female insubordination, a quality these witches have in surplus.

These are not 1980s Womanpower witches. They aren't at all interested in healing the earth, communing with the Great Goddess, or gaining Power-within (as opposed to Power-over).

These are *bad* Witches, and Power-within, as far as they are concerned, is no good at all unless you can zap somebody with it. They are spiritual descendants of the seventeenth-century New England strain and go in for sabbats, sticking pins in wax images, kissing the Devil's backside and phallus worship; this latter though – since it is Updike – is qualified worship. The Great Goddess is present only in the form of Nature itself, or, in this book, Nature herself, with which they, both as women and as witches, are supposed to have special affinities. Nature, however, is far from Wordsworth's big motherly breast. She, or it, is red in tooth, claw and cancer cell, at best lovely and cruel, at worse merely cruel. 'Nature kills constantly, and we call her beautiful.'

How did these middle-class, small-town, otherwise ordinary women get their witchy powers? Simple. They became husbandless. All three are divorcées and embodiments of what American small-town society tends to think about divorcées. Whether you leave your husband or are left 'doesn't make any difference', which will be news to many abandoned women stuck with full child support. Divorced then, and, with the images of their former husbands shrunk and dried and stored away in their minds and kitchens and cellars, they are free to be themselves, an activity Mr Updike regards with some misgivings, as he regards most catchwords and psychofads.

Being yourself involves artistic activity, albeit of minor kinds. Lexa makes ceramic earthmothers, which are sold in the local crafts store, Jane plays the cello, and Sukie writes, badly, a gossip column for the weekly paper, her participles dangling like earrings. All three are dabblers, but their 'creativity' is seen in the same light as that of other, more accomplished female artists. The townspeople of Eastwick, who act as a collective chorus, credit them with 'a certain distinction, an inner boiling such as had in other cloistral towns produced Emily Dickinson's verses and Emily Brontë's inspired novel'.

It's doubtful, however, that either of the Emilys went in for the sexual loop-the-loops indulged in by these three weird sisters.

Sisters in more senses than one because the novel is cunningly set at a precise moment in America's recent history. The women's movement has been around just long enough for some of its phrases to have seeped from New York to the outer darkness of provincial towns like Eastwick, and the witches toss around words like 'chauvinist' in light social repartee. In the public, male world, which is offstage, the Vietnam War goes on, watched by the witches' children on their television sets, and the anti-war activists are making bombs in cellars.

The witches don't busy themselves with 'causes', however. At first, they are merely restless and bored; they amuse themselves with spiteful gossip, playing mischievous tricks and seducing unhappily married men, which Eastwick supplies in strength; for if the witches are bad, the wives are worse, and the men are eviscerated. 'Marriage,' one of the husbands thinks, 'is like two people locked up with one lesson to read, over and over, until the words become madness.'

But enter the Devil, the world's best remedy for women's boredom, in the form of the dark, not very handsome but definitely mysterious stranger Darryl Van Horne, who collects pop art and has an obvious name. Now mischief turns to *maleficio*, real evil occurs and people die, because Van Horne's horn becomes a bone of contention – nothing like not enough men to go around to get the witches' cauldrons bubbling. And when Van Horne is snatched into marriage by a newcomer witchlet, the eye of newt comes out in earnest.

This may sound like an unpromising framework for a serious novelist. Has Mr Updike entered second childhood and reverted to Rosemary's babyland? I don't think so. For one thing, *The Witches of Eastwick* is too well done. Like Van Horne, Mr Updike has always wondered what it would be like to be a woman, and his witches give him a lot of scope for this fantasy. Lexa in particular, who is the oldest, the plumpest, the kindest and the closest to Nature, is a fitting vehicle for some of his most breathtaking similes. In line of descent, he is perhaps closer than any other living American writer to the Puritan view of Nature as a lexicon written by God, but in hieroglyphs, so that unending translation is needed. Mr Updike's prose, here more than ever, is a welter of suggestive metaphors and cross-references, which constantly point toward a meaning constantly evasive.

His version of witchcraft is closely tied to both carnality and mortality. Magic is hope in the face of inevitable decay. The houses and the furniture moulder, and so do the people. The portrait of Felicia Gabriel, victim wife and degenerate after-image of the one-time 'preppy' American cheerleading sweetheart, is gruesomely convincing. Bodies are described in loving detail, down to the last tuft, wart, wrinkle and bit of food stuck in the teeth. No one is better than Mr Updike at conveying the sadness of the sexual, the melancholy of motel affairs – 'amiable human awkwardness', Lexa calls it. This is a book that redefines magic realism.

There's room too for bravura writing. The widdershins dance, portrayed as a tennis game in which the ball turns into a bat, followed by the sabbat as a hot-tub-and-pot session, is particularly fetching. Students of traditional Devil-lore will have as much fun with these transpositions as Mr Updike had. Van Horne, for instance, is part Mephistopheles, offering Faustian pacts and lusting for souls, part alchemist-chemist, and part Miltonic Satan, hollow at the core; but he's also a shambling klutz whose favourite comic book is – what else? – *Captain Marvel*.

Much of *The Witches of Eastwick* is satire, some of it literary playfulness and some plain bitchery. It could be that any attempt to analyse further would be like taking an elephant gun to a puff pastry: an Updike should not mean but be. But again, I don't think so. What a culture has to say about witchcraft, whether in jest or in earnest, has a lot to do with its views of sexuality and power, and especially with the apportioning of powers between the sexes. The witches were burned not because they were pitied but because they were feared.

Cotton Mather and Nathaniel Hawthorne aside, the great American witchcraft classic is *The Wizard of Oz*, and Mr Updike's book reads like a rewrite. In the original, a good little girl and her familiar, accompanied by three amputated males, go seeking a wizard who turns out to be a charlatan. The witches in *Oz* really have superhuman powers, but the male figures do not. Mr Updike's Land of Oz is the real America, but the men in it need a lot more than self-confidence; there's no Glinda the Good, and the Dorothy-like ingenue is a 'wimp' who gets her comeuppance. It's the three witches of Eastwick who go back, in the end, to the equivalent of Kansas – marriage, flat and grey maybe, but at least known.

The Witches of Eastwick could be and probably will be interpreted as just another episode in the long-running American serial called *Blaming Mom*. The Woman-as-Nature-as-magic-as-powerful-as-bad-Mom package has gone the rounds before, sometimes accompanied by the smell of burning. If prattle of witchcraft is heard in the land, can the hunt be far behind? Mr Updike provides no blameless way of being female. Hackles will rise, the word 'backlash' will be spoken; but anyone speaking it should look at the men in this book, who, while proclaiming their individual emptiness, are collectively, offstage, blowing up Vietnam. That's *male* magic. Men, say the witches, more than once, are full of rage because they can't make babies, and even male babies have at their centre 'that aggressive vacuum'. Shazam indeed!

A Martian might wonder at the American propensity for tossing the power football. Each sex hurls it at the other with amazing regularity, each crediting the other with more power than the other thinks it has, and the characters in this book join in the game with glee. The aim seems to be the avoidance of responsibility, the reversion to a childlike state of Huckleberry Finn-like 'freedom'. What the witches want from the Devil is to play without consequences. But all the Devil can really offer is temptation; hot-tubbery has its price, and the Devil must have his due; with the act of creation comes irreversibility, and guilt.

Mr Updike takes 'sisterhood is powerful' at its word and

imagines it literally. What if sisterhood really is powerful? What will the sisters use their 'powers' for? And — given human nature, of which Mr Updike takes not too bright a view — what then? Luckily these witches are only interested in the 'personal', rather than the 'political'; otherwise they might have done something unfrivolous, like inventing the hydrogen bomb.

The Witches of Eastwick is an excursion rather than a destination. Like its characters, it indulges in metamorphoses, reading at one moment like Kierkegaard, at the next like Swift's 'Modest Proposal', and at the next like *Archie* comics, with some John Keats thrown in. This quirkiness is part of its charm, for, despite everything, charming it is. As for the witches themselves, there's a strong suggestion that they are products of Eastwick's — read America's — own fantasy life. If so, it's as well to know about it. That's the serious reason for reading this book.

The other reasons have to do with the skill and inventiveness of the writing, the accuracy of the detail, the sheer energy of the witches and, above all, the practicality of the charms. The ones for getting suitable husbands are particularly useful. You want a rich one, for a change? First you sprinkle a tuxedo with your perfume and your precious bodily fluids and then . . .

8

Introduction to *Roughing It in the Bush*

.   .

The reader will, I hope, forgive me beginning this introduction with my own involvement with Susanna Moodie. I am not a scholar or historian, but a writer of fiction and poetry, and such people are notoriously subjective in their reading.

While I was growing up in the forties and early fifties, Susanna Moodie's *Roughing It in the Bush* sat in our bookcase, which it was my job to dust. It was with the grown-up books, but I always noticed it anyway because of the two interlocking O's of the author's last name, which were featured in the rounded typographical style of 1913 on the cover. I recall opening the book and looking at the fron-tispiece – a snow-covered log cabin – but I did not read this book at the time. For one thing, it was not a novel, and I was not interested in books that were not novels. For another, my father told me that it was a 'classic' and that I would 'find it interesting to read some day'. I tended to shy away from books that were so described. For yet another, it was about people living in a log cabin in the bush. I myself had spent a large part of my childhood in cabins, log and otherwise, in the bush, and did not find anything exotic about the notion. I was more interested in mediaeval castles, or, on the other hand, ray guns. *Roughing It in the Bush*, I thought, would be tame stuff.

My second encounter with this book was in Grade Six, when

part of it appeared in our reader. It was the section in which the Moodies' chimney catches fire and the house does too. This rang true: chimney fires caused by overstuffing were one of the bugbears of my childhood. Still, every author in the Grade Six reader came to us clothed in the dull grey mantle of required reading, and I forgot about Susanna Moodie and went on to other matters, such as Jane Austen.

My third experience with Susanna Moodie was of an altogether different order. When I was a graduate student at the Harvard Department of English Literature, at that time a sort of Jungian hothouse, I had a particularly vivid dream. I had written an opera about Susanna Moodie, and there she was, all by herself on a completely white stage, singing like Lucia de Lammermoor. I could barely read music, but I was not one to ignore portents: I rushed off to the library, where the Canadiana was kept in the bowels of the stacks beneath Witchcraft and Demonology, got out both *Roughing It in the Bush* and Mrs Moodie's later work, *Life in the Clearings*, and read them at full speed.

At first I thought my unconscious had given me a bad tip. Despite the drama of many of the incidents described, the prose was Victorian in a quasi-Dickensian semi-jocular way, veering into Wordsworthian rhapsody when it came to sunsets, and there was a patina of gentility that offended my young soul, as did the asides on the servant question and the lower-classness of many of the emigrants already in place.

However, the Shadow will not be mocked, and Susanna Moodie began to haunt me. About a year and a half later I began a series of poems which became a book, *The Journals of Susanna Moodie*, which by now has doubtless been thrust down many an adolescent throat. What kept bringing me back to the subject – and to Susanna Moodie's own work – were the hints, the gaps between what was said and what hovered, just unsaid, between the lines, and the conflict between what Mrs Moodie felt she ought to think and feel and what she actually did think and feel. Probably my poems were about these tensions. So are her books.

Some years later, I wrote a television play based on a notable murder in *Life in the Clearings*, and later still a short book of social history of the period from 1815 to 1840; and both of these experiences forced me to grapple a little with the background and climate of Susanna Moodie's books. They also made me consider Moodie herself in a newer light. Life in a log cabin in the bush had been normal and pleasant for me, but it was obvious that it was, and had to be, quite otherwise for her. I got culture shock from flush toilets, she got it from mosquitoes, swamps, trackless wildernesses and the thought of bears. In some ways, we were each other's obverse.

The forces that combined to waft Susanna Moodie to Upper Canada in 1832 were wafting many others as well. In 1760, with the capture of Quebec, Britain had acquired the Canadas, Upper and Lower (so called because, though Upper Canada was 'lower' than Lower Canada, travel to both was via the St Lawrence River, and Upper Canada was further upstream). Then came the American Revolution and an influx of immigrant United Empire Loyalists to Upper Canada. Then came the War of 1812 in North America and the Napoleonic Wars in Europe. The end of these wars sent many soldiers back into the potential labour force in Britain, with widespread unemployment as a result. The effects of the Highland Clearances and the Irish potato famine were still being felt. Many of the poor in Britain looked towards emigration to the colonies as a solution that offered them at least the hope of bettering their condition, a belief that was encouraged both by the ruling classes in England and by the ship-owners, merchants and land speculators lying in wait for them along the way. Pamphlets, settlers' guides and other forms of propaganda poured forth, depicting Upper Canada as a bucolic wonderland with a climate much like Britain's, where industry and virtue would inevitably be rewarded.

Rising to these lures or impelled by the pinch of necessity, seven and a half million people crossed the ocean from Britain between 1800 and 1875. In 1832, fifty thousand emigrants entered Upper and Lower Canada. The population of Upper Canada became seven times larger during the first third of the century. 'In 1830,' as Moodie says, 'Canada became the great landmark for the rich in hope and poor in purse.'

Susanna Moodie was not from a poor family, but from the genteel middle-to-upper middle class: however, many from families like hers also chose to emigrate at this time. There was a surplus of younger sons in Britain, of which Mr Moodie was one, and many among the gentry or near-gentry saw a chance, in the colonies, of becoming more nearly what they thought they already were: landed gentry. Susanna Moodie, her sister Catherine Parr Traill, later to become the author of *The Canadian Settler's Guide*, and her brother Samuel Strickland were three who made the choice.

What they may have been expecting beforehand can be gathered from *The Young Emigrants; or, Pictures of Canada*, a children's book written by Catherine Parr Traill in 1826, six years before she and Susanna actually went to Canada. In it, the ideal immigrant family, who are middle class like the Moodies, speedily acquire a prosperous farm, which they tend with the aid of friendly servants and a little discreet poultry-feeding and gardening by the women. They whip up a comfortable and spacious four-bedroom dwelling where they spend the day supervising things and the evenings in practising their musical accomplishments and in 'social chat or innocent gaiety' with their equally genteel neighbours.

The reality, when Susanna Moodie and Catherine Parr Traill actually encountered it, was far otherwise. The most 'English' land in Upper Canada, the fertile and relatively warm Niagara Peninsula, was already taken. After a pleasant enough First Class crossing, far above the horrors of the steerage where the poor travelled in stench-filled, overcrowded semi-darkness, they got their first taste of the Canadas when they landed at Grosse Isle and discovered that to many of the steerage travellers the New World meant a deplorable levelling of social classes. 'Whurrah! my boys! . . . Shure we'll all be jintlemen,' Susanna Moodie heard one Irish labourer shouting. She was to encounter this spirit in many forms later on: saucy servants who wanted to eat at the same table, earlier settlers who looked upon her with contempt, 'Late Loyalists' from the United States who cheated her and borrowed, without returning, anything she was fool enough to lend them. Gentlefolk like her were the target of considerable malice, she found: when the family moved into one dwelling, they found the floor flooded, the fruit trees girdled, and a dead skunk stuffed up the chimney. Later, when she'd had time to mull it over, she came to understand what these people might have had against her: yes, the British class system could be repressive. But at the time this was just one of many obstacles that were set in her path.

There were others. Nature, which Wordsworth had declared, 'never did betray/The heart that loved her', looked quite different in the thickly-treed wilds of Canada from the way it looked in even the craggiest parts of England. Susanna Moodie did her best with vistas and panoramas and picturesque scenery, but she much preferred Canadian Nature from a distance; the deck of a moving boat, for instance. Up close, there were likely to be mosquitoes, mud, ruts, swamps, and stumps. Also, there was winter, which was not like anything she'd encountered before. And there was the nightmare of clearing the land, without the aid of tractors, and of wrenching a few vegetables from the apparently grudging soil.

Above all, there was her own inexperience, her own unfitness for the kind of hardship and labour she found herself compelled to do. Her first home, near Coburg, was rented sight unseen on the understanding that it was 'a delightful summer residence', but it turned out to be a doorless one-room shack which Mrs Moodie took at first sight to be a pigsty. Her second home was even further out in the backwoods. After seven years in the bush, Mrs Moodie had acquired some of the skills necessary for a set-tler's wife – she could make coffee from dandelion roots and bake bread that didn't resemble a cinder, for instance – but, despite her *post facto* sentimentality about her woodland home, she was happy to profit by Mr Moodie's elevation to the position of Sheriff of Belleville and to kiss the wilderness 'adieu'.

We should remember too that the years she spent in the bush were child-bearing ones for her; in those days before modern medicine, when a doctor, even if there had been one available, wouldn't have been much help, not all the children eventually survived. Mrs Moodie is reticent on the subject, but she says at one point, rather chillingly, that she never felt really at home in Canada until she had buried some of her children in it. She may have come to 'love' her rustic house and her new country somewhat, but to get to that point she'd had to pass through 'a hatred so intense that I longed to die, that death might effectually separate us forever'. The point of her book, she more than once reminds us, is to discourage other English gentlefolk from doing what she herself had done. The Canadian frontier, she claims, is for the working classes, who are strong enough to put up with it. Drunkenness, debt, decline and 'hopeless ruin' are more likely to be the lot of the transplanted gentleman.

Now that such warnings are no longer needed, what does *Roughing It in the Bush* have to offer the modern reader? Quite a lot, as it turns out. Although it isn't a novel, but one of those books that purports to tell the plain truth – as, indeed, early novels did too – it's structured like a novel. It has a plot, which combines the journey with the ordeal, as the emigrant-travellers encounter a new land, cope with the strange inhabitants and customs they find there, overcome hardships that range from cholera to starvation. Looked at in this light, *Roughing It in the Bush* can be seen as belonging to a distinct tradition of travel writing – a tradition that perhaps culminates in Eric Newby's *A Short Walk in the Hindu Kush* – in which the horribleness of the journey, the filthiness and squalor of the accommodations, and the awfulness of the food are outdone only by the traveller's self-perceived lunacy in having undertaken the trip at all. It also has a meticulously described setting: the confrontation with a harsh and vast geography was, and was to become, a dominant motif in Canadian writing. It also has characters; 'character sketches', with dialogue included, are something

Mrs Moodie is particularly good at, and 'Brian, the Still Hunter' has frequently been anthologized as a short story. But the most complex and ambiguous character in her book is herself.

If Catherine Parr Traill with her imperturbable practicality is what we like to think we would be under the circumstances, Susanna Moodie is what we secretly suspect we would have been instead. Time and again she rises above the prejudices of her own age and position, but time and again she sinks back into them. She doesn't know how to do things right, she makes mistakes, she's afraid of cows, she gets caught out on the lake in thunderstorms. But (surely like us!) she is not a total ninny; she can keep her head in emergencies, she has an innate decency and a respect for natural virtue and courtesy, and she has a sense of humour and can laugh at her own ineptness.

There is another way of reading Moodie, and that is to place her with three other women writers who were among the first to produce much of anything resembling literature in Upper Canada. One was of course Susanna Moodie's sister, Mrs Traill. Another was Anne Langton, who settled near Sturgeon Lake and wrote *A Gentlewoman in Upper Canada*. The fourth did not settle but passed through quite thoroughly: Anna Jameson, the author of *Winter Studies and Summer Rambles in Canada*. All were gentlewomen, all looked at the growing colony with a critical though not entirely harsh eye, and all demonstrate that gender is not the only thing to be taken into account when accomplishments of one sort or another are being evaluated: their class gave these women a literary edge over those of their less well-educated fellow citizens who happened to be male.

In fact, when you place the early literature of the Canadas beside that of the United States, a curious thing emerges. It's possible to cover American literature from, say, 1625 to 1900, without spending much time at all on women writers, with the exception of Ann Bradstreet and Emily Dickinson. Attention focuses on the 'great' and overwhelmingly male American writers of the period: Melville,

Poe, Hawthorne, Whitman, Thoreau. English Canada produced no such classics at this time – it was settled later – but if you study the literature at all, you can't ignore the women. Possibly the reason for the relative preponderance of women writers in Canada can be found in the different ages in which the two were initially settled: America in the Puritan seventeenth century, English Canada in the nineteenth, the age of the letter and the journal, at a time when many women were already literate. In any case, it's a situation that has persisted until today: the percentage of prominent and admittedly accomplished women writers, in both prose and poetry, is higher in Canada than it is in any of the other English-speaking countries. The same is true of Quebec, in which some of the first writing was done by nuns who had come to convert the Indians (and where, incidentally, the first English-language novel in Canada was written, also by a woman).

Susanna Moodie did not intend to write a Canadian classic, nor would she have anticipated or relished being claimed as an ancestress by the modern women's movement; she was a creature of her own society, and would have disapproved of many feminist principles. But, as others, including T. S. Eliot, have pointed out, a work of literature gains meaning not only from its own context but from those later contexts it may find itself placed within. Susanna Moodie's account of her struggles, failures and survival have resonance for us now partly because we have produced our own literature of struggles, failures and survival. She was not Superwoman, but she coped somehow, and lived to write about it, and even managed to squeeze a kind of wisdom from her ordeal.

9

Haunted by Their Nightmares

Beloved is Toni Morrison's fifth novel, and another triumph. Indeed, Ms Morrison's versatility and technical and emotional range appear to know no bounds. If there were any doubts about her stature as a pre-eminent American novelist, of her own or any other generation, *Beloved* will put them to rest. In three words or less, it's a hair-raiser.

In *Beloved*, Ms Morrison turns away from the contemporary scene that has been her concern of late. This new novel is set after the end of the Civil War, during the period of so-called Reconstruction, when a great deal of random violence was let loose upon blacks, both the slaves freed by Emancipation and others who had been given or had bought their freedom earlier. But there are flashbacks to a more distant period, when slavery was still a going concern in the South and the seeds for the bizarre and calamitous events of the novel were sown. The setting is similarly divided: the countryside near Cincinnati, where the central characters have ended up, and a slave-holding plantation in Kentucky, ironically named Sweet Home, from which they fled eighteen years before the novel opens.

There are many stories and voices in this novel, but the central one belongs to Sethe, a woman in her mid-thirties who is living in an Ohio farmhouse, with her daughter, Denver, and her mother-in-law, Baby Suggs. *Beloved* is such a unified novel that it's difficult to discuss it without giving away the plot, but it must be said at the outset that it is, among other things, a ghost story, for the farmhouse is also home to a sad, malicious and angry ghost, the spirit of Sethe's baby daughter, who had her throat cut under appalling circumstances eighteen years before, when she was two. We never know this child's full name, but we – and Sethe – think of her as Beloved, because that is what is on her tombstone. Sethe wanted 'Dearly Beloved', from the funeral service, but had only enough strength to pay for one word. Payment was ten minutes of sex with the tombstone engraver. This act, which is recounted early in the novel, is a keynote for the whole book: in the world of slavery and poverty, where human beings are merchandise, everything has its price, and price is tyrannical.

'Who would have thought that a little old baby could harbor so much rage?' Sethe thinks, but it does; breaking mirrors, making tiny handprints in cake icing, smashing dishes and manifesting itself in pools of blood-red light. As the novel opens, the ghost is in full possession of the house, having driven away Sethe's two young sons. Old Baby Suggs, after a lifetime of slavery and a brief respite of freedom – purchased for her by the Sunday labour of her son Halle, Sethe's husband – has given up and died. Sethe lives with her memories, almost all of them bad. Denver, her teenage daughter, courts the baby ghost because, since her family has been ostracized by the neighbours, she doesn't have anyone else to play with.

The supernatural element is treated, not in an *Amityville Horror*, watch-me-make-your-flesh-creep mode, but with magnificent practicality, like the ghost of Catherine Earnshaw in *Wuthering Heights*. All the main characters in the book believe in ghosts, so it's merely natural for this one to be there. As Baby Suggs says, 'Not a house in the country ain't packed to its rafters with some dead Negro's grief. We lucky this ghost is a baby. My husband's spirit was to come back in here? or yours? Don't talk to me. You lucky.' In fact, Sethe would rather have the ghost there than not there. It is, after all, her adored child, and any sign of it is better, for her, than nothing.

This grotesque domestic equilibrium is disturbed by the arrival of Paul D., one of the 'Sweet Home men' from Sethe's past. The Sweet Home men were the male slaves of the establishment. Their owner, Mr Garner, is no Simon Legree; instead he's a best-case slave-holder, treating his 'property' well, trusting them, allowing them choice in the running of his small plantation, and calling them 'men' in defiance of the neighbours, who want all male blacks to be called 'boys'. But Mr Garner dies, and weak, sickly Mrs Garner brings in her handiest male relative, who is known as 'the schoolteacher'. This Goebbels-like paragon combines viciousness with intellectual pretensions; he's a sort of master-race proponent who measures the heads of the slaves and tabulates the results to demonstrate that they are more like animals than people. Accompanying him are his two sadistic and repulsive nephews. From there it's all downhill at Sweet Home, as the slaves try to escape, go crazy or are murdered. Sethe, in a trek that makes the ice-floe scene in *Uncle Tom's Cabin* look like a stroll around the block, gets out, just barely; her husband, Halle, doesn't. Paul D. does, but has some very unpleasant adventures along the way, including a literally nauseating sojourn in a nineteenth-century Georgia chain gang.

Through the different voices and memories of the book, including that of Sethe's mother, a survivor of the infamous slave-ship crossing, we experience American slavery as it was lived by those who were its objects of exchange, both at its best – which wasn't very good – and at its worst, which was as bad as can be imagined. Above all, it is seen as one of the most viciously anti-family institutions human beings have ever devised. The slaves are motherless, fatherless, deprived of their mates, their children, their kin. It is a world in which people suddenly vanish and are never seen again, not through accident or covert operation or terrorism, but as a matter of everyday legal policy.

Slavery is also presented to us as a paradigm of how most people behave when they are given absolute power over other people. The first effect, of course, is that they start believing in their own superiority and justifying their actions by it. The second effect is that they make a cult of the inferiority of those they subjugate. It's no coincidence that the first of the deadly sins, from which all the others were supposed to stem, is Pride, a sin of which Sethe is, incidentally, also accused.

In a novel that abounds in black bodies – headless, hanging from trees, frying to a crisp, locked in woodsheds for purposes of rape, or floating downstream drowned – it isn't surprising that the 'white-people', especially the men, don't come off too well. Horrified black children see whites as men 'without skin'. Sethe thinks of them as having 'mossy teeth' and is ready, if necessary, to bite off their faces, and worse, to avoid further mossy-toothed outrages. There are a few whites who behave with something approaching decency. There's Amy, the young runaway indentured servant who helps Sethe in childbirth during her flight to freedom, and incidentally reminds the reader that the nineteenth century, with its child labour, wage slavery and widespread and accepted domestic violence, wasn't tough only for blacks, but for all but the most privileged whites as well. There are also the abolitionists who help Baby Suggs find a house and a job after she is freed. But even the decency of these 'good' whitepeople has a grudging side to it, and even they have trouble seeing the people they are helping as fully-fledged people, though to show them as totally free of their xenophobia and sense of superiority might well have been anachronistic.

Toni Morrison is careful not to make all the whites awful and all the blacks wonderful. Sethe's black neighbours, for instance, have their own envy and scapegoating tendencies to answer for, and Paul D., though much kinder than, for instance, the woman-bashers of Alice Walker's novel *The Color Purple*, has his own limitations and flaws. But then, considering what he's been through, it's a wonder he isn't a mass murderer. If anything, he's a little too huggable, under the circumstances.

Back in the present tense, in chapter one, Paul D. and Sethe make an attempt to establish a 'real' family, whereupon the baby ghost, feeling excluded, goes berserk, but is driven out by Paul D.'s stronger will. So it appears. But then, along comes a strange, beautiful, real flesh-and-blood young woman, about twenty years old, who can't seem to remember where she comes from, who talks like a young child, who has an odd, raspy voice and no lines on her hands, who takes an intense, devouring interest in Sethe, and who says her name is Beloved.

Students of the supernatural will admire the way this twist is handled. Ms Morrison blends a knowledge of folklore — for instance, in many traditions, the dead cannot return from the grave unless called, and it's the passions of the living that keep them alive — with a highly original treatment. The reader is kept guessing; there's a lot more to Beloved than any one character can see, and she manages to be many things to several people. She is a catalyst for revelations as well as self revelations; through her we come to know not only how, but why, the original child Beloved was killed. And through her also Sethe achieves, finally, her own form of self-exorcism, her own self-accepting peace.

Beloved is written in an anti-minimalist prose that is by turns rich, graceful, eccentric, rough, lyrical, sinuous, colloquial and very much to the point. Here, for instance, is Sethe remembering Sweet Home:

> '. . . suddenly there was Sweet Home rolling, rolling, rolling out before her eyes, and although there was not a leaf on that farm that did not want to make her scream, it rolled itself out before her in shameless beauty. It never looked as terrible as it was and it made her wonder if hell was a pretty place too. Fire and brimstone all right, but hidden in lacy groves. Boys hanging from the most beautiful sycamores in the world. It shamed her — remembering the wonderful soughing trees rather than the boys. Try as she might to make it otherwise, the sycamores beat out the children every time and she could not forgive her memory for that.'

In this book, the other world exists and magic works, and the prose is up to it. If you can believe page one – and Ms Morrison's verbal authority compels belief – you're hooked on the rest of the book.

The epigraph to *Beloved* is from the Bible, Romans 9:25: 'I will call them my people, which were not my people; and her beloved, which was not beloved.' Taken by itself, this might seem to favour doubt about, for instance, the extent to which Beloved was really loved, or the extent to which Sethe herself was rejected by her own community. But there is more to it than that. The passage is from a chapter in which the Apostle Paul ponders, Job-like, the ways of God toward humanity, in particular the evils and inequities visible everywhere on the earth. Paul goes on to talk about the fact that the Gentiles, hitherto despised and outcast, have now been redefined as acceptable. The passage proclaims, not rejection, but reconciliation and hope. It continues: 'And it shall come to pass, that in the place where it was said unto them, Ye are not my people; there shall they be called the children of the living God.'

Toni Morrison is too smart, and too much of a writer, not to have intended this context. Here, if anywhere, is her own comment on the goings-on in her novel, her final response to the measuring and dividing and excluding 'schoolteachers' of this world. An epigraph to a book is like a key signature in music, and *Beloved* is written in major.

10

Writing Utopia

How did *The Handmaid's Tale* get written? The answer could be, partly on a rented electric typewriter with a German keyboard in a walk-up flat in West Berlin, and partly in a small house in Tuscaloosa, Alabama – which, it was announced to me with a certain pride, is the *per capita* murder capital of the US. 'Gosh,' I said. 'Maybe I shouldn't be here.' 'Aw, don't y'all worry,' they replied. 'They only shoots family.' But although these two places provided, shall we say, a certain atmosphere, there is more to the story than that.

The Handmaid's Tale, I must explain for the benefit of the one person in the audience who may not have read it yet – out in paperback, and a bargain of creepy thrills for only $4.95 – is set in the future. This conned some people into believing it is Science Fiction, which, to my mind, it is not. I define Science Fiction as fiction in which things happen that are not possible today – that depend, for instance, on advanced space travel, time travel, the discovery of green monsters on other planets or galaxies, or which contain various technologies we have not yet developed. But in *The Handmaid's Tale*, nothing happens which the human race has not already done at some time in the past, or which it is not doing now, perhaps in other countries, or for which it has not yet developed the technology. We've done it, or we're doing it, or we could start doing it tomorrow. Nothing inconceivable takes place, and the projected trends on which my future society is based are already in motion. So I think of *The Handmaid's Tale* not as Science Fiction, but as Speculative Fiction; and, more particularly, as that negative form of Utopian fiction which has come to be known as the Dystopia.

A Utopia is usually thought of as a fictional perfect society, but in fact the word does not mean 'perfect society'. It means 'nowhere', and was used sardonically by Sir Thomas More as the title of his own sixteenth-century fictional discourse on government. Perhaps he meant to indicate that, although his Utopia made more rational sense than the England of his day, it was unlikely to be found anywhere outside a book.

Both the Utopia and the Dystopia concern themselves with the designing of societies; good societies for the Utopias, bad ones for the Dystopias. There is some of the same pleasure in this, for the writer, that we used to get as children when we built sand cities, or dinosaur jungles from Plasticine or drew entire wardrobes for paper dolls. But in a Utopia, you get to plan everything – the cities, the legal system, the customs, even facets of the language. The Dystopian bad design is the Utopian good design in reverse – that is, we the readers are supposed to deduce what a good society is by seeing, in detail, what it isn't.

The Utopia-Dystopia as a form tends to be produced only by cultures based on monotheism – or, like Plato's system, on a single idea of the Good – and which postulate also a single goal-oriented time-line. Cultures based on polytheism and the circularity of time don't seem to produce them. Why bother to try to improve society, or even to visualize it improved, when you know it's all going to go around again, like clothes in the wash? And how can you define a 'good' society as opposed to a 'bad' one if you see good and bad as aspects of the same thing? But Judaeo-Christianity, being a linear monotheism – one God and one plot-line, from Genesis to Revelation – has generated many fictional Utopias, and a good many attempts to create the real thing right here on earth, the venture of the Pilgrim Fathers being one of them – 'We shall be as a city upon a hill, a light to all nations,' unquote – and Marxism being another. In Marxism, history replaces God as a determinant and the classless society replaces the New Jerusalem, but change-through-time, heading in the direction of perfection, is similarly postulated. In the background of every modern Utopia lurk Plato's *Republic* and the Book of Revelations, and modern Dystopias have not been uninfluenced by various literary versions of Hell, especially those of Dante and Milton, which in their turn go right back to the Bible, that indispensable source-book of Western literature.

Sir Thomas More's original *Utopia* has a long list of descendants, many of which I read as I hacked my way through high school, through college, and later through graduate school. This list includes Swift's *Gulliver's Travels*, and, in the nineteenth century, William Morris's *News From Nowhere*, in which the ideal society is a kind of artists' colony; H. G. Wells's *Time Machine*, in which the lower classes actually eat the upper; Butler's *Erewhon*, in which crime is a sickness and sickness is a crime; and W. H. Hudson's *A Crystal Age*. In our own century, the classics are Huxley's *Brave New World*, Bellamy's *Looking Backward*, and, of course, *1984*, to mention a few. Utopias by women are also of note, though not as numerous. There are, for instance, *Herland* by Charlotte Perkins Gilman, and *Woman on the Edge of Time* by Marge Piercey.

Utopias are often satirical, the satire being directed at whatever society the writer is currently living in: that is, the superior arrangements of the Utopians reflect badly on *us*. Dystopias are often more like dire warnings than satires, dark shadows cast by the present into the future. They are what will happen to us if we don't pull up our socks.

What aspects of this life interest such writers? To no one's surprise, their concerns turn out to be much the same as those of society. There are, of course, the superficial matters of clothing and cuisine, partial nudity and vegetarianism making regular appearances. But the main problems are the distribution of wealth, labour relations, power structures, the protection of the powerless,

if any, relations between the sexes, population control, urban planning, often in the form of an interest in drains and sewers, the
rearing of children, illness and its ethics, insanity ditto, the censorship of artists and suchlike riff-raff and anti-social elements,
individual privacy and its invasion, the redefinition of language,
and the administration of justice. If, that is, any such administration is needed. It is a characteristic of the extreme Utopia, at one
end, and the extreme Dystopia at the other, that neither contains
any lawyers. Extreme Utopias are communities of spirit, in which
there cannot be any real disagreements among members because
all are of like and right mind; extreme Dystopias are absolute
tyrannies, in which contention is not a possibility. In Utopia, then,
no lawyers are needed; in Dystopia, no lawyers are allowed.

In between, however, is where most Utopia-Dystopias as well as
most human societies fall, and here the composers of these fictions have shown remarkable fecundity. Relations between the
sexes exhibit perhaps the widest range. Some Utopias go for a sort
of healthy-minded communal sex; others, like W. H. Hudson's
A Crystal Age, for an antlike arrangement in which most citizens are
sexually neutral and only one pair per large country mansion actually breed, which is how they cut down on the birth rate. Still
others, like Marge Piercey's, allow men to participate almost
equally in child-rearing by allowing them to breastfeed via hor-
mone injections, an option that may not rejoice your hearts but at
least has the virtue of novelty. Then there are Huxley's ritualistic
group sex and bottle babies, Skinner's boxes, and various minor
science fictions, written by men I hasten to add, in which women
devour their mates or paralyse them and lay eggs on them, *à la* spi-
ders. Sexual relations in extreme Dystopias usually exhibit some
form of slavery or, as in Orwell, extreme sexual repression.

The details, then, vary, but the Utopia-Dystopia as a form is a
way of trying things out on paper first to see whether or not we
might like them, should we ever have the chance to put them
into actual practice. In addition, it challenges us to re-examine
what we understand by the word 'human', and above all what we

intend by the word 'freedom'. For neither the Utopia nor the Dystopia is open-ended. Utopia is an extreme example of the impulse to order; it's the word 'should' run rampant. Dystopia, its nightmare mirror image, is the desire to squash dissent taken to inhuman and lunatic lengths. Neither are what you'd call tolerant, but both are necessary to the imagination: if we can't visualize the good, the ideal, if we can't formulate what we want, we'll get what we don't want, in spades. It's a sad commentary on our age that we find Dystopias a lot easier to believe in than Utopias: Utopias we can only imagine, Dystopias we've already had. But should we try too hard to enforce Utopia, Dystopia rapidly follows; because if enough people disagree with us we'll have to eliminate or suppress or terrorize or manipulate them, and then we've got *1984*. As a rule, Utopia is only safe when it remains true to its name and stays nowhere. It's a nice place to visit, but do we really want to live there? Which may be the ultimate moral of such stories.

All this was by way of background, to let you know that I'd done the required reading long before launching myself into *The Handmaid's Tale*. There are two other lots of required reading I would like to mention. The first had to do with the literature of the Second World War – I read Winston Churchill's memoirs when I was in high school, not to mention a biography of Rommel, the Desert Fox, and many another tome of military history. I read these books partly because I was an omnivorous reader and they were there; my father was a history buff and these things were just lying around. By extension, I read various books on totalitarian regimes, of the present and the past; the one that sticks out was called *Darkness at Noon*, by Arthur Koestler. (This was not my only reading when I was in high school; I was also reading Jane Austen and Emily Brontë and a particularly lurid book of Sci Fi called *Donovan's Brain*. I would read anything, and still will; when all else is lacking, I read airline in-flight magazines, and I have to say, I am getting tired of those articles on billionaire businessmen. Don't you think it's time for some other kinds of fiction?)

This so-called 'political' area of my reading was reinforced later by travel, to various countries where, to put it mildly, certain things we consider freedoms are not universally in force, and by conversations with many people; I remember in particular meeting a woman who had been in the French Resistance during the war, and a man who had escaped from Poland at the same time.

The other lot of required reading has to do with the history of the seventeenth-century Puritans, especially those who ended up in the United States. At the front of *The Handmaid's Tale* there are two dedications. One is to Perry Miller, who was a professor of mine at the dreaded Harvard Graduate School, and who almost single-handedly was responsible for resurrecting the American Puritans as a field for literary investigation. I had to take a lot of this stuff, and I needed to 'fill my gap' in order to pass my Comprehensives, and this was one area I had not studied as an undergraduate. Perry Miller pointed out that, contrary to what I had been taught earlier, the American Puritans did not come to North America in search of religious toleration, or not what we mean by it. They wanted the freedom to practise *their* religion, but they were not particularly keen on anyone else practising his. Among their noteworthy achievements were the banishing of so-called heretics, the hanging of Quakers and the well-known witchcraft trials. I get to say these bad things about them because they were my ancestors – in a way, *The Handmaid's Tale* is my book about my ancestors – and the second dedication, to Mary Webster, is indeed to one of these very same ancestors. Mary was a well-known witch, or at least she was tried for witchcraft and hanged. But it was before they had invented the drop, which breaks your neck – they merely strung her up and let her dangle, and when they came to cut her down the next morning she was still alive. Under the law of double jeopardy, you couldn't execute a person twice for the same crime, so she lived for another fourteen years. I felt that if I was going to stick my neck out by writing this book, I'd better dedicate it to someone with a very tough neck.

Puritan New England was a theocracy, not a democracy; and the future society proposed in *The Handmaid's Tale* has the form of a

theocracy too, on the principle that no society ever strays completely far from its roots. Stalinist Russia would have been
unthinkable without Czarist Russia to precede it, and so forth.
Also, the most potent forms of dictatorship have always been those
that have imposed tyranny in the name of religion; and even folk
like the French Revolutionaries and Hitler have striven to give a
religious force and sanction to their ideas. What is needed for a
really good tyranny is an unquestionable idea or authority. Political
disagreement is political disagreement; but political disagreement
with a *theocracy* is heresy, and a good deal of gloating self-righteousness
can be brought to bear upon the extermination of heretics, as history has demonstrated, through the Crusades, the forcible
conversions to Islam, the Spanish Inquisition, the burnings-at-the-
stake under the English Queen Bloody Mary, and so on down
through the years. It was in the light of history that the American
constitutionalists in the eighteenth century separated Church
from State. It is also in the light of history that my leaders in *The
Handmaid's Tale* recombine them.

All fictions begin with the question *What if?* The *what if* varies
from book to book – what if John loves Mary, what if John doesn't
love Mary, what if Mary gets eaten by an enormous shark, what if
the Martians invade, what if you find a treasure map, and so forth –
but there is always a *what if*, to which the novel is the answer. The
what if for *The Handmaid's Tale* could be formulated: what if it *can*
happen here? What kind of *it* would it be? (I have never believed any
fictions about the Russians taking over. If they can't get their
refrigerators to work, they wouldn't quite frankly stand much of a
chance. So that, for me, is not a plausible *it*.)

Or *what if* you wanted to take over the US and set up a totalitarian government, the lust for power being what it is? How would
you go about it? What conditions would favour you, and what
slogan would you propose, what flag would you fly, that would
attract the necessary twenty per cent of the population, without
which no totalitarianism can stay in power? If you proposed
Communism, you'd be unlikely to get many takers. A dictatorship

of liberal democrats would be seen even by the slightly dull-witted as a contradiction in terms. Although many dubious acts have been committed, let's face it, in the name of the great god democracy, they've usually been done in secret, or with a good deal of verbal embroidery covering them up. In this country, you'd be more likely to try some version of Puritan Fatherhood if you wanted a takeover. That would definitely be your best plan.

But true dictatorships do not come *in* in good times. They come in in bad times, when people are ready to give up some of their freedoms to someone – anyone – who can take control and promise them better times. The bad times that made Hitler and Mussolini possible were economic, with some extra frills such as a shortage of men in proportion to women, due to the high death rates during the First World War. To make my future society possible, I proposed something a little more complex. Bad economic times, yes, due to a shrinking area of global control, which would mean shrinking markets and fewer sources of cheap raw materials. But also a period of widespread environmental catastrophe, which has had several results: a higher infertility and sterility rate due to chemical and radiation damage (this, by the way, is happening already) and a higher birth-defect rate, which is also happening. The ability to conceive and bear a healthy child would become rare, and thus valued; and we all know who gets most – in any society – of things that are rare and valued. Those at the top. Hence my proposed future society, which, like many human societies before it, assigns more than one woman to its favoured male members. There are lots of precedents for this practice, but my society, being derived from Puritanism, would of course need biblical sanction. Luckily for them, Old Testament patriarchs were notoriously polygamous; the text they chose as their corner-stone is the story of Rachel and Leah, the two wives of Jacob, and their baby competition. When they themselves ran out of babies, they pressed their handmaids into service and counted the babies as their own, thus providing a biblical justification for surrogate motherhood, should anyone need one. Between these five people – not two – the twelve tribes of Israel were produced.

Woman's place, in the Republic of Gilead – so named for the mountain where Jacob promised to his father-in-law Laban that he would protect his two daughters – woman's place is strictly in the home. My problem as a writer was given that my society has stuffed all women back into their homes, how did they go about it? How do you *get* women back into the home, now that they are running around *outside* the home, having jobs and generally flinging themselves around? Simple. You just close your eyes and take several giant steps back, into the not-so-very-distant past – the nineteenth century, to be exact – deprive them of the right to vote, own property or hold jobs, and prohibit public prostitution into the bargain, to keep them from hanging out on street corners, and presto, there they are, back in the home. To stop them from using their gold Amex cards to make quick airplane escapes, I have their credit frozen overnight; after all, if everyone is on computers and cash is obsolete – which is where we're heading – how simple to single out any one group – all those over sixty, all those with green hair, all women. Of the many scary features of my future society, this one seems to have got to the most people. That their beloved, friendly, well-trained credit cards could rise up against them! It is the stuff of nightmares.

This then is part of the core of what I hope you will think is relentless logic running like a spine through *The Handmaid's Tale*. While I was writing it, and for some time after, I kept a scrapbook of clippings from newspapers referring to all sorts of material that fitted in with the premises on which the book was based – everything from articles on the high level of PCBs found in polar bears, to the biological mothers assigned to SS troops by Hitler, in addition to their legal wives, for purposes of child production, to conditions in prisons around the world, to computer technology, to underground polygamy in the state of Utah. There is, as I have said, nothing in the book without a precedent. But this material in itself would not constitute a novel. A novel is always the story of an individual, or several individuals; never the story of a generalized mass. So the real problems in the writing of *The Handmaid's Tale* were the same as the problems involved in the writing of any novel: how to make the story real at a human and individual level. The pitfalls that Utopian writing so frequently stumbles into are the pitfalls of disquisition. The author gets too enthusiastic about sewage systems or conveyor belts, and the story grinds to a halt while the beauties of these are explained. I wanted the factual and logical background to my tale to remain background; I did not want it usurping the foreground.

II

Great Aunts

Aunt J., who was my third and youngest aunt, took me to my first writers' conference. That was in Montreal, in 1958, when I was eighteen. I had already produced several impressive poems; at least I was impressed by them. They had decaying leaves, garbage cans, cigarette butts, and cups of coffee in them. I had been ambushed by T. S. Eliot several months previously, and had wrestled him to a standstill. I did not yet know that it was the done thing, by now, to refer to him as T. S. Idiot.

I didn't show my seedy poems to my mother, who was the oldest of the three sisters and therefore pragmatic, since it was she who had had to tend the others. She was the athlete of the family and was fond of horses and ice-skating and any other form of rapid motion that offered escapes from domestic duties. My mother had only written one poem in her life, when she was eight or nine; it began, 'I had some wings, They were lovely things', and went on, typically for her, to describe the speed of the subsequent flight. I knew that if I forced her to read my butt-and-coffee-ground free verses, she would say they were very nice, this being her standard response to other puzzlements, such as my increasingly dour experiments with wardrobe. Clothing was not a priority of hers either.

But Aunt J. had written reams, according to my mother. She was a romantic figure, as she had once had pleurisy and had been in a San, where she had made flowery shellwork brooches; I had received several of these treasures for Christmas, as a child, in tiny magical boxes with cotton wool in them. Tiny boxes, cotton wool: these were not my mother's style. Aunt J. had to be careful of her health, an infirmity which seemed to go along with writing, from what I knew. She cried at the sad places in movies, as I did, and had flights of fantasy as a child in the Annapolis Valley of Nova Scotia, which was where they had all grown up. Her middle name was Carmen, and to punish what they thought to be her inordinate pride over this, her two older sisters had named the pig Carmen.

Aunt J. was rounded in outline, myopic (as I was), and depicted herself as a sentimental pushover, though this was merely a useful fiction, part of the self-deprecating camouflage adopted by women, then, for various useful purposes. Underneath her façade of lavender-coloured flutter she was tough-minded, like all three of those sisters. It was this blend of soft and hard that appealed to me.

So I showed my poems to Aunt J. She read them and did not laugh, or not in my presence; though knowing her I doubt that she laughed at all. She knew what it was to have ambitions as a writer, though hers had been delayed by Uncle M., who was a bank manager, and by their two children. Much later, she herself would be speaking at conferences, sitting on panels, appearing nervously on talk shows, having authored five books of her own. Meanwhile she wrote children's stories for the weekly Sunday School papers and bided her time.

She sent my gloomy poems to Second Cousin Lindsay, who was an English professor at Dalhousie University. He said I had promise. Aunt J. showed me his letter, beaming with pleasure. This was my first official encouragement.

The writers' conference Aunt J. took me to was put on by the Canadian Authors' Association, which at that time was the only writers' organization in Canada. I knew its reputation – it was the same tea-party outfit about which F. R. Scott had written, 'Expansive puppets percolate self-unction/Beneath a portrait of the Prince of Wales.' It was rumoured to be full of elderly amateurs; I was unlikely to see anyone there sprouting a three-day beard or clad in a black turtle-neck pullover, or looking anything like Samuel Beckett or Eugene Ionesco, who were more or less my idea of real writers. But Aunt J. and I were both so desperate for contact with anything that smacked of the world of letters that we were willing to take our chances with the CAA.

Once at the conference, we opted for a paper to be given by an expert on Fanny Burney. I goggled around the room: there were a lot of what I thought were middle-aged women, in flowered dresses – not unlike Aunt J.'s own dress – and little suits, though there was no one who looked like my idea of a writer: pallid, unkempt, red-eyed. But this was Canada and not France, so what could I expect?

Up to this time I had seen only one Canadian writer in the flesh. His name was Wilson Macdonald and he'd turned up in our high school auditorium, old and wispy and white-haired, where he'd recited several healthy-minded poems about skiing, from memory, and had imitated a crow. I had a fair idea what Jean-Paul Sartre would have thought of him, and was worried that I might end up that way myself: wheeled out for a bunch of spit-ball-throwing teenaged thugs, doing birdcalls. You could not be a real writer and a Canadian too, that much was clear. As soon as I could, I was going to hit Paris and become incomprehensible.

Meanwhile, there I was in Montreal, waiting for the Fanny Burney expert with Aunt J. We were both nervous. We felt like spies of a sort, infiltrators; and so like infiltrators we began to eavesdrop. Right behind us was sitting a woman whose name we recognized because she frequently had poems about snow-covered spruce trees published in the daily Montreal newspaper. She was not discussing spruce trees now, but a hanging that had taken place the day before, at the prison. 'It was so dreadful for him,' she was saying. 'He was so upset.'

Our ears were flapping: had she known the condemned man personally? If so, how creepy. But as we listened on, we gathered that the upset man was not the hanged one; it was her husband, who was the prison Chaplain.

Several gaps opened at my feet: the gap between the sentimentality of this woman's poems and the realities of her life, between the realities of her life and her perceptions of them; between the hangers and the hanged, and the consolers of the hanged, and the consolers of the hangers. This was one of my first intimations that, beneath its façade of teacups and outdoor pursuits and various kinds of trees, Canada – even this literary, genteel segment of Canada, for which I had such youthful contempt – was a good deal more problematic than I had thought.

But I should have known that already.

In the early part of my childhood, I had not known any of my relatives, because they lived in Nova Scotia, two thousand miles away. My parents had left Nova Scotia during the Depression because there were no jobs there. By the time I was born, the Second World War had begun, and nobody travelled great distances without official reasons and gas coupons. But although my aunts were not present in the flesh, they were very much present in the spirit. The three sisters wrote one another every week, and my mother read these letters out loud, to my father but by extension to myself and my brother, after dinner. They were called 'letters from home'. *Home*, for my mother, was always Nova Scotia, never wherever we might be living at the time; which gave me the vague idea that I was misplaced. Wherever I actually was living myself, *home* was not there.

So I was kept up on the doings of my aunts, and also of my cousins, my second cousins, and many other people who fitted in somewhere but were more distantly related. In Nova Scotia, it's not what you do or even who you know that is the most important thing about you. It's which town you're from and who you're related to. Any conversation between two Maritimers who've never met before will begin this way, and go on until both parties discover that they are in fact related to each other. I grew up in a huge extended family of invisible people.

It was not my invisible aunts in their present-day incarnation who made the most impression on me. It was my aunts in the past. There they were as children, in the impossible starched and frilled dresses and the floppy satin hairbows of the first decades of the century, or as teenagers, in black and white in the photograph album, wearing strange clothing – cloche hats, flapper coats up over the knee, standing beside antique motor cars, or posed in front of rocks or the sea in striped bathing suits that came halfway down their legs. Sometimes their arms would be around one another. They had been given captions, by my mother: 'We Three', 'Bathing Belles'. Aunt J. was thin as a child, dark-eyed, intense. Aunt K., the middle sister, looked tailored and brisk. My mother, with huge Pre-Raphaelite eyes and wavy hair and model's cheek-bones, was the beauty, a notion she made light of: she was, and remained, notorious for her bad taste in clothes, a notion she cul-tivated so she wouldn't have to go shopping for them alone. But all three sisters had the same high-bridged noses; Roman noses, my mother said. I pored over these pictures, intrigued by the idea of the triplicate, identical noses. I did not have a sister myself, then, and the mystique of sisterhood was potent for me.

The photo album was one mode of existence for my invisible aunts. They were even more alive in my mother's stories, for, although she was no poet, my mother was a raconteur and deadly mimic. The characters in her stories about 'home' became as famil-iar to me as characters in books; and, since we lived in isolated places and moved a lot, they were more familiar than most of the people I actually encountered.

The cast was constant. First came my strict, awe-inspiring grand-father, a country doctor who drove around the dirt roads in a horse and sleigh, through blizzards, delivering babies in the dead of night and threatening to horse-whip his daughters – especially my mother – for real or imagined transgressions. I did not know what a horse-whip was, so this punishment had the added attraction of the bizarre.

Then came my distracted, fun-loving grandmother, and my

Aunt K., a year younger than my mother but much more intellectual and firm of will, according to my mother. Then Aunt J., sentimental and apt to be left out. These three were 'the girls'. Then, somewhat later, 'the boys', my two uncles, one of whom blew the stove lids off the country schoolhouse with some homemade explosive hidden in a log, the other who was sickly but frequently had everyone 'in stitches'. And the peripheral figures: hired girls who were driven away by the machinations of my mother and Aunt K., who did not like having them around, hired men who squirted them while milking the cows; the cows themselves; the pig; the horses. The horses were not really peripheral characters; although they had no lines, they had names and personalities and histories, and they were my mother's partners in escapades. Dick and Nell were their names. Dick was my favourite; he had been given to my mother as a broken-down, ill-treated hack, and she had restored him to health and glossy beauty. This was the kind of happy ending I found satisfactory.

The stories about these people had everything that could be asked for: plot, action, suspense – although I knew how they would turn out, having heard them before – and fear, because there was always the danger of my grandfather's finding out and resorting to the horse-whip threat, although I don't believe he actually horse-whipped anyone.

What would he find out? Almost anything. There were many things he was not supposed to know, many things the girls were not supposed to know, but did. And what if he were to find out that they knew? A great deal turned, in these stories and in that family, on concealment; on what you did or did not tell; on what was said as distinct from what was meant. 'If you can't say anything good, don't say anything at all,' said my mother, saying a great deal. My mother's stories were my first lesson in reading between the lines.

My mother featured in these stories as physically brave, a walker of fences and also of barn ridge-poles, a sin of horse-whipping proportions – but shy. She was so shy that she would hide from visitors behind the barn, and she could not go to school until Aunt K. was old enough to take her. In addition to the bravery and the shyness, however, she had a violent temper. 'Like Father's,' she said. This was improbable to me, since I could not remember any examples. My mother losing her temper would have been a sight to behold, like the Queen standing on her head. But I accepted the idea on faith, along with the rest of her mythology.

Aunt K. was not shy. Although she was younger than my mother, you would never know it: 'We were more like twins.' She was a child of steely nerves, according to my mother. She was a ringleader, and thought up plots and plans, which she carried out with ruthless efficiency. My mother would be drawn into these, willy-nilly: she claimed she was too weak of will to resist.

'The girls' had to do household chores, more of them after they had driven away the hired girls, and Aunt K. was a hard worker and an exacting critic of the housework of others. Later on in the story, Aunt K. and my mother had a double wedding; the night before this event they read their adolescent diaries out loud to one another and then burnt them. 'We cleaned the kitchen,' said Aunt K.'s diary. 'The others did not do an A-1 job.' My mother and Aunt J. would always laugh when repeating this. It was, as Matthew Arnold would have had it, a touchstone line for them, about Aunt K.

But there was even more to Aunt K. She was a brilliant student, and had her MA in History from the University of Toronto. My grandfather thought my mother was a flighty, pleasure-bent flibbertigibbet until she saved her own money from schoolteaching, and sent herself to college; but he was all set to finance Aunt K. for an advanced degree at Oxford. However, she turned this down in favour of marrying a local Annapolis Valley doctor and having six children. The reason, my mother implied, had something to do with Great-Aunt Winnie, who also had an MA, the first woman to receive one from Dalhousie, but who had never married. Aunt Winnie was condemned – it was thought of as a condemnation – to teach school forever, and turned up at family Christmases, looking wistful. In those days, said my mother, if you did not get married by a certain age, it was unlikely that you ever would. 'You didn't think about not marrying,' said Aunt J. to me, much later. 'There wasn't any *choice* about it. It was just what you did.'

Meanwhile, there was my Aunt K. in the album, in a satin wedding gown and a veil identical to my mother's, and later, with all six children, dressed up as The Old Woman Who Lived in a Shoe in the Apple Blossom Festival Parade. Unlike the stories in books, my mother's stories did not have clear morals, and the moral of this one was less clear than most. Which was better? To be brilliant and go to Oxford, or to have six children? Why couldn't it be both?

When I was six or seven and my brother was eight or nine and the war was over, we began to visit Nova Scotia, every summer or every second summer. We had to: my grandfather had had something called a coronary, more than one of them, in fact, and he could die at any moment. Despite his strictness and what seemed, to me, to be acts of gross unfairness, he was loved and respected. Everyone agreed on that.

These visits were a strain. We reached Nova Scotia from Ontario by driving at breakneck speed and for a great many hours at a time over the postwar highways of Quebec and Vermont and New Brunswick, so that we would arrive cranky and frazzled, usually in the middle of the night. During the visits we would have to be on whispering good behaviour in my grandfather's large white house, and meet and be met by a great many relatives we hardly knew.

But the worst strain of all was fitting these real people – so much smaller and older and less vivid than they ought to have been – into the mythology in my possession. My grandfather was not galloping around the countryside, roaring threats and saving babies. Instead he carved little wooden figures and had to have a nap every afternoon, and his greatest exertion was a stroll around the orchard or a game of chess with my brother. My grandmother was not the harried although comical mother of five, but the caretaker of my grandfather. There were no cows any more, and where were the beautiful horses, Dick and Nell?

I felt defrauded. I did not want Aunt J. and Aunt K. to be the grown-up mothers of my cousins, snapping beans in the kitchen. I wanted them back the way they were supposed to be, in the bobbed haircuts and short skirts of the photo album, playing tricks on the hired girls, being squirted by the hired man, living under the threat of horse-whipping, failing to do an A-1 job.

Once I went on a literary outing with both my aunts.

It was in the early seventies, when I was over thirty and had published several books. Aunt J.'s husband had died, and she'd moved from Montreal back to Nova Scotia to take care of my ageing grandmother. I was visiting, and the aunts and I decided to drive over to nearby Bridgetown, to pay a call on a writer named Ernest Buckler. Ernest Buckler had written a novel called *The Mountain and the Valley*, the mountain being the North Mountain, the Valley being the Annapolis Valley. He'd had some success with it in the States – at that time, in Canada, a sure-fire ticket to hatred and envy – but because he was an eccentric recluse, the hatred and envy quotient was modified. But his success in the States had not been duplicated in Canada, because his Toronto publishers were United Church teetotallers, known for throwing launch parties at which they served fruit juice. (Modernization came finally, with the addition of sherry, doled out in a separate room, into which those who craved it could slink furtively.) These publishers had discovered that there were what my mother referred to as 'goings on' in Buckler's book, and had hidden it in the stock room. If you wanted to actually buy one, it was like getting porn out of the Vatican.

I had read this book as a young adolescent because somebody had given it to my parents under the impression that they would like it because it was about Nova Scotia. My mother's comment was that it was not what things were like when she was growing up. I snuck this book up onto the garage roof, which was flat, where I swiftly located the goings on and then read the rest of the book. It was probably the first novel for adults that I ever did read, with the exception of *Moby Dick*.

So I remembered Ernest Buckler's book with fondness; and by the seventies I'd become involved in a correspondence with him. So over we went to see him in the flesh. My Aunt J. was all agog, because Ernest Buckler was a real writer. My Aunt K. drove. (My Aunt J. never drove, having scraped the doorhandles off the car on one of her few attempts, according to her.)

Aunt K. knew the vicinity well, and pointed out the places of interest as we went by. She had a good memory. It was she who had told me something everyone else had forgotten, including myself: that I had announced, at the age of five, that I was going to be a writer.

During this drive, however, her mind was on other historical matters. 'That's the tree where the man who lived in the white house hanged himself,' she said. 'That's where the barn got burned down. They know who did it but they can't prove a thing. The man in there blew his head off with a shotgun.' These events may have taken place years, decades before, but they were still current in the area. It appeared that the Valley was more like *The Mountain and the Valley* than I had suspected.

Ernest Buckler lived in a house that could not have been changed for fifty years. It still had a horsehair sofa, antimacassars, a woodstove in the living room. Ernest himself was enormously likeable and highly nervous, and anxious that we be pleased. He hopped around a lot, talking a mile a minute, and kept popping out to the kitchen, then popping in again. We talked mostly about books, and about his plans to scandalize the neighbourhood by phoning me up at my grandmother's house, on the party line, and pretending we were having an affair. 'That would give the old biddies something to talk about,' he said. Everyone listened in, of course, whenever he had a call, but not just because he was a local celebrity. They listened in on everyone.

After we left, my Aunt J. said, 'That was something! He said you had a teeming brain!' (He had said this.) My Aunt K.'s comment was, 'That man was oiled.' Of the three of us, she was the only one who had figured out why Mr Buckler had made such frequent trips to the kitchen. But it was understandable that he should have been secretive about it: in the Valley, there were those who drank, and then there were decent people.

Also: there were those who wrote, and then there were decent people. A certain amount of writing was tolerated, but only within limits. Newspaper columns about children and the changing seasons were fine. Sex, swearing and drinking were beyond the pale.

I myself, in certain Valley circles, was increasingly beyond the pale. As I became better known, I also became more widely read there, not because my writing was thought of as having any particular merit but because I was Related. Aunt J. told me, with relish, how she'd hidden behind the parlour door during a neighbour's scandalized visit with my grandmother. The scandal was one of my own books: how, asked the outraged neighbour, could my grandmother have permitted her granddaughter to publish such immoral trash?

But blood is thicker than water in the Valley. My grandmother gazed serenely out the window and commented on the beautiful Fall weather they were having, while my Aunt J. gasped behind the door. My aunts and mother always found the spectacle of my grandmother preserving her dignity irresistible, probably because there was so much dignity to be preserved.

This was the neighbour, the very same one, who as a child had led my aunts astray, sometime during the First World War, inducing them to slide down a red clay bank in their little white lace-edged pantaloons. She had then pressed her nose up against the glass of the window to watch them getting spanked, not just for sliding but for lying about it. My grandmother had gone over and yanked the blind down then, and she was doing it now. Whatever her own thoughts about the goings on in my fiction, she was keeping them to herself. Nor did she ever mention them to me.

For that I silently thanked her. I suppose any person, but especially any woman, who takes up writing has felt, especially at first, that she was doing it against a huge largely unspoken pressure, the pressure of expectation and decorum. This pressure is most strongly felt, by women, from within the family, and more so when the family is a strong unit. There are things that should not be said. Don't tell. If you can't say anything nice, don't say anything at all. Was that counterbalanced adequately by that other saying of my mother's: 'Do what you think is right, no matter what other people think'? And did those other people whose opinion did not matter include the members of one's family?

With the publication of my first real book, I was dreading disapproval. I didn't worry much about my father and mother, who had gracefully survived several other eccentricities of mine – the skirts hand-printed with trilobites and newts, the experiments with beer parlours, the beatnik boyfriends – although they had probably bitten their tongues a few times in the process. Anyway, they lived in Toronto, where goings on of various kinds had now become more common; not in Nova Scotia, where, it was not quite said, things might be a bit more narrow. Instead, I worried about my aunts. I thought they might be scandalized, even Aunt J. Although she had been subjected to some of my early poems, coffee cups and rotting leaves were one thing, but there was more than dirty crockery and mulch in this book. As for Aunt K., so critical of the shoddy housework and drinking habits of others, what would she think?

To my surprise, my aunts came through with flying colours. Aunt J. thought it was wonderful – a real book! She said she was bursting with pride. Aunt K. said that there were certain things that were not done in her generation, but they could be done by mine, and more power to me for doing them.

This kind of acceptance meant more to me than it should have, to my single-minded all-for-art twenty-six-year-old self. (Surely I ought to be impervious to aunts.) However, like the morals of my mother's stories, what exactly it meant is far from clear to me. Perhaps it was a laying-on of hands, a passing of something from one generation to another. What was being passed on was the story itself: what was known, and what could be told. What was between the lines. The permission to tell the story, wherever that might lead.

Or perhaps it meant that I too was being allowed into the magical static but ever-continuing saga of the photo album. Instead of three different-looking young women with archaic clothes and identical Roman noses, standing with their arms around each other, there would now be four. I was being allowed into *home*.

12

Introduction: Reading Blind

Whenever I'm asked to talk about what constitutes a 'good' story, or what makes one well-written story 'better' than another, I begin to feel very uncomfortable. Once you start making lists or devising rules for stories, or for any other kind of writing, some writer will be sure to happen along and casually break every abstract rule you or anyone else has ever thought up, and take your breath away in the process. The word *should* is a dangerous one to use when speaking of writing. It's a kind of challenge to the deviousness and inventiveness and audacity and perversity of the creative spirit. Sooner or later, anyone who has been too free with it will be liable to end up wearing it like a dunce's cap. We don't judge good stories by the application to them of some set of external measurements, as we judge giant pumpkins at the Fall Fair. We judge them by the way they strike us. And that will depend on a great many subjective imponderables, which we lump together under the general heading of taste.

All of which may explain why, when I sat down to read through the large heap of stories from which I was to select for this collection, I did so with misgiving. There were so many stories to choose from, and all of them, as they say, publishable. I knew this because they had already been published. Over the course of the previous year, the indefatigable and devoted series editor, Shannon Ravenel, had read every short story in every known magazine, large or small, famous or obscure, in both the United States and Canada – a total of over two thousand stories. Of these she had chosen one hundred and twenty, from which I was to pick twenty. But how was I to do this? What would be my criteria, if any? How would I be able to tell the best from the merely better? How would I *know*?

I had elected to read these stories 'blind', which meant that Shannon Ravenel had inked out the names of the authors. I had no idea, in advance, how these small black oblongs would transform the act of editing from a judicious task to a gleeful pleasure. Reading through these authorless manuscripts was like playing hooky: with a hundred strokes of a black marker, I had been freed from the weight of authorial reputation. I didn't have to pay any attention to who ought to be in because of his or her general worthiness or previous critical hosannas. I didn't have to worry about who might feel slighted if not included. That weighing, measuring, calculating side of me – and even the most scrupulously disinterested editor has one – had been safely locked away, leaving me to wallow among the ownerless pages unencumbered. Picking up each new story was like a child's game of Fish. You never knew what you would get: it might be a piece of plastic or it might be something wonderful, a gift, a treasure.

In addition to remaining ignorant about authorial worth, I could disregard any considerations about territory. I had no way of knowing, for instance, whether a story with a female narrator was by a female author, whether one with a male narrator was by a man; whether a story about a Chinese immigrant was by a writer with a Chinese background, whether one about a nineteenth-century Canadian poet was by a Canadian. I've recently heard it argued that writers should tell stories only from a point of view that is their own, or that of a group to which they themselves belong. Writing from the point of view of someone 'other' is a form of poaching, the appropriation of material you haven't earned and to which you have no right. Men, for instance, should not write as women; although it's less frequently said that women should not write as men.

This view is understandable but, in the end, self-defeating. Not only does it condemn as thieves and imposters such writers as George Eliot, James Joyce, Emily Brontë and William Faulkner, and, incidentally, a number of the writers in this book; it is also inhibiting to the imagination in a fundamental way. It's only a short step from saying we can't write from the point of view of an 'other' to saying we can't read that way either, and from there to the position that no one can really understand anyone else, so we might as well stop trying. Follow this line of reasoning to its logical conclusion, and we would all be stuck with reading nothing but our own work, over and over; which would be my personal idea of hell. Surely the delight and the wonder come not from who tells the story but from what the story tells, and how.

Reading blind is an intriguing metaphor. When you read blind, you see everything but the author. He or she may be visible intermittently, as a trick of style, a locale about which nobody else is likely to write, a characteristic twist of the plot; but apart from such clues he or she is incognito. You're stranded with the voice of the story.

The Voice of the Story, the Story as Voice

In the houses of the people who knew us we were asked to come in and sit, given cold water or lemonade; and while we sat there being refreshed, the people continued their conversations or went about their chores. Little by little we began to piece a story together, a secret, terrible, awful story.

Toni Morrison, *The Bluest Eye*

It is only the story that can continue beyond the war and the warrior . . . It is only the story . . . that saves our progeny from blundering like blind beggars into the spikes of the cactus fence. The story is our escort; without it, we are blind. Does the blind man own his escort? No, neither do we the story; rather it is the story that owns us.

Chinua Achebe, *Anthills of the Savannah*

How do we learn our notions of what a story is? What sets 'a story' apart from mere background noise, the wash of syllables that surrounds us and flows through us and is forgotten every day? What makes a good story a unified whole, something complete and satisfying in itself? What makes it significant speech? In other words, what qualities was I searching for, perhaps without knowing it, as I read diligently through my pile of tear-sheets?

I've spoken of 'the voice of the story', which has become a sort of catchall phrase; but by it I intend something more specific: a speaking voice, like the singing voice in music, that moves not across space, across the page, but through time. Surely every written story is, in the final analysis, a score for voice. Those little black marks on the page mean nothing without their retranslation into sound. Even when we read silently, we read with the ear, unless we are reading bank statements.

Perhaps, by abolishing the Victorian practice of family reading and by removing from our school curricula those old standbys, the set memory piece and the recitation, we've deprived both writers and readers of something essential to stories. We've led them to believe that prose comes in visual blocks, not in rhythms and cadences; that its texture should be flat because a page is flat; that written emotion should not be immediate, like a drumbeat, but more remote, like a painted landscape: something to be contemplated. But understatement can be overdone, plainsong can get too plain. When I asked a group of young writers, earlier this year, how many of them ever read their own work aloud, not one of them said she did.

I'm not arguing for the abolition of the eye, merely for the reinstatement of the voice, and for an appreciation of the way it carries the listener along with it at the pace of the story. (Incidentally, reading aloud disallows cheating; when you're reading aloud, you can't skip ahead.)

Our first stories come to us through the air. We hear voices.

Children in oral societies grow up within a web of stories; but so do all children. We listen before we can read. Some of our listening is more like listening in, to the calamitous or seductive voices of the adult world, on the radio or the television or in our daily lives. Often it's an overhearing of things we aren't supposed to hear, eavesdropping on scandalous gossip or family secrets. From all these scraps of voices, from the whispers and shouts that surround us, even from the ominous silences, the unfilled gaps in meaning, we patch together for ourselves an order of events, a plot or plots; these, then, are the things that happen, these are the people they happen to, this is the forbidden knowledge.

We have all been little pitchers with big ears, shooed out of the kitchen when the unspoken is being spoken, and we have probably all been tale-bearers, blurters at the dinner table, unwitting violators of adult rules of censorship. Perhaps this is what writers are: those who never kicked the habit. We remained tale-bearers. We learned to keep our eyes open, but not to keep our mouths shut.

If we're lucky, we may also be given stories meant for our ears, stories intended for us. These may be children's Bible stories, tidied up and simplified and with the vicious bits left out. They may be fairy tales, similarly sugared, although if we are very lucky it will be the straight stuff in both instances, with the slaughters, thunderbolts, and red-hot shoes left in. In any case, these tales will have deliberate, moulded shapes, unlike the stories we have patched together for ourselves. They will contain mountains, deserts, talking donkeys, dragons; and, unlike the kitchen stories, they will have definite endings. We are likely to accept these stories as being on the same level of reality as the kitchen stories. It's only when we are older that we are taught to regard one kind of story as real and the other kind as mere invention. This is about the same time we're taught to believe that dentists are useful, and writers are not.

Traditionally, both the kitchen gossips and the readers-out-loud have been mothers or grandmothers, native languages have been mother tongues, and the kinds of stories that are told to children have been called nursery tales or old wives' tales. It struck me as no great coincidence when I learned recently that, when a great number of prominent writers were asked to write about the family member who had had the greatest influence on their literary careers, almost all of them, male as well as female, had picked their mothers. Perhaps this reflects the extent to which North American children have been deprived of their grandfathers, those other great repositories of story; perhaps it will come to change if men come to share in early child care, and we will have old husbands' tales. But as things are, language, including the language of our earliest-learned stories, is a verbal matrix, not a verbal patrix.

I used to wonder why – as seems to be the case – so many more male writers chose to write from a female point of view than the other way around. (In this collection, for instance, male authors with female narrators outnumber the reverse four to one.) But possibly the prevailing gender of the earliest storytelling voice has something to do with it.

Two kinds of stories we first encounter – the shaped tale, the overheard impromptu narrative we piece together – form our idea of what a story is and colour the expectations we bring to stories later. Perhaps it's from the collisions between these two kinds of stories – what is often called 'real life' (and which writers greedily think of as their 'material') and what is sometimes dismissed as 'mere literature' or 'the kinds of things that happen only in stories' – that original and living writing is generated. A writer with nothing but a formal sense will produce dead work, but so will one whose only excuse for what is on the page is that it really happened. Anyone who has been trapped in a bus beside a non-stop talker graced with no narrative skill or sense of timing can testify to that. Or, as Raymond Chandler says in *The Simple Art of Murder*:

> All language begins with speech, and the speech of common men at that, but when it develops to the point of becoming a literary medium it only looks like speech.
>
> Expressing yourself is not nearly enough. You must express the story.

The Uncertainty Principle

All of which gets me no closer to an explanation of why I chose one story over another, twenty stories over the remaining hundred. The uncertainty principle, as it applies to writing, might be stated: *You can say why a story is bad, but it's much harder to say why it's good.* Determining quality in fiction may be as hard as determining the reason for the happiness in families, only in reverse. The old saying has it that happy families are all happy in the same way, but each unhappy family is unique. In fiction, however, excellence resides in divergence, or how else could we be surprised? Hence the trickiness of the formulations.

Here is what I did. I sat on the floor, spread out the stories, and read through them in no particular order. I put each completed story into a 'yes' pile, a 'no' pile, and a 'maybe' pile. By the time I'd gone through them once, I had about twenty-five stories in 'yes', an equal number in 'no', and the rest in 'maybe'.

Here things got harder. The first fourteen yes stories were instant choices: I knew I wouldn't change my mind about them. After that there were gradations, yeses shading to maybes, maybes that could easily be on the low end of yes. To make the final choices, I was forced to be more conscious and deliberate. I went back over my fourteen instant yes stories and tried to figure out what, if anything, they had in common.

They were widely different in content, in tone, in setting, in narrative strategy. Some were funny, others melancholy, others contemplative, others downright sad, yet others violent. Some went over ground that, Lord knows, had been gone over before: the breakdown, the breakup, love and death. Collectively they did not represent any school of writing or propound any common philosophy. I was beginning to feel stupid and lacking in standards. Was I to be thrown back on that old crutch of the Creative Writing Seminar, *It worked for me?*

Perhaps, I thought, my criteria are very simple-minded. Perhaps all I want from a good story is what children want when they listen to tales both told and overheard – which turns out to be a good deal.

They want their attention held, and so do I. I always read to the end, out of some puritanical, and adult, sense of duty owed; but if I start to fidget and skip pages, and wonder if conscience demands I go back and read the middle, it's a sign that the story has lost me, or I have lost it.

They want to feel they are in safe hands, that they can trust the teller. With children this may mean simply that they know the speaker will not betray them by closing the book in the middle, or mixing up the heroes and the villains. With adult readers it's more complicated than that, and involves many dimensions, but there's the same element of keeping faith. Faith must be kept with the language – even if the story is funny, its language must be taken seriously – with the concrete details of locale, mannerism, clothing; with the shape of the story itself. A good story may tease, as long as this activity is foreplay and not used as an end in itself. If there's a promise held out, it must be honoured. Whatever is hidden behind the curtain must be revealed at last, and it must be at one and the same time completely unexpected and inevitable. It's in this last respect that the story (as distinct from the novel) comes closest to resembling two of its oral predecessors, the riddle and the joke. Both, or all three, require the same mystifying buildup, the same surprising twist, the same impeccable sense of timing. If we guess the riddle at once, or if we can't guess it because the answer makes no sense – if we see the joke coming, or if the point is lost because the teller gets it muddled – there is failure. Stories can fail in the same way.

But anyone who has ever told, or tried to tell, a story to children will know that there is one thing without which none of the rest is any good. Young children have little sense of dutifulness or of delaying anticipation. They are longing to hear a story, but only if you are longing to tell one. They will not put up with your lassitude or boredom: if you want their full attention, you must give them yours. You must hold them with your glittering eye or suffer

the pinches and whispering. You need the Ancient Mariner element, the Scheherazade element: a sense of urgency. *This is the story*
I must tell; this is the story you must hear.

Urgency does not mean frenzy. The story can be a quiet story, a
story about dismay or missed chances or a wordless revelation.
But it must be urgently told. It must be told with as much intent-
ness as if the teller's life depended on it. And, if you are a writer, so
it does, because your life as the writer of each particular story is
only as long, and as good, as the story itself. Most of those who hear
it or read it will never know you, but they will know the story.
Their act of listening is its reincarnation.

Is all this too much to ask? Not really; because many stories,
many of these stories, do it superbly.

Down to Specifics

But they do it in a multiplicity of ways. When I was reading through
the stories, someone asked me, 'Is there a trend?' There is no trend.
There are only twenty strong, exciting, and unique stories.

I didn't think anyone could ever write a story about taking
drugs in the sixties that would hold my attention for more than
five minutes, but Michael Cunningham does it brilliantly in 'White
Angel' – because the narrator is a young boy, 'the most criminally
advanced nine-year-old in my fourth-grade class', who is being
initiated into almost everything by his adored sixteen-year-old
brother. The sensual richness of this story is impressive; so is the
way it shifts from out-of-control feverishness and hilarity, as the
two brothers scramble their brains with acid against a background
of Leave-it-to-Beaver Cleveland domesticity ('We slipped the tabs
into our mouths at breakfast, while our mother paused over the
bacon'), to the nearly unbearable poignancy of its tragic ending.

Another story that blindsided me by taking an unlikely subject
and turning it inside out was 'The Flowers of Boredom'. Who could
hope to write with any conviction or panache about working as a
paper-shuffler for a defence contractor? But Rick DeMarinis does.

The visionary glimpse of cosmic horror at the end is come by honestly, step by step, through dailiness and small disgusts. This story is one of those truly original collisions between delicately handled form and banal but alarming content that leaves you aghast and slightly battered.

'Hell lay about them in their infancy,' Graham Greene remarks in *The Lawless Roads*, and this is the tone of Barbara Gowdy's 'Disneyland'. If 'The Flowers of Boredom' views the military enterprise as a giant, superhuman pattern, 'Disneyland' squints at it through Groucho Marx glasses gone rotten. The controlling figure is a domineering father obsessed with his early-sixties fallout shelter. He and his mania would be ludicrous, almost a parody, viewed from a safe distance; but the distance is not safe. This man is seen from beneath by his children, who are forced to play platoon to his drill sergeant in the smelly, dark, tyrannical, and terrifying hell in which he has imprisoned them. The sense of claustrophobia and entrapment are intense.

There are several other fine stories that concern themselves with the terrors, and sometimes the delights, of childhood and with the powerlessness of children caught under the gigantic, heedless feet of the adult world. Mark Richard's 'Strays', with its two poor-white boys abandoned by their runaway mother and rescued, after a fashion, by their rogue gambler of an uncle, is one fine example. Its deadpan delivery of the squalid and the grotesque reminds us that everything that happens to children is accepted as normal by them; or if not exactly normal, unalterable. For them, reality and enchantment are the same thing, and they are held in thrall.

Dale Ray Phillips's 'What Men Love For' contains another child who is under a spell, that cast by his fragile, manic-depressive mother. Against the various rituals she uses to keep herself stuck together, and those the boy himself is in the process of inventing for his own preservation, there's the magic of his father – a magic of luck, risk, hope, and chance embodied in the motorcycle he drives too fast.

'The Boy on the Train' by Arthur Robinson is a wonderful, warped memoir of sorts. Instead of being about one childhood, it's really about two. Two children grow up to be fathers, two fathers misunderstand their sons, and two sons bedevil their fathers in niggling, embarrassing, or nauseating ways designed to get right under their skin: 'In prepubescence, Edward gazed at his face in the mirror a great deal and studied the effects he could get with it. Once he discovered that a strip of toothpaste artfully placed just below a nostril produced an effect that could easily turn his father's queasy stomach. The result was more than he could have hoped for.' The beautiful way this story turns around on itself, loops back, plays variations on three generations, is a delight to follow.

Two of these stories have an almost fablelike simplicity and structure. One of them is M. T. Sharif's 'The Letter Writer' whose hapless protagonist, Haji, is arrested during the Iranian revolution because he is suspected of being the brother of a supposed spy and can't prove he isn't. But the authorities can't prove he is, and since he won't confess and they can't convict him, he is given a make-work job: covering up the bare arms, legs, heads, and necks of women pictured in Western magazines by drawing clothes on them with pen and ink. Earlier, a passing dervish had prophesied that Haji would end up living in a palace, attended by concubines and servants. The manner in which this fate is actually fulfilled is reminiscent of both Kafka and the tradition of the ironic Eastern tale.

Harriet Doerr's 'Edie: A Life' has the plain charm of a sampler. It violates almost every rule I have ever heard about the construction of short stories. It doesn't concentrate, for instance, on an in-depth study of character, or on a short period of time, a single incident that focuses a life. Instead it gives the entire life, in miniature as it were, complete and rounded and unexplained as an apple.

Other stories persuade us and move us in other ways. Larry Brown in 'Kubuku Rides (This Is It)' gives his sad story of an alcoholic wife its edge and drive through the immediacy and vigour of his language, as does Blanche McCrary Boyd in her uneasily uproarious 'The Black Hand Girl'. (The hand, which is a man's, gets black by being sprained in a panty girdle. Read on.) Douglas Glover in 'Why I Decide to Kill Myself and Other Jokes' also draws on the mordant, self-deprecating humour of women. There's a murder with a hammer, a rescue from the snow, an attempted rescue with a skillet. There's a Chinese woman in David Wong Louie's 'Displacement', who is trying to make the best of America, and a native Indian woman in Linda Hogan's 'Aunt Moon's Young Man' who is also trying to make the best of it. There's a left-wing mother whose son rebels by taking up religion. But these are just hints. To get the real story, you have to read the story, as always.

I must admit that, although I was reading blind, I did guess the identities of three of the authors. Bharati Mukherjee's 'The Management of Grief' wasn't even a guess, as I had read it before and it had stayed with me. It's a finely tuned, acutely felt story about an Indian immigrant wife's reactions when the plane carrying her husband and sons is blown up over the Irish Sea by terrorists. The sleepwalking intensity with which she gropes her way through the emotional debris scattered by these senseless deaths and eventually makes a mystic sense out of them for herself is sparely but unsparingly rendered.

When I read 'The Concert Party', I guessed that it was either by Mavis Gallant or by a male writer doing a very good imitation of her. Who else would, or could, write so convincingly and with such interest about a hopeless nerd from Saskatchewan bungling around loose in France in the early fifties? The story did turn out to be by Mavis Gallant, leaving me to admire once again her deftness with a full canvas, her skill at interweaving the fates of her characters, her sharp eye for the details of small pomposities, and her camera work, if it may be called that. Watch the way she shifts, at the end, from closeup to long shot:

> Remembering Edie at the split second when she came to a decision,
> I can find it in me to envy them. The rest of us were born knowing

better, which means we were stuck. When I finally looked away from
her it was at another pool of candlelight, and the glowing, blooming
children. I wonder now if there was anything about us for the children to remember, if they ever later on reminded one another: There
was that long table of English-speaking people, still in bud.

I think I would recognize an Alice Munro story in Braille, even
though I don't read Braille. The strength and distinctiveness of her
voice will always give her away. 'Meneseteung' is, for my money,
one of Alice Munro's best and, in the manner of its telling, quirki-
est stories yet. It purports to be about a minor sentimental
'poetess' – the word, here, is appropriate – living in a small, raw,
cowpat-strewn, treeless nineteenth-century town, which is a far
cry from our idyllic notions of a golden past as the poet's sugary
verses are from real life. Our sweet picture of bygone days is
destroyed, and, in the process, our conceptions of how a story
should proceed. Similarly, the poet herself disintegrates in the
harsh and multiple presence of the vivid life that surrounds her
and that finally proves too huge and real for her. Or does it? Does
she disintegrate or integrate? Does crossing the borders of conven-
tion lead toward insanity or sanity? 'She doesn't mistake that for
reality, and neither does she mistake anything else for reality,' we
are told when the crocheted roses on the tablecloth began to float,
'and that is how she knows that she is sane'.

The last word is not the poet's, however, but the nameless narrator's, the 'I' who has been searching for the poet, or scraps of her,
through time. These last words could be an epigraph for this collection of stories, or for the act of writing itself:

People are curious. A few people are. They will be driven to find
things out, even trivial things. They will put things together,
knowing all along that they may be mistaken. You see them going
around with notebooks, scraping the dirt off gravestones, reading
microfilm, just in the hope of seeing this trickle in time, making a
connection, rescuing one thing from the rubbish.

I thank all the authors in this book for the pleasure their stories have given me, and for what they added to my own sense of what a story is, and can be.

From listening to the stories of others, we learn to tell our own.

13

The Public Woman as Honorary Man

The Warrior Queens, Antonia Fraser's most recent historical essay, is lore-packed, quirky in its approach, and fascinating to read. If non-fiction books can be thought of as detailed answers to unvoiced questions, then the question answered by this one is: How have female political and military leaders gotten away with it? How have they managed to fob themselves off on those hardest to convince soldiers and other politicians, those quintessentially male devisers and players of boys' games – as worthy leaders of the charge or captains of the ship of state, although long of hair and bulgy of breast? Such women have been few enough in number so that the exceptions have very much proven the rule. But what about those exceptions? What was their strategy, their sleight-of-hand? What was their secret?

In pursuit of answers, Fraser has assembled a remarkable group of women for our contemplation. She begins with Boadicea herself, that famed but shadowy first-century British tribal queen who led a revolt against the occupying and oppressive Romans, massacred a lot of them, and was said to have committed suicide when her forces were massacred in return. Fraser provides as faithful an account of the events as is possible, given that information is scarce and reports vary. But she is just as interested in Boadicea's

metamorphoses in historical and literary accounts through the
ages – from pious patriot and martyr, mother of her people, to
unwomanly, bloodthirsty shrew, to symbol of heroic British imperialism, ironic in view of the fact that her own revolt was against an
earlier imperialism. The accounts of her have varied according to
what men considered proper womanly behaviour, and to what
the British considered proper British behaviour; thus Boadicea has
been both slut and saint. Very early on, the myth detached itself
from the real woman in question, and has been floating around
ever since, ready to stick itself like a leech to any woman hardy
enough to brandish a spear or declare for office.

Fraser follows up with a varied assortment of women from
many centuries and civilizations who have held, however briefly,
the reins of power: Zenobia, the third-century Queen of Palmyra
who also challenged Roman rule; Empress Maud, of the twelfth-
century English wars of succession; Queen Tamara of Georgia,
'The Lion of the Caucasus'; Elizabeth I, inspiring her troops to
battle the Spanish Armada; Isabella of Spain; the engaging Queen
Jinga of Angola, who successfully defied the Portuguese colonists;
Catherine the Great of Russia; the Vietnamese heroines, Trung
Trac and Trung Nhi; the amazing Rani of Jhansi, who fought the
British in India; Indira Gandhi, Golda Meir, and a good many more,
concluding with that handy bookend to Boadicea, Margaret
Thatcher. Their childhoods, their paths to leadership, and their
styles vary enormously, but they have one thing in common: All
were instantly mythologized. Male military leaders, taken for all in
all, have been men, and that has been enough; but female ones
cannot be mere women. They are aberrations, and as such are
thought to partake of the supernatural or the monstrous: angels
or devils, paragons of chastity or demons of lust, Whores of
Babylon or Iron Maidens. Sometimes they have profited from the
female saints or goddesses available to them through their cultures, sometimes they have had to work against such images. Their
femininity has been both shackle and banner.

As leaders, they have had to be, like female doctors a decade ago, better than men. They have shamed their male followers by displaying superior courage; they have shamed their male adversaries by inflicting defeat on them at the hands of a mere woman. They have outmanoeuvred, outtalked, outblustered, and in some cases outshot and outridden the cream of the male crop. Altogether they are an impressive lot, and Fraser is to be congratulated for rescuing them from their own myths and for giving them their due as individuals, the lesser-known among them as well as the household words.

But although they have been trotted out like a roll call by many advocates for the equality of women, and presented in many guises – from turn-of-the-century pageants to Judy Chicago's 'Dinner Party' – these women have seldom allied themselves with women in general, or with movements for the improvement of their lot. More typically, they have distanced themselves from women, like Elizabeth I, who was against female rule but saw herself as a divinely placed exception, or like Catherine the Great, who spoke of the 'weak, frivolous, whining species of women'. Many have preferred the status of honorary males. If you're playing boys' games, you need to be one of the boys.

This book should be required reading for any woman going into politics, truck-driving or the Army; indeed, by any woman going into anything, unless her chosen field is uniquely feminine. Public women are put through different tests of nerve, attract different kinds of criticism, and are subject to different sorts of mythologizing than are men, and *The Warrior Queens* indicates what kinds.

Those of us for whom politics is a spectator sport will find it useful, too. It goes a long way toward explaining the various media transformations of, for instance, Margaret Thatcher, from her Attila-the-Hen period through her Iron-Maiden-Falkland-War phase to her incarnation as an editorial-cartoon Boadicea, complete with whip and chariot, triumphant on election day and dragging a clutch of pygmy men in her wake. Women leaders, it seems, find it difficult to be life-sized. For good or ill, they are gigantic.

Part Two

1990–1999

1990–1999

1990 was supposed to be the first year of a brand new era. The Soviet Union was disintegrating. Germany was reunifying, a thing we thought we'd never witness in this lifetime. The West, and that body of practices and values attached to something called 'capitalism' or 'the free-market economy,' seemed triumphant. It was not yet foreseen that, with the disappearance of its enemy, the Western moral balloon would lose helium: it's great to champion freedom in the absence of it, but hard to feel hand-on-heart noble about shopping malls and parking lots and the right to kill yourself through overeating. We approached the last decade before that artificial times-change hinge, The Millennium, in a strange state of disorientation. But, as Roberto Calasso has pointed out, heroes have a need for monsters, though monsters can do very well without heroes; and, unknown to us, the monster-producing energies were gathering themselves together throughout the decade.

Things were quieter on the writing front, mine at least. In 1991 I published *Wilderness Tips*, a collection of stories written during the late 1980s. In the same year we went to France in search of writing time. We could not rent one house for the whole period, so we rented three successive houses – one for fall, one for winter, one for spring – in and around the town of Lourmarin, in Provence. It was in these three houses that I began writing my novel *The Robber Bride*, the occasion for the essay in this volume called 'Spotty-Handed Villainesses'. I also put together a selection of very short fiction called *Good Bones*, a companion to the 1983 *Murder in the Dark*. It was published in 1992, with a cover design I'd pasted together out of issues of French *Vogue* magazine. (The books were done for a small press, and author collage saves money.)

We returned to Canada in time for the summer of 1992. I completed *The Robber Bride* in January of 1993, on a train going across Canada. My father had died earlier that month, right after I myself had been seriously ill with scarlet fever, and it was an effort of will to finish.

A book of poetry, *Morning in the Burned House*, came out in 1995. Also in that year I published a series of four lectures I'd given at Oxford University on the subject of Canadian literature and the north. The title was *Strange Things*, after the first two words in the Robert Service poem 'The Cremation of Dan McGrew'. That poem goes on to talk about the men who moil for gold. It was a moiling sort of decade.

I began the novel *Alias Grace* while I was on a book tour in Europe – in Switzerland, a suitably Freudian/Jungian locale. The process is described in the essay, 'In Search of *Alias Grace*'. What I didn't put in is that right after finishing the book we went to a small village in western Ireland, and I had to edit the book by FedEx – I did not yet have e-mail – which meant that I had to hang a tea towel on the hedge so the deliveryman would know where we were.

A year with three nines in it – one that, in addition, was the last in a thousand-year sequence – this ought to have been potent. The fact that nothing much happened underlines the arbitrariness of numbers, and of the division of time into neat slices such as this one. Nonetheless, it was a satisfying number to write on the left-hand sides of letters. *1999*. How far away it seems already.

14

A Double-Bladed Knife: Subversive Laughter
in Two Stories by Thomas King

'When *Brebeuf and His Brethren* first came out, a friend of mine said
that the thing to do now was to write the same story from the
Iroquois point of view.'

James Reaney, 'The Canadian Poet's Predicament'

Once upon a time long ago, in 1972 to be exact, I wrote a book called
Survival, which was about Canadian literature; an eccentric subject
in those days, when many denied there was any. In this book, there
was a chapter entitled *First People: Indians and Eskimos as Symbols*. What
this chapter examined was the uses made by non-Native writers of
Native characters and motifs, over the centuries and for their own
purposes. This chapter did not examine poetry and fiction written
by Native writers in English, for the simple reason that I could not
at that time find any; although I was able to recommend a small list
of non-fiction titles. The closest thing to 'imaginative' writing by
Natives were 'translations' of Native myths and poetry, which
might turn up at the beginnings of anthologies, or be offered as a
species of indigenous fairy tale in grade-school readers. (Why did I
overlook Pauline Johnson? Perhaps because, being half-white, she
somehow didn't rate as the real thing, even among Natives;
although she is undergoing reclamation today.)

The figures in the stories and poems I analysed ran the gamut. There were Indians and Eskimos seen as closer to Nature and therefore more noble, as closer to Nature and therefore *less* noble, as savage victimizers of whites and as victims of savage whites. There was a strong tendency among younger writers to claim Natives as kin, or as their 'true' ancestors (which may have something to it, since all people on earth are descended from hunter-gatherer societies). There were a lot of adjectives.

Lacking among them was *funny*. Savage irony and morbid humour did sometimes enter the picture as a kind of self-flagellation device for whites, but on the whole Natives were treated by almost everyone with the utmost gravity, as if they were either too awe-inspiring as blood-curdling savages or too sacrosanct in their status of holy victim to allow of any comic reactions either to them or by them. Furthermore, nobody ever seems to have asked them what if anything *they* found funny. The Native as presented in non-Native writing was singularly lacking in a sense of humour; sort of like the 'good' woman of Victorian fiction, who acquired at the hands of male writers the same kind of tragic-eyed, long-suffering solemnity.

Things are changing. Natives are now writing fiction, poetry and plays, and some of the literature being produced by them is both vulgar and hilarious. A good many stereotypes are hitting the dust, a few sensibilities are in the process of being outraged. The comfortable thing about a people who do not have a literary voice, or at least not one you can hear or understand, is that you never have to listen to what they are saying about *you*. Men found it very disconcerting when women started writing the truth about the kinds of things women say about them behind their backs. In particular, they did not appreciate having the more trivial of their human foibles revealed, nor did they appreciate being laughed at. Nobody does, really. But when I heard that the nickname given to a certain priest by the Indians was 'Father Crotchface' because of his beard, it caused me to reflect. For instance, *Father Crotchface and His Brethren* would have altogether a different ring to it, no?

Recently I read, in separate 'little' magazines, two outstanding stories by the same author, Thomas King.[1] They seem to me to be
'perfect' stories — by which I mean that as narrations they are
exquisitely timed, that everything in them appears to be there by
right, and that there is nothing you would want to change or edit
out. Another way of saying this is that they are beautifully written.
But apart from these aesthetic qualities, which they share with
other stories, they impressed me in quite different ways.

They ambush the reader. They get the knife in, not by whacking
you over the head with their own moral righteousness, but by
being funny. Humour can be aggressive and oppressive, as in keep-
'em-in-their-place sexist and racist jokes. But it can also be a
subversive weapon, as it has often been for people who find themselves in a fairly tight spot without other, more physical, weapons.

As these two stories have not yet appeared in a collection
(although they will soon), you'll forgive me for summarizing.

The first one I'd like to discuss is called 'Joe the Painter and the
Deer Island Massacre'. It's set in a small coastal town north of San
Francisco. The narrator is an Indian man; the subject of his narra-
tion is a white man called 'Joe the Painter'. Nobody in the town
except the narrator really likes Joe. He's loud and overly-friendly, and
has the disconcerting habit of blowing his nose into the gutter, one
nostril at a time: 'Whenever he felt a clog in his "breathing-trap", as
he called it, he'd step to the curb, lean over so as not to get his shoes
dirty, hold one nostril shut with his thumb, snort, and blow out the
other one.' But the thing that really gets people about Joe is his honesty. He knows everyone's dirty-underwear business, and announces
it at the top of his lungs in the form of friendly questions, such as,
'"Howdy, Mrs Secord, how's the girls? Looks like you been living off
pudding. Say, you pregnant again?" or, "Howdy, Connie, how's the
boil doing?"'

The action gets going when Joe finds out that the town is planning to have a pageant contest in celebration of its own centennial,
and that there's some grant money available to those who wish to
get up a pageant. Joe is overflowing with civic spirit, and decides to

enter the contest. His entry is to be about the town's founder, one Matthew Larson, and a long-ago incident called 'The Deer Island Massacre', involving a local band of Indians. Joe describes the event as follows: 'Yes, a massacre. Larson's two brothers were killed, but Larson survived and built the town. That's how this place was started. Make a good pageant, huh?'

At this point the narrator – whom we know only as 'Chief' because that's what Joe calls him – assumes that the massacre is the usual movie kind, that is, instigated by treacherous Indians, with heavy losses but with eventual triumph for the whites. He's been asked by Joe to recruit the Indians for this affair, but he isn't so sure his friends and relations will like the idea. However, he's overwhelmed by Joe: 'What's to like? It's all history. You can't muck around with history. It ain't always the way we'd like it to be, but there it is. Can't change it.'

Before the pageant, the Indians congregate on Deer Island – 'Just like the old days,' as the narrator's father says – and begin rehearsing. Joe decides they don't look enough like Indians, and rounds up some wigs and some black yarn braids from the town. The day for the pageant arrives, and Joe introduces it in proper fashion. It is being presented, he says, by the Native Son Players. The narrator likes this. 'Damn, that Joe was creative! Sounded professional,' he thinks. (We, the readers, like it because it's a really vicious touch, and because it twists on a couple of levels. It's the kind of kitschy phrasing Joe would come up with; it plays on 'Native'; and these *are* the Native Sons, although white Americans have often appropriated the designation for themselves alone.)

The first act recounts the arrival of Larson, played by Joe, who is greeted by Redbird, played by the narrator. The second act dramatizes the growing friction between Indians and whites as the latter encroach on Deer Island and want to build things on it. The third is the massacre itself, and here is where we all get a jolt, audience and readers alike – because the massacre is not perpetrated by the Indians. It's done by the whites, sneaking up in the dead of night and butchering the Indians as they lie asleep. The Indians playing the whites open fire, making *bang bang* noises. The Indians playing the Indians leap about, slapping little plastic restaurant ketchup packets on themselves for blood. 'Protect the women and children,' cries Redbird – a line straight from the wagon side of many a Western-movie Indian-and-wagon-train sequence.

The Indian actors thoroughly enjoy themselves. Soon they are all lying 'dead' while flies buzz around the ketchup and Joe soliloquizes over their bodies: 'I abhor the taking of a human life, but civilization needs a strong arm to open the frontier. Farewell, Redman. Know that from your bones will spring a new and stronger community forever.'

The audience is paralysed by Joe's pageant. This is not what they had in mind at all! It seems, somehow, to be in the most outrageous bad taste. It has mentioned – as is Joe's habit – something that has been deemed unmentionable. And it does so with a childlike straightforwardness and honesty that is infuriating. (As the town bartender has said earlier, 'Honesty makes most people nervous.') The town is scandalized. But, after all, what has Joe done? All he has done is to re-enact history, the part of it that is not usually celebrated; and this has called the notion of 'history' itself into question.

Joe's pageant does not win. It is termed 'inappropriate' by the mayor. The pageant that does win – about the founding of the first city council – is entirely 'appropriate' and entirely boring. 'History', the history we choose to recount, is what we find 'appropriate'. The Indians go home, saying that if Joe ever needs some Indians again just give them a call.

The story ends where it begins: the narrator is still the only person in town who likes Joe.

Well now, we say. What are we to make of this apparently artless but secretly designing story? And why are we left sitting, like the audience, with our mouths open? Why do we feel so *sandbagged*? And – because he's never told us – just why *does* the narrator like Joe?

I think the answers will be somewhat different, depending on –
for instance – whether the reader is a white person or a Native
person. But I assume that the narrator likes Joe for a couple of
reasons. First, Joe is entirely although tactlessly honest, and for
this reason he is the only white in the town who can look back at
the town's founding, see that it was based on the ruthless massacre of the earlier incumbents, and say it out loud. Second, Joe is
not sentimental over this. He does not romanticize the slaughtered Indians, or weep crocodile tears over them now that they are
no longer the main competition. He deals with history in the same
practical, unselfconscious way he blows his nose. He doesn't feel
any sanctimonious guilt, either. He lays the actions out and lets
them speak for themselves.

Third, Joe has a high opinion of the narrator. The title 'Chief' is
not a joke for him. He knows the narrator is not a Chief, but he
thinks of him as one anyway. Joe and the 'Chief' each possess qualities that the other one values.

Read in the light of the long North American tradition of
Indians-as-characters-in-white-fiction, this wonderfully satiric but
deadpan story could be seen as a kind of parody-in-miniature of
Fenimore Cooper's Leatherstocking tales, or of the Lone Ranger
and Tonto – the fearless white leader with a penchant for straight
speaking and for seeing justice done, the loyal Indian sidekick who
comes up with the manpower and the sound effects. It would not
work nearly so well as ambush if our minds had not already been
lulled into somnolence by a great deal of storytelling in which
things were seen far otherwise.

The second story gives us an even more radical departure from the
expected. It's called 'One Good Story, That One', and in it Thomas
King invents, not just a new slant on an old story, but a new kind
of narrative voice. The 'Chief' in 'Joe the Painter and the Deer
Island Massacre' lived in a white-folks' town and was familiar with
its vocabulary and ways. Not so the narrator of 'One Good Story',
an older Indian who appears to spend most of his time in the

Canadian bush, although he has been to Yellowknife. It's clear from the outset that English is far from being either his mother-tongue or his language of first choice. It's more like a language of last resort. However, as he uses it to tell his story, it becomes strangely eloquent. King employs this created, truncated voice to suggest, among other things, the pacing of a Native narrator. This storyteller will take his time, will repeat himself, sometimes for emphasis, sometimes for rhythm, sometimes as a delaying tactic, sometimes to get things straight.

His story is about telling a story, and about the kinds of stories that are expected of him, and about the kinds that have been told to him; it's also a story about refusing to tell a story, but we don't know that until the end of the story.

He is minding his own business at his 'summer place' when his friend Napaio arrives with three white men:

> Three men come to my summer place, also my friend Napaio. Pretty loud talkers, those ones. One is big. I tell him maybe looks like Big Joe. Maybe not.
>
> Anyway.
>
> They come and Napaio too. Bring greetings, how are you, many nice things they bring to says. Three.
>
> All white.
>
> Too bad, those.

What do these three want? It turns out they are anthropologists, and they want a story. At first the narrator tries to put them off with stories about people he knows: Jimmy who runs the store, Billy Frank and the dead-river pig. But this will not do.

> Those ones like old story, says my friend, maybe how the world was put together. Good Indian story like that, Napaio says. Those ones have tape recorders, he says.
>
> Okay, I says.
>
> Have some tea.

Stay awake.

Once upon a time.

Those stories start like that, pretty much, those ones, start on time.

The story he proceeds to relate is not what the anthropologists were looking for at all. Instead it is a hilarious version of the Book of Genesis, a white-folk story played back to them in an Indian key, with the narrator's own commentary.

'There was nothing,' he begins. 'Pretty hard to believe that, maybe.' Enter the creator. 'Only one person walk around. Call him god.' God gets tired of walking around, so he begins to create. 'Maybe that one says, we will get some stars. So he does. And then he says, maybe we should get a moon. So, they get one of them too. Someone writes all this down, I don't know. Lots of things left to get.'

The narrator launches into a long list of things god now 'gets', a list which he narrates both in his own language and in English, and which includes several animals, a flint, a television set and a 'grocery store'. God then creates the Garden of 'Evening', and two human beings, Evening herself – the garden is clearly hers – and a man, 'Ah-damn'. 'Ah-damn and Evening real happy, those ones. No clothes, those, you know. Ha, Ha, Ha, Ha. But they pretty dumb, then. New, you know.'

Evening discovers the famous tree, which has a lot of things growing on it, such as potatoes, pumpkins and corn. It also has some 'mee-so', apples. Evening has it in mind to eat some of them, but 'that one, god' re-enters the picture. He has a bad temper and shouts, and is compared by the narrator to a man called Harley James who used to beat up his wife. 'God' orders Evening to leave the apples alone. He is selfish, and will not share.

However, Evening eats an apple, and being a good woman, takes some to share with Ah-damn. The latter is busy writing down the names of the animals as they parade by. 'Pretty boring that,' says the narrator. Writing down does not interest him.

Again, we get a long list of the animals, in two languages. But now the story goes even further off the biblical beaten track, because Coyote comes by a lot of times, in different disguises. 'Gets dressed up, fool around.'

And now the narrator shifts entirely into his own language, which we paleface readers can't follow at all. He even tells a joke, which is presumably about Coyote, but how are we to know? *What kind of a story is this anyway?* Well, it's changing into a story about the coyote. 'Tricky one, that coyote. Walks in circles. Sneaky.'

Evening recognizes immediately, from the tracks on the floor, that the coyote has been around more than once. But she feeds Ah-damn anyway, dumb bunny that he is, like 'white man'. She herself is pointedly identified as an Indian woman, which accounts for her intelligence.

God comes along and is cheesed off because the apples have been eaten. Evening tells him to 'calm down, watch some television', but god wants to kick Evening and Ah-damn out of the garden, 'go somewhere else. Just like Indian today.'

Evening says that's fine with her, there's lots of other good places around, but Ah-damn lies about how many apples he ate, and whines as well. It avails him nothing and he gets thrown out, 'right on those rocks. Ouch, ouch, ouch, that one says.' Evening has to come back and fix him up.

What about the snake? He's been forgotten by the narrator, but is stuck back in at the end. He's in the tree along with the apples, but there's not much to tell about him. The reason he hisses is that Evening stuck an apple in his mouth for trying to get too friendly.

The narrator's story ends with Ah-damn and Evening coming 'out here' and having a bunch of kids. 'That's all. It is ended.'

But Thomas King's story ends another way. The white anthropologists pack up, none too pleased but putting a good face on it. 'All of those ones smile. Nod their head around. Look out window. Make happy noises. Say goodbyes, see you later. Leave pretty quick.' The narrator's last gloss is, 'I clean up all the coyote tracks on the floor.'

If the narrator has a 'good Indian story' to tell, he's kept it to himself. He certainly isn't going to tell it to the white anthropologists, who are seen as sneaky coyotes, mischief-makers, indulging in disguises and fooling around. Instead he's fed them one of their own stories back, but he's changed the moral. No secondary creation of Eve from a rib, no original sin, no temptation by Satan, no guilt, no 'sweat of your brow' curse. The bad behaviour displayed is displayed by 'god', who is greedy, selfish, loud-mouthed and violent. Adam is stupid, and Eve, who is generous, level-headed, peace-loving and nurturing, comes out the hero of the story. In the course of his tale, the Indian narrator is able to convey to the whites more or less what he thinks of white behaviour in general. Nor can they do anything about it, as this is a situation they themselves have sought out – for their own benefit, since, we assume, they wish to use the Indian's story as 'material' – and the etiquette of storytelling prevents them from intervening in the story to protest either its form or its content.

'One Good Story' could be seen as a variant of the Wise Peasant motif, or 'putting one over on the city slicker' by pretending to be a lot dumber than you really are; although, in this case, the city slicker category includes any white reader. We feel 'taken' by the story, in several ways: we get taken in by it, because this narrative voice has considerable charm and straight-faced subtlety; but we also get taken for a ride, just as the three anthropologists are. Perhaps we have been taken for even more of a ride than we realize. How do we know what all those Indian words *really* mean? We don't, and that is very much one of the points. The narrator himself doesn't know what 'Saint Merry' means. Tit for tat. Another tit for tat is that we are forced to experience first hand how it must feel to have your own religious stories retold in a version that neither 'understands' nor particularly reverences them. The biblical Fall of Man has seldom been recounted with such insouciance.

At the same time, and in the midst of our cross-cultural nervousness, we sympathize with the narrator rather than the anthropologists, just as, in 'Joe the Painter' we have taken the side of the odd men out, Joe and the 'Chief', as against the conventional townspeople. Thomas King knows exactly what he's doing.

Both of these stories are about Indians who are expected to 'play Indian', to enact some white man's version of themselves, to serve a symbolic agenda other than their own. Both narrators, in their own ways, refuse: the first by participating in a farcical pageant that undermines the whole 'How-the-West-Was-Won' myth, the second by withholding his authentic 'Indian' tales and hilariously subverting a central and sacrosanct 'white' story.

What other inventive twists of narrative and alarming shifts of viewpoint are in store for us from this author? Time, which begins all stories, will tell.

NOTE

1. Thomas King has published the following works: ed., with Cheryl Calver and Helen Hoy, *The Native in Literature* (Toronto: ECW, 1985); ed., Native Fiction issue of *Canadian Fiction Magazine* No. 60 (1987); *Medicine River* (novel) (Toronto: Penguin, 1990); ed., *'All My Relations': An Anthology of Contemporary Canadian Native Prose* (Toronto: McClelland & Stewart, 1990); *One Good Story, That One* (story cycle, in progress).

15

Nine Beginnings

1. *Why do you write?*

I've begun this piece nine times. I've junked each beginning.

I hate writing about my writing. I almost never do it. Why am I doing it now? Because I said I would. I got a letter. I wrote back *no*. Then I was at a party and the same person was there. It's harder to refuse in person. Saying *yes* had something to do with being nice, as women are taught to be, and something to do with being helpful, which we are also taught. Being helpful to women, giving a pint of blood. With not claiming the sacred prerogatives, the touch-me-not self-protectiveness of the artist, with not being selfish. With conciliation, with doing your bit, with appeasement. I was well brought up. I have trouble ignoring social obligations. Saying you'll write about your writing is a social obligation. It's not an obligation to the writing.

2. *Why do you write?*

I've junked each of nine beginnings. They seemed beside the point. Too assertive, too pedagogical, too frivolous or belligerent, too falsely wise. As if I had some special self-revelation that would encourage others, or some special knowledge to impart, some pithy saying that would act like a talisman for the driven, the obsessed. But I have no such talismans. If I did, I would not continue, myself, to be so driven and obsessed.

3. *Why do you write?*

I hate writing about my writing because I have nothing to say about it. I have nothing to say about it because I can't remember what goes on when I'm doing it. That time is like small pieces cut out of my brain. It's not time I myself have lived. I can remember the details of the rooms and places where I've written, the circumstances, the other things I did before and after, but not the process itself. Writing about writing requires self-consciousness; writing itself requires the abdication of it.

4. *Why do you write?*

There are a lot of things that can be said about what goes on around the edges of writing. Certain ideas you may have, certain motivations, grand designs that don't get carried out. I can talk about bad reviews, about sexist reactions to my writing, about making an idiot of myself on television shows. I can talk about books that failed, that never got finished, and about why they failed. The one that had too many characters, the one that had too many layers of time, red herrings that diverted me when what I really wanted to get at was something else, a certain corner of the visual world, a certain voice, an inarticulate landscape.

I can talk about the difficulties that women encounter as writers. For instance, if you're a woman writer, sometime, somewhere, you will be asked: *Do you think of yourself as a writer first, or as a woman first?* Look out. Whoever asks this hates and fears both writing and women.

Many of us, in my generation at least, ran into teachers or male writers or other defensive jerks who told us women could not really write because they couldn't be truck drivers or Marines and therefore didn't understand the seamier side of life, which included sex with women. We were told we wrote like housewives, or else we were treated like honorary men, as if to be a good writer was to suppress the female.

Such pronouncements used to be made as if they were the simple truth. Now they're questioned. Some things have changed for the better, but not all. There's a lack of self-confidence that gets instilled very early in many young girls, before writing is even seen as a possibility. You need a certain amount of nerve to be a writer, an almost physical nerve, the kind you need to walk a log across a river. The horse throws you and you get back on the horse. I learned to swim by being dropped into the water. You need to know you can sink, and survive it. Girls should be allowed to play in the mud. They should be released from the obligations of perfection. Some of your writing, at least, should be as evanescent as play.

A ratio of failures is built into the process of writing. The wastebasket has evolved for a reason. Think of it as the altar of the Muse Oblivion, to whom you sacrifice your botched first drafts, the tokens of your human imperfection. She is the tenth Muse, the one without whom none of the others can function. The gift she offers you is the freedom of the second chance. Or as many chances as you'll take.

5. *Why do you write?*
In the mid-eighties I began a sporadic journal. Today I went back through it, looking for something I could dig out and fob off as pertinent instead of writing this piece about writing. But it was useless. There was nothing in it about the actual composition of anything I've written over the past six years. Instead there are exhortations to myself – to get up earlier, to walk more, to resist lures and distractions. *Drink more water*, I find. *Go to bed earlier.* There were lists of how many pages I'd written per day, how many I'd retyped, how many yet to go. Other than that, there was nothing but descriptions of rooms, accounts of what we'd cooked and/or eaten and with whom, letters written and received, notable sayings of children, birds and animals seen, the weather. What came

up in the garden. Illnesses, my own and those of others. Deaths, births. Nothing about writing.

> *January 1, 1984. Blakeney, England. As of today, I have about 130 pp. of the novel done and it's just beginning to take shape & reach the point at which I feel that it exists and can be finished and may be worth it. I work in the bedroom of the big house, and here, in the sitting room, with the wood fire in the fireplace and the coke fire in the dilapidated Raeburn in the kitchen. As usual I'm too cold, which is better than being too hot — today is grey, warm for the time of year, damp. If I got up earlier maybe I would work more, but I might just spend more time procrastinating — as now.*
> And so on.

6. *Why do you write?*

You learn to write by reading and writing, writing and reading. As a craft it's acquired through the apprentice system, but you choose your own teachers. Sometimes they're alive, sometimes dead.

As a vocation, it involves the laying on of hands. You receive your vocation and in your turn you must pass it on. Perhaps you will do this only through your work, perhaps in other ways. Either way, you're part of a community, the community of writers, the community of storytellers that stretches back through time to the beginning of human society.

As for the particular human society to which you yourself belong — sometimes you'll feel you're speaking for it, sometimes — when it's taken an unjust form — against it, or for that other community, the community of the oppressed, the exploited, the voiceless. Either way, the pressures on you will be intense; in other countries, perhaps fatal. But even here — speak 'for women', or for any other group which is feeling the boot, and there will be many at hand, both for and against, to tell you to shut up, or to say what they want you to say, or to say it a different way. Or to save them. The billboard awaits you, but if you succumb to its temptations you'll end up two-dimensional.

Tell what is yours to tell. Let others tell what is theirs.

7. *Why do you write?*

Why are we so addicted to causality? *Why do you write?* (Treatise by child psychologist, mapping your formative traumas. Conversely: palm-reading, astrology and genetic studies, pointing to the stars, fate, heredity.) *Why do you write?* (That is, why not do something useful instead?) If you were a doctor, you could tell some accept-able moral tale about how you put Band-Aids on your cats as a child, how you've always longed to cure suffering. No one can argue with that: But writing? What is it *for*?

Some possible answers: *Why does the sun shine? In the face of the absurd-ity of modern society, why do anything else? Because I'm a writer. Because I want to discover the patterns in the chaos of time. Because I must. Because someone has to bear witness. Why do you read?* (This last is tricky: maybe they don't.) *Because I wish to forge in the smithy of my soul the uncreated conscience of my race. Because I wish to make an axe to break the frozen sea within.* (These have been used, but they're good.)

If at a loss, perfect the shrug. Or say: *It's better than working in a bank.* Or say: *For fun.* If you say this, you won't be believed, or else you'll be dismissed as trivial. Either way, you'll have avoided the question.

8. *Why do you write?*

Not long ago, in the course of clearing some of the excess paper out of my workroom, I opened a filing cabinet drawer I hadn't looked into for years. In it was a bundle of loose sheets, folded, creased, and grubby, tied up with leftover string. It consisted of things I'd written in the late fifties, in high school and the early years of university. There were scrawled, inky poems, about snow, despair, and the Hungarian Revolution. There were short stories dealing with girls who'd had to get married, and dispirited, mousy-haired high-school English teachers – to end up as either was at that time my vision of Hell – typed finger-by-finger on an ancient machine that made all the letters half-red.

There I am, then, back in grade twelve, going through the writers' magazines after I'd finished my French Composition homework, typing out my lugubrious poems and my grit-filled stories. (I was big on grit. I had an eye for lawn-litter and dog turds on sidewalks. In these stories it was usually snowing damply, or raining; at the very least there was slush. If it was summer, the heat and humidity were always wiltingly high and my characters had sweat marks under their arms; if it was spring, wet clay stuck to their feet. Though some would say all this was just normal Toronto weather.)

In the top right-hand corners of some of these, my hopeful seventeen-year-old self had typed, 'First North American Rights Only'. I was not sure what 'First North American Rights' were; I put it in because the writing magazines said you should. I was at that time an aficionado of writing magazines, having no one else to turn to for professional advice.

If I were an archeologist, digging through the layers of old paper that mark the eras in my life as a writer, I'd have found, at the lowest or Stone Age level – say around ages five to seven – a few poems and stories, unremarkable precursors of all my frenetic later scribbling. (Many children write at that age, just as many children draw. The strange thing is that so few of them go on to become writers or painters.) After that there's a great blank. For eight years, I simply didn't write. Then, suddenly, and with no missing links in between, there's a wad of manuscripts. One week I wasn't a writer, the next I was.

Who did I think I was, to be able to get away with this? What did I think I was doing? How did I get that way? To these questions I still have no answers.

9. *Why do you write?*
There's the blank page, and the thing that obsesses you. There's the story that wants to take you over and there's your resistance to it. There's your longing to get out of this, this servitude, to play hooky, to do anything else: wash the laundry, see a movie. There are words and their inertias, their biases, their insufficiencies, their glories. There are the risks you take and your loss of nerve, and the help that comes when you're least expecting it. There's the

laborious revision, the scrawled-over, crumpled-up pages that drift across the floor like spilled litter. There's the one sentence you know you will save.

Next day there's the blank page. You give yourself up to it like a sleepwalker. Something goes on that you can't remember afterwards. You look at what you've done. It's hopeless.

You begin again. It never gets any easier.

16

A Slave to His Own Liberation

The general of the title of Gabriel García Márquez's new novel is Simón Bolívar, 'The Liberator', who in the years 1811–24 led the revolutionary armies of South America in a brilliant and gruelling series of campaigns that swept the Spaniards from their former colonies. In the process many rich and long-established cities were devastated, vast wealth was captured and squandered, whole populations were laid waste through slaughter, famine and disease, and, in the aftermath, the unified South America Bolívar so fervently desired – a country that would have balanced, and challenged, the United States – fell apart in a series of jealous bickerings, intrigues, assassinations, secessions, local feuds and military coups.

Had Bolívar not existed, Mr García Márquez would have had to invent him. Seldom has there been a more fitting match between author and subject. Mr García Márquez wades into his flamboyant, often improbably and ultimately tragic material with enormous gusto, heaping detail upon sensuous detail, alternating grace with horror, perfume with the stench of corruption, the elegant language of public ceremony with the vulgarity of private moments, the rationalistic clarity of Bolívar's thought with the malarial intensity of his emotions, but tracing always the main compulsion that drives his protagonist: the longing for an independent and unified South America. This, according to Bolívar himself, is the clue to all his contradictions.

Just now, when empires are disintegrating and the political map is being radically redrawn, the subject of *The General in His Labyrinth* is a most timely one. It is noteworthy that Mr García Márquez has chosen to depict his hero not in the days of his astonishing triumphs, but in his last months of bitterness and frustration. One feels that, for the author, the tale of Bolívar is exemplary, not just for his own turbulent age but for ours as well. Revolutions have a long history of eating their progenitors.

Each book by Mr García Márquez is a major literary event. Each has also been quite different from its predecessors, and the new novel, ably translated by Edith Grossman, is no exception. It is set in the past, but to call it a historical novel would be to do it an injustice. Nor is it one of those fictions – such as, for instance, *A Maggot* by John Fowles – in which a few real personages are mingled with the imagined ones. In this book the element of the real is front and centre: most of the people in it actually lived; all of the events and most of the incidents actually took place, and the rest have their foundation in voluminous research: if someone eats a guava, then guavas existed, in that place and at that season.

But Mr García Márquez avoids a chronological narrative (although, very helpfully, the linear sequence of events is provided in a note at the end). Instead he begins his book at the point at which General Bolívar, an old man at the age of forty-six, literally shrunken by the unspecified illness that will soon kill him, is rejected as president of the new government he himself has helped to create. Cold-shouldered by the elite, jeered by the rabble, he leaves the Colombian city of Bogotá for a meandering journey by barge down the Magdalena River with the stated intention of sailing to Europe.

He never makes it. Thwarted by the oppressive and calamitous weather, by the machinations of his enemies – in particular his fellow revolutionary and arch-rival, Francisco de Paula Santander –

by the political ambitions of his friends, by his illness and above all by his own reluctance to leave the scene of his former glories, he wanders from city to city, house to house, refuge to refuge, dragging his increasingly baffled and restless entourage in his wake. In some places he is treated with scorn, in others with veneration; he endures endless celebrations in his honour, pleas for his intercession, fiestas and official receptions, punctuated by the brutal interventions of nature – floods, heat waves, epidemics – and by fresh episodes in the decay of his own body.

Always he is dogged by a question he refuses to answer: will he recapture the presidency in order to suppress the anarchy and civil war that are threatening to tear the continent apart? In other words, is he willing to purchase unity at the expense of a rudimentary democracy, and at the price of a dictatorship headed by himself? Possibly he is waiting for the right moment to make a comeback; but this moment never arrives. 'The headlong race between his misfortunes and his dreams' is won by the misfortunes, and the monster at the centre of his 'labyrinth' gets him in the end.

The structure of the book is itself labyrinthine, turning the narrative back on itself, twisting and confusing the thread of time until not only the general but the reader cannot tell exactly where or when he is. Woven into the present, as memory, reveries, dream or feverish hallucination, are many scenes from the general's earlier life: near catastrophes in war, splendid triumphs, superhuman feats of endurance, nights of orgiastic celebration, portentous turns of fate and romantic encounters with beautiful women, of which there seem to have been a large number. There is the deeply suppressed image of his young wife, dead after eight months of marriage; there is his devoted, cigar-smoking Amazonian mistress, Manuela Sáenz, who once saved him from assassination. But there were also – according to his faithful valet, José Palacios, who plays Leporello to Bolívar's Don Juan – thirty-five other serious affairs, 'not counting the one-night birds, of course'.

Of course: because Bolívar is not only a prime exponent of the

well-known Latin American machismo but a true child of the
Romantic age. His political imagination was formed by the French
Revolution; his heroes were Napoleon and Rousseau. Like Byron,
he was a romantic ironist, a sceptic in religion, a flouter of social
norms, a philanderer — a man capable of great self-sacrifice in the
pursuit of large and glorious goals, but otherwise a worshipper at
the altar of his own ego. He approached each new woman as a
challenge; 'once satisfied, he [would] . . . send them extravagant
gifts to protect himself from oblivion, but, with an emotion that
resembled vanity more than love, he would not commit the least
part of his life to them.'

On the subject of politics, Mr García Márquez's Bolívar is little
short of prophetic. Just before his death, he proclaims that South
America 'is ungovernable, the man who serves a revolution plows
the sea, this nation will fall inevitably into the hands of the unruly
mob and then will pass into the hands of almost indistinguishable
petty tyrants'. He foresees the perils of debt: 'I warned Santander
that whatever good we had done for the nation would be worth-
less if we took on debt because we would go on paying interest till
the end of time. Now it's clear: debt will destroy us in the end.' He
has something to say, as well, about the role of the United States in
Latin American affairs: inviting the United States to the Congress
of Panama is 'like inviting the cat to the mice's fiesta'. 'Don't go . . .
to the United States,' he warns a colleague. 'It's omnipotent and
terrible, and its tale of liberty will end in a plague of miseries for us
all.' As Carlos Fuentes has remarked, the patterns of Latin
American politics, and of United States' intervention in them, have
not changed much in 160 years.

In addition to being a fascinating literary tour de force and a
moving tribute to an extraordinary man, *The General in His Labyrinth*
is a sad commentary on the ruthlessness of the political process.
Bolívar changed history, but not as much as he would have liked.
There are statues of 'The Liberator' all over Latin America, but in
his own eyes he died defeated.

17

Angela Carter: 1940–1992

Intelligence and kindness don't always go hand in hand – very smart people being notoriously easily irritated by the dumbness of others – but in Angela Carter, who died last Sunday, they did. When you skinned your knee on the British press, as sometimes happens to authors, she was ready with the Band-Aid and cup of tea; so that you wouldn't feel like a whiny, self-indulgent brat, she was quite ready to join in with some plaints of her own. Few writers understand this procedure, which requires tact and balance, but Angela had it down to a fine art.

The amazing thing about her, for me, was that someone who looked so much like the Fairy Godmother – the long, prematurely-white hair, the beautiful complexion, the benign, slightly blinky eyes, the heart-shaped mouth – should actually *be* so much like the Fairy Godmother. She seemed always on the verge of bestowing something – some talisman, some magic token you'd need to get through the dark forest, some verbal formula useful for the opening of charmed doors.

You kept waiting for her to address you as 'my child', though in an absent-minded rather than a patronizing way. And since she had an infinite fund of goodies up her sleeve – facts, oddities, books to be read, snippets of gossip, heaps of stuff in general – you were never disappointed. You always came away feeling that you'd received more than you had given.

But this innate graciousness was not a matter of conventional manners. You got your cup of tea in the kitchen, not the sitting-room, and you got it in a mug. Several of our conversations took place while feeding deep-dish pizzas to our respective young children, in establishments that were far from posh. There was something of *Alice*'s White Queen about her, too: if she had had any hairpins, they certainly would have been coming out, constantly. Although possessed of a thoroughly organized mind, she lived in the midst of what could be called welter or profusion, depending on point of view, and made few concessions to anyone else's ideas of what should be bought, worn or sat on.

Nor was she in any way mealy-mouthed. As you might expect from reading her books – she was, among other things, a quirky, original and baroque stylist, a trait especially marked in *The Bloody Chamber* – her vocabulary was a mix of finely-tuned phrase, luscious adjective, witty aphorism, and hearty, up-theirs vulgarity, so evident in her novels *Wise Children* and *Nights at the Circus*.

But she was devoid of the knee-jerk sneer reflex. If an opinion came up that cried out to be sneered at, there would be a pause, while she considered it from all sides. Then she would give a beatific but impish smile and proceed – in her high, quizzical, oddly child-like voice – to play devil's advocate, arguing the sneer-worthy position just to see if there was anything in it. Perhaps *play* is the operative word – not as in *trivial activity*, but as in word-play, play of thought, or play of light. Despite her scepticism, her down-to-earth practicality, and an undertone of muted and sometimes fatalistic sadness, the imagination at work was mercurial, multi-sided, and more than faintly Gothic.

She was born subversive, in the sense of its original root: *to overturn*. She had an instinctive feeling for the other side, which included also the underside, and for the other hand, the sinister one. Only she could have written *The Sadeian Woman*, which interprets the Marquis de Sade's badly-behaved heroines as early feminists. The other side is also the irrational side, and she was, per-haps and in part, an inheritor of the fanciful Scottish or Celtic tradition, as exemplified by, say, George Macdonald. The Scottish element in her background – of which she was proud – might explain as well her openness to ex-colonies, such as Australia, which she adored, and Canada, where she had a devoted readership.

In a country where the all-too-frequent response to any men-tion of Canada is a polite yawn, this last especially endeared her to me. Although she possessed a detailed – even an anthropologi-cal – knowledge of Britain, she was the opposite of parochial. Nothing, for her, was outside the pale: she wanted to know about everything and everyone, and every place and every word. She rel-ished life and language hugely, and revelled in the diverse.

It was part of her kindness that she made the process of her dying easy for her many friends, as easy as she could. I hope she had even a small idea of how much she will be missed.

18

Afterword to *Anne of Green Gables*

Anne of Green Gables is one of those books you feel almost guilty liking, because so many other people seem to like it as well. If it's that popular, you feel, it can't possibly be good, or good for you.

Like many others, I read this book as a child, and absorbed it so thoroughly that I can't even remember when. I read it to my own daughter when she was eight, and she read it again to herself later, and acquired all the sequels – which she, like everyone else including the author, realized were not on quite the same level as the original. I saw the television series too, and, despite rewrites and excisions, the central story was as strong and as appealing as ever.

And several summers ago, when my family and I were spending some time on Prince Edward Island, I even saw the musical. The theatre gift-store was offering *Anne* dolls, an *Anne* cookbook, and *Anne* paraphernalia of all kinds. The theatre itself was large but crowded; in front of us was a long row of Japanese tourists. During one especially culture-specific moment – a dance in which a horde of people leapt around holding eggs glued on to spoons clenched between their teeth – I wondered what the Japanese tourists could possibly be making of it. Then I took to wondering what they could be making of the whole phenomenon. What did they make of the *Anne* dolls, the *Anne* knick-knacks, the *Anne* books themselves? Why was Anne Shirley, the talkative red-haired orphan, so astonishingly popular among them?

Possibly it was the red hair: that must be exotic, I thought. Or possibly Japanese women and girls found Anne encouraging: in danger of rejection because she is not the desired and valued boy, she manages to win over the hearts of her adoptive parents and to end the book with a great deal of social approval. But she triumphs without sacrificing her sense of herself: she will not tolerate insult, she defends herself, she even loses her temper and gets away with it. She breaks taboos. On a more conventional level, she studies hard at school and wins a scholarship, she respects her elders, or at least some of them, and she has a great love of Nature (although it is Nature in its more subdued aspect; hers is a pastoral world of gardens and blossoming trees, not mountains and hurricanes).

It was helpful for me to try looking at *Anne*'s virtues through other eyes, because for a Canadian woman – once a Canadian girl – *Anne* is a truism. Readers of my generation, and of several generations before and since, do not think of *Anne* as 'written'. It has simply always been there. It is difficult not to take the book for granted, and almost impossible to see it fresh, to realize what an impact it must have had when it first appeared.

It is tempting to think of *Anne* as just a very good 'girls' book', about – and intended for – pre-adolescents. And on one level, it is just that. Anne's intense friendship with the ever-faithful Diana Barry, the hatefulness of Josie Pye, the schoolroom politics, the tempest-in-a-teapot 'scrapes', Anne's overdone vanity and her consciousness of fashion in clothes and bookmarks – all are familiar to us, both from our own observation and experience and from other 'girls' books'.

But *Anne* draws on a darker, and, some would say, a more respectable literary lineage. Anne Shirley is, after all, an orphan and the opening chapters of *Jane Eyre* and *Oliver Twist* and *Great Expectations*, and, later and closer to Anne, the bad-tempered, unhappy, sallow-faced little Mary of *The Secret Garden*, have all contributed both to Anne Shirley's formation as orphan-heroine and to the reader's understanding of the perils of orphanhood in the nineteenth and early twentieth centuries. Unless she had been allowed to stay at Green Gables, Anne's fate would have been to be passed around as a cheap drudge from one set of uncaring adults to another. In the real world, as opposed to the literary one, she would have been in great danger of ending up pregnant and disgraced, raped – like many of the Barnardo Homes female orphans – by the men in the families in which they had been 'placed'. We have forgotten, by now, that orphans were once despised, exploited, and feared, considered to be the offspring of criminals or the products of immoral sex. Rachel Lynde, in her tales of orphans who have poisoned and set fire to the families who have taken them in, is merely voicing received opinion. No wonder Anne cries so much when she thinks she will be 'returned', and no wonder Marilla and Matthew are considered 'odd' for keeping her!

But Anne partakes of another 'orphan' tradition as well: the folk-tale orphan who wins despite everything, the magic child who appears, as it seems, from nowhere – like King Arthur – and proves to have qualities far superior to anyone around her.

Such literary echoes may form the structural underpinnings of Anne's tale, but the texture is relentlessly local. L. M. Montgomery stays within the parameters of the conventions available to her: nobody goes to the bathroom in this book, and although we are in the country, no pigs are visibly slaughtered. But, that said, she remains faithful to her own aesthetic credo, as set forth by Anne's beloved schoolteacher Miss Stacy, who 'won't let us write anything but what might happen in Avonlea in our own lives'. Part of the current interest in 'Avonlea' is that it appears to be a 'jollier', more innocent world, long-gone and very different from our own; but for Montgomery, 'Avonlea' was simply reality edited. She was determined to write from what she knew: not the whole truth, perhaps, but not a total romanticization either. Rooms and clothes and malicious gossip are described much as they were, and people talk in the vernacular, minus the swear words – but then, the people we hear speaking are mostly 'respectable' women, who would not have sworn anyway. This world was familiar to me through the stories told to me by my Maritime parents and aunts: the sense of community and 'family', the horror of being 'talked about', the smug rectitude, the distrust of outsiders, the sharp division between what was 'respectable' and what was not, as well as the pride in hard work and the respect for achievement, all are faithfully depicted by Montgomery. Marilla's speech to Anne – 'I believe in a girl being fitted to earn her own living whether ever she has to or not' – may sound like radical feminism to some, but in fact it is just a sample of Maritime self-reliance. My mother was brought up like that; consequently, so was I.

Montgomery wrote from her own experience in another and more profound way as well. Knowing what we now know about her life, we realize that Anne's story was a mirror-image of her own, and gathers much of its force and poignancy from thwarted wish-fulfilment. Montgomery, too, was virtually an orphan, abandoned by her father after her mother's death to a set of strict, judgemental grandparents, but she never gained the love she grants so lavishly to Anne. Anne's experience of exclusion was undoubtedly hers; the longing for acceptance must have been hers as well. So was the lyricism; so was the sense of injustice; so was the rebellious rage.

Children identify with Anne because she is what they often feel themselves to be – powerless and scorned and misunderstood. She revolts as they would like to revolt, she gets what they would like to have, and she is cherished as they themselves would like to be. When I was a child, I thought – as all children do – that Anne was the centre of the book. I cheered her on, and applauded her victories over the adults, her thwartings of their wills. But there is another perspective.

Although *Anne* is about childhood, it is also very much centred on the difficult and sometimes heartbreaking relationship between children and adults. Anne seems to have no power, but in reality she has the vast though unconscious power of a beloved child.

Although she changes in the book – she grows up – her main transformation is physical. Like the Ugly Duckling, she becomes a swan; but the inner Anne – her moral essence – remains much what it has always been. Matthew, too, begins as he means to go on: he is one of those shy, child-like men who delight Montgomery's heart (like Cousin Jimmy in the *Emily* books), he loves Anne from the moment he sees her, and he takes her part in every way and on every occasion.

The only character who goes through any sort of essential transformation is Marilla. *Anne of Green Gables* is not about Anne becoming a good little girl: it is about Marilla Cuthbert becoming a good – and more complete – woman. At the book's beginning, she is hardly even alive; as Rachel Lynde, the commonsense voice of the community, puts it, Marilla is not *living*, just *staying*. Marilla takes Anne on, not out of love as Matthew does, but out of a cold sense of duty. It is only in the course of the book that we realize there is a strong family resemblance between the two. Matthew, as we have always known, is a 'kindred spirit' for Anne, but the kinship with Marilla goes deeper: Marilla, too, has been 'odd', ugly, unloved. She, too, has been the victim of fate and injustice.

Anne without Marilla would – admit it – be sadly one-dimensional, an over-talkative child whose precocious cuteness might very easily pall. Marilla adds the saving touch of lemon juice. On the other hand, Anne acts out a great many of Marilla's concealed wishes, thoughts, and desires, which is the key to their relationship. And, in her battles of will with Anne, Marilla is forced to confront herself, and to regain what she has lost or repressed: her capacity to love, the full range of her emotions. Underneath her painful cleanliness and practicality, she is a passionate woman, as her outpouring of grief at Matthew's death testifies. The most moving declaration of love in the book has nothing to do with Gilbert Blythe: it is Marilla's wrenching confession in the penultimate chapter:

Oh, Anne, I know I've been kind of strict and harsh with you maybe – but you mustn't think I didn't love you as well as

Matthew did, for all that. I want to tell you now when I can. It's never been easy for me to say things out of my heart, but at times like this it's easier. I love you as dear as if you were my own flesh and blood and you've been my joy and comfort ever since you came to Green Gables.

The Marilla we first meet could never have laid herself bare like this. Only when she has recovered – painfully enough, awkwardly enough – her capacity to feel and express, can she become what Anne herself has lost long ago, and truly wants: a mother. But to love is to become vulnerable. At the beginning of the book, Marilla is all-powerful, but by the end, the structure has been reversed, and Anne has much more to offer Marilla than the other way around.

It may be the ludicrous escapades of Anne that render the book so attractive to children, but it is the struggles of Marilla that give it resonance for adults. Anne may be the orphan in all of us, but then, so is Marilla. Anne is the fairy-tale wish-fulfilment version, what Montgomery longed for. Marilla is, more likely, what she feared she might become: joyless, bereft, trapped, hopeless, unloved. Each of them saves the other. It is the neatness of their psychological fit – as well as the invention, humour, and fidelity of the writing – that makes *Anne* such a satisfying and enduring fable.

19

Introduction: The Early Years

For we are great statements in our days
And on the basis of that we can expect small audiences.

Gwendolyn MacEwen was born in Toronto in September 1941, during the darkest days of World War II. She died, unexpectedly and far too young, in 1987, at the age of forty-five.

Due to family disruptions – her mother was frequently hospitalized for mental illness, her father became an alcoholic – her childhood was stressful; but the conviction that she would be a poet came to her as a saving grace in early adolescence. She began publishing poetry in the well-respected journal *The Canadian Forum* when she was sixteen, and at the age of eighteen – although warned against such a rash step by more practical heads – she left high school to pursue her vocation.

The late fifties was not the best time for such a move, especially if you were a woman. In the world of conventional North American popular culture, Doris Day and Betty Crocker ruled supreme and Mom-and-Dad domesticity was the norm; rebellion against the bourgeoisie was embodied by Marlon Brando and his all-boy *Wild Ones* motorbike gang. The music was rock 'n' roll or jazz, heavily male both. 'Artist' meant male painter; any woman rash enough to take brush in hand was regarded as a dabbler. The Beat Generation writers had a place for women, true, but only as complaisant helpmeets; they were expected to keep on cookin' and smilin' and payin' the rent, and to keep out of the hair of their genius men. Women artists of any kind, in that still heavily-Freudian era, were assumed to have adjustment problems. *Man Does, Woman Is*, as Robert Graves so dauntingly put it; and if women insisted on doing rather than being, they were likely to end up with their heads in the oven.

For Gwendolyn MacEwen, all of this was compounded you would think by location. Toronto was not exactly a centre of cosmopolitan artistic energy at the time. Montreal was considered to be the cultural heartland, for both English-speaking and French-speaking artists alike, whereas Toronto was thought of as a puritanical provincial backwater, a boring, constipated place where you couldn't get wine with dinner. Persons of taste sneered at it, even and especially those who lived there. Colonialism lingered on, and it was assumed that first-rate cultural products were imported from abroad – from Europe if you were old-fashioned, from New York if you thought of yourself as the cutting edge.

But for young writers, even young female writers, there were compensations. Cultural trends are never as oppressively homogeneous in the outbacks as they are in the centres, and in Canada there was a generation of women poets just before MacEwen's who hadn't heard yet that they were supposed to just be: Phyllis Webb, Anne Wilkinson, Jay Macpherson, P. K. Page, Margaret Avison. And the writing community was so small, beleaguered, and desirous of reinforcements that it was welcoming to any newcomer with talent, especially such an outstanding talent as MacEwen's. Oddly enough, this period – so forbidding and desertlike to the casual view – was, for writing, an age of youthful successes. In addition to Leonard Cohen it produced Daryl Hine, who published his first major collection when he was under twenty; James Reaney, the boy wonder from Stratford; Marie-Claire Blais, the girl wonder from Quebec; Jay Macpherson, who won the country's foremost literary award when she was twenty-seven; Michael Ondaatje, b. p. nichol, Joe Rosenblatt, bill bissett – all early publishers; and many others. So although Gwendolyn MacEwen started publishing very early, she wasn't alone.

Nor was it unusual for her to begin with poetry. Like many of her contemporaries, she eventually produced several novels and collections of short stories, and during the course of her career she also produced radio plays, translations for the theatre, and travel writing; but the poetry appeared first. Indeed, for most of the sixties poetry was the predominant literary form in Canada: the few existing publishers were reluctant to take chances with new novelists, as novels were expensive to produce and were thought to have a severely limited audience inside Canada and none whatsoever outside it. But poems could be published as broadsheets, or in one of the five or six 'little' magazines then extant, or by very small, frequently self-operated presses; or they could be broadcast on the radio – notably on the CBC's pivotal programme, *Anthology*. Or they could be read aloud.

I first met Gwendolyn MacEwen in the fall of 1960, at The Bohemian Embassy, a coffee house – it was, by then, the age of coffee houses – that featured jazz and folksinging, and, on Thursday nights, poetry readings. The Embassy had the décor of its period – the checked tablecloths, the candles in the chianti bottles; it was also a smoke-filled firetrap. But it was mecca to the poetry community, and MacEwen, who must have been nineteen then, was already a regular reader there. She was a slight-figured, doe-eyed person with long dark hair, who read in an accomplished, sultry, caressing voice that owed, perhaps, a little to Lauren Bacall. The combination of the child-like appearance, the rich voice, and the poetic authority were compelling – you came away from a MacEwen reading feeling you'd been let in on a unique and delicious secret.

MacEwen's primary interest as a poet was in language, and in its corollary, myth-making. In this she was not alone: the late fifties and the early sixties comprised a sort of minor Age of Myth, though there were, of course, other influences around. Northrop Frye's *Anatomy of Criticism* held critical centre stage, with Marshall McLuhan and his structural analysis of popular culture moving up strongly. Leonard Cohen's first volume was called *Let Us Compare Mythologies*; James Reaney's magazine *Alphabet* was entirely devoted to the 'mythopoeic' approach, or to correspondences between 'real life' and 'story'; and Canadian poets were endlessly telling each other that what they really needed to do was to create an 'indigenous mythology'. In this context, MacEwen's interest in what we might call a mythic structuring of reality – or the structuring of a mythic reality, in opposition to the disappointing world of mundane experience she often refers to as 'Kanada' – seems less bizarre. True, no one else settled on Ancient Egypt and the Middle East with quite the same intensity as she does, but her imaginative otherworld is not limited to one time or place. In general – and especially in her earlier poetry – she opposes the works of children, magicians, adventurers, escape artists, the hierarchical and splendid past, the divinely mad, the 'barbaric', and poetry, to that of grown-ups, materialists, bureaucrats, the modern daily grind, stolid sanity, the 'tame', and newspaper prose.

One of the paradoxes of MacEwen's work is that the protagonists she chooses – in Yeatsean terms, the *personae* – are almost invariably male. She speaks in a female voice when addressing, as the lyric 'I', a male 'You', but when she uses a more dramatic form, or writes a poem about a heroic figure, the central character is usually a man, such as the escape artist Manzini, or Sir John Franklin, or – in a later, major work – Lawrence of Arabia. When female figures from history or story do appear as speakers, they are likely to be exceptions to their sex; Egyptian princesses, not ordinary Egyptian women; Rider Haggard's *She*, with her supernatural powers.

But this is not really surprising. The roles available to women at the time lacked energy; and if what interested you was magic, risk, and exploration, rather than, say, quiet contemplation in the garden between meals, the choice of a male voice was almost inevitable. MacEwen wanted to be out on the sharp edge with the boys, not back in the kitchen with the girls; she was entranced with cosmic predicaments, and the time for female astronauts had not yet come. She might have analysed the female condition and then tapped the resulting anger, like Sylvia Plath; but then she would have been a very different kind of poet. Power – including the dark side of power – was much more interesting to her than powerlessness. Even in the love poems, in which she repeatedly invokes and extols what appears to be a transcendent male figure – a kind of male muse – it's evident who is doing the invoking; and invoking is after all a kind of conjuring, with success dependent on the expertise and verbal skill of the conjuror. What engaged her was not complaint but exuberance, not descent but ascent: not the fire, but the *rising* fire.

The first volume of Gwendolyn MacEwen's selected poems covers the first fifteen years of her poetic career, from the late fifties to the early seventies. It traces the bright trajectory of her early verse, followed by the astonishingly rapid development and exfoliation of her talent. In these poems her range and craft, her poetic strength and intelligence, speak for themselves. Over these years she created, in a remarkably short time, a complete and diverse poetic universe and a powerful and unique voice, by turns playful, extravagant, melancholy, daring and profound. To read her remains what it has always been: an exacting but delightful pleasure, though not one without its challenges and shadows.

Deal, infidel, the night is indeed difficult.

20

Spotty-Handed Villainesses: Problems of Female Bad Behaviour in the Creation of Literature

My title is 'Spotty-Handed Villainesses'; my subtitle is 'Problems of Female Bad Behaviour in the Creation of Literature'. I should probably have said, 'in the creation of novels, plays and epic poems'. Female bad behaviour occurs in lyric poems, of course, but not at sufficient length.

I began to think about this subject at a very early age. There was a children's rhyme that went:

There was a little girl
Who had a little curl
Right in the middle of her forehead;
When she was good, she was very, very good,
And when she was bad, she was horrid!

No doubt this is a remnant of the Angel/Whore split so popular among the Victorians, but at the age of five I did not know that. I took this to be a poem of personal significance – I did after all have curls – and it brought home to me the deeply Jungian possibilities of a Dr Jekyll–Mr Hyde double life for women. My older brother used this verse to tease me, or so he thought. He did manage to make 'very, very good' sound almost worse than 'horrid', which remains an accurate analysis for the novelist. Create a flawless character and you create an insufferable one; which may be why I am interested in spots.

Some of you may wonder whether the spotty-handedness in my title refers to age spots. Was my lecture perhaps going to centre on that once-forbidden but now red-hot topic, The Menopause, without which any collection of female-obilia would be incomplete? I hasten to point out that my title is not age-related; it refers neither to age spots nor to youth spots. Instead it recalls that most famous of spots, the invisible but indelible one on the hand of wicked Lady Macbeth. Spot as in guilt, spot as in blood, spot as in 'out, damned'. Lady Macbeth was spotted, Ophelia unspotted; both came to sticky ends, but there's a world of difference.

But is it not, today – well, somehow *unfeminist* – to depict a woman behaving badly? Isn't bad behaviour supposed to be the monopoly of men? Isn't that what we are expected – in defiance of real life – to somehow believe, now? When bad women get into literature, what are they doing there, and are they permissible, and what, if anything, do we need them for?

We do need something like them; by which I mean, something disruptive to static order. When my daughter was five, she and her friend Heather announced that they were putting on a play. We were conscripted as the audience. We took our seats, expecting to see something of note. The play opened with two characters having breakfast. This was promising – an Ibsonian play perhaps, or something by G. B. Shaw? Shakespeare is not big on breakfast openings, but other playwrights of talent have not disdained them.

The play progressed. The two characters had more breakfast. Then they had more. They passed each other the jam, the corn-flakes, the toast. Each asked if the other would like a cup of tea. What was going on? Was this Pinter, perhaps, or Ionesco, or maybe Andy Warhol? The audience grew restless. 'Are you going to do anything except have breakfast?' we said. 'No,' they said. 'Then it isn't a play,' we said. 'Something else has to happen.'

And there you have it, the difference between literature – at least literature as embodied in plays and novels – and life. *Something else has to happen.* In life we may ask for nothing more than a kind of eternal breakfast – it happens to be my favourite meal, and certainly it is the most hopeful one, since we don't yet know what atrocities the day may choose to visit upon us – but if we are going to sit still for two or three hours in a theatre, or wade through two or three hundred pages of a book, we certainly expect something more than breakfast.

What kind of something? It can be an earthquake, a tempest, an attack by Martians, the discovery that your spouse is having an affair; or, if the author is hyperactive, all of these at once. Or it can be the revelation of the spottiness of a spotty woman. I'll get around to these disreputable folks shortly, but first let me go over some essentials which may be insulting to your intelligence, but which are comforting to mine, because they help me to focus on what I'm doing as a creator of fictions. If you think I'm flogging a few dead horses – horses which have been put out of their pain long ago – let me assure you that this is because the horses are not in fact dead, but are out there in the world, galloping around as vigorously as ever.

How do I know this? I read my mail. Also, I listen to the questions people ask me, both in interviews and after public readings. The kinds of questions I'm talking about have to do with how the characters in novels ought to behave. Unfortunately, there is a widespread tendency to judge such characters as if they were job applicants, or public servants, or prospective roommates, or somebody you're considering marrying. For instance, I sometimes get a question – almost always, these days, from women – that goes something like, 'Why don't you make the men stronger?' I feel that this is a matter which should more properly be taken up with God. It was not, after all, I who created Adam so subject to temptation that he sacrificed eternal life for an apple; which leads me to believe that God – who is, among other things, an author – is just

as enamoured of character flaws and dire plots as we human writers are. The characters in the average novel are not usually folks
you would want to get involved with at a personal or business
level. How then should we go about responding to such creations?
Or, from my side of the page, which is blank when I begin – how
should I go about creating them?

What is a novel, anyway? Only a very foolish person would
attempt to give a definitive answer to that, beyond stating the more
or less obvious facts that it is a literary narrative of some length
which purports, on the reverse of the title page, not to be true, but
seeks nevertheless to convince its readers that it is. It's typical of
the cynicism of our age that, if you write a novel, everyone assumes
it's about real people, thinly disguised; but if you write an autobiography everyone assumes you're lying your head off. Part of this is
right, because every artist is, among other things, a con-artist.

We con-artists do tell the truth, in a way; but, as Emily
Dickinson said, we tell it slant. By indirection we find direction
out – so here, for easy reference, is an elimination-dance list of
what novels are not.

— Novels are not sociological textbooks, although they may
contain social comment and criticism.

— Novels are not political tracts, although 'politics' – in the
sense of human power structures – is inevitably one of their subjects. But if the author's main design on us is to convert us to
something – whether that something be Christianity, capitalism, a
belief in marriage as the only answer to a maiden's prayer, or feminism – we are likely to sniff it out, and to rebel. As André Gide
once remarked, 'It is with noble sentiments that bad literature gets
written.'

— Novels are not how-to books; they will not show you *how to*
conduct a successful life, although some of them may be read this
way. Is *Pride and Prejudice* about how a sensible middle-class
nineteenth-century woman can snare an appropriate man with a
good income, which is the best she can hope for out of life, given
the limitations of her situation? Partly. But not completely.

— Novels are not, primarily, moral tracts. Their characters are not all models of good behaviour — or, if they are, we probably won't read them. But they *are* linked with notions of morality, because they are about human beings and human beings divide behaviour into good and bad. The characters judge each other, and the reader judges the characters. However, the success of a novel does not depend on a Not Guilty verdict from the reader. As Keats said, Shakespeare took as much delight in creating Iago — that arch-villain — as he did in creating the virtuous Imogen. I would say probably more, and the proof of it is that I'd bet you're more likely to know which play Iago is in.

— But although a novel is not a political tract, a how-to book, a sociology textbook or a pattern of correct morality, it is also not merely a piece of Art for Art's Sake, divorced from real life. It cannot do without a conception of form and a structure, true, but its roots are in the mud; its flowers, if any, come out of the rawness of its raw materials.

— In short, novels are ambiguous and multi-faceted, not because they're perverse, but because they attempt to grapple with what was once referred to as the human condition, and they do so using a medium which is notoriously slippery — namely, language itself.

Now, let's get back to the notion that in a novel, something else has to happen — other than breakfast, that is. What will that 'something else' be, and how does the novelist go about choosing it? Usually it's backwards to what you were taught in school, where you probably got the idea that the novelist had an overall scheme or idea and then went about colouring it in with characters and words, sort of like paint-by-numbers. But in reality the process is much more like wrestling a greased pig in the dark.

Literary critics start with a nice, clean, already-written text. They then address questions to this text, which they attempt to answer; 'What does it mean?' being both the most basic and the most difficult. Novelists, on the other hand, start with the blank page, to which they similarly address questions. But the questions are different. Instead of asking, first of all, 'What does it mean?' they work at the widget level; they ask, 'Is this the right word?' 'What does it mean?' can only come when there is an 'it' to mean something. Novelists have to get some actual words down before they can fiddle with the theology. Or, to put it another way: God started with chaos – dark, without form and void – and so does the novelist. Then God made one detail at a time. So does the novelist. On the seventh day, God took a break to consider what he'd done. So does the novelist. But the critic starts on Day Seven.

The critic, looking at plot, asks, 'What's happening here?' The novelist, creating plot, asks, 'What happens next?' The critic asks, 'Is this believable?' The novelist, 'How can I get them to believe this?' The novelist, echoing Marshall McLuhan's famous dictum that art is what you can get away with, says, 'How can I pull this off?' – as if the novel itself were a kind of bank robbery. Whereas the critic is liable to exclaim, in the mode of the policeman making the arrest, 'Aha! You can't get away with that!'

In short, the novelist's concerns are more practical than those of the critic; more concerned with 'how to,' less concerned with metaphysics. Any novelist – whatever his or her theoretical interests – has to contend with the following how-to questions:

— What kind of story shall I choose to tell? Is it, for instance, comic or tragic or melodramatic, or all? How shall I tell it? Who will be at the centre of it, and will this person be a) admirable or b) not? And – more important than it may sound – will it have a happy ending, or not? No matter what you are writing – what genre and in what style, whether cheap formula or high-minded experiment – you will still have to answer – in the course of your writing – these essential questions. Any story you tell must have a conflict of some sort, and it must have suspense. In other words: something other than breakfast.

Let's put a woman at the centre of the something-other-than-breakfast, and see what happens. Now there is a whole new set of questions. Will the conflict be supplied by the natural world? Is our female protagonist lost in the jungle, caught in a hurricane, pursued by sharks? If so, the story will be an adventure story and her job is to run away, or else to combat the sharks, displaying courage and fortitude, or else cowardice and stupidity. If there is a man in the story as well, the plot will alter in other directions: he will be a rescuer, an enemy, a companion in struggle, a sex bomb, or someone rescued by the woman. Once upon a time, the first would have been more probable, that is, more believable to the reader; but times have changed and art is what you can get away with, and the other possibilities have now entered the picture.

Stories about space invasions are similar, in that the threat comes from outside and the goal for the character, whether achieved or not, is survival. War stories *per se* – ditto, in that the main threat is external. Vampire and werewolf stories are more complicated, as are ghost stories; in these, the threat is from out-side, true, but the threatening thing may also conceal a split-off part of the character's own psyche. Henry James's *The Turn of the Screw* and Bram Stoker's *Dracula* are in large part animated by such hidden agendas; and both revolve around notions of female sexu-ality. Once all werewolves were male, and female vampires were usually mere sidekicks; but there are now female werewolves, and women are moving in on the star bloodsucking roles as well. Whether this is good or bad news I hesitate to say.

Detective and espionage stories may combine many elements, but would not be what they are without a crime, a criminal, a tracking-down, and a revelation at the end; again, all sleuths were once male, but sleuthesses are now prominent, for which I hope they lay a votive ball of wool from time to time upon the tomb of the sainted Miss Marple. We live in an age not only of gender cross-over but of *genre* crossover, so you can throw all of the above into the cauldron and stir.

Then there are stories classed as 'serious' literature, which centre not on external threats – although some of these may exist – but on relationships among the characters. To avoid the eternal breakfast, some of the characters must cause problems for some of the others. This is where the questions really get difficult.

As I've said, the novel has its roots in the mud, and part of the mud is history; and part of the history we've had recently is the history of the women's movement, and the women's movement has influenced how people read, and therefore what you can get away with, in art.

Some of this influence has been beneficial. Whole areas of human life that were once considered non-literary or sub-literary – such as the problematical nature of homemaking, the hidden depths of motherhood, and of daughterhood as well, the once-forbidden realms of incest and child abuse – have been brought inside the circle that demarcates the writeable from the non-writeable. Other things, such as the Cinderella happy ending – the Prince Charming one – have been called into question. (As one lesbian writer remarked to me, the only happy ending she found believable any more was the one in which girl meets girl and ends up with girl; but that was fifteen years ago, and the bloom is off even that romantic rose.)

To keep you from being too depressed, let me emphasize that none of this means that you, personally, cannot find happiness with a good man, a good woman or a good pet canary; just as the creation of a bad female character doesn't mean that women should lose the vote. If bad male characters meant that, for men, all men would be disenfranchised immediately. We are talking about what you can get away with in art; that is, what you can make believable. When Shakespeare wrote his sonnets to his dark-haired mistress, he wasn't saying that blondes were ugly, he was merely pushing against the notion that only blondes were beautiful. The tendency of innovative literature is to include the hitherto excluded, which often has the effect of rendering ludicrous the conventions that have just preceded the innovation. So the form of the ending, whether happy or not, does not have to do with how people live their lives – there is a great deal of variety in that department (and, after all, in life every story ends with death, which is not true of novels). Instead it's connected with what literary conventions the writer is following or pulling apart at the moment. Happy endings of the Cinderella kind do exist in stories, of course, but they have been relegated largely to genre fiction, such as Harlequin romances.

To summarize some of the benefits to literature of the women's movement – the expansion of the territory available to writers, both in character and in language; a sharp-eyed examination of the way power works in gender relations, and the exposure of much of this as socially constructed; a vigorous exploration of many hitherto-concealed areas of experience. But as with any political movement which comes out of real oppression – and I do empha-size the *real* – there was also, in the first decade at least of the present movement, a tendency to cookie-cut: that is, to write to a pattern and to oversugar on one side. Some writers tended to polarize morality by gender – that is, women were intrinsically good and men bad; to divide along allegiance lines – that is, women who slept with men were sleeping with the enemy; to judge by tribal markings – that is, women who wore high heels and makeup were instantly suspect, those in overalls were acceptable; and to make hopeful excuses – that is, defects in women were ascribable to the patriarchal system and would cure themselves once that system was abolished. Such oversimplifications may be necessary to some phases of political movements. But they are usually prob-lematical for novelists, unless the novelist has a secret desire to be in billboard advertising.

If a novelist writing at that time was also a feminist, she felt her choices restricted. Were all heroines to be essentially spotless of soul – struggling against, fleeing from or done in by male oppres-sion? Was the only plot to be The Perils of Pauline, with a lot of moustache-twirling villains but minus the rescuing hero? Did suf-fering prove you were good? (If so – think hard about this – wasn't it all for the best that women did so much of it?) Did we face a sit-uation in which women could do no wrong, but could only have wrong done to them? Were women being confined yet again to that alabaster pedestal so beloved of the Victorian age, when Woman as better-than-man gave men a licence to be gleefully and enjoyably worse than women, while all the while proclaiming that they couldn't help it because it was their nature? Were women to be condemned to virtue for life, slaves in the salt-mines of goodness? How intolerable.

Of course, the feminist analysis made some kinds of behaviour available to female characters which, under the old dispensation – the pre-feminist one – would have been considered bad, but under the new one were praiseworthy. A female character could rebel against social strictures without then having to throw herself in front of a train like Anna Karenina; she could think the unthinkable and say the unsayable; she could flout authority. She could do new bad-good things, such as leaving her husband and even deserting her children. Such activities and emotions, however, were – according to the new moral thermometer of the times – not really bad at all; they were good, and the women who did them were praiseworthy. I'm not against such plots. I just don't think they are the only ones.

And there were certain new no-no's. For instance: was it at all permissible, any more, to talk about women's will to power, because weren't women supposed by nature to be communal egalitarians? Could one depict the scurvy behaviour often practised by women against one another, or by little girls against other little girls? Could one examine the Seven Deadly Sins in their female versions – to remind you, Pride, Anger, Lust, Envy, Avarice, Greed and Sloth – without being considered anti-feminist? Or was a mere mention of such things tantamount to aiding and abetting the enemy, namely the male power structure? Were we to have a warning hand clapped over our mouths, yet once again, to prevent us from saying the unsayable – though the unsayable had changed? Were we to listen to our mothers, yet once again, as they intoned – If You Can't Say Anything Nice, Don't Say Anything At All? Hadn't men been giving women a bad reputation for centuries? Shouldn't we form a wall of silence around the badness of women, or at best explain it away by saying it was the fault of Big Daddy, or – permissible too, it seems – of Big Mom? Big Mom, that agent of the patriarchy, that pronatalist, got it in the neck from certain seven-ties feminists; though mothers were admitted into the fold again once some of these women turned into them. In a word: were women to be homogenized – one woman is the same as another – and deprived of free will – as in, *The patriarchy made her do it?*

Or, in another word – were men to get all the juicy parts? Literature cannot do without bad behaviour, but was all the bad behaviour to be reserved for men? Was it to be all Iago and Mephistopheles, and were Jezebel and Medea and Medusa and Delilah and Regan and Goneril and spotty-handed Lady Macbeth and Rider Haggard's powerful superfemme fatale in *She*, and Toni Morrison's mean Sula, to be banished from view? I hope not. Women characters, arise! Take back the night! In particular, take back The Queen of the Night, from Mozart's *Magic Flute*. It's a great part, and due for revision.

I have always known that there were spellbinding evil parts for women. For one thing, I was taken at an early age to see 'Snow White and the Seven Dwarfs'. Never mind the Protestant work ethic of the dwarfs. Never mind the tedious housework-is-virtuous motif. Never mind the fact that Snow White is a vampire – anyone who lies in a glass coffin without decaying and then comes to life again must be. The truth is that I was paralysed by the scene in which the evil queen drinks the magic potion and changes her shape. What power, what untold possibilities!

Also, I was exposed to the complete, unexpurgated *Grimms' Fairy Tales* at an impressionable age. Fairy tales had a bad reputation among feminists for a while – partly because they'd been cleaned up, on the erroneous supposition that little children don't like gruesome gore, and partly because they'd been selected to fit the fifties Prince Charming is Your Goal ethos. So 'Cinderella' and 'The Sleeping Beauty' were okay, though 'The Youth Who Set Out to Learn What Fear Was', which featured a good many rotting corpses, plus a woman who was smarter than her husband, were not. But many of these tales were originally told and retold by women, and these unknown women left their mark. There is a wide range of heroines in these tales; passive good girls, yes, but adventurous, resourceful women as well, and proud ones, and slothful ones, and foolish ones, and envious and greedy ones, and also many wise women and a variety of evil witches, both in disguise and not, and bad stepmothers and wicked ugly sisters and false brides as well. The stories, and the figures themselves, have immense vitality, partly because no punches are pulled – in the versions I read, the barrels of nails and the red-hot shoes were left intact – and also because no emotion is unrepresented. Singly, the female characters are limited and two-dimensional. But put all together, they form a rich five-dimensional picture.

Female characters who behave badly can of course be used as sticks to beat other women – though so can female characters who behave well, witness the cult of the Virgin Mary, better than you'll ever be, and the legends of the female saints and martyrs – just cut on the dotted line, and, minus one body part, there's your saint, and the only really good woman is a dead woman, so if you're so good, why aren't you dead?

But female bad characters can also act as keys to doors we need to open, and as mirrors in which we can see more than just a pretty face. They can be explorations of moral freedom – because everyone's choices are limited, and women's choices have been more limited than men's, but that doesn't mean women can't make choices. Such characters can pose the question of responsibility, because if you want power you have to accept responsibility, and actions produce consequences. I'm not suggesting an agenda here, just some possibilities; nor am I prescribing, just wondering. If there's a closed-off road, the curious speculate about why it's closed off, and where it might lead if followed; and evil women have been, for a while recently, a somewhat closed-off road, at least for fiction-writers.

While pondering these matters, I thought back over the numerous bad female literary characters I have known, and tried to sort them into categories. If you were doing this on a blackboard, you might set up a kind of grid: bad women who do bad things for bad reasons, good women who do good things for good reasons, good women who do bad things for good reasons, bad women who do bad things for good reasons, and so forth. But a grid would just be a beginning, because there are so many factors involved: for instance, what the character thinks is bad, what the reader thinks is bad, and what the author thinks is bad, may all be different. But let me define a thoroughly evil person as one who intends to do evil, and for purely selfish reasons. The Queen in 'Snow White' would fit that.

So would Regan and Goneril, Lear's evil daughters; very little can be said in their defence, except that they seem to have been against the patriarchy. Lady Macbeth, however, did her wicked murder for a conventionally acceptable reason, one that would win approval for her in corporate business circles – she was furthering her husband's career. She pays the corporate-wife price, too – she subdues her own nature, and has a nervous breakdown as a result. Similarly, Jezebel was merely trying to please a sulky husband; he refused to eat his dinner until he got hold of Naboth's vineyard, so Jezebel had its owner bumped off. Wifely devotion, as I say. The amount of sexual baggage that has accumulated around this figure is astounding, since she doesn't do anything remotely sexual in the original story, except put on make-up.

The story of Medea, whose husband Jason married a new princess, and who then poisoned the bride and murdered her own two children, has been interpreted in various ways. In some versions Medea is a witch and commits infanticide out of revenge; but the play by Euripides is surprisingly neo-feminist. There's quite a lot about how tough it is to be a woman, and Medea's motivation is commendable – she doesn't want her children to fall into hostile hands and be cruelly abused – which is also the situation of the child-killing mother in Toni Morrison's *Beloved*. A good woman, then, who does a bad thing for a good reason. Hardy's *Tess of the D'Urbervilles* kills her nasty lover due to sexual complications; here too we are in the realm of female-as-victim, doing a bad thing for a good reason. (Which, I suppose, places such stories right beside the front page, along with women who kill their abusive husbands. According to a recent *Time* story, the average jail sentence in the US for men who kill their wives is four years, but for women who kill their husbands – no matter what the provocation – it's twenty. For those who think equality is already with us, I leave the statistics to speak for themselves.)

These women characters are all murderers. Then there are the seducers; here again, the motive varies. I have to say too that with the change in sexual mores, the mere seduction of a man no longer rates very high on the sin scale. But try asking a number of women what the worst thing is that a woman friend could possibly do to them. Chances are the answer will involve the theft of a sexual partner.

Some famous seductresses have really been patriotic espionage agents. Delilah, for instance, was an early Mata Hari, working for the Philistines, trading sex for military information. Judith, who all but seduced the enemy general Holofernes and then cut off his head and brought it home in a sack, was treated as a heroine, although she has troubled men's imaginations through the centuries – witness the number of male painters who have depicted her – because she combines sex with violence in a way they aren't accustomed to and don't much like. Then there are figures like Hawthorne's adulterous Hester Prynne, she of *The Scarlet Letter*, who becomes a kind of sex-saint through suffering – we assume she did what she did through Love, and thus she becomes a good woman who did a bad thing for a good reason – and Madame Bovary, who not only indulged her romantic temperament and voluptuous sensual appetites, but spent too much of her husband's money doing it, which was her downfall. A good course in double-entry bookkeeping would have saved the day. I suppose she is a foolish woman who did a stupid thing for an insufficient reason, since the men in question were dolts. Neither the modern reader nor the author consider her very evil, though many contemporaries did, as you can see if you read the transcript of the court case in which the forces of moral rectitude tried to get the book censored.

One of my favourite bad women is Becky Sharpe, of Thackeray's *Vanity Fair*. She makes no pretensions to goodness. She is wicked, she enjoys being wicked, and she does it out of vanity and for her own profit, tricking and deluding English society in the process – which, the author implies, deserves to be tricked and deluded, since it is hypocritical and selfish to the core. Becky, like Undine Spragg in Edith Wharton's *The Custom of the Country*, is an adventuress; she lives by her wits and uses men as ambulatory bank-accounts. Many literary adventurers are male – consider Thomas Mann's *Felix Krull, Confidence Man* – but it does make a difference if you change the gender. For one thing, the nature of the loot changes. For a male adventurer, the loot is money and women; but for a female one, the loot is money and men.

Becky Sharpe is a bad mother too, and that's a whole other subject – bad mothers and wicked stepmothers and oppressive aunts, like the one in *Jane Eyre*, and nasty female teachers, and depraved governesses, and evil grannies. The possibilities are many.

But I think that's enough reprehensible female behaviour for you today. Life is short, art is long, motives are complex, and human nature is endlessly fascinating. Many doors stand ajar; others beg to be unlocked. What is in the forbidden room? Something different for everyone, but something you need to know and will never find out unless you step across the threshold. If you are a man, the bad female character in a novel may be – in Jungian terms – your anima; but if you're a woman, the bad female character is your shadow; and as we know from the Offenbach opera *Tales of Hoffmann*, she who loses her shadow also loses her soul.

Evil women are necessary in story traditions for two much more obvious reasons, of course. First, they exist in life, so why shouldn't they exist in literature? Second – which may be another way of saying the same thing – women have more to them than virtue. They are fully dimensional human beings; they too have subterranean depths; why shouldn't their many-dimensionality be given literary expression? And when it is, female readers do not automatically recoil in horror. In Aldous Huxley's novel *Point Counter*

Point, Lucy Tantamount, the man-destroying vamp, is preferred by the other female characters to the earnest, snivelling woman whose man she has reduced to a wet bath sponge. As one of them says, 'Lucy's obviously a force. You may not like that kind of force. But you can't help admiring the force in itself. It's like Niagara.' In other words, awesome. Or, as one Englishwoman said to me recently, 'Women are tired of being *good* all the time.'

I will leave you with a final quotation. It's from Dame Rebecca West, speaking in 1912 – 'Ladies of Great Britain . . . we have not enough evil in us.'

Note where she locates the desired evil. In *us*.

21

The Grunge Look

I first went to Europe on May the 13th, 1964. I had been told I was going to do this five months earlier by a male psychic working out of a Toronto tea shop. 'You will be going to Europe in May,' he said.

'No I won't,' I said.

'Yes you will,' he said, smugly reshuffling his cards.

I did.

Fleeing a personal life of Gordian complexity, and leaving behind a poetry manuscript rejected by all, and a first novel ditto, I scraped together what was left after a winter of living in a Charles Street rooming-house and writing *tours-de-force* of undiscovered genius while working by day at a market research company, borrowed six hundred dollars from my parents, who were understandably somewhat nervous about my choice of the literary life by then, and climbed onto a plane. In the Fall I would be teaching grammar to Engineering students at eight-thirty in the morning in a Quonset hut at the University of British Columbia, so I had about three months. In this period of time I intended to become – what? I wasn't sure exactly, but I had some notion that the viewing of various significant pieces of architecture would improve my soul – would fill in a few potholes in it, get rid of a few cultural hangnails, as it were. Here, I had been studying English literature for six years – I even had an MA, which had got me rejected for employment by the Bell Telephone Company on the grounds of overqualification – and I had never even seen, well, things. Stonehenge, for instance. A visit to Stonehenge would surely improve my understanding of Thomas Hardy. Or someone. Anyway, a lot of my friends from college had already run to England, intending to be actors and the like. So England was my first stop.

The truth is that I didn't have much idea of what I was really doing. Certainly, I had almost no idea at all of where I was really going, and how much it had changed since I'd last checked in via the pages of Charles Dickens. Everything was so much smaller and shabbier than I had imagined. I was like the sort of Englishman who arrives in Canada expecting to find a grizzly bear on every street corner. 'Why are there so many *trucks*?' I thought. There were no trucks in Dickens. There weren't even any in T. S. Eliot. 'I did not know Death had undone so many,' I murmured hopefully, as I made my way across Trafalgar Square. But the people there somehow refused to be as hollow-cheeked and plangent as I'd expected. They appeared to be mostly tourists, like myself, and were busy taking pictures of one another with pigeons on their heads.

My goal, of course, was Canada House, the first stop of every jet-stunned, impecunious young Canadian traveller in those days. But before I go on, let me say a few words about those days. What sort of year was 1964?

It was the year after 1963, in which John Kennedy had been so notably shot. It was the year before the first (to my knowledge) anti-Vietnam peace march; it was roughly four years before the great hippie explosion, and five years before the onset of the early-seventies wave of feminism. Miniskirts had not yet arrived; pantihose were approaching, but I don't believe they had as yet squeezed out the indigenous population of garter-belts and stockings. In hair, something called the bubble-cut was favoured: women rolled their hair in big bristle-filled rollers to achieve a smoothly swollen look, as if someone had inserted a tube into one of their ears and blown up their heads like balloons. I indulged in this practice too, though with mixed results, since my hair was

ferociously curly. At best it resembled a field of weeds gone over
with a lawn roller – still squiggly, though somewhat mashed. At
worst it looked as if I'd stuck my finger in a light socket. This sil-
houette was later to become stylish, but was not so yet. As a result
I went in for head scarves, of the Queen-Elizabeth-at-Balmoral
type. Paired with the slanty-eyed, horned-rimmed glasses I wore in
an attempt to take myself seriously, they were not at all flattering.

Come to think of it, neither was anything in my suitcase.
(Hitchhiking backpackers had not yet overrun Europe, so it was, still,
a suitcase.) Fashion-wise, 1964 was not really my year. Beatniks had
faded, and I hadn't discovered the romantic raggle-taggle gypsy mode;
but then, neither had anyone else. Jeans had not yet swept all before
them, and for ventures to such places as churches and museums,
skirts were still required; grey-flannel jumpers with Peter-Pan-col-
lared blouses were my uniform of choice. High heels were the norm
for most occasions, and about the only thing you could actually walk
in were some rubber-soled suede items known as Hush Puppies.

Lugging my suitcase, then, I Hush-Puppied my way up the
imposing steps of Canada House. At that time it offered – among
other things, such as a full shelf of Geological Surveys – a reading
room with newspapers in it. I riffled anxiously through the Rooms
To Let, since I had no place to stay that night. By pay telephone, I
rented the cheapest thing available, which was located in a suburb
called Willesden Green. This turned out to be about as far away
from everything as you could get, via the London Underground,
which I promptly took (here at last, I thought, looking at my
intermittently-bathed, cadaverous and/or dentally-challenged
fellow passengers, were a few people Death had in fact undone, or
was about to). The rooming-house furnishings smelled of old, sad
cigarette smoke, and were of such hideous dinginess that I felt I'd
landed in a Graham Greene novel; and the sheets, when I finally
slid between them, were not just cold and damp, they were wet.
('North Americans like that kind of thing,' an Englishwoman said
to me, much later. 'Unless they freeze in the bathroom they think
they've been cheated of the English experience.')

The next day I set out on what appears to me in retrospect a dauntingly ambitious quest for cultural trophies. My progress through the accumulated bric-a-brac of centuries was marked by the purchase of dozens of brochures and postcards, which I collected to remind myself that I'd actually been wherever it was I'd been. At breakneck speed I gawped my way through Westminster Abbey, the Houses of Parliament, St Paul's Cathedral, the Tower of London, the Victoria and Albert Museum, the National Portrait Gallery, the Tate, the house of Samuel Johnson, Buckingham Palace, and the Albert Memorial. At some point I fell off a double-decker bus and sprained my foot, but even this, although it slowed me down, did not stop me in my headlong and reckless pursuit. After a week of this, my eyes were rolling around like loose change, and my head, although several sizes larger, was actually a good deal emptier than it had been before. This was a mystery to me.

Another mystery was why so many men tried to pick me up. It was hardly as if I was, in my little grey-flannel jumpers, dressed to kill. Museums were the usual locale, and I suppose there was something about a woman standing still with her head tilted at a ninety-degree angle that made solicitation more possible. None of these men was particularly rude. 'American?' they would ask, and when I said Canadian, they would look either puzzled or disappointed, and would proceed only tentatively to the next question. When they got no for an answer, they simply moved along to the next upstretched neck. Possibly, they hung around tourist lodestones on the theory that female travellers travelled for the same kinds of sexual-adventure reasons they would have travelled, had they been travelling themselves. But in this there was – and possibly still is – a gender difference. Ulysses was a sailor, Circe was a stay-at-home with commodious outbuildings.

When not injecting myself with culture, I was looking for something to eat. In England in 1964, this was quite difficult, especially if you didn't have much money. I made the mistake of trying a hamburger and a milkshake, but the English didn't yet have the concept: the former was fried in rancid lamb fat, the latter fortified with what tasted like ground-up chalk. The best places were the fish-and-chip shops, or, barring that, the cafés, where you could get eggs, sausages, chips, and peas, in any combination. Finally, I ran into some fellow Canadians, who'd been in England longer than I had, and who put me onto a Greek place in Soho, which actually had salads, a few reliable pubs, and the Lyons' Corner House on Trafalgar Square, which had a roast-beef all-you-can-eat for a set price. A mistake, as the Canadian journalists would starve themselves for a week, then hit the Lyons' Corner House like a swarm of locusts. (The Lyons' Corner House did not survive.)

It must have been through these expatriates that I hooked up with Alison Cunningham, whom I'd known at university and who was now in London, studying modern dance and sharing a second-floor flat in South Kensington with two other young women. Into this flat, Alison – when she heard of my wet-sheeted Willesden Green circumstances – generously offered to smuggle me. 'Smuggle' is appropriate; the flat was owned by aristocratic twins called Lord Cork and Lady Hoare, but as they were ninety and in nursing homes, it was actually run by a suspicious dragon of a housekeeper; so for purposes of being in the flat I had to pretend I didn't exist.

In Alison's flat I learned some culturally useful things that have stuck with me through the years: how to tell a good kipper from a bad one, for instance; how to use an English plate-drying rack; and how to make coffee in a pot when you don't have any other device. I continued with my tourist programme – stuffing in Cheyne Walk, several lesser-known churches, and the Inns of Court – and Alison practised a dance, which was a reinterpretation of *The Seagull*, set to several of the Goldberg Variations as played by Glenn Gould. I can never hear that piece of music without seeing Alison, in a black leotard and wearing the severe smile of a Greek caryatid of the Archaic period, bending herself into a semi-pretzel on that South Kensington sitting-room floor. Meanwhile, I was not shirking in the salt-mines of Art. Already, my notebook contained several new proto-gems, none of which, oddly, busied itself with the age-old masterworks of Europe. Instead, they were about rocks.

When things got too close for comfort with the dragon house-keeper, I would have to skip town for a few days. This I did by cashing in some miles on the rail pass I had purchased in Canada – one of the few sensible preparations for my trip I had managed to make. (Why no Pepto-Bismol, I ask myself; why no acetaminophen with codeine; why no Gravol? I would never think of leaving the house without them now.) On this rail pass you could go anywhere the railways went, using up miles as you did so. My first journeys were quite ambitious. I went to the Lake District, overshooting it and getting as far north as Carlisle before I had to double back; whereupon I took a bus tour of the Lakes, viewing them through fumes of cigar smoke and nausea, and, although surprised by their smallness, was reassured to hear that people still drowned in them every year. Then I went to Glastonbury, where after seeing the Cathedral, I was waylaid by an elderly lady who got five pounds out of me to help save King Arthur's Well, which – she said – was in her backyard and would be ruined by a brewery unless I contributed to the cause. I made it to Cardiff with its genuine-ersatz castle, and to Nottingham and the ancestral home of the Byrons, and to York, and to the Brontë manse, where I was astonished to learn, from the size of their tiny boots and gloves, that the Brontës had been scarcely bigger than children. As a writer of less than Olympian stature, I found this encouraging.

But as my rail pass dwindled, my trips became shorter. Why did I go to Colchester? To the Cheddar Gorge? To Ripon? My motives escape me, but I went to these places; I have the postcards to prove it. Julius Caesar visited Colchester, too, so there must have been something to it; but I was driven by frugality rather than by the historicist imperative: I didn't want any of my rail pass miles to go to waste.

Around about July, Alison decided that France would be even more improving for me than England had been, so in the company of a male friend of mine from Harvard, in full retreat from a Southern girlfriend who had brought several ball gowns to a student archeological graveyard excavation, we took the night boat-train. It was an average Channel crossing, during which we all turned gently green. Alison bravely continued to discourse on intellectual matters, but finally turned her head and, with a dancer's casual grace, threw up over her left shoulder. These are the moments one remembers.

Benefits of European Travel

BEFORE
(*photo credit: unknown*)

DURING
A Pre-Raphaelite pose
(*photo credit: photo machine,*
Gare du Nord, Paris)

AFTER
Montreal, 1968
(*photo credit: Jim Polk*)

By the time we'd been two days in Paris, where we subsisted on a diet of baguettes, *café au lait*, oranges, pieces of cheese, and the occasional bean-heavy bistro meal, I was in an advanced state of dysentery. We were shunting around from cheap *pension* to cheap *pension*; the rooms were always up gloomy flights of stairs, with lights that went off when you were halfway up and cockroaches that rustled and crackled underfoot. None of these establishments allowed you to stay in them during the day; so I lay moaning softly on hard French park benches, in gravelly French parks, while Alison, with a sense of duty Florence Nightingale would have envied, read me long improving passages from Doris Lessing's *The Golden Notebook*. Every fifteen minutes a policeman would come by and tell me I had to sit up, since lying on the park benches was forbidden; and every half hour I would make a dash for the nearest establishment with a toilet, which featured, not the modern plumbing that has taken over today, but a hole in the ground and two footrests, and many previous visitors with imperfect aims.

A diet of bread and water, and some potent French emulsion, administered by Alison, improved my condition, and I dutifully hiked around to Notre Dame, the Eiffel Tower, and the Louvre. In Paris, the men bent on pickups didn't bother to wait until you had stopped and were craning your neck; they approached at all times, even when you were crossing the street. '*Americaine?*' they would ask hopefully. They were polite – some of them even used the subjunctive, as in '*Voudriez-vous coucher avec moi?*' – and, when refused, would turn away with a beagle-like melancholy which I chose to find both existential and Gallic.

When we had only a week and a half left, the three of us pooled our resources and rented a car, with which we toured the Châteaux of the Loire, viewing a great many eighteenth-century gilded chairs and staying in youth hostels, and living on more cheese. By this time I was supersaturated with culture; waterlogged, so to speak. If someone had stepped on my head, a stream of dissolved brochures would have poured forth.

Then, for some reason now lost in the mists of history, I decided to go to Luxembourg. On the way there, a middle-aged conductor chased me around the train compartment; when I explained that I was not in fact American, as he had supposed, he shrugged and said 'Ah', as if that explained my reluctance. By this time I was getting somewhat fed up with the excess of dog-and-fire-hydrant male attention, and I let my irritation spill over onto the cultural agenda; when I finally got to Luxembourg, I did not go to visit a single church. Instead, I saw *Some Like It Hot*, with subtitles in Flemish, French, and German, where I was the only person in the theatre who laughed in the right places.

This seemed an appropriate point of re-entry to North America. Culture is as culture does, I thought to myself, as I returned to England, steered myself and my Hush Puppies towards the plane, and prepared for decompression.

At that moment my trip in retrospect felt a lot like stumbling around in the dark, bumping into heavy, expensive pieces of furniture, while being mistaken for someone else. But distance adds perspective, and in the months that followed, I tried hard for it. Had my soul been improved? Possibly, but not in the ways I'd anticipated. What I took back with me was not so much the churches and museums and the postcards of them I'd collected, but various conversations, in buses, on trains, and with the pickup men at the museums. I remembered especially the general bafflement when it turned out that I was not what I appeared to be; namely, an American. For the Europeans, there was a flag-shaped blank where my nationality should have been. What was visible to me was invisible to them; nor could I help them out by falling back on any internationally-famous architectural constructs. About all I had to offer as a referent was a troop of horsey policemen, which hardly seemed enough.

But one person's void is another person's scope, and that was where the new poems I'd brought back squashed at the bottom of my suitcase would come in, or so I thought. Speaking of which, my grey-flannel wardrobe – I could see it now – definitely had to go.

As a deterrent to stray men it was inadequate, as a disguise irrelevant, as a poetic manifesto incoherent. I did not look serious in it, merely earnest, and also – by now – somewhat grubby. I had picked up a brown suede vest, on sale at Liberty's, which, with the addition of a lot of black and some innovation with the hair, would transform me into something a lot more formidable; or so I intended.

I did get to Stonehenge, incidentally. I felt at home with it. It was pre-rational, and pre-British, and geological. Nobody knew how it had arrived where it was, or why, or why it had continued to exist; but there it sat, challenging gravity, defying analysis. In fact, it was sort of Canadian. 'Stonehenge,' I would say to the next mournful-looking European man who tried to pick me up. That would do the trick.

22

Not So Grimm: The Staying Power
of Fairy Tales

The accomplished British novelist Marina Warner is also the author of several intriguing works of non-fiction, including *Alone of All Her Sex*, an examination of the Virgin Mary cult, and *Monuments and Maidens*, an analysis of female allegorical figures. Her new book inhabits roughly the same territory – the widespread icon, the popular image, the much-told tale – but is even more ambitious in scope.

From the Beast to the Blonde is what its subtitle proclaims; a book about fairy tales and also about those who have told them. As befits its subject, it is a thing of splendour – marvellous, bizarre, exotic – but at the same time familiar as porridge. It's crammed full of goodies – stick your thumb into it anywhere, and out comes a plum – and profusely illustrated. It is also simply essential reading for anyone concerned, not only with fairy tales, myth, and legends, but also with how stories of all kinds get told.

Like many children, I devoured fairy tales. Having cut my milk teeth on the unexpurgated Grimms' – despite my parents' fears that the red-hot shoes and poked-out eyeballs might be too much for a six-year-old – I went on to the Andrew Lang collections, the *Arabian Nights*, and anything else I could get my hands on – if eerily illustrated by Arthur Rackham or Edmund Dulac, so much the better. By the time I hit college I was well-prepared for the more Jungian of my professors, who, in those myth-oriented days of the late fifties, referred casually to such fairy-tale denizens as WOMs (Wise Old Men) and WOWs (Wise Old Women).

Fairy tales were said to contain universal archetypes, and to teach deep and timeless psychic lessons. Of course, a WOM could just as easily be a Wandering Old Molester and a WOW, a Wicked Old Witch, and if encountered in the forest, or, say, the corner drugstore, a girl was hard-pressed to know whether to give them her crust of bread or a very wide berth. Still, there was a definite mystique.

Then fairy tales fell on hard times. Despite such thoughtful studies as Bruno Bettelheim's *The Uses of Enchantment*, they were prettied up and weeded – adventurous heroines as well as grisly doings were downplayed, and the prone or Sleeping Beauty position was favoured. After that, the tales were – understandably – attacked by feminists as brainwashing devices, aimed at turning women into beautiful, dutiful automatons, at extolling the phallic power of sword-sporting princes, and at slandering non-biological parental units and the chronologically enhanced. Like corsets, they were designed to confine, and as such were reprehensibly outmoded.

But now Marina Warner rides to the rescue. Fiddle-dee-dee, says she, in true Wise Woman fashion, as she rolls up her sleeves and sets to work salvaging things from the closet of discards. Look! Not musty old straw at all, she proclaims. Real gold! You just have to know how to spin it. And quicker than you can say Rumpelstiltskin backward, out the window goes the theory of timeless archetypes, as well as the Volkish idea that these stories were authentic, indigenous, preliterate, out-of-the-soul-of-the-soil emanations. (Her impressive collection of sources and variants puts paid to that.)

Away, too, goes the recent school of disparagement. If you want a feminist heroine, she suggests, how about Mother Goose?

Reconsider the beaky nose, the funny bonnet, and the nursery pinafore. Mother Goose dresses like a featherbrain for the same reason that female 'tourists' are favoured as espionage couriers: Both disarm suspicion. But underneath, what surprises! Disguise! Ambiguity! Subversion!

Warner's theory of narrative, once put forth, is eminently sensible: For any tale told, there is a teller, but also a tellee. Also a social context, which changes over time: 'Historical realism' is a term she favours. Even when the narrative events themselves remain constant, the moral spin put on them may not, for both the tellers and the tellees have their own fluctuating agendas.

Is it a coincidence that 'old wives' tales' about the advisability of being nice to elderly women were once told by elderly women, who needed all the help they could get? Or that Bluebeard stories about young girls being married off to murderous husbands should have peaked during a reaction against made-for-money forced nuptials? Or that the beastliness of the fur-bearing Beast, he of Beauty-and-the, should once have been held against him, but in these green times is seen as a plus? (This book surely contains the definitive in-depth analysis of the Disney film of the tale, if 'in-depth' here is not oxymoronic.)

The first section of Warner's book is about the tellers. It deals engagingly with those who collected, rewrote and concocted such stories, from Marie-Jeanne L'Heritier to Perrault, to the studious Grimm brothers and the melancholy Hans Andersen. But also, even more entertainingly, it considers the imagined teller-of-tales, she (and it is mostly a 'she') from whom story itself was perceived to flow. Who would have suspected that the Mother Goose, whose comical portrait adorned so many early collections, had such an ancient and august lineage? The cackly voiced bird-woman, it appears, goes all the way back to the feather-bodied sirens. The sibyl figures in her genealogy too, as does the Queen of Sheba, who was thought by medieval artists to have a bird's foot. So do such disparate figures as the hard-pressed but cool Scheherazade, the pious and instructive Saint Anne, and a bevy of raucous crones, who, like Juliet's nurse, are vulgar in their speech and erotic in their interests.

But the more women as a group were misprized by society, the greater the level of disguise required by any who dared to break silence. In times of oppression, wisdom of certain kinds can safely be spoken only through the mouths of those playing the fool. Thus the goose-face.

The second part of the book deals with the tales themselves – not only in their verbal forms, but also as they feature in plays, operas, films and pictures. Warner focuses on stories with female protagonists – beanstalk Jack and his bravely bladed brethren get short shrift, while maiden-devouring ogres, demon lovers and incest-inclined fathers are bathed in the lurid spotlight – but then, this book does not pretend to be an encyclopedia. Nor are all the girls in it goody-goodies: Unpleasant females such as ugly sisters, bad fairies and wicked stepmothers get a thorough going-over, with the caveat that stepmothers in our changed socio-economic times need no longer be wicked. (I was relieved to hear that, being one.)

Why so many dead mothers? Why so many blonde heroines? Why indeed a chapter called, enticingly, 'The Language of Hair'? From which Rapunzel-like German hair-water ad did the Dadaists pinch their name? Only list, Dear Reader – Warner herself is a dab hand at lists – and you shall know all. Or if not all, at least a good deal more than you did when you came in.

At times, you may feel you're at risk of falling into a charmed sleep, having pricked your finger on one spinster too many, but that just means you've been reading too fast. This is a complex tapestry woven of many yarns, and you shouldn't try to unravel all of its threads at once.

Although Warner is entranced by the vitality and metamorphic properties of the fairy tale as form, she does not try to make a case for it as at all times politically appropriate. She recognizes 'the contrary directions of the genre', which pull it 'toward acquiescence on the one hand and rebellion on the other'. Because a

story – any story, but especially one that exists in such a vernacular domain – is a negotiation between teller and audience, the
listeners are accomplices. The aim of the tale may well be to
instruct, but if it does not also delight, it will play to empty houses.
As Warner says, 'Fairystorytellers know that a tale, if it is to
enthrall, must move the listeners to pleasure, laughter or tears . . .
The sultan is always there, half asleep, but quite awake enough to
rouse himself and remember that death sentence he threatened.'

We the audience are the collective sultan. If we want insipid
heroines, that's what we'll get, and ditto for bigotries and prejudices and superheated shoes. But not forever. As Warner also says,
'What is applauded and who sets the terms of the recognition and
acceptance are always in question.' We need not content ourselves
with limp compliance or sullen revenge: The creative retelling,
the utopian dream, the mischievous reversal, the rightly-chosen
wish, and the renewed sense of wonder may instead be ours.

This is a happy ending – and Warner knows her genre far too
well not to give us one – but it is also a challenge. The uses of
enchantment, it seems, are in our hands.

23

'Little Chappies with Breasts'

Hilary Mantel's seventh novel, *An Experiment in Love*, is only the second to be published in the United States. This is a shame, because Ms Mantel is an exceptionally good writer. Her book's title, however, is somewhat misleading. 'Experiment' suggests clinical detachment; but if experiments are going on, they're more like what Dr Frankenstein got up to with the body parts: intense, unholy and messy. As for 'love', the inaccuracy is that it's singular: there are many kinds of love in this book, almost all contaminated. 'Enter the Dragoness' might be a more likely title, for this is a story about emotional kung fu, female style – except that by the end although all are wounded or worse, there's no clear winner.

The playing field is England, with its bafflingly complex and minutely calibrated systems of class and status, of region and religion; the players are little girls, larger girls, young women and, looming huge over all, mothers. The weapons are clothing, schools, intelligence, friendships, insults, accents, trophy boyfriends, material possessions and food. The battle cry is *'Sauve qui peut!'*

The narrator is Carmel McBain, who – having somehow survived to adulthood – kicks off the action with a Proustian time-warp experience, triggered by a newspaper photograph of her former roommate. Back she goes, sucked through the plug hole of memory into her dire childhood. One of her quirks is that she's dogged by lines from the poems she's learned at school, 'The Rime of the Ancient Mariner' among them. Carmel is both the Mariner, doomed to relate, and the Wedding Guest, doomed to listen; and we too are held enthralled while she unwraps her own personal albatross and tells us how she got sadder but wiser.

'I wanted to separate myself from the common fate of girls who are called Carmel,' she tells us, 'and identify myself with girls with casual names, names which their parents didn't think about too hard.' Carmel is the name of the mountain where the prophet Elijah slaughtered the priests of Baal: it's not quite like being called Linda. Indeed, Carmel is sometimes less a person than a geographic site, where embattled forces play themselves out despite her.

It's her mother who saddled her with this weighty name: a formidable north-of-England working-class mother, of wrathful temperament and Irish Catholic descent, who covers her daughter with her own elaborate embroidery, crams her with homework and launches her like a missile at the social establishment she both despises and envies. Carmel's mother expects her to climb the heights: 'The task in life that she set for me was to build my own mountain, build a step-by-step success: the kind didn't matter as long as it was high and it shone. And as she had told me that it is ruthless people who rise highest in this life, I would slash through the ropes of anyone who tried to climb after me . . . and jump about on the summit alone.'

Carmel's forced climb leads from the grim 1950s Catholic primary school of her small, decrepit mill town to the Holy Redeemer, a superior establishment run by sarcastic nuns. There she wears a uniform that includes both a tie and a girdle, and is 'stuffed with education', though other nutrients are scarce. The aim is to turn women into 'little chappies with breasts'. 'Women were forced to imitate men, and bound not to succeed at it.' Nevertheless, Carmel achieves a meagre scholarship and a bed in Tonbridge Hall, a neo-Brontëan women's residence at London

University. Among other things, this novel is a *Bildungsroman*, and one of the issues raised is the form of education appropriate for women.

All along the way, Carmel has a fellow climber, her *doppelgänger* and nemesis, the stolid and implacable Karina. Karina's parents are immigrants. They have undergone the war – cattle cars are mentioned – although they are not Jewish. Out of compunction, Carmel's mother insists on a friendship between the girls; thereafter Karina is linked to Carmel, and where Carmel goes Karina follows. Like Carmel's mother, she too envies and despises, but the object of these emotions is Carmel herself. Whatever Carmel has, Karina takes or else destroys, though it is not a one-sided war. Carmel gets her licks in too, and may even have started it all in kindergarten by kicking Karina's baby doll: an early recognition, perhaps, that all was not well in the world of mums and tots. Over the years, Karina is Carmel's enemy, but also – when the girls enter the alien territory of upmarket nuns and middle-class southerners – her oldest friend and grudging ally. 'I never thought she was dangerous, except to me,' thinks Carmel, wrongly, as it turns out.

They are a Jack-Spratt-and-his-wife couple: Carmel thin and childish, not even allowed to help burn the sparse family dinner; Karina rotund and prematurely competent, a little housewife at the age of twelve. Carmel is cold and hungry and watery, and dreams of drowning; Karina is warm and wool-covered, associated with Catherine wheels and fire. Above all, Karina is the protégée and voice of the mothers, especially Carmel's mother: angry, self-righteous, annihilating.

Although she is acquiescent and browbeaten, Carmel has ways of rebelling. At school she practises 'dumb insolence', and her first act on reaching university is to chop off her hair, which, via the torturing use of curl rags, has been one of the instruments of maternal control. But she also takes over her mother's role. Her mother has deprived her not only of affection and approval but of actual nourishment, and now Carmel begins to deprive herself. Karina, on the other hand, is gorging herself to blimp-like proportions. As one character comments, 'More and more of Karina. Less and less of Carmel.'

We are warned against considering this a story about anorexia; too middle class. Rather, claims the narrator, it is a story about 'appetite'. Well, perhaps. This portion of the book is set in 1970, at the precise time when anorexia was becoming common but was not yet common knowledge; any later and Carmel could not have been so unselfconscious about her plight. In any case, the dwindling of Carmel has complex causes. There is the nuns' connection of eating with sin and their emphasis on self-denial – but how much self can you do without and still remain alive? There's also Carmel's poverty, and the dreadful food of Tonbridge Hall. But the difficulty for Carmel goes well beyond the pinched pennies and the underdone vegetables: How much of life does she dare to eat? How much enjoy? The pleasure principle has not been exactly fostered.

The pleasures of the novel, however, are many. The women's-residence portions of *An Experiment in Love* are as harshly delicious as those in *The Group*; the childhood sections are immediate and vivid, funny and bleak, and the intricate love and love-hate relationships among the women, which as the narrator says, have nothing to do with sex, are right on target. This is Carmel's story, but it is that of her generation as well: girls at the end of the sixties, caught between two sets of values, who had the pill but still ironed their boyfriends' shirts.

Moral confusion reigns, and moral questions also: What makes bad people bad? Even more mysteriously, what makes good people good? Why Karina, and why the heartbreakingly kind Lynette, Karina's affluent roommate, rebuffed by her at every turn? Carmel's weak father, who has retreated into jigsaw puzzles, can't find the missing part of Judas, and neither can Carmel.

'Descriptions are your strong point,' Carmel is told, and they are Ms Mantel's as well. Never have dripping tights hung over a radiator or the smell of a child's wooden ruler been so meticulously rendered. The similes and metaphors glint brightly: the sheets in the dormitory are 'tucked strap-tight into the bed's frame, as if to harness a lunatic'; the residence soup is 'an uncleaned aquarium, where vegetable matter swam'. Much of this verbal dexterity is exercised on food, but as a narrator Carmel is like her mother: she does a little embroidery on everything.

If there's any complaint, it's that we want to know more; like Carmel herself, the book could have been a little fatter. What happened to Karina and Carmel after the horrifying denouement? But perhaps that's the point: it's what you'll never know that haunts you; and with all its brilliance, its sharpness and its clear-eyed wit, *An Experiment in Love* is a haunting book.

24

In Search of *Alias Grace*: On Writing Canadian Historical Fiction

What I am going to talk about this evening has to do with the Canadian novel, and more particularly, the Canadian historical novel. I will address the nature of this genre insofar as it has to do with the mysteries of time and memory; I will meditate on why so many of this kind of novel have been written by English-speaking Canadian authors lately; and after that I'll talk a little about my own recent attempt to write such a novel. At the end I'll attempt some sort of meaning-of-it-all nugget or philosophical summation, as such a thing is implicitly called for in the list of ingredients on the cookie box.

Fiction is where individual memory and experience and collective memory and experience come together, in greater or lesser proportions. The closer the fiction is to us, the more we recognize and claim it as individual rather than collective. Margaret Laurence used to say that her English readers thought *The Stone Angel* was about old age, the Americans thought it was about some old woman they knew, and the Canadians thought it was about their grandmothers. Each character in fiction has an individual life, replete with personal detail – the eating of meals, the flossing of teeth, the making of love, the birthing of children, the attending of funerals, and so forth – but each also exists within a context, a fictional world comprised of geology, weather, economic forces, social classes, cultural references, and wars and plagues and such big public events; you'll note that, being Canadian, I put the geology first. This fictional world so lovingly delineated by the writer may bear a more obvious or a less obvious relation to the world we actually live in, but bearing no relation to it at all is not an option. We have to write out of who and where and when we are, whether we like it or not, and disguise it how we may. As Robertson Davies has remarked, '. . . we all belong to our own time, and there is nothing whatever that we can do to escape from it. Whatever we write will be contemporary, even if we attempt a novel set in a past age . . .'[1] We can't help but be modern, just as the Victorian writers – whenever they set their books – couldn't help but be Victorian. Like all beings alive on Middle Earth, we're trapped by time and circumstance.

What I've said about fictional characters is, of course, also true of every real human being. For example: here I am, giving this Bronfman Lecture in Ottawa. By what twists of coincidence or fate – how novelistic these terms sound, but also how faithful to real experience they are – do I find myself back here in my city of origin?

For it was in Ottawa that I was born, fifty-seven years, three days and several hours ago. The place was the Ottawa General Hospital; the date, November 18, 1939. About the exact hour, my mother – to the despair of many astrologers since – is a little vague, that being a period when women were routinely conked out with ether. I do know that I was born after the end of the Grey Cup football game. The doctors thanked my mother for waiting; they'd all been following the game on the radio. In those days most doctors were men, which may explain their sportive attitude.

'In those days' – there I am, you see, being born in *those* days, which are not the same as these days; no ether now, and many a woman doctor. As for Ottawa, I wouldn't have been there at all if it hadn't been for the Great Depression: my parents were economic refugees from Nova Scotia – there's your economic force – from which they were then cut off by the Second World War – there's your big public event.

We lived – here's your personal detail – in a long, dark, railroad-car-shaped second-storey apartment on Patterson Avenue, near the Rideau Canal – there's your geology, more or less – an apartment in which my mother once caused a flood by rinsing the diapers in the toilet, where they got stuck – in *those* days there were no disposable diapers, and not even any diaper services. In *those* days, as I'm sure some of you believe you remember, there was much more snow – there's your weather – and it was much whiter and more beautiful than any snow they ever come up with nowadays. As a child I helped to build snow forts that were much bigger than the Parliament Buildings, and even more labyrinthine – there's your cultural reference. I remember this very clearly, so it must be true, and there's your individual memory.

What's my point? It's out of such individual particulars that fiction is constructed; and so is autobiography, including the kind of autobiography we are each always writing, but haven't yet got around to writing down; and so, too, is history. History may intend to provide us with grand patterns and overall schemes, but without its brick-by-brick, life-by-life, day-by-day foundations it would collapse. Whoever tells you that history is not about individuals, only about large trends and movements, is lying. The shot heard round the world was fired on a certain date, under certain weather conditions, out of a certain rather inefficient type of gun. After the Rebellion of 1837, William Lyon Mackenzie escaped to the United States dressed in women's clothing; I know the year, so I can guess the style of his dress. When I lived in the rural Ontario countryside north of Toronto, a local man said, 'There's the barn where we hid the women and children, that time the Fenians invaded.' An individual barn; individual women and children. The man who told me about the barn was born some sixty years after the Fenian attack, but he said *we* not *they*: he was remembering as a personal experience an event at which he had not been present in the flesh, and I believe we have all done that. It's at such points that memory, history and story all intersect; it would take only one step more to bring all of them into the realm of fiction.

We live in a period in which memory of all kinds, including the sort of larger memory we call history, is being called into question. For history as for the individual, forgetting can be just as convenient as remembering, and remembering what was once forgotten can be distinctly uncomfortable. As a rule, we tend to remember the awful things done to us, and to forget the awful things we did. The Blitz is still remembered; the fire-bombing of Dresden, well, not so much, or not by us. To challenge an accepted version of history – what we've decided it's proper to remember – by dredging up things that society has decided are better forgotten, can cause cries of anguish and outrage, as the makers of a recent documentary about the Second World War could testify. Remembrance Day, like Mother's Day, is a highly ritualized occasion; for instance, we are not allowed, on Mother's Day, to commemorate *bad* mothers, and even to acknowledge that such persons exist would be considered – on that date – to be in shoddy taste.

Here is the conundrum, for history and individual memory alike, and therefore for fiction also: How do we *know* we know what we think we know? And if we find that after all we don't know what it is that we once thought we knew, how do we know we are who we think we are, or thought we were yesterday, or thought we were – for instance – a hundred years ago? These are the questions one asks oneself, at my age, whenever one says *Whatever happened to old what's-his-name?*; they are also the questions that arise in connection with Canadian history, or indeed with any other kind of history. They are also the questions that arise in any contemplation of what used to be called 'character'; they are thus central to any conception of the novel. For the novel concerns itself, above all, with time. Any plot is a *this* followed by a *that*; there must be change in a novel, and change can only take place over time, and this change can only have significance if either the character in the book, or, at the very least, the reader, can remember what came before. As Henry James's biographer Leon Edel has said, if there's a clock in it, you know it's a novel.

Thus there can be no history, and no novel either, without memory of some sort; but when it comes right down to it, how reliable is memory itself – our individual memory, or our collective memory as a society? Once, memory was a given. You could lose it and you could recover it, but the thing lost and then recovered was as solid and all-of-a-piece, was as much a *thing*, as a gold coin. 'Now it all comes back to me,' or some version of it, was a staple of the recovering-from-amnesia scenes in Victorian melodramas – indeed, even so late as the recovering-from-amnesia scene in Graham Greene's *The Ministry of Fear*; and there was an *it*, there was an *all*. If the seventeenth century revolved around faith – that is, what you believed – and the eighteenth around knowledge – that is, what you could prove – the nineteenth could be said to have revolved around memory. You can't have Tennyson's *Tears, idle tears . . . Oh death in life, the days that used to be*, unless you can remember those days that used to be and are no more. Nostalgia for what once was, guilt for what you once did, revenge for what someone else once did to you, regret for what you once might have done, but didn't do – how central they all are to the previous century, and how dependent each one of them is on the idea of memory itself. Without memory, and the belief that it can be recovered whole, like treasure fished out of a swamp, Proust's famous *madeleine* is reduced to a casual snack. The nineteenth-century novel would be unimaginable without a belief in the integrity of memory; for what is the self without a more or less continuous memory of itself, and what is the novel without the self? Or so they would have argued, back then.

As for the twentieth century, at least in Europe, it has been on the whole more interested in forgetting – forgetting as an organic process, and sometimes as a willed act. Dali's famous painting *The Persistence of Memory* features a melting clock and a parade of destructive ants; Beckett's famous play *Krapp's Last Tape* is relentless in its depiction of how we erase and re-write ourselves over time; Milan Kundera's novel *The Book of Laughter and Forgetting* has a touchstone twentieth-century title; the horrifying film *Night and Fog* is only one of many twentieth-century statements about how we industriously and systematically obliterate history to suit our own vile purposes; and in Orwell's *1984*, the place where documents are sent to be destroyed is called, ironically, the Memory Hole. The twentieth century's most prominent theories of the psyche – those that evolved from Freud – taught us that we were not so much the sum of what we could remember, as the sum of what we had forgotten;[2] we were controlled by the Unconscious, where unsavoury repressed memories were stored in our heads like rotten apples in a barrel, festering away but essentially unknowable, except for the suspicious smell. Furthermore, twentieth-century European art as a whole gradually lost faith in the reliability of time itself. No longer an evenly-flowing river, it became a collage of freeze-frames, jumbled fragments, and jump-cuts.[3]

The hero of Spanish writer Javier Marias's 1989 novel *All Souls* represents a host of twentieth-century European spiritual relatives when he says,

> ... I must speak of myself and of my time in the city of Oxford, even though the person speaking is not the same person who was there. He seems to be, but he is not. If I call myself 'I', or use a name which has accompanied me since birth and by which some will remember me ... it is simply because I prefer to speak in the first person and not because I believe that the faculty of memory alone is any guarantee that a person remains the same in different times and different places. The person recounting here and now what he saw and what happened to him then is not the same person who saw those things and to whom those things happened; neither is he a prolongation of that person, his shadow, his heir or his usurper.[4]

End of quote. Fine and dandy, we say, with our streetwise postmodern consciousness. However, problems do arise. If the I of now has nothing to do with the I of then, where did the I of now come from? Nothing is made from nothing, or so we used to believe. And, to get back to Canadian Studies – why is it that it's now – within the last fifteen or twenty years, and so near the end of the fragmenting and memory-denying twentieth century – that the Canadian historical novel has become so popular, with writers and readers alike?

But what exactly do we mean by 'historical novel'? All novels are in a sense 'historical' novels; they can't help it, insofar as they have to, they *must*, make reference to a time that is not the time in which the reader is reading the book. (A reference to science fiction novels will not save us here, as the writer has of course written the book in a time that is already past to the reader.) But there is the past tense – yesterday and yesterday and yesterday, full of tooth flossing and putting the antifreeze into the car, a yesterday not so long ago – and then there is The Past, capital P and T.

Charles Dickens' Scrooge timorously asks the Ghost of Christmas Past whether the past they are about to visit is 'long past', and is told, 'No – *your* past.' For a considerable period it was only 'your past' – the personal past of the writer, and, by extension, that of the reader – that was at issue in the Canadian novel. I don't recall any serious writer in the sixties writing what we think of as historical romances proper, that is, the full-dress petticoat-and-farthingale kind, which were associated with subjects like Mary Queen of Scots. Perhaps it was thought that Canada lacked the appropriate clothing for such works; perhaps the genre itself was regarded as a form of trash writing, like bodice rippers – which, like any other genre, it either is or it isn't, depending on how it's done.

Once, we as a society were not so squeamish. Major Richardson's hugely popular nineteenth-century novel *Wacousta* was, among other things, an historical novel along the lines of Sir Walter Scott, granddaddy of the form, and Fenimore Cooper, his even more prolix descendant. These were nineteenth-century novelists, and the nineteenth century loved the historic novel. *Vanity Fair, Middlemarch, A Tale of Two Cities, Ivanhoe, Treasure Island* – all are historic novels of one kind or another, and these are only a few. Perhaps the question to be asked is not why we're writing historic novels now, but why we didn't do it before.

In any case, by the 1960s it was as if we'd forgotten that on this continent, and especially north of the 49th parallel, there was ever a bodice to be ripped or a weak-minded lady to be rendered hysterical by the experience. We were instead taken up by the momentous discovery that we actually existed, in what was then the here and now, and we were busily exploring the implications of that.

Our generation of English-speaking Canadians — those of us who were children in the forties and adolescents in the fifties — grew up with the illusion that there was not then and never had been a Canadian literature. I say 'illusion', because there had in fact been one; it's just that we weren't told about it. The collapse of old-style English colonial imperialism had abolished the old-style school reader — the kind that used to contain excerpts from English literature, mingled with bits from our native singers and songstresses, usually so termed. Thus you could go through twelve years of schooling, back then, and come out with the impression that there had only ever been one Canadian writer, and that was Stephen Leacock.

The fifties came right after the forties and the thirties; and the double-whammy of the Depression followed by the War had wiped out what in the teens and twenties had been a burgeoning indigenous publishing industry, complete with best-sellers. (Remember Mazo De La Roche? We didn't. We were told nothing about her.) Add to that the weight of the paperback book industry — completely controlled, back then, from the United States — and the advent of television, most of which came from south of the border, and you get the picture. There was radio, of course. There was the CBC. There were Simon and Schuster and Our Pet, Juliet. But it wasn't much of a counterbalance.

When we hit university in the late fifties and encountered intellectual magazines, we found ourselves being fed large doses of anxiety and contempt, brewed by our very own pundits and even by some of our very own poets and fiction writers, concerning our own inauthenticity, our feebleness from the cultural point of view, our lack of a real literature, and the absence of anything you could dignify by the name of history – by which was meant interesting and copious bloodshed on our own turf. In Quebec, people were more certain of their own existence, and especially of their own persistence, although they had lots of Parisian-oriented voices to tell them how substandard they were. In Angloland, Earle Birney's famous poem that concludes 'It's only by the lack of ghosts we're haunted' sums up the prevailing attitude of the time.

Well, we young writers charged ahead anyway. We thought we were pretty daring to be setting our poems and stories in Toronto and Vancouver and Montreal, and even Ottawa, rather than in London or Paris or New York. We were, however, relentlessly contemporary: history, for us, either didn't exist, or it had happened elsewhere, or if ours it was boring.

This is often the attitude among the young, but it was especially true of us, because of the way we'd encountered our own history. Quebec has always had its own version of history, with heroes and villains, and struggle, and heartbreak, and God; God was a main feature until recently. But those of us in English Canada who went to high school when I did weren't dosed with any such strong medicine. Instead we were handed a particularly anaemic view of our past, insofar as we were given one at all. For others on more troubled shores the epic battles, the heroes, the stirring speeches, the do-or-die last stands, the freezing to death during the retreat from Moscow. For us the statistics on wheat and the soothing assurances that all was well in the land of the cow and potato, not to mention – although they *were* mentioned – the vein of metallic ore and the stack of lumber. We looked at these things, and saw that they were good, if tedious, but we didn't really examine how they'd been obtained or who was profiting by them, or who did the actual work, or how much they got paid for it. Nor was much said about who inhabited this space before white

Europeans arrived, bearing gifts of firearms and smallpox, because weren't we nice people? You bet we were, and nice people do not dwell on morbid subjects. I myself would have been much more interested in Canadian history if I'd known our dull Prime Minister, Mackenzie King, had believed that the spirit of his mother was inhabiting his dog, which he always consulted on public policy – it explains so much – but nobody knew about such things back then.

The main idea behind the way we were taught Canadian history seemed to be reassurance: as a country, we'd had our little differences, and a few embarrassing moments – the Rebellion of '37, the hanging of Louis Riel, and so forth – but these had just been unseemly burps in one long gentle after-dinner nap. We were always being told that Canada had come of age. This was even a textbook title: *Canada Comes of Age.* I'm not sure what it was supposed to mean – that we could vote and drink and shave and fornicate, perhaps; or that we had come into our inheritance, and could now manage our own affairs.

Our inheritance. Ah yes – the mysterious sealed box handed over by the family solicitor when young master comes into his majority. But what was inside it? Many things we weren't told about in school, and this is where the interest in historical writing comes in. For it's the very things that *aren't* mentioned that inspire the most curiosity in us. *Why* aren't they mentioned? The lure of the Canadian past, for the writers of my generation, has been partly the lure of the unmentionable – the mysterious, the buried, the forgotten, the discarded, the taboo.

This digging up of buried things began perhaps in poetry; for instance, E. J. Pratt's narrative poems on subjects like the sinking of the *Titanic* and the life of the French Jesuit missionary, Brébeuf. Pratt was followed by certain younger writers; I think of Gwendolyn MacEwen's mid-sixties verse play *Terror and Erebus*, about the failure of the Franklin expedition. I blush to mention Margaret Atwood's *The Journals of Susanna Moodie* of 1970, but since I'll need to mention it later on anyway, I'll get the blushing over with now.

Other poets – Doug Jones and Al Purdy in particular, but there were more – used historic events as the subject for individual poems. James Reaney was a pioneer in the use of local history – he was writing the Donnelly trilogy in the late '60s, although the plays were not produced until later. There were other plays in the 1970s too – Rick Salutin's *The Farmers' Rebellion*, about the Upper Canadian Rebellion, springs to mind.

Then came the novels. These weren't historical romances of the bodice-ripping kind; instead they were what we should probably term 'novels set in the historic past', to distinguish them from the kind of thing you find in drugstores that have cloaks on them and raised silver scrollwork titles. When is the past old enough to be considered historic? Well, roughly, I suppose you could say it's anything before the time at which the novel-writer came to consciousness; that seems fair enough.

In the novel, then, we had Anne Hébert's excellent *Kamouraska* as early as 1970. It was written in French, but it was translated, and many English-speaking writers read it. As far back as Margaret Laurence's *The Diviners* in 1974 and Marian Engel's *Bear* in 1976, figures from the Canadian past were used as a point of reference for the Canadian present – Catherine Parr Traill by Laurence, an obscure and probably invented nineteenth-century English emigrant by Engel. Rudy Wiebe's *The Temptations of Big Bear* in 1973, and *The Scorched Wood People* in 1977 are usually thought of as being enclosed by the parentheses *Native People*, but they are of course set entirely in the past. Then there's Timothy Findley's *The Wars* in 1977.

In the eighties and nineties, the trend intensified. Graeme Gibson's *Perpetual Motion* was published in 1982. After that their names are legion. Robertson Davies' *Murther and Walking Spirits* is an historical novel. So – using my definition of historic – are Michael Ondaatje's *In the Skin of a Lion* and *The English Patient*, and Brian Moore's *Blackrobe*. So are Alice Munro's two stories 'Meneseteung' and 'A Wilderness Station'. So are George Bowering's *Burning Waters* and Daphne Marlatt's *Ana Historic*, and Jane Urquhart's *The Whirlpool* and *Away*; so is Carol Shield's *The Stone Diaries*; so is Timothy Findley's *The*

Piano Man's Daughter. In this year alone, we have Findley's *You Went Away*, Anne Marie Macdonald's *Fall on Your Knees*, Katherine Govier's *Angel Walk*, Anne Michaels' *Fugitive Pieces*, Gail Anderson-Dargatz's *The Cure for Death by Lightning* and Guy Vanderhaeghe's *The Englishman's Boy.*

All of these are set in the past – Dickens' *long* past – but not all use the past for the same purposes. Of course not; the authors of them are individuals, and each novel has its own preoccupations. Some attempt to give more or less faithful accounts of actual events, in answer perhaps to such questions as 'Where did we come from and how did we get here?' Some attempt restitution of a sort, or at least an acknowledgement of past wrongs – I'd put the Rudy Wiebe novels and Guy Vanderhaeghe's book in this category, dealing as they do with the deplorable North American record on the treatment of Native peoples. Others, such as Graeme Gibson's, look at what we have killed and destroyed in our obsessive search for the pot of gold. Others delve into class structure and political struggles – Ondaatje's *In the Skin of a Lion*, for instance. Yet others unearth a past as it was lived by women, under conditions a good deal more stringent than our own; yet others use the past as background to family sagas – tales of betrayal and tragedy and even madness. 'The past is another country,' begins the English novel *The Go-Between*;[5] 'they do things differently there.' Yes, they do, and these books point that out; but they also do quite a few things the same, and these books point that out as well.

Why then has there been such a spate of historical novels in the past twenty years, and especially in the past decade? Earlier, I gave some possible reasons as to why this trend didn't occur earlier; but why is it happening now?

Some might say that we're more confident about ourselves – that we're now allowed to find ourselves more interesting than we once did; and I think they would be right. In this, we're part of a worldwide movement that has found writers and readers, especially in ex-colonies, turning back towards their own roots, while not rejecting developments in the imperial centres. London and

Paris are still wonderful places, but they are no longer seen as the only homes of the good, the true and the beautiful, as well as of those more typical twentieth-century tastes, the bad, the false and the ugly. You want squalor, lies and corruption? Hell, we've got 'em home-grown, and not only that, we always have had, and there's where the past comes in.

Some might say that, on the other hand, the past is safer; that at a time when our country feels very much under threat – the threat of splitting apart, and the threat of having its established institutions and its social fabric and its sense of itself literally torn apart – it feels comforting to escape backwards, to a time when these things were not the problems. With the past, at least we know what happened: while visiting there, we suffer from no uncertainties about the future, or at least the part of it that comes in between them and us; we've read about it. The *Titanic* may be sinking, but we're not on it. Watching it subside, we're diverted for a short time from the leaking lifeboat we're actually in right now.

Of course the past was not really safer. As a local museum custodian has commented, 'Nostalgia is the past without the pain,'[6] and for those living in it, the past was their present, and just as painful as our present is to us – and perhaps more so, considering the incurable diseases and the absence of anaesthesia, central heating and indoor plumbing back then, to mention a few of the drawbacks. Those who long for a return to the supposed values of the nineteenth century should turn away from the frilly-pillow magazines devoted to that era and take a good hard look at what was really going on. So although cosiness may be an attraction, it's also an illusion; and not many of the Canadian historical novels I've mentioned depict the past as a very soothing place.

There's also the lure of time travel, which appeals to the little cultural anthropologist in each one of us. It's such fun to snoop, as it were; to peek in the windows. What did they eat, back then? What did they wear, how did they wash their clothes, or treat their sick, or bury their dead? What did they think about? What lies did they tell, and why? Who were they really? The questions, once they begin, are endless. It's like questioning your dead great-grandparents – does any of what they did or thought live on in us?

I think there's another reason for the appeal, and it has to do with the age we are now. Nothing is more boring to a fifteen-year-old than Aunt Agatha's ramblings about the family tree; but often, nothing is more intriguing to a fifty-year-old. It's not the individual authors who are now fifty – some of them are a good deal younger than that. I think it's the culture.

I once took a graduate course entitled 'The Literature of the American Revolution', which began with the professor saying that there actually *was* no literature of the American Revolution, because everyone was too busy being too revolting during that period to write any, so we were going to study the literature just before it, and the literature just after it. What came after it was a lot of hand-wringing and soul-searching on the part of the American artistic community, such as it was. Now that we've had the Revolution, they fretted, where is the great American genius that ought to burst forth? What should the wondrous novel or poem or painting be like, to be truly American? Why can't we have an American fashion industry? And so on. When *Moby Dick* and Walt Whitman finally did appear, most right-thinking people wiped their feet on them; but such is life.

However, it was out of this questioning and assessing climate – where did we come from, how did we get from there to here, where are we going, who are we now – that Nathaniel Hawthorne wrote *The Scarlet Letter*, an historic novel set in seventeenth-century New England. The eighteenth century had mostly been embarrassed by the Puritans, and especially by their crazed zeal during the Salem witchcraft trials, and had tried to forget about them; but Hawthorne dug them up again, and took a long hard look at them. *The Scarlet Letter* is not of course seventeenth-century in any way the Puritans would have recognized; in good nineteenth-century style, it's far too admiring and respectful of that adulterous baggage, Hester Prynne. Instead it's a novel that uses a seventeenth-century English Colonial setting for the purposes of a newly-forged nineteenth-century American Republic. And I think that's part of the interest for writers and readers of Canadian historical fiction, now: by taking a long hard look backwards, we place ourselves.

Having more or less delivered two of the three main things I promised you, I'll now turn to the third, that is, my own attempt to write a piece of fiction set in the past. I didn't plan to do it, but I somehow ended up doing it anyway; which is how my novels generally occur. Nor was I conscious of any of the motives I've just outlined. I think novelists begin with hints and images and scenes and voices, rather than with theories and grand schemes. It's individual characters interacting with and acted upon by the world that surrounds them that the novel has to do; with the details, not the large pattern; although a large pattern may then of course emerge.

The book in question is *Alias Grace*, and here is how it came about. In the sixties, for reasons that can't be rationally explained, I found myself writing a sequence of poems called *The Journals of Susanna Moodie*, which was about an English emigrant who came to what is now Ontario in the 1830s and had a truly awful time in a swamp north of Peterborough, and wrote about her experiences in a book called *Roughing It in the Bush*, which warned English gentlefolk not to do the same. Canada, in her opinion, was a land suited only to horny-handed peasants, otherwise known as honest sons of toil. After she escaped from the woods she wrote *Life in the Clearings*, which contains her version of the Grace Marks story.

Susanna Moodie describes her meeting with Grace in the Kingston Penitentiary in 1851; she then re-tells the double murder in which Grace was involved. The motive, according to Moodie, was Grace's passion for her employer, the gentleman Thomas Kinnear, and her demented jealousy of Nancy Montgomery, Kinnear's housekeeper and mistress. Moodie portrays Grace as the driving engine of the affair – a scowling, sullen teenage temptress – with the co-murderer, the manservant James McDermott, shown as a mere dupe, driven on by his own lust for Grace as well as by her taunts and blandishments.

Thomas Kinnear and Nancy Montgomery ended up dead in the cellar, and Grace and McDermott made it across Lake Ontario to the States with a wagonful of stolen goods. They were caught and brought back, and tried for the murder of Thomas Kinnear; the murder of Nancy was never tried, as both were convicted and condemned to death for the murder of Kinnear. McDermott was hanged. Grace was sentenced as an accessory, but as a result of petitions by her well-wishers, and in consideration of her feebler sex and extreme youth – she was barely sixteen – her sentence was commuted to life.

Moodie saw Grace again, this time in the violent ward of the newly built Lunatic Asylum in Toronto; and there her account ends, with a pious hope that perhaps the poor girl was deranged all along, which would explain her shocking behaviour and also afford her forgiveness in the Afterlife. That was the first version of the story I came across, and being young, and still believing that 'non-fiction' meant 'true', I did not question it.

Time passed. Then, in the seventies, I was asked by CBC producer George Jonas to write a script for television. My script was about Grace Marks, using Moodie's version, which was already highly dramatic in form. In it, Grace is brooding and obsessive, and McDermott is putty in her hands. I did leave out Moodie's detail about Grace and McDermott cutting Nancy up into four pieces before hiding her under a washtub. I thought it would be hard to film, and anyway why would they have bothered?

I then received an invitation to turn my television script into a theatre piece. I did give this a try. I hoped to use a multi-levelled stage, so the main floor, the upstairs, and the cellar could all be seen at once. I wanted to open it in the Penitentiary and close it in the Lunatic Asylum, and I had some idea of having the spirit of Susanna Moodie flown in on wires, in a black silk dress, like a cross between Peter Pan and a bat; but it was all too much for me, and I gave it up, and then forgot about it.

More time passed. Soon enough it was the early 1990s, and I was on a book tour, and sitting in a hotel room in Zurich. A scene came to me vividly, in the way that scenes often do. I wrote it down on a piece of hotel writing paper, lacking any other kind; it was much the same as the opening scene of the book as it now exists. I recognized the locale: it was the cellar of the Kinnear house, and the female figure in it was Grace Marks. Not immediately, but after a while, I continued with the novel. This time however I did what neither Moodie nor I had done before: I went back to the past.

The past is made of paper; sometimes, now, it's made of microfilm and CD ROMs, but ultimately they too are made of paper. Sometimes there's a building or a picture or a grave, but mostly it's paper. Paper must be taken care of; archivists and librarians are the guardian angels of paper; without them there would be a lot less of the past than there is, and I and many other writers owe them a huge debt of thanks.

What's on the paper? The same things that are on paper now. Records, documents, newspaper stories, eyewitness reports, gossip and rumour and opinion and contradiction. There is – as I increasingly came to discover – no more reason to trust something written down on paper then than there is now. After all, the writers-down were, and are, human beings, and are subject to error, intentional or not, and to the very human desire to magnify a scandal, and to their own biases. I was often deeply frustrated as well, not by what those past recorders had written down, but by what they'd left out. History is more than willing to tell you who won the Battle of Trafalgar and which world leader signed this or that treaty, but it's more reluctant about the now-obscure details of daily life. Nobody wrote these things down, because everybody knew them, and considered them too mundane and unimportant to record. Thus I found myself wrestling not only with who said what about Grace, but also with how to clean a chamber pot, what footgear would have been worn in winter, the origins of quilt pattern names, and how to store parsnips. If you're after the truth, the whole and detailed truth, and nothing but the truth, you're going to have a thin time of it if you trust to paper; but with the past, it's almost all you've got.

Susanna Moodie said at the outset of her account that she was writing the story from memory, and as it turns out, her memory was no better than most. She got the location wrong, and the names of some of the participants, just for starters. Not only that, the story was much more problematic, although less neatly dramatic, than the one Moodie had told. For one thing, the witnesses – even eye-witnesses, even at the trial itself – could often not agree; but then, how is this different from most trials? For instance, one says the Kinnear house was left in great disarray by the criminals, another says it was tidy and it was not realized at first that anything had been taken. Confronted with such discrepancies, I tried to deduce which account was the most plausible.

Then there was the matter of the central figure, about whom opinion was very divided indeed. All commentators agreed that Grace was uncommonly good-looking, but they could not agree on her height or the colour of her hair. Some said Grace was jealous of Nancy, others that Nancy was, on the contrary, jealous of Grace. Some viewed Grace as a cunning female demon, others considered her a simple-minded and terrorized victim, who had only run away with McDermott out of fear for her own life.

I discovered as I read that the newspapers of the time had their own political agendas. Canada West was still reeling from the effects of the 1837 Rebellion, and this influenced both Grace's life before the murders and her treatment at the hands of the press. A large percentage of the population – some say up to a third – left the country after the Rebellion; the poorer and more radical third, we may assume, which may account for the Tory flavour of those who remained. The exodus meant a shortage of servants, which in turn meant that Grace could change jobs more frequently than her counterparts in England. In 1843 – the year of the murder – editorials were still being written about the badness or worthiness of William Lyon Mackenzie; and as a rule, the Tory newspapers that vilified him also vilified Grace – she had after all been involved in the murder of her Tory employer, an act of grave insubordination; but the Reform newspapers that praised Mackenzie were also

inclined to clemency towards Grace. This split in opinion continued through later writers on the case, right up to the end of the
nineteenth century.

I felt that, to be fair, I had to represent all points of view. I devised
the following set of guidelines for myself: when there was a solid
fact, I could not alter it; long as I might want to have Grace witness
McDermott's execution, it could not be done, because, worse luck,
she was already in the Penitentiary on that day. Also, every major
element in the book had to be suggested by something in the writing about Grace and her times, however dubious such writing
might be; but in the gaps left unfilled, I was free to invent. Since
there were a lot of gaps, there is a lot of invention. *Alias Grace* is very
much a novel rather than a documentary.

As I wrote, I found myself considering the number and variety
of the stories that had been told: Grace's own versions – there
were several – as reported in the newspapers and in her
'Confession'; McDermott's versions, also multiple; Moodie's version; and those of the later commentators. For each story, there
was a teller, but – as is true of all stories – there was also an audience; both were influenced by received climates of opinion, about
politics, but also about criminality and its proper treatment, about
the nature of women – their weakness and seductive qualities, for
instance – and about insanity; in fact about everything that had a
bearing on the case.

In my fiction, Grace too – whatever else she is – is a story-teller,
with strong motives to narrate, but also strong motives to with-
hold; the only power left to her as a convicted and imprisoned
criminal comes from a blend of these two motives. What is told by
her to her audience of one, Dr Simon Jordan – who is not only a
more educated person than she is, but a man, which gave him an
automatic edge in the nineteenth century, and a man with the
potential to be of help to her – is selective, of course. It's dependent
on what she remembers; or is it what she says she remembers,
which can be quite a different thing? And how can her audience tell
the difference? Here we are, right back at the end of the twentieth

century, with our own uneasiness about the trustworthiness of memory, the reliability of story, and the continuity of time. In a Victorian novel, Grace would say, 'Now it all comes back to me'; but as *Alias Grace* is not a Victorian novel, she does not say that; and if she did, would we – any longer – believe her?

These are the sorts of questions that my own fictional excursion into the nevertheless real Canadian past left me asking. Nor did it escape me that a different writer, with access to exactly the same historical records, could have – and without doubt would have – written a very different sort of novel. I'm not one of those who believes there is no truth to be known; but I have to conclude that, although there undoubtedly was a truth – somebody did kill Nancy Montgomery – truth is sometimes unknowable, at least by us.

What does the past tell us? In and of itself, it tells us nothing. We have to be listening first, before it will say a word; and even so, listening means telling, and then re-telling. It's we ourselves who must do such telling, about the past, if anything is to be said about it; and our audience is one another. After we in our turn have become the past, others will tell stories about us, and about our times; or not, as the case may be. Unlikely as it seems, it's possible we may not interest them.

But meanwhile, while we still have the chance, what should we ourselves tell? Or rather, what *do* we tell? Individual memory, history, and the novel, are all selective: no one remembers everything, each historian picks out the facts he or she chooses to find significant, and every novel, whether historical or not, must limit its own scope. No one can tell all the stories there are. As for novelists, it's best if they confine themselves to the Ancient Mariner stories; that is, the stories that seize hold of them and torment them until they've grabbed a batch of unsuspecting Wedding Guests with their skinny hands, and held them with their glittering eyes or else their glittering prose, and told them a tale they cannot choose but hear.

Such stories are not about this or that slice of the past, or this or that political or social event, or this or that city or country or nationality, although of course these may enter into it, and often do. They are about human nature, which usually means they are about pride, envy, avarice, lust, sloth, gluttony, and anger. They are about truth and lies, and disguises and revelations; they are about crime and punishment; they are about love and forgiveness and long-suffering and charity; they are about sin and retribution and sometimes even redemption.

In the recent film *Il Postino*, the great poet Pablo Neruda upbraids his friend, a lowly postman, for having filched one of Neruda's poems to use in his courtship of a local girl. 'But,' replies the post-man, 'poems do not belong to those who write them. Poems belong to those who need them.' And so it is with stories about the past. The past no longer belongs only to those who lived in it; the past belongs to those who claim it, and are willing to explore it, and to infuse it with meaning for those alive today. The past belongs to us, because we are the ones who need it.

NOTES

1. Robertson Davies, *The Merry Heart*, McClelland and Stewart, Toronto, 1996, p. 358.

2. See, for instance, Ian Hacking, *Rewriting the Soul*, Princeton University Press, Princeton, 1995.

3. See, for instance, Paul Fussell's *The Great War and Modern Memory*, OUP, Oxford, 2000.

4. Javier Marias, *All Souls*, The Harvill Press, London, 1995.

5. L.P. Hartley, *The Go-Between*, Penguin Modern Classics, 2004.

6. CBC show about local museums, summer 1996.

25

Why I Love *The Night of the Hunter*

I'm incapable of choosing my single favourite anything, so I picked *The Night of the Hunter* for other reasons. First, it's among those films that made an indelible impression on me when it came out. That was in 1955, when I was a teenager and the theatres were blue with smoke: your boyfriend held his cigarette in one hand and attempted to sneak the other into your Peter Pan bra. What was on the screen was the secondary action, and it's a tribute to *The Night of the Hunter* that I can't remember which boyfriend I saw it with. So gripping was it that it warped my young brain, and several of its images have haunted me ever since. The underwater Shelley Winters, for instance, in her aspect of wrecked mermaid, has made several disguised appearances in my own writing.

My second reason was that The Word is an English event, and this film has an English connection. It was directed by Charles Laughton, who had a noteworthy stage career in London and made many English films before joining the European exiles who illuminated Hollywood from the thirties to the fifties. A bleak romantic trapped in an odd body, he often played monsters, which doubtless informed his direction of *The Night of the Hunter* — as did his interest in art and his wide literary and biblical background. Surely it's his sympathy with the material that enabled him to extract such extraordinary performances from the cast – Robert Mitchum, Shelley Winters, and Lillian Gish in particular.

The film came out in the same year as *The Blackboard Jungle* and *Rebel without a Cause*, so did not have the impact it deserved, although it has gathered a serious following since. European critics in particular have delved into its filmic influences, supplied Freudian analyses (frail mothers, sons and their torn loyalties to fathers, whether dead, fake, or ideal – *vide* the portrait of Abraham Lincoln tucked into the trial scene), and made Bettleheimian references to its fairy-tale depth-psychology, not to mention the depth-psychology of Laughton himself.

This film and its director appear made for each other – paradoxical, because *The Night of the Hunter* is such a profoundly American film. It is also a writers' film, another reason I chose it for a literary festival. For many films, the scenario serves only as a skeleton upon which the director hangs his own ideas and effects, but almost every image in this film – every rabbit, owl and so forth – was thoroughly described in the scenario. A script like this probably wouldn't get to first base in Hollywood today: it would be considered too wordy.

The film was adapted from a novel by Davis Grubb, and was written by James Agee, the author of *Let Us Now Praise Famous Men* and *A Death in the Family*, and of the film *The African Queen*. Both Grubb and Agee grew up in the Ohio valley during the Depression, which is where and when the film is set. Both were part of a general movement that turned away from the cosmopolitanism of the twenties to focus on the dark, poverty-stricken heartland of America. But Agee and Grubb, although they remembered the thirties, were not writing then. By their time, they would have had the benefit of a generation of literary scholars dedicated to the unravelling of the twisted, Gothic skeins of American Puritanism, through such earlier writers as Hawthorne, Poe, Melville and Twain. It shows.

The film has a double framework. It opens with Rachel – an older woman whom we later meet as a rescuer of stray children – invoking the world of bedtime stories and dreams. (One might say that if this is her idea of a restful tale for kiddies she's a sadistic bitch, because this dream is a nightmare; but then, folk tales have always been nightmares. Her job as narrator is to render the nightmare at least partially safe.) The next framework is a social one: the Depression, cause of the desperation that drives the film's initial robbery.

Within this double frame is the folkloric tale itself, with its ogre (played by Mitchum). His name is Harry, as in 'Old Harry', vernacular for the Devil. Cross Richard the Third with Milton's Satan and enclose him in a Southern psychopath posing as a preacher, and this character is what you'd get. He cannot be explained by the Depression – he is simply radical evil – but, in Laughton's hands, he's a complex figure as well, one of those fast-talking conmen who recur throughout American art, embraced by society, then torn apart by it. He's a monster, but finally a sacrificial one.

On one level the plot is simplicity itself: Dad has done a stick-up and stashed the money in a doll. This Mammonish idol, a Venus of Willendorf with its tummy stuffed with cash, becomes the desired treasure in the struggle between evil and innocence. The robber's two children – a girl and an older boy – have been sworn not to tell the doll's secret to anybody, especially not to their mother, the fleshly and therefore wilful Willa. Wolfish fellow-prisoner Harry knows about the money, but not where it's hidden; so after Dad is hanged he puts on his sheep's clothing and goes off to romance the widow, oozing sexual power from every pore but especially from his lower eyelids. Willa falls for it and marries him, but Harry's not interested in her body. He cuts her throat and sinks her in the river, then claims she's run off, as demonish women do.

Now he can get his hands on the kids. He forces the secret of the doll, but the children make their escape in a boat and go down the Ohio river, with the enraged preacher hunting them. It's a quintessential American image – the two floating innocents recall Huckleberry Finn and Jim, and, behind them, that favourite American biblical image, the Ark riding the Deluge with its Saving Remnant – in this case, the deluge that has overwhelmed the children's mother. That this particular deluge is all mixed up with adult sexuality, and also with the repression of it, is quintessentially American as well – it being the nature of Puritanism to produce a world which repudiates sexuality but is also thoroughly sexualized.

The children are sheltered by Rachel (who's a good woman, since she's well past sex), and stalked by their pursuer. Finally there's a standoff, a capture and a trial, and the villain is dead. But we can't breathe easy: the metaphysics are too unsettling. The film is punctuated by images of hands: towards the beginning, the preacher makes a puppet show with his knuckles, which have LOVE and HATE tattooed on them. Will love win out over hate? If so, what kind of love? Does God himself love you or hate you, and if you place yourself in his hands, what is the nature of those hands?

The hands return at the end, when there's a duet sung by Harry the monster and Rachel the saviour – incidentally, perhaps the only time Jesus has appeared in the guise of a sweet little old lady with a gun. They sing the hymn 'Leaning on the Everlasting Arms' – they both sing it, but each is referring to a different arm; and at the end of every arm there's a hand, and for every right hand there's also a left.

But for every Song of Experience there's a Song of Innocence, and it's the child's-eye view that gives this film its translucence and candour. Its crucial perspective is that of the young boy, John Harper, poised between innocence and experience. He alone distrusts the preacher from the beginning, he alone realizes what's become of his mother; but, tellingly, he refuses to testify against her murderer. Son of a hanged killer and a butchered mother, stepson of a maniac, he has strong reason to distrust the adult world, but Rachel's house can shelter him only while he remains a child. Perhaps he will grow up to become a robber. Or perhaps, as his name suggests, a singer of blood-spattered sagas and the author of apocalyptic revelations?

There's a happy ending complete with Christmas presents, but we don't credit it and neither should John. He knows too much. In other words, if it's the night of the hunter, what will it be the day of, once that morning sun comes up?

Part Three

2000–2005

2000–2005

On New Year's Eve 2000, the millennium was ushered in. Our computers were all supposed to go into meltdown, but they didn't. My mother was by this time very old and nearly blind, but she could still see bright lights. We arranged some fireworks outside her picture window so she could participate, and my sister accidentally set fire to the back yard. That's my image of the grand event – my sister jumping up and down in the dry weeds, attempting to stamp out the conflagration.

On my journal page that began the Year 2000, I scribbled: *The fireworks were very good on TV except for the fatuous commentary. Nothing leaked. The church bells rang. It was quite warm. There was a half moon. The angels did not arrive, or at least none visible to the naked eye. No bombs fell. No snow. No terrorists around here.*

Famous last words.

I completed *The Blind Assassin* after several false starts, one of them in Canada, one of them in a curious rented-by-Internet flat in London. The breakthrough came in France, where I was writing on the assemblage of end-tables that served as a desk. I finished the novel in late 1999 and did the editing in the February of 2000, in Madrid, where I was also finishing the six lectures I gave that spring at Cambridge University on the subject of writers and writing. (These were later published as *Negotiating with the Dead*.) So during the early months of that first year of the twenty-first century, it was bright blue skies and sunlight and the eating of *churros*, followed by the Cambridge gardens in full bloom, and bluebells in the woods, and mist.

The Blind Assassin came out in the fall of 2000. It was the fourth of my novels to be shortlisted for the Booker Prize. To my surprise the book committed what Oscar Wilde would have called an unpardonable solecism of style by actually winning.

In the first part of 2001 I was still on the book tour for *The Blind Assassin*. I'd got as far as New Zealand and Australia and was taking a break in Queensland to do some bird-watching with friends when I unaccountably found myself beginning another novel – a process described in the short piece, 'Writing *Oryx and Crake*'.

I continued with this novel back in Canada. I wrote part of it on an island in Lake Erie, where my novel-writing was sadly interrupted by the untimely death of Mordecai Richler. Several other friends and fellow-writers also died during this period, and I wrote about some of them.

I composed several chapters of *Oryx and Crake* on a boat in the Arctic, a good location for writing as nobody can phone. In September of 2001, I was in Toronto airport waiting for a plane to New York for the paperback launch of *The Blind Assassin* when the 9/11 catastrophe took place.

One of the pieces in this section is connected with that event. At that period I was working on an introduction to Rider Haggard's peculiar novel *She*; the editor on this quixotic project was a young man called Benjamin Dreyer, and it was from him that I was able to learn – via e-mail, during that time of blocked phone lines – that my friends and colleagues in New York were safe.

In times of crisis, the temptation is to throw everything into defense mode, to believe that the best defense is offense – which can lead, in the human body, to death from your own immune response – and to jettison the very values you thought you were defending in the first place. Too often, the operation can be a success, but the patient dies. Urgers of moderation and multilateralism are seen as wimps, and chest-thumping becomes the order of the day. My 'Letter to America' was written because I made a promise to Victor Navasky, the editor of *The Nation*, to write such a thing, back in the summer of 2002, before the invasion of Iraq was even mentioned. 'Letter' appeared just before that invasion began. It was widely reprinted and generated a great deal of response from around the world. The essay on Napoleon's mistakes came from my reading of history and my sense of caution.

This section might well be called 'A Fistful of Editors', in tribute to the many editors I have worked with over the years. In occasional writing, it is usually the editors who come up with the occasions. Then they cajole you into writing about them, hold your hand while you're doing it, and attempt to save you from your more embarrassing mistakes. There have been magazine editors, newspaper editors, editors of anthologies, and editors in charge of introductions and afterwords. They've all been wonderful. Some new editors came into my life at this period – Erica Wagner of *The Times*, Robert Silvers of *The New York Review of Books*. Mr Silvers is the only editor I know who seems to be at his most elegant and charming – at least on the subject of semi-colons – over the phone and in the middle of the night. That is probably why he always gets his way. Ms Wagner is the only editor I know who has a brush-cut and tattoos.

Whenever I think I'm coming to resemble Melmoth the Ponderer, or The Restless Unread, prowling by night and pouncing on unwary readers, or one of the Scribes of Dracula, chained in a cellar, eating flies, and doomed to scribble endlessly – whenever I resolve to write less and do something healthful instead, like ice dancing – some honey-tongued editor is sure to call me up and make me an offer I can't refuse. So in some ways this book is simply the result of an under-developed ability to say no.

But no one succumbs to a temptation they find unattractive. What is it, this compulsion to scrawl things on blank pages? Why this boundless outflowing of words? What drives us to it? Is writing some sort of disease, or – being speech in visual form – is it simply a manifestation of being human?

26

Pinteresque

Harold Pinter was already a strong presence, when, at the age of seventeen, I moved out of the Victorian penumbra of the high school curriculum and into the world where people who were actually alive were writing. There, in the bookstore where they sold exciting volumes with modern-looking soft but glossy covers, were Beckett and Sartre and Ionesco and Camus, and Pinter. Of course I thought Pinter was very old, considering the company he was keeping, but he was not. He had only started very young.

And what an astonishing trajectory it has been ever since. A comet, but a comet shaped like a hedgehog or a burr. Not a cosy presence: not comforting, not cuddly, not flannel. Prickly, bothersome, mordant and dour. Always unexpected: coming up on you sideways with an alarming glare.

But always itself, this body of work we now call *Pinter*. A singular accomplishment. It has spawned its own adjective: Pinteresque.

I was trying to think what we might mean by this adjective, or what I might mean, and two things came to mind. One was deafness, and the other was silence. In Pinter, people don't hear one another, or they mis-hear, and sometimes this is deliberate and sometimes not. Paradoxically, Pinter thus makes us listen; he makes us listen very carefully, and very hard. As for silence, no one has ever used it better. The long pause, the reply that isn't there, the absence of expected speech. Pinter's characters are frequently at a loss for words, and this loss stands for loss in general.

I said *Pinteresque* to myself again, just to see what would come up, and two figures presented themselves. One was Job, who has had everything taken away from him and who is complaining quite rightfully to God about God's injustice towards him. *Why me?* says Job, *I don't deserve this*. God doesn't answer the question. Instead he comes up with a bunch of questions of his own designed to show how great he is. The deafness of God: man outraged by a universe that either pays no attention to him or squashes him like a bug. Not to mention the other men in this universe, who are equally deaf and frequently shits as well.

The other figure is Abraham, especially the Abraham in Kierkegaard's essay about him. Abraham is ordered by God to cut his only son's throat. In the face of this cruel and unnatural request, Abraham does not protest. Neither does he agree. He is silent. But it is a huge silence with a haunting echo.

One of these echoes is Pinter – the silences in Pinter.

Reverberating silences.

Pinteresque.

27

Mordecai Richler: 1931–2001:
Diogenes of Montreal

Mordecai Richler is gone, and a major light has been snuffed out. But what sort of light? No athlete's torch, no angel's halo. Picture instead the lantern of grumpy, scathing, barrel-dwelling Diogenes, who walked around in daylight searching for an honest man.

Mordecai was the searcher and the honest man both, and equally distrustful of fine feathers. Tarted up for grand events, he somehow gave the impression that he'd be happier in the barrel. Rumpled, tie askew, glass of Scotch at his elbow, thin cigar in mouth, his sad bloodhound's gaze fixed on the bogusness of the passing scene, while in one hand he held the pen that was both lance (as in chivalry, as in boil) and balloon-puncturing pin – this is the image of him beloved by his public and perfected by his friend Aislin, the celebrated cartoonist. Mordecai seemed so permanent, so substantial, so on top of things, so much to be depended on when each new hot-air blimp loomed into view, that it's difficult to believe in his mortality.

But – as with all fine writers – mortality was his subject. Human nature, in all its nakedness, paltriness, silliness, avariciousness, crassness, meanness, and downright evil – he knew it inside out, having had a ringside view as he came of age in a poor Jewish area of Montreal during the Depression and then witnessed, not only the atrocities but also the hypocrisies of the Second World War, followed – for him – by the hard scrabbling of the literary life in London, as seen from the bottom.

He'd paid – as we say – his dues. His bullshit radar was acute, his hopes for the innate goodness of the human species not very high, and in this he was a satirist, a true child of Jonathan Swift. When he went after separatism in Quebec, he rubbed fur the wrong way; but all of his fur-rubbing was deliberate – he would have been horrified to have wounded the innocent, unintentionally. Quebec was hardly alone: Anyone was fair game, so long as the target had committed the ultimate sin in his eyes, which was – or so I'd guess – pomposity.

His propensity for skewering the inflated, coupled with a wonderful sense of mischief, produced some of the most hilarious moments in Canadian literature. The pretentious 'art' film of a bar mitzvah in *The Apprenticeship of Duddy Kravitz*, the travesty of the Franklin expedition in *Solomon Gursky Was Here*, in which the heroic sailors dress up in ladies' frillies – this is Mordecai at his most inventively outrageous. But every satirist cherishes an alternative to the vices and follies he depicts, and so did Mordecai. His alternative was not so far from that of Charles Dickens – the warm-hearted, sane and decent human being – and this side of him comes to the fore in his novels, most particularly in his tragi-comic meditation on fallibility, *Barney's Version*. Behind the formidable public persona was a shy and generous man, who gave his time to efforts he believed in – most recently, the 'best-book-only' Giller Prize, for which he served as an architect and first-year juror.

He was a consummate professional with high standards and no time for fools, but he was also a dear man who was loved by everyone who knew him well, respected by his fellow-writers, and trusted by his many devoted readers to tell it straight. For my generation, he was a trailblazer who went on to create and occupy a unique place in our national life and literature, and we will miss him very much.

28

When Afghanistan Was at Peace

In February 1978, almost twenty-three years ago, I visited Afghanistan with my spouse, Graeme Gibson, and our eighteen-month-old daughter. We went there almost by chance: we were on our way to the Adelaide Literary Festival in Australia. Pausing at intervals, we felt, would surely be easier on a child's time clock. (Wrong, as it turned out.) We thought Afghanistan would make a fascinating two-week stopover. Its military history impressed us – neither Alexander the Great nor the British in the nineteenth century had stayed in the country long because of the ferocity of its warriors.

'Don't go to Afghanistan,' my father said when told of our plans. 'There's going to be a war there.' He was fond of reading history books. 'As Alexander the Great said, Afghanistan is easy to march into but hard to march out of.' But we hadn't heard any other rumours of war, so off we went.

We were among the last to see Afghanistan in its days of relative peace – relative, because even then there were tribal disputes and superpowers in play. The three biggest buildings in Kabul were the Chinese Embassy, the Soviet Embassy and the American Embassy, and the head of the country was reportedly playing the three against one another.

The houses of Kabul were carved wood, and the streets were like a living *Book of Hours*: people in flowing robes, camels, donkeys, carts with huge wooden wheels being pushed and pulled by men at either end. There were few motorized vehicles. Among them were buses covered with ornate Arabic script, with eyes painted on the front so the buses could see where they were going.

We managed to hire a car in order to see the terrain of the famous and disastrous British retreat from Kabul to Jalalabad. The scenery was breathtaking: jagged mountains and the *Arabian Nights* dwellings in the valleys – part houses, part fortresses – reflected in the enchanted blue-green of the rivers. Our driver took the switch-back road at breakneck speed since we had to be back before sundown because of bandits.

The men we encountered were friendly and fond of children: our curly-headed, fair-haired child got a lot of attention. The winter coat I wore had a large hood so that I was sufficiently covered and did not attract undue notice. Many wanted to talk; some knew English, while others spoke through our driver. But they all addressed Graeme exclusively. To have spoken to me would have been impolite. And yet when our interpreter negotiated our entry into an all-male teahouse, I received nothing worse than uneasy glances. The law of hospitality toward visitors ranked higher than the no-women-in-the-teahouse custom. In the hotel, those who served meals and cleaned rooms were men, tall men with scars either from duelling or from the national sport, played on horseback, in which gaining possession of a headless calf is the aim.

Girls and women we glimpsed on the street wore the chador, the long, pleated garment with a crocheted grill for the eyes that is more comprehensive than any other Muslim coverup. At that time, you often saw chic boots and shoes peeking out from the hem. The chador wasn't obligatory back then; Hindu women didn't wear it. It was a cultural custom, and since I had grown up hearing that you weren't decently dressed without a girdle and white gloves, I thought I could understand such a thing. I also knew that clothing is a symbol, that all symbols are ambiguous and that this one might signify a fear of women or a desire to protect them from the gaze of strangers. But it could also mean more negative things, just as the colour red can mean love, blood, life, royalty, good luck – or sin.

I bought a chador in the market. A jovial crowd of men gathered around, amused by the spectacle of a Western woman picking out such a non-Western item. They offered advice about colour and quality. Purple was better than light green or the blue, they said. (I bought the purple.) Every writer wants the Cloak of Invisibility – the power to see without being seen – or so I was thinking as I donned the chador. But once I had put it on, I had an odd sense of having been turned into negative space, a blank in the visual field, a sort of anti-matter – both there and not there. Such a space has power of a sort, but it is a passive power, the power of taboo.

Several weeks after we left Afghanistan, the war broke out. My father was right, after all. Over the next years, we often remembered the people we met and their courtesy and curiosity. How many of them are now dead, through no fault of their own?

Six years after our trip, I wrote *The Handmaid's Tale*, a speculative fiction about an American theocracy. The women in that book wear outfits derived in part from nuns' costumes, partly from girls' school hemlines and partly – I must admit – from the faceless woman on the Old Dutch Cleanser box, but also partly from the chador I acquired in Afghanistan and its conflicting associations. As one character says, there is freedom to and freedom from. But how much of the first should you have to give up in order to assure the second? All cultures have had to grapple with that, and our own – as we are now seeing – is no exception. Would I have written the book if I never visited Afghanistan? Possibly. Would it have been the same? Unlikely.

29

Introduction to *She*

When I first read Rider Haggard's highly famous novel *She*, I didn't know it was highly famous. I was a teenager, it was the 1950s, and *She* was just one of the many books in the cellar. My father unwittingly shared with Jorge Luis Borges a liking for nineteenth-century yarns with touches of the uncanny coupled with rip-roaring plots; and so, in the cellar, where I was supposed to be doing my homework, I read my way through Rudyard Kipling and Conan Doyle, and *Dracula* and *Frankenstein*, and Robert Louis Stevenson and H. G. Wells, and also Henry Rider Haggard. I read *King Solomon's Mines* first, with its adventures and tunnels and lost treasure, and then *Allan Quartermain*, with its adventures and tunnels and lost civilization. And then I read *She*.

I had no socio-cultural context for these books then – the British Empire was the pink part of the map, 'imperialism and colonialism' had not yet acquired their special negative charge, and the accusation 'sexist' was far in the future. Nor did I make any distinctions between great literature and any other kind. I just liked reading. Any book that began with some mysterious inscriptions on a very old broken pot was fine with me, and that is how *She* begins. There was even a picture at the front of my edition – not a drawing of the pot, but a *photograph* of it, to make the yarn really convincing. (The pot was made to order by Haggard's sister-in-law; he intended it to function like the pirate map at the beginning of *Treasure Island* – a book the popularity of which he hoped to rival – and it did.)

Most outrageous tales state at the very beginning that what follows is so incredible the reader will have trouble believing it, which is both a come-on and a challenge. The messages on the pot stretch credulity, but having deciphered them, the two heroes of *She* – the gorgeous but none-too-bright Leo Vincey and the ugly but intelligent Horace Holly – are off to Africa to hunt up the beautiful, undying sorceress who is supposed to have killed Leo's distant ancestor. Curiosity is their driving force, vengeance is their goal. Many a hardship later, and after having narrowly escaped death at the hands of the savage and matrilineal tribe of the Amahagger, they find not only the ruins of a vast and once-powerful civilization and the numerous mummified bodies of the same, but also, dwelling among the tombs, the self-same undying sorceress, ten times lovelier, wiser, and more ruthless than they had dared to imagine.

As Queen of the Amahagger, 'She-who-must-be-obeyed' wafts around wrapped up like a corpse in order to inspire fear; but once tantalizingly peeled, under those gauzy wrappings is a stunner, and – what's more – a virgin. 'She', it turns out, is two thousand years old. Her real name is Ayesha. She claims she was once a priestess of the Egyptian nature-goddess Isis. She's been saving herself for two millennia, waiting for the man she loves: one Kallikrates, a very good-looking priest of Isis and the ancestor of Leo Vincey. This man broke his vows and ran off with Leo's ancestress, whereupon Ayesha slew him in a fit of jealous rage. For two thousand years she's been waiting for him to be reincarnated; she's even got his preserved corpse enshrined in a side room, where she laments over it every night. A point-by-point comparison reveals – what a surprise! – that Kallikrates and Leo Vincey are identical.

Having brought Leo to his knees with her knockout charms, and having polished off Ustane, a more normal sort of woman with whom Leo has formed a sexual pair-bond, and who just happens to be a reincarnation of Ayesha's ancient Kallikrates-stealing enemy, She now demands that Leo accompany her into the depths of a nearby mountain. There, She says, is where the secret of extremely long and more abundant life is to be found. Not only that, She and Leo can't be One until he is as powerful as She – the union might otherwise kill him (as it does, in the sequel *Ayesha: The Vengeance of She*). So off to the mountain they go, via the ruins of the ancient, once-imperial city of Kôr. To get the renewed life, all one has to do – after the usual Haggard adventures and tunnels – is to traverse some caverns measureless to man, step into a very noisy rolling pillar of fire, and then make one's getaway across a bottomless chasm.

This is how She acquired her powers two thousand years before, and to show a hesitating Leo how easy it is, She does it again. Alas, this time the thing works backward, and in a few instants Ayesha shrivels up into a very elderly bald monkey and then crumbles into dust. Leo and Holly, both hopelessly in love with She and both devastated, totter back to civilization, trusting in her promise that She will return.

As a good read in the cellar, this was all very satisfactory, despite the overblown way in which She tended to express herself. *She* was an odd book in that it placed a preternaturally powerful woman at the centre of things: the only other such woman I'd run into so far had been the Wonder Woman of the comics, with her sparkly lasso and bar-spangled panties. Both Ayesha and Wonder Woman went all weak-kneed when it came to the man they loved – Wonder Woman lost her magic powers when kissed by her boyfriend, Steve Trevor; Ayesha couldn't focus on conquering the world unless Leo Vincey would join her in that dubious enterprise – and I was callow enough, at fifteen, to find this part of it not only soppily romantic but pretty hilarious. Then I graduated from high school and discovered good taste, and forgot for a while about *She*.

For a while, but not forever. In the early sixties I found myself in graduate school, in Cambridge, Massachusetts. There I was exposed to Widener Library, a much larger and more organized version of the cellar; that is, it contained many sorts of books, not all of which bore the Great Literature Seal of Approval. Once I was let loose in the stacks, my penchant for not doing my homework soon reasserted itself, and it wasn't long before I was snuffling around in Rider Haggard and his ilk once more.

This time, however, I had some excuse. My field of specialization was the nineteenth century, and I was busying myself with Victorian quasi-goddesses; and no one could accuse Haggard of not being Victorian. Like his age, which practically invented archeology, he was an amateur of vanished civilizations; also like his age, he was fascinated by the exploration of unmapped territories and encounters with 'undiscovered' native peoples. As an individual, he was such a cookie-cutter county gentleman – albeit with some African travelling in his past – that it was hard to fathom where his overheated imagination had come from, though it may have been this by-the-book-English-establishment quality that allowed him to bypass intellectual analysis completely. He could sink a core-sampling drill straight down into the great English Victorian unconscious, where fears and desires – especially male fears and desires – swarmed in the darkness like blind fish. Or so claimed Henry Miller, among others.

Where did it all come from? In particular, where did the figure of She come from – old-young, powerful-powerless, beautiful-hideous, dweller among tombs, obsessed with an undying love, deeply in touch with the forces of Nature and thus of Life and Death? Haggard and his siblings were said to have been terrorized by an ugly rag doll that lived in a dark cupboard and was named 'She-who-must-be-obeyed', but there is more to it than that. *She* was published in 1887, and thus came at the height of the fashion for sinister but seductive women. It looked back also on a long tradition of the same. Ayesha's literary ancestresses include the young-but-old supernatural women in George MacDonald's *Curdie* fantasies, but also various Victorian femmes fatales: Tennyson's Vivien in *The Idylls of the King*, bent on stealing Merlin's magic; the

Pre-Raphaelite temptresses created in both poem and picture by Rossetti and William Morris; Swinburne's dominatrixes; Wagner's nasty pieces of female work, including the very old but still tooth-some Kundry of *Parsifal*; and, most especially, the Mona Lisa of Walter Pater's famous prose poem, older than the rocks upon which she sits, yet young and lovely, and mysterious, and filled to the brim with experiences of a distinctly suspect nature.

As Sandra Gilbert and Susan Gubar pointed out in their 1989 book, *No Man's Land*, the ascendancy in the arts of these potent but dangerous female figures is by no means unconnected with the rise of 'Woman' in the nineteenth century, and with the hotly debated issues of her 'true nature' and her 'rights', and also with the anxi-eties and fantasies these controversies generated. If women ever came to wield political power – to which they were surely, by their natures, unsuited – what would they do with it? And if they were beautiful and desirable women, capable of attacking on the sexual as well as the political front, wouldn't they drink men's blood, sap their vitality, and reduce them to grovelling serfs? As the century opened, Wordsworth's Mother Nature was benign, and 'never would betray / The heart that loved her'; but by the end of the cen-tury, Nature and the women so firmly linked to her were much more likely to be red in tooth and claw – Darwinian goddesses rather than Wordsworthian ones. When, in *She*, Ayesha appropri-ates the fiery phallic pillar at the heart of Nature for the second time, it's just as well that it works backward. Otherwise men could kiss their own phallic pillars goodbye.

'You are a whale at parables and allegories and one thing reflect-ing another,' wrote Rudyard Kipling in a letter to Rider Haggard, and there appear to be various hints and verbal signposts scattered over the landscape of *She*. For instance, the Amahagger, the tribe ruled by She, bear a name that not only encapsulates *hag* but also conflates the Latin root for *love* with the name of Abraham's ban-ished wilderness-dwelling concubine, Hagar, and thus brings to mind a story of two women competing for one man. The ancient city of Kôr is named perhaps for *core*, cognate with the French *coeur*, but suggesting also *corps*, for body, and thus *corpse*, for dead body; for She is in part a Nightmare Life-in-Death. Her horrid end is reminiscent of Darwinian evolution played backward – woman into monkey – but also of vampires after the stake-into-the-heart manoeuvre. (Bram Stoker's *Dracula* appeared after *She*, but Sheridan LeFanu's *Carmilla* predates it, as does many another vampire story.) These associations and more point toward some central significance that Haggard himself could never fully explicate, though he chalked up a sequel and a couple of prequels trying. '*She*,' he said, was 'some gigantic allegory of which I could not catch the meaning.'

Haggard claimed to have written *She* 'at white heat', in six weeks – 'It came,' he said, 'faster than my poor aching hand could set it down,' which would suggest hypnotic trance or possession. In the heyday of Freudian and Jungian analysis, *She* was much explored and admired, by Freudians for its womb-and-phallus images, by Jungians for its anima figures and thresholds. Northrop Frye, proponent of the theory of archetypes in literature, says this of *She* in his 1975 book, *The Secular Scripture: A Study of the Structure of Romance*:

> In the theme of the apparently dead and buried heroine who comes to life again, one of the themes of Shakespeare's *Cymbeline*, we seem to be getting a more undisplaced glimpse of the earth-mother at the bottom of the world. In later romance there is another glimpse of such a figure in Rider Haggard's *She*, a beautiful and sinister female ruler, buried in the depths of a dark continent, who is much involved with archetypes of death and rebirth . . . Embalmed mummies suggest Egypt, which is preeminently the land of death and burial, and, largely because of its biblical role, of descent to a lower world.

Whatever *She* may have been thought to signify, its impact upon publication was tremendous. *Everyone* read it, especially men; a whole generation was influenced by it, and the generation after that. A dozen or so films have been based on it, and a huge amount of the pulp-magazine fiction churned out in the teens, twenties, and thirties of the twentieth century bears its impress. Every time a young but possibly old and/or dead woman turns up, especially if she's ruling a lost tribe in a wilderness and is a hypnotic seductress, you're looking at a descendant of She.

Literary writers too felt her foot on their necks. Conrad's *Heart of Darkness* owes a lot to her, as Gilbert and Gubar have indicated. James Hilton's Shangri-La, with its ancient, beautiful, and eventually crumbling heroine, is an obvious relative. C. S. Lewis felt her power, fond as he was of creating sweet-talking, good-looking evil queens; and in Tolkien's *The Lord of the Rings*, She splits into two: Galadriel, powerful but good, who's got exactly the same water-mirror as the one possessed by She; and a very ancient cave-dwelling, man-devouring spider-creature named, tellingly, Shelob.

Would it be out of the question to connect the destructive Female Will, so feared by D. H. Lawrence and others, with the malign aspect of She? For Ayesha is a supremely transgressive female who challenges male power; though her shoe size is tiny and her fingernails are pink, she's a rebel at heart. If only she hadn't been hobbled by love, she would have used her formidable energies to overthrow the established civilized order. That the established civilized order was white and male and European goes without saying; thus She's power was not only female – of the heart, of the body – but barbaric, and 'dark'.

By the time we find John Mortimer's Rumpole of the Bailey referring to his dumpy, kitchen-cleanser-conscious wife as 'she who must be obeyed', the once-potent figure has been secularized and demythologized, and has dwindled into the combination of joke and rag doll that it may have been in its origins. Nevertheless, we must not forget one of Ayesha's preeminent powers – the ability to reincarnate herself. Like the vampire dust at the end of Christopher Lee movies, blowing away only to reassemble itself at the outset of the next film, She could come back. And back. And back.

No doubt this is because She is in some ways a permanent feature of the human imagination. She's one of the giants of the
nursery, a threatening but compelling figure, bigger and better
than life. Also worse, of course. And therein lies her attraction.

SOURCES

Atwood, Margaret. 'Superwoman Drawn and Quartered: The Early Forms of
    She'. *Alphabet* magazine, vol. 10, July 1965.

Frye, Northrop. *The Secular Scripture: A Study of the Structure of Romance*. Cambridge,
    Mass.: Harvard University Press, 1976.

Gilbert, Sandra M., and Gubar, Susan. *No Man's Land: The Place of the Woman
    Writer in the Twentieth Century*, vol. 2: *Sexchanges*. New Haven: Yale University
    Press, 1989.

Karlin, Daniel. Introduction, in Haggard, H. Rider, *She*. Oxford: Oxford
    University Press, 1991.

30

Introduction to *Doctor Glas*

Now I sit at my open window, writing — for whom? Not for any friend or mistress. Scarcely for myself even. I do not read today what I wrote yesterday; nor shall I read this tomorrow. I write simply so my hand can move, my thoughts move of their own accord. I write to kill a sleepless hour. Why can't I sleep? After all, I've committed no crime.

Doctor Glas was first published in Sweden in 1905, when it caused a scandal, largely because of its handling of those two perennially scandalous items, sex and death. I first read it in the form of a tattered paperback sent to me by Swedish friends — a reissue of a 1963 translation, published to coincide with the film based on it. On the back of my copy are various well-deserved encomiums from newspaper reviews: 'a masterpiece', 'the most remarkable book of the year', 'a book of rare quality developed with true skill'. Nevertheless, *Doctor Glas* has long been out of print in this English version. It's a pleasure to welcome it back.

The uproar around *Doctor Glas* stemmed from the perception that it was advocating abortion and euthanasia, and was perhaps even rationalizing murder. Its protagonist is a doctor, and he has some strong things to say about the hypocrisy of his own society concerning these matters. But Hjalmar Söderberg, its author —

already a successful novelist, playwright, and short-story writer –
may have been somewhat taken aback by this, because *Doctor Glas* is
not a polemic, not a work of advocacy. Instead it is an elegant, vigorous, and tightly knit psychological study of a complex individual
who finds himself at a dangerous but compelling open doorway
and can't decide whether or not to go through it, or why he
should.

The novel's protagonist, Doctor Tyko Gabriel Glas, is a thirtyish
medical man whose journal we read over his shoulder as he com-
poses it. His voice is immediately convincing: intelligent, wistful,
opinionated, dissatisfied, by turns rational and irrational, and
unnervingly modern. We follow him through his memories, his
desires, his opinions of the mores of his social world, his lyrical
praises or splenetic denunciations of the weather, his prevarica-
tions, his self-denunciations, his boredom, and his yearning. Glas is
a romantic idealist turned solitary and sad, and afflicted with *fin de
siècle* malaise – a compound of fastidious aestheticism, longing for
the unobtainable, scepticism concerning the established systems of
morality, and disgust with the actual. He would like only beautiful
things to exist, but has the sordid forced on him by the nature of
his profession. As he himself says, he's the last person on earth
who should have been a doctor: it brings him into too much contact with the more unpleasant aspects of human carnality.

What he wants above all is action, a feat to perform which might
fit the hero he hopes he may carry around inside him. In romances,
such deeds often involve a knight, a troll, and a captive maiden
who must be rescued, and this is the sort of situation that fate
serves up to Doctor Glas. The troll is a flesh-creepingly loathsome
and morally repulsive pastor called Gregorius, whom Glas hates
even before he finds he has good reason for his hatred. The maiden
in captivity is his young and beautiful wife, Helga, who confides to
Doctor Glas that she has married Gregorius out of mistaken religious notions, and can no longer stand his sexual attentions.
Divorce is impossible: a 'respectable' clergyman convinced of his

own righteousness, as the Reverend Gregorius is, would never consent to it. Mrs Gregorius will be enslaved to this toadstool-faced goblin forever unless Doctor Glas will help her.

Doctor Glas has now been given a chance to prove himself. But will he discover that he is a brave knight, an ordinarily timorous nobody, or just as much of a troll as Gregorius, only a murderous one? He contains within himself the possibilities of all three. His name, too, is threefold. *Tyko* refers to the great Danish astronomer Tycho Brahe, who kept his eyes on the stars, far away from the earthiness of the earth – as Doctor Glas so often does throughout the novel. *Gabriel* is the name of the Angel of the Annunciation, proclaimer of the Holy Birth, who is also credited with being the Destroying Angel, sent to wipe out Sodom and Sennacherib, and thought to be the angel of the Last Judgement as well. Thus it's a good name for a medical practitioner, who holds the keys to life and death, but it's also a good name for Doctor Glas, who must decide whether or not to take judgement into his own hands.

And *Glas* is glass: like the diary form itself, it's a reflecting surface, a mirror in which one sees oneself. It's hard and impermeable, but easily shattered; and, from certain angles, it's transparent. This last quality is one of Glas's complaints: he can only fall in love with women who are in love with someone else, because their love makes them radiant; but their love for other men means that Glas himself is invisible to them. So it is with Mrs Gregorius: she is having an adulterous affair with another man, and can't 'see' Doctor Glas. She can only see through him, making of him a means to the end she longs for. As for Doctor Glas's nemesis, it's worth noting that although 'Gregorius' is the name of a saint and of a couple of popes, it's also the name of a certain kind of telescope. Like Glas, Gregorius is glassy; he wears glasses, and looking into them, Glas sees the reflection of his own bespectacled self. Perhaps he hates Gregorius so much because the man unconsciously reminds Glas of the father who used to punish him, and whose physicality repelled him as a young boy; or perhaps it's because Gregorius is his ogrish double, the sly, whining, selfish, and self-justifying personification of the lust he can't permit himself to act out.

At first glance the structure of *Doctor Glas* is disarmingly casual, almost random. The device of the diary allows us to follow events as they unfold, but allows us also to listen in on Glas's reactions to them. The workings of the novel are so subtle that the reader doesn't notice at first that it has any: so immediate, even blunt, is the voice that we appear to be reading the uncensored thoughts of a real person. Glas promises candour: he won't set down everything, he says, but he will record nothing that isn't true. 'Anyway,' he adds, 'I can't exorcise my soul's wretchedness – if it is wretched – by telling lies.' Chance encounters and trivial conversations alternate with fits of midnight scribbling; jokes and pleasant convivial meals are followed by hours of anguish; night and dreamtime counterpoint the world of purposeful daylight. Unanswered questions punctuate the text – 'By the way, why do the clergy always go into church by a back door?' – as do odd moments of hilarity verging on the burlesque, as when Gregorius considers administering the communion wine in the form of pills, to avoid germs. (The pill idea soon recurs in a much more evil form.)

Söderberg had read his Dostoevsky: he too is interested in the disgruntlements of underground men, and in charting impulse and rationalization and motive, and in the fine line that runs between the violent thought and the criminal act. He'd read his ghost-ridden Ibsen and that master of bizarre obsession, Poe. He'd also read his Freud, and he knows how to make use of the semi-conscious motif, the groundswells of the unspoken. There are two hints in the text that point us toward the book's methods: Glas's meditation on the nature of the artist, who to him is not an originator but an aeolean harp, who makes music only because the winds of his own time play over him – thus the discursiveness; and his invocation of Wagner, who used the leitmotif to connect large swathes of disparate music into a unified whole. A tracing of all the red roses – from dead mother to out-of-reach beloved to

rejected potential sweetheart – reveals some of these interconnec-
tions, as does a survey of all the astronomical images, from moon
to stars to sun to the sunny, starry-eyed Mrs Gregorius. 'Truth is
like the sun,' says Glas's friend Markel, 'its value wholly depends
upon our being at a correct distance away from it.' And so it would
be, we suspect, with Mrs Gregorius: she can be valuable for Glas as
an ideal only as long as she is kept at a correct distance.

Doctor Glas is deeply unsettling, in the way certain dreams are – or,
no coincidence, certain films by Bergman, who must have read it.
The eerie blue northern nights of midsummer combined with an
unexplained anxiety, the nameless Kirkegaardean dread that
strikes Glas at the most ordinary of moments, the juxtaposition of
pale spirituality with an almost comic vulgar sensuality – these
are from the same cultural context. The novel launches itself from
the ground of naturalism set in place by French writers of the nineteenth century, but goes beyond it. Some of Söderberg's
techniques – the mix of styles, the collage-like snippets – anticipate,
for instance, *Ulysses*. Some of his images anticipate the Surrealists:
the disturbing dreams with their ambiguous female figures, the
sinister use of flowers, the glasses with no eyes behind them, the
handless watchcase in which Doctor Glas carries around his little
cyanide pills. A few decades earlier and this novel would never have
been published; a few years later and it would have been dubbed a
forerunner of the stream-of-consciousness technique.

   Doctor Glas is one of those marvellous books that appear as fresh
and vivid now as on the day it was published. As the English writer
William Sansom has said, 'In most of its writing and much of the
frankness of its thought, it might have been written tomorrow.' It
occurs on the cusp of the nineteenth and the twentieth centuries,
but it opens doors the novel has been opening ever since.

31

Mystery Man:
Some clues to Dashiell Hammett

The Selected Letters of Dashiell Hammett, 1921–1960
edited by Richard Layman with Julie M. Rivett

Dashiell Hammett: A Daughter Remembers
by Jo Hammett, edited by Richard Layman with Julie M. Rivett

Dashiell Hammett: Crime Stories & Other Writings
selected and edited by Steven Marcus

When I was a pre-adolescent spending summers in northern Canada, I read a lot of old detective fiction because it was there. When I'd got through the pile I read some of it over again, there being no library where I could go and get more. I didn't reread Erie Stanley Gardner or Ellery Queen: I found them dry. But I did reread Dashiell Hammett.

What was it about these books that intrigued me as an avid but ignorant child reader? Their world was fast-paced, sharp-edged, and filled with zippy dialogue and words I'd never heard pronounced – slang words like 'gunsel', fancy words like 'punctilious'. This was not the Agatha Christie sort of story – there were fewer clues, and these were more likely to be lies people told rather than cuff buttons they'd left strewn around. There were more corpses, with less importance bestowed on each: a new character would appear, only to be gunned down by a fire-spitting revolver. In a 'clues' novel, everything depended on who was where; in a Hammett one, it was more likely to be who was who, given to disguises and false names as these folk were. The action was dispersed, not sealed up as in a nobody-leaves-this-house puzzle: dark mean streets were prowled, cars were driven at speed, people blew in from elsewhere and hid out and skipped town. Oddly enough, clothing was described in more detail than in many country-house murders – a feature I appreciated. There was a lot of drinking, of substances I had never heard of, and a great deal of smoking. As an eleven-year-old I found this world very, very sophisticated.

It's odd to think that in July of 1951, while I was trying to figure out why a man would turn a strange shade of yellow, with bloodshot eyes, while telling a woman that maybe he loved her and maybe she loved him but he wasn't going to play the sap for her, the author of the books that so fascinated me was about to be jailed. The McCarthy Red Scare was at its height, and Hammett had been called into US district court as a representative of the Civil Rights Congress Bail Fund to be questioned about four fugitives. Notoriously, he refused to testify. He wouldn't even give his name. The man whose books had been legends in their time had now become a legend of a different kind: exemplary, not only of a certain kind of American fiction, but also of a certain kind of American life.

Forty years after his death, Dashiell Hammett continues to intrigue. While he was still alive, Raymond Chandler wrote his famous 1944 tribute to him, 'The Simple Art of Murder'. After his death, his companion of many years and literary executrix, Lillian Hellman, served him up as a dreamlife portrait in her 1973 memoir, *Pentimento*. Attempting to control the legend, Hellman then authorized a biography;[1] there have been several unauthorized biographies as well. In 2001, there were three new additions to works by and about Hammett: *The Selected Letters of Dashiell Hammett, 1921–1960*, edited by Richard Layman with Hammett's granddaughter Julie M. Rivett; *Dashiell Hammett: A Daughter Remembers*, a personal memoir by Hammett's second daughter, Josephine, who also supplied a foreword for the *Letters*; and *Dashiell Hammett: Crime Stories & Other Writings*, selected and edited by Steven Marcus.

The man who created and solved so many mysteries left quite a few of his own behind him, it seems: many have been the attempts to explicate him. Where did his talent come from? Why the extreme drinking, the reckless spending? Why the communism, in such a patriotic American? Why the sudden creative silence, and then that other silence, the one that landed him in jail? Did Lillian Hellman exhaust him, or was she on the contrary his right-hand gal and kindly keeper? These are the sorts of questions that have raised themselves over time.

Those who have read even a little about Hammett know the main outlines of the plot. It's laid before us in condensed form at the end of *Dashiell Hammett: Crime Stories & Other Writings*, and again in the excellent summaries dividing the periods of his life in the *Selected Letters*, and yet again, in a different mode, in Jo Hammett's memoir.

This last is exactly what the jacket says it is: a reminiscence presented in 'straightforward prose, with unaffected charm'. It contains a lot of photos, and some new, suggestive information about Hammett's family background. It also tells the story of how the photos came to light – one of those proverbial stashes of old cardboard boxes in the garage that turn out to be a treasure trove. Jo Hammett writes concisely, with much personal anecdote and wry observation. She sees her father from a necessarily intimate angle, and though she adored him, she also naturally resented his treatment of the family – of her mother Jose, her older sister Mary, and herself. Hammett wasn't evil or violent, and he tried to send sufficient money; he gave the daughters lavish treats; he wrote them loving, funny letters; but he was seldom there.

Jo Hammett saves the largest part of her resentment for Lillian Hellman, who seems to have deserved it. Ms Hammett tries her best to acknowledge Hellman's virtues – she was smart, she had good taste, she took care of Hammett during his last, broke decade – but it costs her a lot of teeth-grinding to do so. Hellman, it seems, was close to being a mythomaniac, and a ruthless power player; gaining control of Hammett's copyrights was one of her milder gambits. No Other Woman would have come out well from the daughter's point of view, but this portrait of Hellman does raise a question: What did Hammett see in her? As his daughter says, he appreciated people who went too far, as he often did himself; and his admiration for attractive women who lied outrageously – so evident in *The Maltese Falcon* and elsewhere – predates Hellman. It's another of Hammett's enigmas, for otherwise he set great store by speaking honestly.

Samuel Dashiell Hammett was born in rural Maryland in 1894. As a boy he wanted to read all the books in the Baltimore Public Library, but he had to quit high school at the age of fourteen to help out with the shaky family finances. (His father, whom he didn't like, was a spendthrift, drinker, sharp dresser, and womanizer; but unlike Hammett, who resembled him in all these respects, he was mean and stingy.) At twenty-one, Hammett got a job as a Pinkerton's detective agency operative, which he left in 1918 to join the army. He suffered the first of many severe respiratory illnesses then. During one recuperation he married a nurse he met at the infirmary; then he signed on at Pinkerton's once more, but his health broke down. It was then that he began writing crime stories for the pulps.[2]

Once Hammett had teamed up with the magazine *Black Mask*, an astonishing burst of creativity followed. He turned out stories at an amazing rate, followed by five highly successful novels, including *Red Harvest*, *The Dain Curse*, *The Glass Key*, and *The Maltese Falcon*, this last perhaps the best-known American crime novel of all time. By that time he was famous and rich, but he was also drinking and

spending money, both at a prodigal rate. Then followed the liaison
with Lillian Hellman and his silence as a writer. Later in the thirties
he became involved in the activities of the Communist Party of
America, as did many who were appalled by the rise of fascism.
That he had been a witness to violent union-busting during his
Pinkerton days may also have played a part.[3] After serving in the
army during World War Two – he edited an army paper in the
Aleutians – he was caught in the Red Scare dragnet and jailed for
contempt of court. His books and the radio shows based on them
were blacklisted and the IRS went after him for back taxes. He
came out of prison minus his health and his money, neither of
which he ever regained. He died in 1961, at the age of sixty-six.

The *Selected Letters* was made possible by the same lucky garage
find that enabled Jo Hammett to piece together her memoir. All of
the letters are by Hammett: the answers to them have disappeared.
Most of the letters are to women – his wife, his daughters, Lillian
Hellman, other mistresses and women friends – either because
women saved the letters, or because Hammett felt more comfortable writing to women than to men. Reading them is like reading
the letters of anyone you don't know – first names you can't place,
books you've never heard of, private jokes you don't get – but then
some *bon mot* or caustic remark will liven things up again. ('Bruce
Lockwood, who has been borrowing money from me, sent me a
dozen of his wife's horrible watercolours, from which I'm supposed to select a couple to be gifted with.') Many letters are
ornamented with drawings or stuck with newspaper clippings;
some are whimsical pieces of wordplay. They're the letters of a
man who loved to write, to flirt, and to amuse others. It's plain to
see why women liked him.

The letters have been meticulously edited, and among them
are some documents that will be very helpful to anyone studying –
for instance – American intellectual and political life of the thirties
and forties. The letters to Hammett's first daughter, Mary, in which
he tries to answer her questions about the chief issues of the day –
why support the Republican side in the Spanish Civil War, what's

the scoop on Hitler – are particularly sober and thoughtful. The letters to Lillian Hellman show that the two of them had – whatever their respective failings – a deep-rooted, enduring, and often frisky relationship, though it's somewhat unnerving to come across the tough and ambitious Hellman being addressed as 'my little cabbage'.

The letters begin in 1921, with a series to Josephine Dolan, soon to become Hammett's wife. Anyone who was around in the first half of the twentieth century will recognize the young-man-to-girlfriend style. He teases her and sweet-talks, and brags about how much hell he's been raising. Presumably she scolded him about his health and teased him in return. It's a sweet beginning.

Another sweet beginning is his letters to the editor of *Black Mask*. Already, in 1923, he's making fun of himself: Creda Dexter in 'The Tenth Clew' is described as looking like a kitten, but Hammett confesses to the *Black Mask* editor that her original looked 'exactly like a young white-faced bull pup'. Then, he claims, his nerve failed him: 'Nobody will believe you if you write a thing like that, I told myself. They'll think you're trying to spoof them. So, for the sake of plausibility, I lied about her . . .'

But such gentle ridicule of the genre alternates with earnestness: in a 1928 letter to his book publisher, he says he wants to try adapting the 'stream-of-consciousness method' to the detective story. 'I'm one of the few – if there are any more – people moderately literate who take the detective story seriously,' he says. 'I don't mean that I necessarily take my own or anybody else's seriously – but the detective story as a form. Some day somebody's going to make "literature" out of it . . . and I'm selfish enough to have my hopes . . .'

Dashiell Hammett: Crime Stories & Other Writings contains the foundation for those hopes. The 'other writings' are two small and admired non-fiction pieces, 'From the Memoirs of a Private Detective' and 'Suggestions to Detective Story Writers'. The first is a string of anecdotes about human stupidity and bits of cynical, tongue-in-cheek wisdom reminiscent of Ambrose Bierce: 'Pocket-picking is the easiest to master of all the criminal trades. Anyone who is not crippled can become an adept in a day.' The second – the 'Suggestions' – displays the practical seriousness with which Hammett viewed his craft, while at the same time it's hilariously scathing at the expense of other, sloppier detective story writers. 'A pistol, to be a revolver, must have something on it that revolves,' he remarks. '"Youse" is the plural of "you."' 'A trained detective shadowing a subject does not ordinarily leap from doorway to doorway . . .'

This approach brings to mind that other American Samuel, Sam Clemens (Mark Twain), who so famously took the stuffing out of Fenimore Cooper's standards of accuracy. Indeed, the two Samuels[4] have a lot in common: the combination of steely-eyed observation of the dirty underbelly of America and the idealistic wish that it would live up to its founding principles, the deadpan humour, and above all the dedication to language. This last, in both, took the form of an attempt to capture the tone and cadence of the American vernacular in literature, of which *Huckleberry Finn* is surely the first fully triumphant example.

Seen in this light, Hammett, with his word-collecting and ear for slang dialects,[5] is part of the project of American linguistic self-definition that began with Noah Webster's 1783 *Spelling Book* and his later dictionary. The effort was continued through Fenimore Cooper's Natty Bumppo of the *Leatherstocking Tales*, and gathered speed with various dialect and regional writers of the nineteenth century, as well as Whitman and his barbaric yawp. Owen Wister and his creation of the western – its *ur*-plot, its tall tales and talk – belongs here too, and Bret Harte, and many after them. The hard-boiled detective story lent itself to this sort of exploration, criminal slang being not only colourful but often indigenous.

If this is Hammett's literary ancestry, or part of it, his subsequent family tree is equally noteworthy. He was an admirer of Sherwood Anderson, who wrote concisely about hitherto overlooked corners of small-town life. He respected Faulkner as one might respect a very bright but weird second cousin.[6] He found Hemingway irritating, like a brother who is also a rival, and took little pokes at him – in 'The Main Death' he has a particularly vacuous rich girl reading *The Sun Also Rises*. He must have found it gratifying to be called 'better than Hemingway' in the 1930 publisher's ad for *The Maltese Falcon*.

Like Wister's *Virginian*, the grand-daddy of all westerns, Hammett's work had incalculable influence. He was one of those writers whom everyone of a certain age read as a matter of course. He himself said, 'I've been as bad an influence on American literature as anyone I can think of.' Raymond Chandler is the younger brother: he inherited the battered office furniture and the type of the romantic-loner detective, though Philip Marlowe is more of an intellectual than Sam Spade, and more fascinated with upholstery. Nathanael West was arguably a melancholy cousin. Elmore Leonard – who, like Hammett, began in magazines – has Hammett's pace, descriptive eye, and dead-on ear for dialogue. Carl Hiassen has the outrageousness, the taste for the hilariously bizarre, and the manic inventiveness.[7]

The Hammett prize for experimenting with language in a criminal setting must surely go to Jonathan Lethem's beguiling *Motherless Brooklyn*, in which the sleuth has Tourette's syndrome. And there are many, many more. Even the pratfalling body pile-ups were inherited by an unlikely third cousin: read Hammett's 'Dead Yellow Women' or 'The Big Knockover', then the riot-in-the-bar sequence in the first chapter of Thomas Pynchon's *V*, just for fun. The most recent addition is the fine Spanish thriller writer Pérez-Reverte, who pays direct homage to *The Maltese Falcon*.

Dashiell Hammett: Crime Stories & Other Writings takes us back to the beginning of the line. Twenty-four of the early magazine stories have been selected. In addition, there's the manuscript of *The Thin Man*, much shorter and almost completely different from the published book. (No Nick and Nora Charles tossing back the booze in their chic apartment, no Asta the dog.) The stories give us a good look at the young Hammett staking out his territory. They're best read one at a time, with pauses between, since too much at once dulls the edge. They are very much of their period and genre – 'hard-boiled' was the term used of this kind of side-of-the-mouth crime fiction. (Hard-boiled eggs were what blue-collar workers had in their lunch boxes.) But despite their adherence to formulas it's easy to see from the stories why Hammett rose so rapidly.

Low life and high life are his interests: each set is motivated largely by money, power, and sex, and each behaves badly, though the highlifes are less likely to have poor complexions, perhaps because they don't eat at grease joints – about the only places in Hammett stories where people consume food. The cosy middle-class Norman Rockwell front-porch folks do not concern him; when their representatives appear, they are likely to be thugs in disguise, like the 'affectionate old couple' with their twinkling eyes in 'The House in Turk Street' who are fronting for a mob, or the entire population of the town of Izzard, in 'Nightmare Town', including the jolly banker and the kindly doctor, who are all part of a huge criminal conspiracy.[8]

'Realism' is a word often used to describe Hammett's writing, but the stories are realistic only in their settings and details – the pimples on nasty youths, the dingy office furniture of the cheap private eyes – and in their forthright use of the vernacular. The dialogue was influenced by its period, when the wisecrack and the vaudeville one-liner were valued and a smart mouth like Dorothy Parker's was an asset. The plots are Jacobean in their doubled and redoubled vengeance, and also in their carnage: they resemble multiple car crashes. This was the age of the Keystone Cops, when mayhem was first being portrayed on the screen,[9] and surely some of the brawls and corpse-fests in Hammett were intended to be funny in this quasi-slapstick way. The exuberance of language, the relish with which seediness is described, the playing with aphorisms, the joy of bizarre invention – it's a pleasure to imagine the young Hammett cutting loose with whatever rascally highjinks he could cook up and put over. The aim was not realism, but to make things seem real – 'real as a dime', as one narrator says of a far-fetched yarn he's been reading.

For the pulp adventure-crime stories of this era are not real realism. Instead they're romances in the Northrop Frye sense, with knights-errant disguised as detectives, and treasures with criminal-mastermind ogres guarding them. There are trolls in the guise of goons with huge chins, pasty faces, dead eyes, or other physical dis-tortions, and threatened maidens who sometimes really are maidens – innocent heiresses transgressing social boundaries – but most likely instead *femmes fatales* with silver eyes or other enchant-ments. These latter turn into clawing cats or foul-mouthed banshees when the hero calls their bluff. Quite often the spell-breaking words are 'You are a liar', or words to that effect; for like Sam Spade after him, the hero always resists female blandishments in pursuit of his higher mission. This mission is not exactly justice; it's more like professionalism. The hero has a job to do and is good at his job. He's a working man, and this kind of toughness and thoroughness gets Hammett's respect. Also this kind of tough-ness, for toughness was a cardinal virtue for him.[10]

The hero who most frequently appears in these stories, and the one that made Hammett so popular with his readers, is a man without a name. He's known as the Continental Op – an operative working for the Continental Detective Agency. The Op reports to The Old Man – surely the original of James Bond's M, George Smiley's Control, and Charlie of *Charlie's Angels*. This hero makes a point of avoiding heroics, as his aim is not to get himself killed but to catch the criminals. He's short and fat and down-to-earth, play-ing a grouchy Sancho Panza to the thin, idealistic tilter at windmills who was lurking inside Hammett and would make such a decisive appearance in the courtroom in his later life.

Fatness and thinness are distinguishing markers in the stories and novels, but they're also recurring motifs in the letters. Time and again Hammett tells his correspondents that he's eating again, that he's gaining weight, or – when illness or drink have got the better of him – that he hasn't been able to eat at all. In the light of this constant struggle with his thinness – at bottom a struggle to remain alive – the title of Hammett's last novel, *The Thin Man*, may have been a wry joke, the subject of which was Hammett himself. The thin man in the book is a mad genius who's dead before the book begins. He appears to be alive only because other people say he is; in reality, he's so thin he isn't there at all. 'Count me out,' Hammett may have been saying. 'I've run out of energy, I'm gone.' And he was gone, from the writing scene at least.

Which brings us to the two silences: the literary silence, and the dramatic public one in federal court. Of the literary one – the absence of any new books after the mid-thirties – Jo Hammett makes short work. 'He didn't stop writing. Not until the very last. What he stopped was finishing.' And indeed the letters are sprinkled with references to books he was beginning or continuing, and to possibilities for having the free time and the space in which to write.[11] This part of the story makes painful reading for anyone who's trying to write books, since the moves – the setting out with optimism, the evasion, the fading away of purpose – are so familiar.

None of the attempts came to anything. Drink has been suggested as the reason, and illness, and other activities that interfered, though it was Hammett's choice to let them. Then there were ambition and high standards: Hammett wanted to go 'mainstream' – to get outside what he felt was the limiting circle of crime writing – and that was a big leap. Perhaps, however, his fundamental problem was with language. 'I stopped writing because I was repeating myself,' he said in 1956. 'It is the beginning of the end when you discover you have style.' And he did have style, or rather a style – a mannered implement he'd worked up and polished, but an implement very much of its time. Possibly he could no longer settle on a language equal to the occasion; or rather, the occasion itself had passed by. By the forties and fifties the scene had changed radically, and he must have felt out of his element. He couldn't go to town on the language any more, because that kind of town no longer existed.

Then there's the other silence, the one in court. The virtues of silence as a stratagem had occurred to Hammett early. 'It doesn't matter how shrewd a man is, or how good a liar,' the Op says in the 1924 story 'ZigZags of Treachery': 'If he'll talk to you and you play your cards right, you can hook him – can make him help you convict him. But if he won't talk you can't do a thing with him.'

Also, if Hammett kept silent, he wouldn't implicate anyone else: only he would suffer. Strangely enough, there's a literary precedent even for that. The young boy who'd wanted to read all the books in the Baltimore Public Library can hardly have escaped Longfellow, then the most revered of American poets. Longfellow's poem 'The Children's Hour'[12] was chosen by Hammett as the title of the play attributed to Lillian Hellman, though Hammett had provided the story for it and did much of the work. So Hammett more than likely knew Longfellow's verse drama, *Giles Corey of the Salem Farms*.

Giles Corey was the man who refused to plead either guilty or not guilty during the Salem witchcraft episode. If he plead, he'd have been tried, and if tried, he'd have been found guilty – all those accused were. His property would then have been confiscated by the state, and his family deprived. He took his stand on principle, but also out of consideration for others, as Hammett himself did. The penalty for failure to plead was 'pressing' – stones were piled on top of you until you either plead or died. Giles Corey did the latter.[13] If Hammett considered the Salem trials as a paradigm for the McCarthy 'witchhunt', he was not alone. Many used that metaphor, including Arthur Miller in his play *The Crucible*.

In Longfellow's play, the last words spoken about Corey before his death are, 'I wonder now/If the old man will die, and will not speak? He's obstinate enough and tough enough/For anything on earth.' Silence equals toughness. Could it be that this verbal equation was first planted in young Hammett's head by the author of *Evangeline*?

Well, it's one more clue.

NOTES

1 . Diane Johnson, *Dashiell Hammett: A Life*, New York: Random House, 1983.

2.   The term 'pulp' didn't refer to the sleaziness of the writing, but to the quality of the paper: the 'pulps' were printed on uncoated paper, as opposed to the more upmarket 'slicks'. But many good writers got their start in the pulps, and they were a source of income if you could write quickly.

3.   As he was already a star by then, he evidently didn't have to suffer the mind-bending and humiliation dished out to lesser CPUSA members, such as Richard Wright.

4.   The third Samuel in the trio is Sam Spade. Hammett was very conscious of names, and would have given his own to this character quite deliberately.

5.   As Jo Hammett remarks, 'Papa loved all kinds of word play: thieves' cant, convict argot, Yiddish expressions, restaurant and cowboy talk, Cockney rhyming slang, gangster-lowlife speak.'

6.   In 1931 he was reading *Sanctuary*, which – with its twisted Popeye and its socialite who plays with the toughs – is probably Faulkner's most Hammett-like book. Hammett didn't think highly of it, but revised his opinion of Faulkner upward in later years.

7.   Hiassen's amazing 'Velcro-Face' of *Skin Tight* and his road-kill-eating ex-senator exist on a continuum that leads from Hammett's squinty or big-chinned grotesques through Faulkner's twisted Popeye through *Dick Tracy* of the comics, with its gargoyle thugs such as 'Anyface', who looked like Swiss cheese.

8.   This strain – awfulness behind the apple-pie façade – runs through Hawthorne's 'Young Goodman Brown', in which the wholesome townsfolk are in league with the Devil, through Hammett, through Ray Bradbury's *Martian Chronicles*, where the town conceals murderous Martians, through the film *The Stepford Wives*, in which robot wife doubles have replaced real wives, to the television show *Twin Peaks* and certain episodes of *The X Files*. In real life it has played itself out in versions of Satanic cults, as well as its *ur*-form, the infamous Salem witchcraft trials.

9.   Hammett was a moviegoer. It's endearing to find him giving his opinion of the relative merits of *Pinocchio* versus *Snow White*. Needless to say, he liked *Pinocchio* better.

10.   Jo Hammett describes all the kinds of toughness Hammett admired: tough men, tough women, tough sports. It was a quality of character as

well as a physical quality. 'Toughness,' she says, 'would take him through the last bad years.'

11.   There were three main attempts: *My Brother Felix*, which was 'going to be pretty good for both magazines and movies'; *The Valley Sheep Are Fatter*, a title that comes from one of Thomas Love Peacock's novels; and *Tulip*, this last about a writer who can no longer write.

12.   Thought of as a piece of syrupy kitsch by those who haven't read it closely. But Hammett was a good reader, and must have seen it for the creepy poem it is.

13.   The only words Corey is said to have uttered were: 'Put on more stones,' but Longfellow has the pressing take place offstage and so does not use them.

32

Of Myths and Men

Atanarjuat: The Fast Runner is the first feature film ever to be made in Inuktitut. It's also the first to be made almost entirely by Inuit – *made* in many ways, for the clothing, the artifacts such as spears and kayaks, and the dwellings, were all painstakingly researched and then handmade by artisans to recreate the world of almost a thousand years ago, long before the coming of Europeans. For the people of the community out of which this film emerged, it will be what they have lacked for so many years: a validation of their roots.

The danger might have been that such a film would have only a curio value, but nothing could be farther from the truth. *Atanarjuat* won the *Camera d'or* at Cannes for best first feature and then went on to collect six Genie Awards, and no wonder. It's already being called a masterpiece. This film is a knockout.

I've seen it, or parts of it, on three occasions. I'll talk about them in reverse order.

The film was viewable in England before its release in Canada, so I saw it in its entirety in London, at the Institute of Contemporary Arts. We went to the matinee, but even so we were lucky to get in: The place was packed. During the screening, my English pal and I – supposed mistresses of sang-froid, both of us – did a lot of arm-clutching, and, at the end, some unseemly snivelling. As we staggered out of the theatre, red-eyed and wobbly-kneed, she said: 'My god! What a film!' Speechlessness is the beat tribute.

I'd known *Atanarjuat* was going to be on in London because, while I'd been in Paris doing my bad imitation of a person who can speak French, we'd happened to turn on the BBC, and the film was being reviewed, complete with excerpts. I don't think I've ever heard an English film critic indulging in this kind of breathless rhapsody. 'If Homer had been given a video camera, this is what he would have done,' said he, and there's something to that.

Which bit of Homer? The story of the House of Atreus would be my guess, for this is a generational saga with many Homeric elements — love, jealousy, rivalry between young contenders, extraordinary feats of strength, resentments passed from fathers to sons, and crimes that beget consequences years later. The world of Greek myth is one in which gods interact with human beings, dreams have significance, grudges are held, vengeance is exacted, the ways of Fate are dark, food can cast a spell, and animals aren't always what they seem; and if you substitute the word 'spirits' for the word 'gods', these things are true as well of *Atanarjuat*.

It helps going into the film to know a couple of things. First, this is not a 'made-up' story, any more than Homer would have said *The Iliad* was made up. It's based on oral tradition — on a series of events said to have really happened, in real places. (You can follow the travels of the characters on the film's website.) So it would be beside the point to fault someone called 'the author' for something you don't like about 'the plot'.

Second, a newborn child was thought to be a reincarnation of someone who'd died. Thus, when the grandmother addresses a young woman as 'little mother' — which throws you the first time you hear it — it's not just that the girl is named after the old woman's mother: She is that mother.

Third, spirits are all around. They can confer extra strength, and they can enter into people, and make them behave badly (like the demons cast out by Christ). But they can be mastered to some extent by shamans, who can also call on the dead for help. So, as in Homer, this story isn't just about conflict between human rivals. It's a battle between one lot of spirits and another, kicked off when an evil spirit arrives and sows discord among the members of a hunting group, and enters into one of them.

Fourth, it was forbidden for a woman to speak to or even look at her brother-in-law. That's why the bad sex scene between the wayward second wife of the hero and the hero's brother isn't just any old roll in the fur. It's really bad.

Fifth, there are various kinds of strength. There's the strength conferred by the position of leadership – keep your eye on the teeth-and-tusk necklace, the equivalent of the crown in *Richard III* – and this position is always held by a man, because the group is a hunting group and it's the men who hunt. There's the strength conferred by shamanistic power, which can be used for good or ill; but it helps to know that both the woman (later the grandmother) who gives a talismanic rabbit's foot to her brother, and the brother himself, possess this power.

And finally, there's moral authority. This can be earned or lost. (Watch out for the moment when, in any western genre film, the hero – his enemies finally at his mercy – would blow them to bits. This doesn't happen. Instead, Atanarjuat says, 'The killing stops here,' thus gaining moral authority. We could use a little of that right now.) But the ultimate moral authority resides with the elders, who wield it sparingly, though to crushing effect. Keep your eye on the grandmother.

These were things I would have liked to have known the first time I saw this film. It was the summer before it was to preview at the Toronto International Film Festival (on Sept. 12, 2001: the preview was cancelled). I was on an icebreaker in the Arctic, with a tour group called Adventure Canada. They'd asked me to come along and give a couple of talks, a small price to pay for the experience of seeing places I'd only ever dreamed about. Everything about this voyage was magic; the Arctic light effects alone – the mirages, the Fats Morgana, the 'glories' – were worth the trip. At one point we all got out and stood on an ice pan, looking foreboding-ly like a David Blackwood lithograph.

If we'd taken off all our clothes and leapt from floe to floe, we might have resembled instead – from a distance – the spectacular scene in which the hero of *Atanarjuat* runs stark naked across miles and miles of broken pan ice. I didn't get as far as this during my first viewing. It wasn't that the film was being shown in episodes on a TV set and it was hard to read the subtitles. But Pakak Innuksuk – the man who plays the Strong One, the hero's older brother – was on the ship with us. He was a man of few but cogent words, a hunter from much farther north, and in the film he was much as he seemed in life; more brusque, but recognizable. So I watched up to the place where Pakak was sleeping in a skin tent along with his brother and the three murderous rivals were sneaking up on them. I knew Pakak was about to be horribly speared, and I didn't think I could go through with it. (It was okay to watch Pakak being speared in London. I hadn't just had pancakes with him.)

There's a permeable boundary between reality and art. We know there's a connection, we know there's a difference, but there's no stone wall. When I think of *Atanarjuat*, of course I will always think of Pakak. While we were scrambling around on the Arctic land-scape one day, I recalled with some embarrassment having been told that a native band, lacking a word for 'northern tourism', had come up with an expression that means 'white men playing in the woods'. So there we were, mostly white people playing on the rocks, and there was Pakak, standing on a cliff where he had a good view.

He had a large bear gun. He was watching out for animals. As he, and all the men of whom (says the lore) he is an incarnation, have been doing for thousands of years.

33

Cops and Robbers

Tishomingo Blues is Elmore Leonard's thirty-seventh novel. At that number you'd think he'd be flagging, but no, the maestro is in top form. If, like Graham Greene, he were in the habit of dividing his books into 'novels' and 'entertainments' – with, for instance, *Pagan Babies* and *Cuba Libre* in the former list, and *Glitz*, *Get Shorty*, and *Be Cool* in the latter – this one might fall on the 'entertainment' side; but, as with Greene, those that might be consigned to the 'entertainment' section are not necessarily of poorer quality.

Those offended by what my grandmother called 'language', and by what used to be termed, in adventure stories, 'fearful oaths', and by the derogatory epithets and salacious jokes that used to pass from mouth to ear in the smoking cars of trains and now whiz to and fro over the Internet, should avoid *Tishomingo Blues*. But Leonard is often and justly praised for his mastery of the demotic, and the demotic would not be itself without this kind of thing. Anyway it's pretty much always apt: each character speaks in character. Here's one of the more villainous heavies:

> No mention of the smoke or the two greasers – Newton thinking
> of the one he'd asked that time where the nigger was and the one

said he'd gone to fuck your wife. It had set him off, sure, even
knowing it wasn't true. One, Myrna wasn't ever home, she played
bingo every night of her life. And two, not even a smoke'd want to
fuck her, Myrna going four hundred pounds on the hoof. Try and
find the wet spot on her.

This is an object lesson in economy worthy of a short essay in
Maladicta, the defunct scholarly journal devoted to foul language
(still available on the Internet): three racial slurs, two F-words,
misogyny combined with lookism, and a sneer at bingo players, all
wrapped up in five terse lines. The man who speaks this will surely
die. ('Good' characters in Leonard swear differently from the way
'bad' characters do.)

As to what Leonard is up to beyond the texture of his prose, it's
what he's been up to for some time. A good deal of any Leonard
novel – or those of, say, the last twenty years – consists of deadpan
social observation. John Le Carré has maintained that, for the late
twentieth century at least, the spy novel is the central fictional
form, because it alone tackles the implementation of the hidden
agendas that – we suspect, and as the evening news tends to con-
firm – surround us on all sides.[1] Similarly, Elmore Leonard might
argue – if he were given to argument, which he is not – that a
novel without some sort of crime or scam in it can hardly claim to
be an accurate representation of today's reality. He might add that
this is especially true when that reality is situated in America, home
of Enron and of the world's largest privately held arsenal, where
casual murders are so common that most aren't reported, and
where the CIA encourages the growing and trading of narcotics to
finance its foreign adventures.

Not only that – Leonard might continue, and it's a point he's copi-
ously illustrated – the line between the law and the lawbreakers is,
in his native land at any rate, not a firm one. (One of the nasties in
this book is an ex-sheriff's deputy, an employment category about
which few have a good word to say.) In fact, the uncertainties about

this division – law enforcers vs lawbreakers, with coins tossed over who the villains are to be – goes far back, and is firmly embedded in American folklore. The Revolutionaries of 1776 were in essence rebels against the established government of their time, and ever since then there has been some question about who is entitled to impose what sort of legal code upon whom, and by what means. The Klan vigilantes and the lynch mob have been – as Leonard reminds us in this book – two of the less pleasant historical responses.

There are righteous causes in aid of which breaking the law is surely the moral thing to do, but who is to decide what those causes are? It's a series of short steps from the rude bridge that spanned the flood, where the embattled and incidentally law-breaking Concord farmers stood, to John Brown's celebrated abolitionist and also homicidal Body, to Thoreau's classic 'Civil Disobedience', to Darlin' Corrie of the well-known folk song, who has to wake up and get her shotgun because the Revenooers are a-comin' to tear her still-house down.

Like all writers who concern themselves with crimes and punishments, Leonard is interested in moral issues, but these issues are for him by no means clear-cut. Having been born in 1925, he entered the scene as a conscious observer during the half-century when this tendency – the questioning of law, the admiration of its breakers – was at its peak. It was the thirties, and the Depression was causing much real desperation. No wonder that many followed the exploits of the James brothers and Bonnie and Clyde with a great deal of interest – young Leonard, by his own account, among them. For if oppression is economic, and the bank has grabbed your farm and turfed out your family, isn't it at least slightly heroic to stick your hand in the till? The father who hangs in connection with such a crime in Davis Grubb's thirties-era novel *The Night of the Hunter* is not a bad guy: he's a good guy, and it's the system that hangs him that bears the moral taint.

But the James brothers and Bonnie and Clyde were not Robin Hoods, even in mythologized retellings. The American version of the robber as folk hero is very potent, but it doesn't include giving to the poor: that would be sappy, and perhaps Communist as well. The best thing to do with the poor is to remove yourself from their number by any means at your disposal, and this is largely what Leonard's crooks set out to accomplish. Thus, quite often in Leonard's books you don't get a choice between good non-criminals and bad criminals: instead, you get a choice between good guys and bad guys, period. There are many factors that determine whether a guy is good or bad – more specifically, whether he is an asshole, a pompous blowhard, a coward, a condescending jerk, a moron, or a man a man can respect – but which side of the legal line he happens to be on is not among them.

As every child who has ever played cops and robbers knows, it was more fun being a robber, because you could fool people and get away with forbidden behaviour, and there was more risk. In *Tishomingo Blues*, fun, risk, forbidden behaviour, and fooling people go together. There are two main characters. The first is not a criminal. Instead he's an edge-dweller and risk-taker of another sort. He's a professional high-diver called Dennis Lenahan, who makes a living at amusement parks going off an eighty-foot tower into a tank that looks, from above, to be the size of a fifty-cent piece. He does this, as far as we can tell, for three reasons: it gives him a rush, it helps him to pick up girls, and he has no other marketable skills. When we enter his picture he's beginning to worry about how much longer he'll be able to keep up the performances without breaking his neck. (Or rupturing his anus and ruining his genitalia, two other hazards of high-diving about which we are duly informed on the first page.) Dennis is not someone who's ever given a thought to stock options or gated retirement communities – his first marriage failed because he was 'too young', and, although nearing forty, he's still too young – so these are new and depressing thoughts for the likeable lad.

Dennis soothes his anxieties by wafting into bed with nice women who never turn him down – well, he's very fit – and this is the one matter that may give the female reader thoughtful pause. Leonard is precise about physicality in other respects. His characters piss, take dumps, fart, have bad breath, and much else. Unlike some fictional characters, they eat and drink, and they do this accurately, brand names and all. (Early Times, Pepsis, and Lean Cuisines are featured.) But Dennis floats into the sack with nary a question and nary a precaution: no thoughts of STDs trouble his enthusiastic head. Maybe this is accurate, too – probably it is, or there wouldn't be so many cases of herpes, not to mention AIDS. But you want to whisper – especially when Dennis is tumbling around with the disaffected wife of a morally disgusting man who's done hard time in an unsanitary prison – 'Dennis honey, don't you know who's been in there before you?' Dennis, we fear, will wake up one morning with a dose of something he can't get rid of. But such dismal futures lie outside the margins of the book, and to dwell too long on them would be like anticipating Cinderella's wedding night, when she will pop out of her trance and realize that Prince Charming is a shoe fetishist.

The second main character has a lot more bulbs in his chandelier. The name he's going by is Robert Taylor – we assume it's assumed[2] – and he's definitely a criminal element. He's handsome, slick, personable, cool, well-dressed, Jaguar-driving, and from Detroit. (He also carries an attaché case with a gun in it, but this is a part of the country – Tunica, Mississippi – where people have guns the way most people have noses, so it elicits scant surprise.) In addition to all of the above, Robert is black. Add in the setting and an upcoming historical re-enactment of a Civil War battle, and you've got the nitroglycerine for the dynamite.

When I started reading about Tunica, Mississippi, as described by Elmore Leonard, it seemed so extravagantly over the top – even just architecturally – that I thought I'd stumbled upon a made-up place, like the Emerald City of Oz, which it somewhat resembles. (Oz too is a city of illusions controlled by a scam artist who deceives people and holds out false promises.) But I should have known better, because Leonard doesn't make up this sort of stuff. He does-n't need to: it's right there for the taking, in all its full-blown weirdness. Tunica is real – it's 'The Casino Capital of the South'. But it's *also* made up, because the business of gambling is nothing if not the successful selling of illusion.

The connection between illusion and reality, lies and truth – and also the gap between them – is one of the leitmotivs that runs through *Tishomingo Blues*. Everything in Tunica is *faux*, including the whore-in-a-trailer pretending to be Barbie, and the 'Southern Living Village', a complex in the throes of development where all the dwellings are imitations of something else and the entire oper-ation is a front for the drug trade. The focus of the story is the Tishomingo Lodge & Casino. Its name is ripped off from a real Native American chief; its form is a kitschy tepee; its cocktail wait-resses wear fringed fake-buckskin miniskirts; its foyer mural is horrendously inaccurate. But though the décor in Tunica may be fake, the danger is real.

Dennis the diver lands in Tunica because he's talked the man-ager of the casino into engaging his high-dive act as a customer attraction. Almost immediately he's in trouble. While up on his tower and about to do a test dive, he sees two men down below shoot a third man. They see him seeing them. They're about to pot him, but they get distracted. Robert Taylor, the black criminal, has witnessed the shooting too. He has also witnessed Dennis wit-nessing it. They strike up a curious symbiotic palship.

What does each want of the other? What Dennis ought to want is a goodbye handshake and a bus ticket to Nome, Alaska, but he's a bit of an innocent and doesn't know how afraid he ought to be. Also he doesn't want to abandon his tower and his tank. So he sticks around, and Robert Taylor presents himself as a fellow who can help Dennis do that. Without Robert present, we fear, young Dennis's brain will shortly be 'red Cream of Wheat', as other brains have been before. So Robert is our man.

But what does Robert Taylor want of Dennis? That's more com-plicated. First version, he wants Dennis and his diving act to function as the laundry for his drug money, because he plans to take over the market from the local-yokel Dixie Mafia. Second version, he wants to buy Dennis's soul. He puts that right on the table. 'You at the crossroads, Dennis. I'm about to make an offer to buy your soul.' 'Like Faust, man. Sell your soul, you get anything you want.' If Dennis sells, what he'll get is mojo, and this mojo will enable him to realize his innermost dreams; but he'll have to really believe it – otherwise it won't work – and they have the one chance to grab it.[3]

For Robert isn't just any old gangster. He's invested with more significance than that. He's the Master of the Crossroads, the deceiving prankster born and bred in the briar patch, the man who makes things happen. He's the fast-talking salesman selling himself and riding on a shoeshine and a smile;[4] he's the gambler with his sleeves stuffed with aces. He's the deity you pray to when you want change and action, though there's no guarantee of what kind of action you will get. He's Mercury, god of thieves and commerce and communication and conductor of souls to the underworld, and he's Anansi, African web-spinner, catcher of flies in traps. He teases Dennis by implying he's the Devil, but if so he's hardly the biblical Satan. Instead he's the devil of folklore, whose bargains could work out in your favour, especially if you do what Dennis is urged to do – no matter what you see, keep your mouth shut.[5] Robert is – in other words – a particularly engaging example of a trickster figure.[6] 'You gonna miss me, you know it?' he says toward the end of the book, as much to the reader as to the lady he's taking leave of. 'You gonna miss the fun.'

And he's on solid home ground in Tunica. His roots – he claims – are right here, on the banks of the Mississippi River, the *ur*-river, the Old Man River. The Mississippi divides and binds all elements – North and South, white, black, and Indian, rich and poor, travellers and gamblers. It's the river of *Showboat*, and, yes, Leonard dutifully supplies a beautiful quadroon who's concealing her ancestry. It's the river of Huck and Jim, the first white–black pair out to beat the odds and the scoundrels. It's the river of the

King and the Duke, seedy but amusing scammers-for-profit; and it's the river of Melville's Confidence Man, an elusive and ambiguous figure whose masquerades result – sometimes – in good.

Robert Taylor is the inheritor, then, of a long and many-stranded tradition. To watch him in action as he mines this rich lode is a pleasure, though it's somewhat like what Monty Python did with Botticelli's *Venus* – part humorous travesty, part straight aggression. Robert, for instance, is a history buff. 'History can work for you,' he says, 'you know how to use it,' and he does know how. He's gone to college – he paid his tuition by dealing, but he wouldn't sell to students because he figured their minds were already too addled:

> I took eighteen hours of history – ask me a question about it, anything, like the names of famous assassins in history. Who shot Lincoln, Grover Cleveland. I took history 'cause I loved it, man, not to get a job from it. I knew about the Civil War even before I saw it on TV, the one Ken Burns did. I stole the entire set of videos from Blockbuster.

Robert's first history trick is to get hold of a 1915 souvenir postcard of a lynching, and to tell two different Tunica white bad guys that it's his great-grandpa dangling from the bridge and their great-grandpa doing the hanging:

> I thought maybe you already knew your great-granddaddy lynched that man in the picture, my own great-granddaddy, rest his soul. And cut his dick off. Can you imagine a man doing that to another man . . .? . . . I thought to myself, Lookit how our heritage is tied together, going back to our ancestors. Yeah, I'm gonna show him the historical fact of it.

Robert says this to a diehard racist and violent creep. This is *Roots* with a vengeance. 'You only used it to set [him] up,' says Dennis of the postcard. 'That don't mean it ain't real,' Robert replies.

Robert's aim is to scam his way as an 'African Confederate' into the re-enactment of the Battle of Brice's Cross Roads (which will not take place at the real Brice's Cross Roads, needless to say). That way, he can arrange for his opponents to be dispatched with real bullets – putting the history back into History, you might say. The Dixie Mafia's tribute to authenticity, on the other hand, is to attempt to re-enact the postcard lynching, with Robert playing the role of dickless corpse. As usual, Leonard has done his research; he has the rules and attitudes of the re-enactment movement down pat, and he plays them for all they're worth. If you didn't know about Naughty Child Pie and the Robert E. Lee and Stonewall Jackson salt-and-pepper shakers, and what farbs and hard-cores are, you'll find out here.

Leonard doesn't write whodunits – we always know who done it because we see them doing it. You might say he writes howdunits. His plots are like chess games – the pieces are all out in the open, we can watch the setup, but it's the rapid moves of the endgame that surprise. They're also like Feydeau farces, which is in no way to disparage them. Such performances are very hard to pull off successfully, and timing is everything: Feydeau used to compose with a stopwatch. The reader knows who is in which cupboard and under what bed and behind which bush, but the characters don't know. Then they start figuring it out, and things move very quickly after that. The sleight-of-hand machinery in this book is engineered by Robert, of course: as chief trickster, he is after all the Master of Illusion.

But in this world of the amusement park and the dress-ups and the re-enactment, of the façade, the disguise, and the sham, where does reality lie, and what's actually worth having, and who has it? I'd say there's one main thing, and that is the respect – not of everyone, because men who want that are vain and foolish – but of a man whose respect counts for something. (These are boys' rules. Women aren't players in the respect game, in the world of *Tishomingo Blues*: they earn favourable attention in other ways.) The ways of obtaining and evaluating this and other kinds of man-to-man respect could form the basis for a dissertation in sociobiology – the male primate stare, for instance, or who looks at whom, and how, and what it means.

Apart from being able to do the stare, you get respect – as far as I can figure out – by being serious about things that count, by not talking too much, by knowing what you're talking about – there's a lot of lore-exchanging in this book, about the blues and their singers, about the Civil War, about how to set up a diving tank, and, rather less enchantingly, about baseball games of yore.[7] If you already have respect, and especially if you're a criminal kingpin, you have to keep the respect by not getting lazy and arrogant, or it'll be the Cream of Wheat brain for you.

But most of all you get the respect by making a hard thing look easy. This is how Dennis gets Robert's respect. 'I love to watch people who make what they do look easy. No flaws, nothing sticking out,' he says about Dennis's act. A third party comments, 'The guy high in the air, twisting and turning, is in control of himself, showing how cool he is. And Robert's cool. He keeps Dennis around because he respects him as a man.' Women don't evaluate this kind of behaviour in quite the same way. When Dennis douses his clothing in high-test gasoline and torches himself for a fireball jump, Robert says, 'Man.' But his female companion says, 'Big fucking deal.' When women do admire Dennis, they're looking at his body – what might be in it for them. But Robert's admiring the guts and the technique.

Billy Darwin, Dennis's employer, has his own version of 'big fucking deal'. He makes the mistake of thinking that the thing is easy because it looks easy. He belittles what Dennis does, 'sounding like a nice guy while putting you in your place, looking down at what you did for a living', and then he tries diving off the tower himself to demonstrate his cool and to show what a snap it is. He comes to grief.

And this, possibly, is our one small peek behind the scenes, to the shadows where the author lurks. Could it be that Mr Leonard has heard a few too many times that the thing he's done professionally now for four decades, or thirty-seven times, is really easy because he makes it look easy? Just because it's an amusement park and people are entertained by what you do, does that mean it's not a serious skill? Could it be that he'd like to see a few of those kinds of commentators try jumping off the tower themselves? If you've been to the crossroads, and made the deal, and got the mojo – which turns out to be dependent on a great deal of hard work and practice, just like sleight-of-hand – wouldn't you maybe get a trifle riled by that kind of misjudgement from time to time?

Not so as to lose your cool, mind you. Not so much as that.

NOTES

1. Le Carré gave these views in his acceptance speech when granted an honorary degree by the University of Edinburgh.

2. 'Robert Taylor' was the assumed name of the actor who, besides being a famous romantic lead, starred in a huge number of crime and western films. He played, for instance, Billy the Kid in the eponymous film in 1941. As someone says in *Tishomingo Blues*, 'working for Robert . . . was like being in the fucking movies'.

3. It's odd to find the sentiments of the Blue Fairy in *Pinocchio* on the lips of Robert Taylor. But then, wishing upon a star, makes no difference who you are, is partly what distinguishes Taylor from the bad guys: he's dreaming his own version of the American Dream.

4. Robert Taylor is the mirror image of Willy Loman of *Death of a Salesman*. The latter is the dishonest 'honest' man, the former the honest dishonest one.

5. See for instance the Grimms' tale 'The Devil's Sooty Brother'. In such stories the hero, if lucky and prompt, can obtain the Devil's bounty and keep his own soul too, and this is what Dennis does.

6. For much more, see Lewis Hyde's thorough study, *Trickster Makes This World*, New York: Farrar, Straus and Giroux, 1998. Hyde makes the point however that in a nation paved from end to end with snake-oil salesmen, the Trickster doesn't function quite as usual.

7. The character who drones on about baseball is intended to be boring. The trick is to see how he interjects his obsession into any topic whatsoever. If you get tired of it you can do what Dennis does – tune out.

34

The Indelible Woman

I first read Virginia Woolf's *To the Lighthouse* when I was nineteen. I had to. It was on a course – 'The Twentieth-Century Novel', or some such. I got on all right with the nineteenth-century novel – the works of Dickens were, I felt, just as such things should be, at least in England: lots of mad people and fog. Nor did I do too badly with certain twentieth-century novels. Hemingway I could more or less fathom – I'd played war as a child, I'd gone fishing a lot, I knew the approximate rules of both, I was aware that boys were laconic. Camus was depressing enough for the late-adolescent me, with existential angst and gritty, unpleasant sex into the bargain. Faulkner was my idea of what could be possible for – well, for myself as a writer (which was what I wanted to be), hysteria in steaming, bug-infested swamps being my notion of artistic verisimilitude. (I knew those bugs. I knew those swamps, or swamps very like them. I knew that hysteria.) That Faulkner could also be outrageously funny went – at the age I was then – right past me.

But Virginia Woolf was off on a siding as far as my nineteen-year-old self was concerned. Why go to the lighthouse at all, and why make such a fuss about going or not going? What was the book about? Why was everyone so stuck on Mrs Ramsay, who went around in floppy old hats and fooled around in her garden, and indulged her husband with spoonfuls of tactful acquiescence, just like my surely boring mother? Why would anyone put up with Mr Ramsay, that Tennyson-quoting tyrant, eccentric disappointed genius though he might be? Someone had blundered, he shouts, but this did not cut any ice with me. And what about Lily Briscoe, who wanted to be an artist and made much of this desire, but who didn't seem to be able to paint very well, or not to her own satisfaction? In Woolfland, things were so tenuous. They were so elusive. They were so inconclusive. They were so deeply unfathomable. They were like the line written by a wispy poet in a Katherine Mansfield short story: 'Why must it always be tomato soup?'

At nineteen, I'd never known anyone who had died, with the exception of my grandfather, who'd been old and far away. I'd never been to a funeral. I understood nothing of that kind of loss – of the crumbling of the physical texture of lives lived, the way the meaning of a place could change because those who used to be in it were no longer there. I knew nothing about the hopelessness and the necessity of trying to capture such lives – to rescue them, to keep them from vanishing altogether.

Although I'd been guilty of many artistic failures, such was my callowness that I did not yet recognize them as such. Lily Briscoe suffers the aggression of an insecure man who keeps telling her that women can't paint and women can't write, but I didn't see why she should be so upset about it: the guy was obviously a drip, so who cared what he thought? Anyway, no one had ever said that sort of thing to me, not yet. (Little did I know they would soon begin.) I didn't realize what weight such pronouncements could have, even when uttered by fools, because of the many centuries of heavily respectable authority that lay behind them.

This past summer, forty-three years later, I read *To the Lighthouse* again. No particular reason: I was in that very Canadian space, 'the cottage', and so was the book, and I'd read all the murder mysteries. So I thought I'd try again.

How was it that, this time, everything in the book fell so completely into place? How could I have missed it — above all, the patterns, the artistry — the first time through? How could I have missed the resonance of Mr Ramsay's Tennyson quotation, coming as it does like a prophecy of the First World War? How could I not have grasped that the person painting and the one writing were in effect the same? ('Women can't write, women can't paint . . .') And the way time passes over everything like a cloud, and solid objects flicker and dissolve? And the way Lily's picture of Mrs Ramsay — incomplete, insufficient, doomed to be stuck in an attic — becomes, as she adds the one line that ties it all together at the end, the book we've just read?

Some books have to wait until you're ready for them. So much, in reading, is a matter of luck. And what luck I'd just had! (Or so I muttered to myself, putting on my floppy old hat, going out to fool around in my unfathomable garden . . .)

35

The Queen of Quinkdom

The Birthday of the World is Ursula K. Le Guin's tenth collection of stories. In it she demonstrates once again why she is the reigning queen of . . . but immediately we come to a difficulty, for what is the fitting name of her kingdom? Or, in view of her abiding concern with the ambiguities of gender, her queendom, or perhaps – considering how she likes to mix and match – her quinkdom? Or may she more properly be said to have not one such realm, but two?

'Science fiction' is the box in which her work is usually placed, but it's an awkward box: it bulges with discards from elsewhere. Into it have been crammed all those stories that don't fit comfortably into the family room of the socially realistic novel or the more formal parlour of historical fiction, or other compartmentalized genres: westerns, gothics, horrors, gothic romances, and the novels of war, crime, and spies. Its subdivisions include science fiction proper (gizmo-riddled and theory-based space travel, time travel, or cybertravel to other worlds, with aliens frequent); science-fiction fantasy (dragons are common; the gizmos are less plausible, and may include wands); and speculative fiction (human society and its possible future forms, which are either much better than what we have now, or much worse). However, the membranes separating these subdivisions are permeable, and osmotic flow from one to another is the norm.

The lineage of 'science fiction', broadly considered, is very long, and some of its literary ancestors are of the utmost respectability. Alberto Manguel has catalogued many in *The Dictionary of Imaginary Places*: Plato's account of Atlantis is among them, and Sir Thomas More's *Utopia* and Jonathan Swift's *Gulliver's Travels*. Accounts of voyages to unknown realms with bizarre inhabitants are as old as Herodotus in his wilder moments, as old as *The Thousand and One Nights*, as old as Thomas the Rhymer. Folk tales, the Norse Sagas, and the adventure-romances of chivalry are not-so-distant cousins of such tales, and have been drawn on by hundreds of imitators of *The Lord of the Rings* and/or *Conan the Conqueror* – works which previously fetched their water from the same wells, as did their precursors, George MacDonald and the H. Rider Haggard of *She*.

Jules Verne is probably the best known of the early gizmo-fictionalists, but Mary Shelley's *Frankenstein* could be thought of as the first 'science fiction' – that is, the first fiction that had real science in it – inspired as it was by experiments with electricity, in particular the galvanizing of corpses. Some of her preoccupations have stayed with the genre (or genres) ever since: most specifically, what is the price that must be paid by Promethean Man for stealing fire from Heaven? Indeed, some commentators have proposed 'science fiction' as the last fictional repository for theological speculation. Heaven, Hell, and aerial transport by means of wings having been more or less abandoned after Milton, outer space was the only remaining neighbourhood where beings resembling gods, angels, and demons might still be found. J. R. R. Tolkien's friend and fellow fantasist C. S. Lewis even went so far as to compose a 'science fiction' trilogy – very light on science, but heavy on theology, the 'space ship' being a coffin filled with roses and the temptation of Eve being re-enacted on the planet of Venus, complete with luscious fruit.

Rearranged human societies have been a constant in the tradition as well, and they have been used both to criticize our present state of affairs and to suggest more pleasant alternatives. Swift depicted an ideal civilization, although – how English! – it was populated by horses. The nineteenth century, cheered on by its successes with sewage systems and prison reform, produced a number of earnestly hopeful speculative fictions. William Morris's *News from Nowhere* and Edward Bellamy's *Looking Backward* are foremost among them, but this approach became such a vogue that it was satirized, not only by Gilbert and Sullivan's operetta *Utopia Limited*, but also by Samuel Butler's *Erewhon*, where illness is a crime and crime is an illness.

However, as the optimism of the nineteenth century gave way to the Procrustean social dislocations of the twentieth – most notably in the former Soviet Union and the former Third Reich – literary utopias, whether serious or sardonic, were displaced by darker versions of themselves. H. G. Wells's *The Time Machine*, *The War of the Worlds*, and *The Island of Dr Moreau* prefigure what was shortly to follow. *Brave New World* and *1984* are of course the best known of these many prescient badlands, with Karel Čapek's *R.U.R.* and the nightmarish fables of John Wyndham running close behind.

It's too bad that one term – 'science fiction' – has served for so many variants, and too bad also that this term has acquired a dubious if not downright sluttish reputation. True, the proliferation of sci-fi in the twenties and thirties gave rise to a great many bug-eyed-monster-bestrewn space operas that were published in pulp magazines and followed by films and television shows that drew heavily on this odoriferous cache. (Who could ever forget *The Creeping Eye*, *The Head That Wouldn't Die*, or *The Attack of the Sixty-Foot Woman*? A better question: Why can't we forget them?)

In brilliant hands, however, the form can be brilliant, as witness the virtuoso use of sci-trash material in Kurt Vonnegut's *Slaughterhouse Five*, or Russell Hoban's linguistically inventive *Riddley Walker*, or Ray Bradbury's *Fahrenheit 451* and *The Martian Chronicles*.

(Jorge Luis Borges was a fan of this last book, which is no surprise.) Sci-fi is sometimes just an excuse for dressed-up
swashbuckling and kinky sex, but it can also provide a kit for
examining the paradoxes and torments of what was once fondly
referred to as the human condition: What is our true nature,
where did we come from, where are we going, what are we doing
to ourselves, of what extremes might we be capable? Within the
frequently messy sandbox of sci-fi fantasy, some of the most
accomplished and suggestive intellectual play of the last century
has taken place.

Which brings us to Ursula K. Le Guin. No question about her literary quality: her graceful prose, carefully thought-through
premises, psychological insight, and intelligent perception have
earned her the National Book Award, the Kafka Award, five Hugos,
five Nebulas, a Newbery, a Jupiter, a Gandalf, and an armful of
other awards, great and small. Her first two books, *Planet of Exile* and
Rocannon's World, were published in 1966, and since then she has published sixteen novels, as well as ten collections of stories.

Collectively, these books have created two major parallel universes: the universe of the Ekumen, which is sci-fi proper – space
ships, travel among worlds, and so forth – and the world of
Earthsea. The latter must be called 'fantasy', I suppose, since it
contains dragons and witches and even a school for wizards,
though this institution is a long way from the Hogwarts of Harry
Potter. The Ekumen series may be said – very broadly – to concern itself with the nature of human nature: How far can we
stretch and still remain human? What is essential to our being,
what is contingent? The Earthsea series is occupied – again, very
broadly speaking – with the nature of reality and the necessity of
mortality, and also with language in relation to its matrix. (That's
heavy weather to make of a series that has been promoted as
suitable for age twelve, but perhaps the fault lies in the marketing directors. Like *Alice in Wonderland*, these tales speak to readers
on many levels.)

Le Guin's preoccupations are not divided into two strictly separate packages, of course: both of her worlds are scrupulously attentive to the uses and misuses of language; both have their characters fret over social gaffes and get snarled up in foreign customs; both worry about death. But in the Ekumen universe, although there is much strangeness, there is no magic, apart from the magic inherent in creation itself.

The astonishing thing about Le Guin as a writer is that she managed to create these two realms, not only in parallel, but at the same time. The first Earthsea book, *A Wizard of Earthsea*, appeared in 1968, and *The Left Hand of Darkness*, the famous classic from the Ekumen series, in 1969. Either one would have been sufficient to establish Le Guin's reputation as a mistress of its genre; both together make one suspect that the writer has the benefit of arcane drugs or creative double-jointedness or ambidexterity. Not for nothing did Le Guin invoke handedness in her fourth title: as soon as we start talking about the *left* hand, all sorts of biblical connotations gather. (Although the left hand is the sinister one, God too has a left hand, so left hands can't be all bad. Should your right hand know what your left hand is doing, and if not, why not? And so forth.) As Walter Benjamin once said, the decisive blows are struck left-handed.

Ursula K. Le Guin has continued to explore and describe and dramatize both of her major fictional realms over the thirty-six years that have passed since her first novel was published. But since the stories in *The Birthday of the World* are Ekumen stories – with two exceptions – it's as well to concentrate on the science-fiction world rather than on the fantasy one. The general premises of the Ekumen series are as follows. There are many habitable planets in the universe. Long, long ago they were 'seeded' by a people called the Hainish, space travellers from an earth-like planet, after which time passed, disruptions occurred, and each society was left alone to develop along different lines.

Now, a benevolent federation called the Ekumen having been established, explorers are being sent out to see what has become of these far-flung but still hominid or perhaps even human societies. Conquest is not the aim, nor is missionary work: non-invasive, non-directive understanding and recording are the functions required of such explorers or ambassadors, who are known as Mobiles. Various gizmos are provided to allow them to function amid the alien corn, and they are provided with a handy widget called the 'ansible', a piece of technology we should all have because it allows for instantaneous transmission of information, thus cancelling out the delaying effects of the fourth dimension. Also, it never seems to crash like your Internet email programme. I'm all for it.

Here it is necessary to mention that Le Guin's mother was a writer, her husband is a historian, and her father was an anthropologist; thus she has been surrounded all her life by people whose interests have dovetailed with her own. The writing connection, through her mother, is obvious. Her husband's historical knowledge must have come in very handy: there's more than an echo in her work of the kinds of usually unpleasant events that change what we call 'history'. But her father's discipline, anthropology, deserves special mention.

   If the 'fantasy' end of science fiction owes a large debt to folk tale and myth and saga, the 'science fiction' end owes an equally large debt to the development of archeology and anthropology as serious disciplines, as distinct from the tomb-looting and exploration-for-exploitation that preceded them and continued alongside them. Layard's discovery of Nineveh in the 1840s had the effect of a can opener on Victorian thinking about the past; Troy and Pompeii and ancient Egypt were similarly mesmerizing. Through new discoveries and fresh excavations, European concepts of past civilizations were rearranged, imaginative doors were opened, wardrobe choices were expanded. If things were once otherwise, perhaps they could be otherwise again, especially where clothing and sex were concerned – two matters that particularly fascinated Victorian and early-twentieth-century imaginative writers, who longed for less of the former and more of the latter.

Anthropology arrived a little later. Cultures were discovered in remote places that were very different from the modern West, and rather than being wiped out or subjugated, they were taken seriously and studied. How are these people like us? How are they different? Is it possible to understand them? What are their foundation myths, their beliefs about an afterlife? How do they arrange their marriages, how do their kinship systems work? What are their foods? How about their (a) clothing and (b) sex? Which were usually discovered – through the work of various perhaps over-eager inquirers such as Margaret Mead – to be (a) scantier and (b) more satisfactory than ours?

Anthropologists do – or are supposed to do – more or less what the Mobiles in Le Guin's Ekumen construction are supposed to do: they go to distant shores, they look, they explore foreign societies and try to figure them out. Then they record, and then they transmit. Le Guin knows the tricks of the trade, and also the pitfalls: her Mobiles are mistrusted and misled while they are in the field, just as real anthropologists have been. They're used as political pawns, they're scorned as outsiders, they're feared because they have unknown powers. But they are also dedicated professionals and trained observers, and human beings with personal lives of their own. This is what makes them and the stories they tell believable, and Le Guin's handling of them engaging as writing in its own right.

It's informative to compare two of Le Guin's introductions: the one she wrote for *The Left Hand of Darkness* in 1976, seven years after the book was first published, and the foreword she's now written for *The Birthday of the World*. *The Left Hand of Darkness* takes place on the planet of Gethen, or Winter, where the inhabitants are neither men nor women nor hermaphrodites. Instead they have phases: a nonsexual phase is followed by a sexual phase, and during the latter each person changes into whichever gender is suitable for the occasion. Thus anyone at all may be, over a lifetime, both mother and father, both penetrator and penetree. As the story opens, the 'king'

is both mad and pregnant, and the non-Gethenian observer from
the Ekumen is nothing if not confused.

This novel appeared at the beginning of the hottest period of
1970s feminism, when emotions were running very high on subjects
having to do with genders and their roles. Le Guin was accused of
wanting everyone to be an androgyne and of predicting that in
the future they would be; conversely, of being anti-feminist
because she'd used the pronoun 'he' to denote persons not in
'kemmer' – the sexual phase.

Her introduction to *The Left Hand of Darkness* is therefore somewhat brisk. Science fiction should not be merely extrapolative, she
says; it should not take a present trend and project it into the
future, thus arriving via logic at a prophetic truth. Science fiction
cannot predict, nor can any fiction, the variables being too many.
Her own book is a 'thought-experiment', like *Frankenstein*. It begins
with 'Let's say,' follows that with a premise, and then watches to see
what happens next. 'In a story so conceived,' she says, 'the moral
complexity proper to the modern novel need not be sacrificed . . .
thought and intuition can move freely within bounds set only by
the terms of the experiment, which may be very large indeed.'

The purpose of a thought-experiment, she writes, is to 'describe
reality, the present world'. 'A novelist's business is lying' – lying
interpreted in the novelist's usual way, that is, as a devious method
of truth-telling. Consequently the androgyny described in her
book is neither prediction nor prescription, just description:
androgyny, metaphorically speaking, is a feature of all human
beings. With those who don't understand that metaphor is
metaphor and fiction is fiction, she is more than a little irritated.
One suspects she's received a lot of extremely odd fan mail.

The foreword to *The Birthday of the World* is mellower. Twenty-six
years later, the author has fought her battles and is an established
feature of the sci-fi landscape. She can afford to be less didactic,
more charmingly candid, a little scattier. The universe of the
Ekumen now feels comfortable to her, like 'an old shirt'. No sense
in expecting it to be consistent, though: 'Its Time Line is like

something a kitten pulled out of the knitting basket, and its history consists largely of gaps.' In this foreword, Le Guin describes process rather than theory: the genesis of each story, the problems she had to think her way through. Typically, she doesn't concoct her worlds: she finds herself in them, and then begins to explore them, just like, well, an anthropologist. 'First to create difference,' she says, '. . . then to let the fiery arc of human emotion leap and close the gap: this acrobatics of the imagination fascinates and satisfies me as almost no other.'

There are seven shorter stories in *The Birthday of the World*, and one that might qualify as a novella. Six of the first seven are Ekumen stories – they're part of the 'old shirt'. The seventh probably belongs there, though its author isn't sure. The eighth is set in a different universe altogether – the generic, shared, science-fiction 'future'. All but the eighth are largely concerned with – as Le Guin says – 'peculiar arrangements of gender and sexuality'.

All imagined worlds must make some provision for sex, with or without black leather and tentacles, and the peculiarity of the arrangements is an old motif in science fiction: one thinks not only of Charlotte Perkins Gilman's *Herland*, where the genders live separately, but also of W. H. Hudson's *A Crystal Age*, featuring an ant-like neuter state, or John Wyndham's 'Consider Her Ways', also based on a hymenoptera model, or Marge Piercey's *Woman on the Edge of Time*, which tries for absolute gender equality. (Men breastfeed: watch for this trend.) But Le Guin takes things much farther. In the first story, 'Coming of Age in Karhide', we see Gethen/Winter not through the eyes of a Mobile, but through those of a Gethenian just coming into adolescence: Which gender will s/he turn into first? This story is not only erotic, but happy. Why not, in a world where sex is always either spectacular or of no concern whatsoever?

Things aren't so jolly in 'The Matter of Seggri', where there's a gender imbalance: far more women than men. The women run everything, and marry each other as life partners. The rare boy children are spoiled by the women, but as men they must live a segregated life in castles, where they dress up, show off, stage public fights, and are rented out as studs. They don't have much fun. It's like being trapped in the World Wrestling Federation, forever.

'Unchosen Love' and 'Mountain Ways' take place on a world called O, created by Le Guin in *A Fisherman of the Inland Sea*. On O, you must be married to three other people, but can have sex with only two of them. The quartets must consist of a Morning man and a Morning woman – who can't have sex – and an Evening man and an Evening woman, who also can't have sex. But the Morning man is expected to have sex with the Evening woman and also the Evening man, and the Evening woman is expected to have sex with the Morning man and also the Morning woman. Putting these quartets together is one of the problems the characters face, and keeping them straight – who's for you, who's taboo – is a problem for both reader and writer. Le Guin had to draw charts. As she says, 'I like thinking about complex social relationships which produce and frustrate highly charged emotional relationships.'

'Solitude' is a meditative story about a world in which conviviality is deeply distrusted. Women live alone in their own houses in an 'auntring' or village, where they make baskets and do gardening, and practise the non-verbal art of 'being aware'. Only the children go from house to house, learning lore. When girls come of age they form part of an auntring, but boys must go off to join adolescent packs and scratch a living in the wilderness. They fight it out, and those who survive become breeding males, living shyly in hermit huts, guarding the auntrings from a distance, and being visited by the women, who 'scout' for purposes of mating. This setup, despite its spiritual satisfactions, would not suit everyone.

'Old Music and the Slave Women' comes very close to home, inspired as it was by a visit to a former plantation in the American South. On the planet of Werel, slavers and anti-slavers are at war, and sex among the slavers is a matter of raping the field hands. The chief character, an intelligence officer with the Ekumen embassy, gets into arguments over human rights and then bad trouble. Of all the stories, this one comes closest to substantiating Le Guin's claim that science fiction describes our own world. Werel could be any society torn by civil war: wherever it's happening, it's always brutal, and Le Guin, although at times a movingly lyrical writer, has never shied away from necessary gore.

The title story is constructed on an Inca base, with a splash of ancient Egypt. A man and a woman together form God. Both positions are hereditary and created by brother–sister marriage; the duties of God include divination by dancing, which causes the world to be born anew each year. Governance is carried out by God's messengers, or 'angels'. What happens when a foreign but powerful presence enters this highly structured world and the belief system that sustains it crumbles? You can imagine, or you can read 'The Conquest of Peru'. Nevertheless, this delicate story is strangely courageous, strangely hopeful: the world ends, but then, too, it is always beginning.

The last story, 'Paradises Lost', continues the note of renewal. Many generations have been born and have died on board a long-distance space ship. During the voyage a new religion has sprung up, whose adherents believe they are actually, now, in Heaven. (If so, Heaven is just as boring as some have always feared.) Then the ship reaches the destination proposed for it centuries earlier, and its inhabitants must decide whether to remain in 'Heaven' or to descend to a 'dirtball' whose flora, fauna, and microbes are completely alien to them. The most enjoyable part of this story, for me, was the release from claustrophobia: Try as I might, I couldn't imagine why anyone would prefer the ship.

Le Guin is on the side of the dirtball, too; and, by extension, of our very own dirtball. Whatever else she may do – wherever her curious intelligence may take her, whatever twists and knots of motive and plot and genitalia she may invent – she never loses touch with her reverence for the immense *what is*. All her stories are, as she has said, metaphors for the one human story; all her fantastic planets are this one, however disguised. 'Paradises Lost' shows us our own natural world as a freshly discovered Paradise Regained, a realm of wonder; and in this, Le Guin is a quintessentially American writer, of the sort for whom the quest for the Peaceable Kingdom is ongoing. Perhaps, as Jesus hinted, the kingdom of God is within; or perhaps, as William Blake glossed, it is within a wild flower, seen aright.

The story – and the book – ends with a minimalist dance, as an old woman and a crippled old man celebrate, indeed worship, the ordinary dirt that sustains them after they have left the ship. 'Swaying, she lifted her bare feet from the dirt and set them down again while he stood still, holding her hands. They danced together that way.'

36

Victory Gardens

When I was small, people had Victory Gardens. This was during the Second World War, and the idea was that if people grew their own vegetables, then the food produced by the farmers would be freed up for use by the army. There was another strong motivator: rationing was in effect for things you were unlikely to be able to grow yourself, such as sugar, butter, milk, tea, cheese and meat, so the more you could grow, the better you would eat, and the better the soldiers would eat, too. Thus, by digging and hoeing and weeding and watering, you too could help win the war.

But people did not live on vegetables and fruit alone. Anything resembling protein or fat was precious. Shortening, margarine and bacon drippings were cherished; gizzards, livers, feet and necks were not scorned. Bits and scraps that today would be carelessly tossed into the trash were hoarded and treasured, making their way from their first appearance as, say, a roasted chicken, through various other incarnations as noodle-and-leftovers casseroles, soups and stews, and mystery ingredients in pot pies. A housewife's skill was measured by the number of times she could serve up the same thing without your knowing it.

Careful planning was required; waste was frowned on. This

meant that everything, not only from such things as chickens but from the garden, had to be used, and, if necessary, preserved. Home freezing hadn't arrived yet, so canning and preserving were major activities, especially in the late summer, when the garden would produce more than the family could eat. Housewives cooked up vast quantities of tomato sauce, pickles, green beans, strawberries, applesauce – vegetables and fruits of all kinds. These would be eaten in the winter, along with the cabbages and the winter squash and the root vegetables – beets, carrots, turnips and potatoes – that had been stored in a cool place.

As children growing up in this era, we knew that every seedling was precious. We were part of the system: we weeded and watered, we picked off cabbage worms and tomato worms and potato bugs. We dug peelings and cores and husks back into the soil; we fended off woodchucks; we sprinkled wood ashes. If lucky enough to be near a source of blueberries, we picked them; and we picked peas and beans, and we dug potatoes. I can't claim that all of this was spontaneous labour, joyfully performed: such tasks were chores. But the connection between tending the vegetables and eating the results was clear. Food did not come wrapped in plastic from the supermarket – there were hardly any supermarkets, anyway. It came out of the ground or it grew on a bush or tree, and it needed water and sunlight and proper fertilization.

My mother's generation was brought up strictly: children were expected to finish everything on their plates, whether they liked it or not, and if they failed to do this they were made to sit at the dinner table until they did. Frequently they were told to remember other children who were starving – the Armenians, the Chinese. I used to think this was both harsh – why force a child to eat when it wasn't hungry? – and ridiculous – what good would eating your bread crusts do for the Armenians? But this method doubtless had at its heart an insistence on respect. Many people had laboured to produce the food on the plate, among them the parents, who had either grown it or paid hard-earned cash for it. You could not snub this food. You should show a proper gratitude.

Hence the once-widespread practice of saying grace at meals, which has fallen into disuse. Why be grateful for something – now – so easy to come by?

In the plotline of life on earth, gardens are a recent twist. They date back to perhaps ten thousand years ago, when the gathering and hunting that had been the prevailing model for 99 per cent of human history could no longer sustain societies in the face of diminishing game and wild food supplies.

When the total population of the earth was less than four million people – before, the experts estimate, about ten thousand years ago – the gathering and hunting way of life was still viable. The myth of the Golden Age appears to have some foundation in fact: food was there in the wild, for the taking, and people didn't have to spend much of their time obtaining it. After that point, conditions became harder, as communities had to adapt more labour-intensive stratagems to feed themselves. 'Agriculture' is sometimes used to denote any form of cultivation or domestication – of herd animals for meat and milk, of garden crops and fruit trees, of field crops such as wheat and barley. Sometimes a distinction is made between 'agriculture', in which large areas are farmed using the plough to break the ground – traditionally a male activity – and 'horticulture', in which smaller, individual garden plots are cultivated, traditionally by women. 'Horticulture' is thought to have come first, but all agree that there was a long period of transition in which gathering and hunting, horticulture and agriculture, existed side by side.

Many ills have been ascribed to agriculture. In gathering and hunting cultures, food was – as a rule – obtained and eaten as needed. But once agriculture became firmly established – once crops could be harvested and stored, once surpluses could be accumulated, and, not incidentally, transported, exchanged, destroyed, and stolen – social strata became possible, with slaves at the lower end, peasants above them, and a ruling class on top that made no physical effort in order to eat. Armies could march on surplus food supplies; religious hierarchies could tithe; kings could preside; taxes could be levied. Crop monocultures became widespread, with a dependence on only a few kinds of food, resulting not only in mal-nutrition, but in famine at times of crop failure.

A city-dweller's relation to food is – as a system – closer to the gathering–hunting model than to the horticultural–agricultural one. You don't grow the food yourself, or raise it in the form of an animal. Instead you go to the place where the food is – the super-market, most likely. Someone else has done the killing, in the case of animal food, or the primary picking, in the case of vegetables, but essentially the shopper is a gatherer. His or her skills consist in knowing where the good stuff is and tracking it down if it's rare. The shopping experience is given all the trappings of a walk in a magic forest – soft music plays, the colours of packages are super-naturally bright, food is displayed as if it's there by miracle. All you have to do is reach out your hand, as in the Golden Age. And then pay, of course.

Such a system disguises origins. The food in shops is dirt-free, and as bloodless as possible. Yet everything we eat comes – in one way or another – out of the earth.

The first garden I can remember was in northern Quebec, where my father ran a small field insect research station. The area was a glacial scrape – a region where the glaciers had removed the top-soil thousands of years ago, scraping down to the granite bedrock. Thousands of years after their retreat, the soil was just a thin layer on top of sand or gravel. My parents used this sandy soil as the basis for their garden. Luckily they had a source of manure, from a lumber camp – in those days, horses were still used in winter, to drag the felled trees down to the lake for eventual transport to the mill by water. My parents ferried boatloads of this manure to their fenced-in sandy patch, where they dug it in. From this unpromis-ing ground they raised – among other things – peas, beans, carrots, radishes, lettuce, spinach, Swiss chard, and even the occasional flower. Nasturtiums are what I remember, and the vivid blossoms of the scarlet runner beans, a favourite with hummingbirds. The moral: almost any patch of dirt can be a garden, with enough elbow grease and horse manure.

That garden occurred in the 1940s, when the war was still going on, horticulture in the form of Victory Gardens was still widely practised, and every morsel of food was treasured.

After the war the post-war boom set in, and attitudes underwent a major change. After a long period of anxiety and hard work and tragedy, people wanted more ease in their lives. Military production switched off, the manufacture of consumer goods switched on. Home appliances proliferated: the outdoor clothesline was replaced by the dryer, the wringer washer by the automatic. Supermarkets sprang up. Pre-packaging arrived. Simple-minded abundance was the order of the day.

The period from 1950 to 2000 might be characterized as the Disposable Period. Waste – including pre-planned obsolescence – was no longer seen as an evil and a sin. It became a positive thing, because the more you threw out, the more you would consume, and that would drive the economy, and everyone would become more prosperous. Wouldn't they?

This model works fine as long as there's an endless supply of goods funnelling into the in end of the pipe. But it breaks down when the source of supply becomes exhausted. The ultimate source of supply is the biosphere itself. But in the fifties, that too appeared to be inexhaustible. And so the party continued. What a thrill, to eat only half of your hamburger, then toss the rest!

There was an undeniable emotional charge to throwing stuff out. Scrimping, saving and hoarding make a person feel poor – think of Scrooge, in *A Christmas Carol* – whereas dispensing largesse, whether in the form of a prize goose, as in Scrooge's case, or in the form of filling up your garbage can with junk you no longer want, makes you feel rich. Saving is heavy, discarding is light. Why do we feel this way? Once we were nomads, and nomads don't carry around grand pianos. They don't hoard food; instead they move to where food is. They leave a light footprint, as the green folk say. Well, it's a theory.

But we can't all be nomads any more. There isn't enough space left for that.

Many people gave up their gardens after the war. My parents kept on with theirs, because they said fresh food tasted better. (This is actually true.) The age of full-blown pesticides was just arriving, and that may have had something to do with it as well. My father was an early opponent of widespread pesticide use, partly because this was his field of study. According to him, spraying forests to kill infestations of budworm and sawfly simply arrested the infestation, after which the insects would develop a resistance to the poisons used on them and would continue on their rampage. Meanwhile you'd have killed off their natural enemies, which would no longer be around to fight them. The effects of these poisons on human beings was unknown, but could not be discounted. At that time his views were considered quaint.

Thus the second major garden in my life was in Toronto. Again, the soil was unpromising: heavy clay, which was sticky in the rain but would bake to a hard finish during dry spells. The soil was particularly good for growing giant dandelions and huge clumps of couch grass. It took a lot of work to turn it into anything resembling a garden. Kitchen scraps were composted, fall leaves were dug into the ground by the bushel.

By this time I was a teenager, and was expected to do quite a lot of weeding and watering. News for parents: weeding and watering someone else's garden is not quite as engaging as weeding and watering your own. The high points were the time when I shot a marauding woodchuck with my bow (the arrow was a target arrow, not a hunting arrow, so it bounced off) and the other time when I pulled up all of my father's experimental Jerusalem artichokes by mistake.

Once past my teenage years, I gave up gardening for a time. I'd had enough of it. Also I wasn't in a location that permitted it: I was an itinerant student and sometime teacher and market researcher and writer, and I moved fifteen times in ten years. In the early seventies, however, I found myself on a farm that had a barn with a large supply of well-rotted horse manure, and the temptation was too great to resist. For eight years we grew everything imaginable. To the staples we added corn, kohlrabi, asparagus, currants – red and white – and elderberries. We tried out new methods – potatoes grown in straw, marigolds to catch slugs. We canned, froze, dried; we made sauerkraut, not an experiment I would choose to repeat. We made wine, jams and jellies, beer. We raised our own chickens and ducks and sheep; we buried parsnips in holes in the ground, and carrots in boxes of sand in the root cellar.

It was a lot of work. This is one reason people don't do more home gardening.

The other, of course, is lack of land. The number of pumpkins you can raise on your apartment balcony is finite, and your wheat crop in this location would not be large.

Lack of land. Lack of *arable* land. To that we may add 'lack of sea', because the sea's resources are being destroyed as fast as the earth's. Soon we may have to add 'lack of fresh water' and even 'lack of breathable air'. There's no free lunch after all.

As a species, we're suffering from our own success. From a population of four million ten thousand years ago, we've increased to six billion today, and growing. The exponential population explosion that has occurred since 1750 was unprecedented in human history, and it will never be repeated. We must slow our growth rate as a species, or face a series of unimaginable environmental and human catastrophes. Arable land is finite, and much of it is rapidly being paved over, eroded, polluted, or depleted. The same rules apply to us as to other animals: no biological population can outlive the exhaustion of its resource base. It's an easy thing to demonstrate to children. Get them an ant farm, feed the ants, watch the ants increase in number. Then cut off the food supply. End of ants.

For *homo sapiens*, the major question of the twenty-first century will be, *How will we eat?* Already 80 per cent of the world's people exist on the starvation borderline. Will we see a sudden enormous crash, as in the mouse-and-lemming cycle? And if so, what then?

These are alarming thoughts to place in the foreword to a kindly and attractive book on school gardening. Such an admirable demonstration of care and careful planning, so much variety, such a symbol of hope. I don't apologize for these thoughts, however: the world I have just described is the one today's children will be facing unless there are some fairly large changes of direction.

The reasons for encouraging the school gardening movement are many. Gardens are educational, teaching as they do many lessons. Food grows in the ground, not in supermarkets; air, soil, sun and water are the four necessary ingredients; composting is a fine notion; front lawns are a water-gobbling waste of space; the individual can be an instrument for positive change; unless you're a geologist, plants are more interesting than gravel; beetles come in many forms; worms are good; nature must be respected; we are part of nature.

All of these are positive concepts, but fifty years ago – even thirty years ago – they would have been viewed as extra, frilly, prissy, goody-goody. Even now, some in our society would place them in this slot: the hard stuff, the right stuff to grind into the minds of children, is how to make a lot of money.

But money's useless when there's nothing to eat. So there's another set of skills to be learned from school gardens: how to grow your own food. Perhaps today's children will need these skills. Perhaps they'll find themselves in some grim collective dedicated to turning golf courses back into market gardens and superhighways into very long grain fields, and front lawns into potato plots. Perhaps the Victory Garden will make a forced comeback due to scarcity.

Or perhaps our species will solve its problems before droughts and famines become endemic.

Then again, perhaps not.

37

Mortification

Mortifications never end. There is always a never-before-experienced one waiting just around the corner. As Scarlett O'Hara might have said, 'Tomorrow is another mortification.' Such anticipations give us hope: God isn't finished with us yet, because these things are sent to try us. I've never been entirely sure what that meant. Where there is blushing, there is life? Something like that.

While waiting for the mortifications yet to come, when I'll have dentures and they'll shoot out of my mouth on some august public occasion, or else I will topple off the podium or be sick on my presenter, I'll tell you of three mortifications past.

Early period

Long, long ago, when I was only twenty-nine and my first novel had just been published, I was living in Edmonton, Alberta, Canada. It was 1969. The women's movement had begun, in New York City, but it had not yet reached Edmonton, Alberta. It was November. It was freezing cold. I was freezing cold, and I went about wearing a secondhand fur coat – muskrat, I think – that I'd bought at the Salvation Army for $25. I also had a fur hat I'd made out of a rabbit shruggie – a shruggie was a sort of fur bolero – by deleting the arms and sewing up the armholes.

My publisher arranged my first-ever book signing. I was very excited. Once I'd peeled off the muskrats and rabbits, there I would be, inside the Hudson's Bay Company Department Store, where it was cosily warm – this in itself was exciting – with lines of eager, smiling readers waiting to purchase my book and have me scribble on it.

The signing was at a table set up in the Men's Sock and Underwear Department. I don't know what the thinking was behind this. There I sat, at lunch hour, smiling away, surrounded by piles of a novel called *The Edible Woman*. Men in overcoats and galoshes and toe rubbers and scarves and earmuffs passed by my table, intent on the purchase of boxer shorts. They looked at me, then at the title of my novel. Subdued panic broke out. There was the sound of a muffled stampede as dozens of galoshes and toe rubbers shuffled rapidly in the other direction.

I sold two copies.

Middle period

By this time I'd achieved a spoonful or two of notoriety, enough so that my US publisher could arrange to get me onto an American TV talk show. It was an afternoon show, which in those days – could it have been the late seventies? – meant variety. It was the sort of show at which they played pop music, and then you were supposed to sashay through a bead curtain, carrying your trained koala bear, or Japanese flower arrangement, or book.

I waited behind the bead curtain. There was an act on before me. It was a group from the Colostomy Association, who were talking about their colostomies, and about how to use the colostomy bag.

I knew I was doomed. No book could ever be that riveting.

W.C. Fields vowed never to share the stage with a child or a dog; I can add to that, 'Never follow the Colostomy Association.' (Or any other thing having to do with frightening bodily items, such as the port-wine-stain removal technique that once preceded me in Australia.) The problem is, you lose all interest in yourself and your so-called 'work' – 'What did you say your name was? And tell us the plot of your book, just in a couple of sentences, please' – so immersed are you in picturing the gruesome intricacies of . . . but never mind.

Modern period

Recently I was on a TV show in Mexico. By this time I was famous, insofar as writers are, although perhaps not quite so famous in Mexico as in other places. This was the kind of show where they put make-up on you, and I had eyelashes that stood out like little black shelves.

The interviewer was a very smart man who had lived – as it turned out – only a few blocks from my house, in Toronto, when he'd been a student and I'd been elsewhere, being mortified at my first book signing in Edmonton. We went merrily along through the interview, chatting about world affairs and such, until he hit me with the F-question. The do-you-consider-yourself-a-feminist question. I lobbed the ball briskly back over the net ('Women are human beings, don't you agree?'), but then he blindsided me. It was the eyelashes: they were so thick I didn't see it coming.

'Do you consider yourself *feminine?*' he said.

Nice Canadian middle-aged women go all strange when asked this by Mexican talk-show hosts somewhat younger than themselves, or at least I did. 'What, at my age?' I blurted. Meaning: *I used to get asked this in 1969 as part of being mortified in Edmonton, and after thirty-four years I shouldn't have to keep on dealing with it!* But with eyelashes like that, what could I expect?

'Sure, why not?' he said.

I refrained from telling him why not. I did not say: *Geez Louise, I'm sixty-three and you still expect me to wear pink, with frills?* I did not say: *feminine, or feline, pal? Grr, meow.* I did not say: *This is a frivolous question.*

Whacking my eyelashes together, I said: 'You really shouldn't be asking *me*. You should be asking the men in my life.' (Implying there were hordes of them.) 'Just as I would ask the women in *your* life if you are masculine. They'd tell me the truth.'

Time for the commercial.

A couple of days later, still brooding on this theme, I said, in public, 'My boyfriends got bald and fat and then they died.' Then I said, 'That would make a good title for a short story.' Then I regretted having said both.

Some mortifications are, after all, self-inflicted.

38

Writing *Oryx and Crake*

Oryx and Crake was begun in March, 2001. I was still on a book tour for my previous novel, *The Blind Assassin,* but by that time I had reached Australia. After I'd finished the book-related events, my spouse and I and two friends travelled north, to Max Davidson's camp in the monsoon rain forest of Arnheimland. For the most part we were bird-watching, but we also visited several open-sided cave complexes where Aboriginal people had lived continuously, in harmony with their environment, for tens of thousands of years. After that we went to Cassowary House, near Cairns, operated by Philip Gregory, an extraordinary birder; and it was while looking over Philip's balcony at the red-necked crakes scuttling about in the underbrush that *Oryx and Crake* appeared to me almost in its entirety. I began making notes on it that night.

I hadn't planned to begin another novel so soon after the previous one. I'd thought I might take some time off, write a few short pieces, clean out the cellar. But when a story appears to you with such insistence you can't postpone it.

Of course, nothing comes out of nothing. I'd been thinking about *what if* scenarios almost all my life. I grew up among the scientists — 'the boys at the lab' mentioned in the Acknowledgements are the graduate students and post-docs who worked with my father in the late 1930s and early 1940s at his forest-insect research station in northern Quebec, where I spent my early childhood. Several of my close relatives are scientists, and the main topic at the annual family Christmas dinner is likely to be intestinal parasites or sex hormones in mice, or, when that makes the non-scientists too queasy, the nature of the Universe. My recreational reading – books I read for fun, magazines I read in airplanes – is likely to be pop science of the Stephen Jay Gould or *Scientific American* type, partly so I'll be able to keep up with the family dialogue and maybe throw a curve or two. ('Supercavitation?') So I'd been clipping small items from the back pages of newspapers for years, and noting with alarm that trends derided ten years ago as paranoid fantasies had become possibilities, then actualities. The rules of biology are as inexorable as those of physics: run out of food and water and you die. No animal can exhaust its resource base and hope to survive. Human civilizations are subject to the same law. I continued to write away at *Oryx and Crake* during the summer of 2001. We had some other travels planned, and I wrote several chapters of this book on a boat in the Arctic, where I could see for myself how quickly the glaciers were receding. I had the whole book mapped out and had reached the end of Part 7 when I was due to go to New York for the paperback publication of *The Blind Assassin*.

I was sitting in Toronto airport, daydreaming about Part 8. In ten minutes my flight would be called. An old friend of mine came over and said, 'We're not flying.' 'What do you mean?' I said. 'Come and look at the television,' he replied. It was September 11.

I stopped writing for a number of weeks. It's deeply unsettling when you're writing about a fictional catastrophe and then a real one happens. I thought maybe I should turn to gardening books – something more cheerful. But then I started writing again, because what use would gardening books be in a world without gardens, and without books? And that was the vision that was preoccupying me.

Like *The Handmaid's Tale*, *Oryx and Crake* is a speculative fiction, not a science fiction proper. It contains no intergalactic space travel, no teleportation, no Martians. As with *The Handmaid's Tale*, it invents nothing we haven't already invented or started to invent. Every novel begins with a *what if*, and then sets forth its axioms. The *what if* of *Oryx and Crake* is simply, *What if we continue down the road we're already on? How slippery is the slope? What are our saving graces? Who's got the will to stop us?*

'Perfect storms' occur when a number of different forces coincide. So it is with the storms of human history. As novelist Alistair MacLeod has said, writers write about what worries them, and the world of *Oryx and Crake* is what worries me right now. It's not a question of our inventions – all human inventions are merely tools – but of what might be done with them; for no matter how high the tech, *homo sapiens* remains at heart what he's been for tens of thousands of years – the same emotions, the same preoccupations. To quote poet George Meredith:

> . . . In tragic life, God wot,
> No villain need be! Passions spin the plot:
> We are betrayed by what is false within.

39

Letter to America

Dear America:

This is a difficult letter to write, because I'm no longer sure who you are. Some of you may be having the same trouble.

I thought I knew you: We'd become well acquainted over the past fifty-five years. You were the Mickey Mouse and Donald Duck comic books I read in the late 1940s. You were the radio shows – Jack Benny, *Our Miss Brooks*. You were the music I sang and danced to: the Andrews Sisters, Ella Fitzgerald, the Platters, Elvis. You were a ton of fun.

You wrote some of my favourite books. You created Huckleberry Finn, and Hawkeye, and Beth and Jo in *Little Women*, courageous in their different ways. Later, you were my beloved Thoreau, father of environmentalism, witness to individual conscience; and Walt Whitman, singer of the great Republic; and Emily Dickinson, keeper of the private soul. You were Hammett and Chandler, heroic walkers of mean streets; even later, you were the amazing trio, Hemingway, Fitzgerald and Faulkner, who traced the dark labyrinths of your hidden heart. You were Sinclair Lewis and Arthur Miller, who, with their own American idealism, went after the sham in you, because they thought you could do better.

You were Marlon Brando in *On the Waterfront*, you were

Humphrey Bogart in *Key Largo*, you were Lillian Gish in *Night of the Hunter*. You stood up for freedom, honesty and justice; you protected the innocent. I believed most of that. I think you did, too. It seemed true at the time.

You put God on the money, though, even then. You had a way of thinking that the things of Caesar were the same as the things of God: That gave you self-confidence. You have always wanted to be a city upon a hill, a light to all nations, and for a while you were. Give me your tired, your poor, you sang, and for a while you meant it.

We've always been close, you and us. History, that old entangler, has twisted us together since the early seventeenth century. Some of us used to be you; some of us want to be you; some of you used to be us. You are not only our neighbours: In many cases – mine, for instance – you are also our blood relations, our colleagues and our personal friends. But although we've had a ringside seat, we've never understood you completely, up here north of the 49th parallel. We're like Romanized Gauls – look like Romans, dress like Romans, but aren't Romans – peering over the wall at the real Romans. What are they doing? Why? What are they doing now? Why is the haruspex eyeballing the sheep's liver? Why is the soothsayer wholesaling the Bewares?

Perhaps that's been my difficulty in writing you this letter: I'm not sure I know what's really going on. Anyway, you have a huge posse of experienced entrail-sifters who do nothing but analyse your every vein and lobe. What can I tell you about yourself that you don't already know?

This might be the reason for my hesitation: embarrassment, brought on by a becoming modesty. But it is more likely to be embarrassment of another sort. When my grandmother – from a New England background – was confronted with an unsavoury topic, she would change the subject and gaze out the window. And that is my own inclination: Keep your mouth shut, mind your own business.

*

But I'll take the plunge, because your business is no longer merely your business. To paraphrase Marley's Ghost, who figured it out too late, mankind is your business. And vice versa: When the Jolly Green Giant goes on the rampage, many lesser plants and animals get trampled underfoot. As for us, you're our biggest trading partner: We know perfectly well that if you go down the plug-hole, we're going with you. We have every reason to wish you well.

I won't go into the reasons why I think your recent Iraqi adventures have been – taking the long view – an ill-advised tactical error. By the time you read this, Baghdad may or may not be a pancake, and many more sheep entrails will have been examined. Let's talk, then, not about what you're doing to other people but about what you're doing to yourselves.

You're gutting the Constitution. Already your home can be entered without your knowledge or permission, you can be snatched away and incarcerated without cause, your mail can be spied on, your private records searched. Why isn't this a recipe for widespread business theft, political intimidation and fraud? I know you've been told that all this is for your own safety and protection, but think about it for a minute. Anyway, when did you get so scared? You didn't used to be easily frightened.

You're running up a record level of debt. Keep spending at this rate and pretty soon you won't be able to afford any big military adventures. Either that or you'll go the way of the USSR: lots of tanks, but no air conditioning. That will make folks very cross. They'll be even crosser when they can't take a shower because your shortsighted bulldozing of environmental protections has dirtied most of the water and dried up the rest. Then things will get hot and dirty indeed.

You're torching the American economy. How soon before the answer to that will be not to produce anything yourselves but to grab stuff other people produce, at gunboat-diplomacy prices? Is the world going to consist of a few mega-rich King Midases, with the rest being serfs, both inside and outside your country? Will the biggest business sector in the United States be the prison system? Let's hope not.

If you proceed much further down the slippery slope, people around the world will stop admiring the good things about you. They'll decide that your city upon the hill is a slum and your democracy is a sham, and therefore you have no business trying to impose your sullied vision on them. They'll think you've abandoned the rule of law. They'll think you've fouled your own nest.

The British used to have a myth about King Arthur. He wasn't dead, but sleeping in a cave, it was said; and in the country's hour of greatest peril, he would return. You too have great spirits of the past you may call upon: men and women of courage, of conscience, of prescience. Summon them now, to stand with you, to inspire you, to defend the best in you. You need them.

40

Edinburgh and Its Festival

We lived in Edinburgh in 1978–9, the fall, winter and spring months. That was the year the train tunnel fell in between Edinburgh and London, and the truckers went on strike, and so in the absence of food coming in we had to live on Brussels sprouts, salmon, and wool. And haggis, of course, with a lot of whisky poured on. Then it snowed, and everyone said 'It never does this,' and people would not venture out, though there was not much snow at all by our Canadian double-drift standards, and then the gritters, who hardly ever got a chance to go on strike, went on strike as well. The atmosphere was festive. The Scots were in their element, because life had become so grindingly but bracingly Presbyterian, just the way it was supposed to be.

I was writing a book at the time. I wrote in our bedroom, which had three necessary appliances but only two wall plugs. So I could have the heater and the light, or the light and the electric typewriter. Having the heater and the typewriter was no use because it was dark. I would plug in the heater to achieve warmth, then unplug it and plug in the typewriter and work until frost set in. Then recycle.

We were there because my novelist partner, Graeme Gibson, was the first Scotland–Canada Literary Exchange writer from

Canada. Liz Lochhead was the Scottish one. This programme has since been cancelled due to political correctness – the Canadians insisted on sending the Scots to Fredricton rather than Toronto or Montreal, and so forth. Too bad, because it was worthwhile. Graeme was in ecstasy most of the time: he'd gone to the University of Edinburgh back in the fifties, when there were still gas lights. All he had to do was partake in the cultural life, and he did this with a vengeance. He tried every single malt he could get his hands on. He went around the Highlands and Island and talked in schools. The Scots were wildly generous, unlike their reputation. They wouldn't let him pay for drinks, and they even took him to a football game, with the advice that he wear rubber boots, because of the rivers of piss that would come pouring down the stands. Which they did.

When I wasn't writing my book with the aid of the two wall plugs, I was on Mom and Tot duty, as our daughter was three. I used to take her to James Thin's, which must have had the first Bookstore Café in existence. It was way ahead of its time, although it did not seem so then, as the clientele were mostly elderly ladies. You could get a scone and read your purchases. Or we would go to the Mothers and Tots morning group, complete with sandbox and Wendy house, where I picked up every child's cold going and ended up with an impressive bronchitis. Oh well.

I also learned a song which has stayed with me ever since:

> Here's a box, put on the lid,
> I wonder what's inside of it!
> Why, it's a (cow, fire engine, Shi'ite protest march, etc.) without a doubt!
> Let's open the box and let it out!
>   (Loud mooing, mee-mo-ing, enraged shouting, from the assembled tots.)

I have often felt since that this is a useful song for the understanding of rapidly unfolding historical events.

For Hallowe'en – a Scottish festival in its origins, more or less –
I was determined to carve a pumpkin. There weren't any. 'What do
you use instead?' I asked. 'Turnips,' was the reply. I got a turnip and
carved it out – hard work, took days. It then sagged gradually in a
sinister way until it looked like Mr Hyde in the last chapter. A
Scottish vegetable, the turnip. I had a deep suspicion that my leg
had been pulled, in that straight-faced way that ought to have been
familiar to me, as it is a cultural trope that made its way to Canada
via Nova Scotia, and turns up quite frequently in my relatives.

Dr Johnson was wrong – the Scots love good food, when they
can get it. Our favourite restaurants then were The Café Royal
with its wonderful mosaic murals, and the Shamiyana – an Indian
restaurant – and Henderson's, a vegetarian but non-Puritanical
restaurant then in its glory. There were other festive events, as
well. For instance, in December I took my daughter to the largest
department store on Princes Street, in search of Santa Claus. I'd
been warned that Christmas was not a big Scottish thing – that
position was held by New Year's, First Footings and all – but yes, I
was told, there was a Santa on duty. He was up in Men's Overcoats.
We made our way through the coats as through a thicket, and
sighted a Santa throne, on a dais. Santa himself was off to the side
having a fag, as there were no customers. Spotting us, he hastily
butted out and adjusted his beard, and leapt into his chair. 'What
do you want for Christmas, little girl?' he growled. 'A goat,' said my
daughter. I'll never know where that came from.

We didn't go to the Edinburgh Festival then. The Festival was in the
summer, and we had to go back before it started. I couldn't even
get into Holyrood to see the site of the Darnley murder. ('Murder's
off, dear,' I was told. I'm happy to say the murder scene has since
been viewed by me in all its sombre brown-varnished splendour. If
I'd seen it earlier, the blood would have been red, and easily
chipped off, and in a different room. 'Amazing how these murders
move around,' I said to the guide who'd explained all this. 'Yes,' he
said. 'It's miraculous!')

My first trip back to Edinburgh after my year there was not auspicious. It was a book tour for *Bodily Harm* — the early eighties, then — and I was supposed to do a reading in a bookstore. Readings were not yet all the rage, and neither was I. It was raining. Three people came. Oh well.

But since, of course, things have changed. For Edinburgh, and for me as well. Edinburgh has become — well, chic. Apparently it is one of the three chic cities of Britain. Gone are the long, musty expanses of woeful maroon carpeting, the freezing rooms, the decaying grandeur. Instead there are boutique hotels, with wonderful food and sesame seeds everywhere. I on the other hand am approaching the decaying grandeur. Oh well.

So we both came back to Edinburgh in — when? August of 2001, it must have been. The air was fresh, the hotel was adorable, it rained some of the time. We wandered around looking at old haunts, buying tartan vests, and having nostalgia in pubs. The literary part of the Festival took place in a tent; the writers' green room was a yurt, and I fell in love with yurts. (But a *yurt*, in Edinburgh? How chic can you get?)

What else can I say? It was all wonderful. Edinburgh is the handsomest city in Europe. Edinburgh Castle is haunted. The Scots are grand. One of my fondest memories of them is when I was in Edinburgh on a book tour for *The Blind Assassin*, and the Booker shortlist had just been announced. I was doing a radio broadcast, and at its end a very large, very bashful Scotsman shuffled up with a great fistful of beautiful heart-melting white roses. 'Congratulations,' said he, from somewhere way, way down in his throat. He was bright red, and not from drink.

The turnip was forgiven.

41

George Orwell: Some Personal Connections

I grew up with George Orwell. I was born in 1939, and *Animal Farm* was published in 1945. Thus I was able to read it at the age of nine. It was lying around the house, and I mistook it for a book about talking animals, sort of like *The Wind in the Willows*. I knew nothing about the kind of politics in the book — the child's version of politics then, just after the war, consisted of the simple notion that Hitler was bad but dead. So I gobbled up the adventures of Napoleon and Snowball, the smart, greedy, upwardly-mobile pigs, and Squealer the spin-doctor, and Boxer the noble but thick-witted horse, and the easily-led, slogan-chanting sheep, without making any connection with historical events.

To say that I was horrified by this book would be an understatement. The fate of the farm animals was so grim, the pigs were so mean and mendacious and treacherous, the sheep were so stupid. Children have a keen sense of injustice, and this was the thing that upset me the most: the pigs were so *unjust*. I cried my eyes out when Boxer the horse had an accident and was carted off to be made into dog food, instead of being given the quiet corner of the pasture he'd been promised.

The whole experience was deeply disturbing to me, but I am forever grateful to George Orwell for alerting me early to the danger flags I've tried to watch out for since. In the world of *Animal Farm*, most speechifying and public palaver is bullshit and instigated lying, and though many characters are good-hearted and mean well, they can be frightened into closing their eyes to what's really going on. The pigs browbeat the others with ideology, then twist that ideology to suit their own purposes: their language games were evident to me even at that age. As Orwell taught, it isn't the labels – Christianity, Socialism, Islam, Democracy, Two Legs Bad, Four Legs Good, the works – that are definitive, but the acts done in their names.

I could see, too, how easily those who have toppled an oppressive power take on its trappings and habits. Jean-Jacques Rousseau was right to warn us that democracy is the hardest form of government to maintain; Orwell knew that in the marrow of his bones, because he'd seen it in action. How quickly the precept 'All Animals are Equal' is changed into 'All Animals are Equal, but Some are More Equal than Others.' What oily concern the pigs show for the welfare of the other animals, a concern that disguises their contempt for those they are manipulating. With what alacrity do they put on the once-despised uniforms of the tyrannous humans they have overthrown, and learn to use their whips. How self-righteously they justify their actions, helped by the verbal web-spinning of Squealer, their nimble-tongued press agent, until all power is in their trotters, and pretence is no longer necessary, and they rule by naked force. A *revolution* often means only that: a revolving, a turn of the wheel of fortune, by which those who were at the bottom mount to the top, and assume the choice positions, crushing the former power-holders beneath them. We should beware of all those who plaster the landscape with large portraits of themselves, like the evil pig, Napoleon.

Animal Farm is one of the most spectacular Emperor-Has-No-Clothes books of the twentieth century, and it got George Orwell into trouble accordingly. People who run counter to the current popular wisdom, who point out the uncomfortably obvious, are likely to be strenuously baa-ed at by herds of angry sheep. I didn't have all that figured out at the age of nine, of course – not in any conscious way. But we learn the patterns of stories before we learn their meanings, and *Animal Farm* has a very clear pattern.

Then along came *Nineteen Eighty-Four*, which was published in 1949. Thus I read it in paperback a couple of years later, when I was in high school. Then I read it again, and again: it was right up there among my favourite books, along with *Wuthering Heights*. At the same time, I absorbed its two companions, Arthur Koestler's *Darkness at Noon* and Aldous Huxley's *Brave New World*. I was keen on all three of them, but I understood *Darkness at Noon* to be a tragedy about events that had already happened, and *Brave New World* to be a satirical comedy, with events that were unlikely to unfold in exactly that way. ('Orgy-Porgy', indeed.) *Nineteen Eighty-Four* struck me as more realistic, probably because Winston Smith was more like me – a skinny person who got tired a lot and was subjected to physical education under chilly conditions – this was a feature of my school – and who was silently at odds with the ideas and the manner of life proposed for him. (This may be one of the reasons *1984* is best read when you are an adolescent: most adolescents feel like that.) I sympathized particularly with Winston Smith's desire to write his forbidden thoughts down in a deliciously tempting secret blank book: I had not yet started to write, myself, but I could see the attractions of it. I could also see the dangers, because it's this scribbling of his – along with illicit sex, another item with considerable allure for a teenager of the fifties – that gets Winston into such a mess.

Animal Farm charts the progress of an idealistic movement of liberation towards a totalitarian dictatorship headed by a despotic tyrant; *Nineteen Eighty-Four* describes what it's like to live entirely within such a system. Its hero, Winston Smith, has only fragmentary memories of what life was like before the present dreadful regime set in: he's an orphan, a child of the collectivity. His father died in the war that has ushered in the repression, and his mother has disappeared, leaving him with only the reproachful glance she gave him as he betrayed her over a chocolate bar – a small betrayal

that acts both as the key to Winston's character and as a precursor
to the many other betrayals in the book.

The government of Airstrip One, Winston's 'country', is brutal.
The constant surveillance, the impossibility of speaking frankly to
anyone, the looming, ominous figure of Big Brother, the regime's
need for enemies and wars – fictitious though both may be – which
are used to terrify the people and unite them in hatred, the mind-
numbing slogans, the distortions of language, the destruction of
what has really happened by stuffing any record of it down the
Memory Hole – these made a deep impression on me. Let me re-
state that: they frightened the stuffing out of me. Orwell was
writing a satire about Stalin's Soviet Union, a place about which I
knew very little at the age of fourteen, but he did it so well that I
could imagine such things happening anywhere.

There is no love interest in *Animal Farm*, but there is one in
Nineteen Eighty-Four. Winston finds a soulmate in Julia, outwardly a
devoted Party fanatic, secretly a girl who enjoys sex and make-up
and other spots of decadence. But the two lovers are discovered,
and Winston is tortured for thought-crime – inner disloyalty to
the regime. He feels that if he can only remain faithful in his heart
to Julia, his soul will be saved – a romantic concept, though one we
are likely to endorse. But like all absolutist governments and reli-
gions, the Party demands that every personal loyalty be sacrificed
to it, and replaced with an absolute loyalty to Big Brother.
Confronted with his worst fear in the dreaded Room 101, where
there's a nasty device involving a cage-full of starving rats which
can be fitted to the eyes, Winston breaks – 'Don't do it to me,' he
pleads, 'do it to Julia.' (This sentence has become shorthand in our
household for the avoidance of onerous duties. Poor Julia – how
hard we would make her life if she actually existed. She'd have to
be on a lot of panel discussions, for instance.)

After his betrayal of Julia, Winston Smith becomes a handful of
malleable goo. He truly believes that two and two make five, and
that he loves Big Brother. Our last glimpse of him shows him sitting drink-sodden at an outdoor café, knowing he's a dead man

walking and having learned that Julia has betrayed him, too, while he listens to a popular refrain: 'Under the spreading chestnut tree/I sold you and you sold me . . .'

Orwell has been accused of bitterness and pessimism – of leaving us with a vision of the future in which the individual has no chance, and the brutal, totalitarian boot of the all-controlling Party will grind into the human face, forever. But this view of Orwell is contradicted by the last chapter in the book, an essay on Newspeak – the doublethink language concocted by the regime. By expurgating all words that might be troublesome – 'bad' is no longer permitted, but becomes 'double-plus-ungood' – and by making other words mean the opposite of what they used to mean – the place where people get tortured is the Ministry of Love, the building where the past is destroyed is the Ministry of Information – the rulers of Airstrip One wish to make it literally impossible for people to think straight. However, the essay on Newspeak is written in standard English, in the third person, and in the past tense, which can only mean that the regime has fallen, and that language and individuality have survived. For whoever has written the essay on Newspeak, the world of *1984* is over. Thus it's my view that Orwell had much more faith in the resilience of the human spirit than he's usually been given credit for.

Orwell became a direct model for me much later in my life – in the real 1984, the year in which I began writing a somewhat different dystopia, *The Handmaid's Tale*. By that time I was forty-four, and I'd learned enough about real despotisms – through the reading of history, through travel, and through my membership in Amnesty International – so that I didn't need to rely on Orwell alone.

The majority of dystopias – Orwell's included – have been written by men, and the point of view has been male. When women have appeared in them, they have been either sexless automatons or rebels who've defied the sex rules of the regime. They've acted as the temptresses of the male protagonists, however welcome this temptation may be to the men themselves. Thus Julia, thus the cami-knicker-wearing, orgy-porgy seducer of the Savage in *Brave New World*, thus the subversive *femme fatale* of Yvgeny Zamyatin's 1924 seminal classic, *We*. I wanted to try a dystopia from the female point of view – the world according to Julia, as it were. However, this does not make *The Handmaid's Tale* a 'feminist dystopia', except insofar as giving a woman a voice and an inner life will always be considered 'feminist' by those who think women ought not to have these things.

In other respects, the despotism I describe is the same as all real ones and most imagined ones. It has a small powerful group at the top that controls – or tries to control – everyone else, and it gets the lion's share of available goodies. The pigs in *Animal Farm* get the milk and the apples, the élite of *The Handmaid's Tale* get the fertile women. The force that opposes the tyranny in my book is one in which Orwell himself – despite his belief in the need for political organization to combat oppression – always put great store: ordinary human decency, of the kind he praised in his essay on Charles Dickens. The biblical expression of this quality is probably in the verse, 'Insofar as you do it unto the least of these, you do it unto me.' Tyrants and the powerful believe, with Lenin, that you can't make an omelette without breaking eggs, and that the end justifies the means. Orwell, when push came to shove, would have believed – on the contrary – that the means defines the end. He wrote as if he sided with John Donne who said, 'Every man's death diminishes me.' And so say – I would hope – all of us.

At the end of *The Handmaid's Tale*, there's a section that owes much to *1984*. It's the account of a symposium held several hundred years in the future, in which the repressive government described in the novel is now merely a subject for academic analysis. The parallels with Orwell's essay on Newspeak should be evident.

Orwell has been an inspiration to generations of writers in another important respect – his insistence on the clear and exact use of language. 'Prose like a window pane,' he said, opting for plainsong rather than ornament. Euphemisms and skewed terminology should not obscure the truth. 'Acceptable megadeaths' rather than 'millions of rotting corpses, but hey, it's not us that's dead'; 'untidiness' instead of 'massive destruction' – this is the beginning of Newspeak. Fancy verbiage is what confuses Boxer the horse and underpins the chantings of the sheep. To insist on *what is*, in the face of ideological spin, popular consensus, and official denial: Orwell knew this takes honesty, and a lot of guts. The position of odd man out is always an uneasy one, but the moment we look around and find that there are no longer any odd men among our public voices is the moment of most danger – because that's when we'll be in lockstep, ready for the Three Minutes' Hate.

The twentieth century could be seen as a race between two versions of man-made hell – the jackbooted state totalitarianism of Orwell's *Nineteen Eighty-Four*, and the hedonistic ersatz paradise of *Brave New World*, where absolutely everything is a consumer good and human beings are engineered to be happy. With the fall of the Berlin Wall in 1989, it seemed for a time that *Brave New World* had won – from henceforth, state control would be minimal, and all we'd have to do was go shopping and smile a lot, and wallow in pleasures, popping a pill or two when depression set in.

But with the legendary 9/11 World Trade Center attack in the year 2001, all that changed. Now it appears we face the prospect of two contradictory dystopias at once – open markets, closed minds – because state surveillance is back again with a vengeance. The torturer's dreaded Room 101 has been with us for millennia. The dungeons of Rome, the Inquisition, the Star Chamber, the Bastille, the proceedings of General Pinochet and of the junta in Argentina – all have depended on secrecy and on the abuse of power. Lots of countries have had their versions of it – their ways of silencing troublesome dissent. Democracies have traditionally defined themselves by, among other things, openness and the rule of law. But now it seems that we in the West are tacitly legitimizing the methods of the darker human past, upgraded technologically and sanctified to our own uses, of course. For the sake of freedom, freedom must be renounced. To move us towards the improved world – the utopia we're promised – dystopia must first hold sway. It's a concept worthy of doublethink. It's also, in its ordering of events, strangely Marxist. First the Dictatorship of the Proletariat, in which lots of heads must roll; then the pie-in-the-sky Classless Society, which oddly enough never materializes. Instead we just get pigs with whips.

What would George Orwell have to say about it? I often ask myself.

Quite a lot.

42

Carol Shields, Who Died Last Week, Wrote Books That Were Full of Delights

The beloved Canadian author Carol Shields died on July 16 at her home in Victoria, British Columbia, after a long battle with cancer. She was sixty-eight. The enormous media coverage given to her and the sadness expressed by her many readers paid tribute to the high esteem in which she was held in her own country, but her death made the news all around the world.

Conscious as she was of the vagaries of fame and the element of chance in any fortune, she would have viewed that with a certain irony, but she would also have found it deeply pleasing. She knew about the darkness, but – both as an author and as a person – she held on to the light. 'She was just a luminous person, and that would be important and persist even if she hadn't written anything,' said her friend and fellow author Alice Munro.

Earlier in her writing career, some critics mistook this quality of light in her for lightness, light-mindedness, on the general principle that comedy – a form that turns on misunderstanding and confusion, but ends in reconciliation, of however tenuous a kind – is less serious than tragedy, and that the personal life is of lesser importance than the public one. Carol Shields knew better. Human life is a mass of statistics only for statisticians: the rest of us

live in a world of individuals, and most of them are not prominent.
Their joys however are fully joyful, and their griefs are real. It was
the extraordinariness of ordinary people that was Shields' forte,
reaching its fullest expression in her novels *Swann*, *The Republic of Love*,
and especially *The Stone Diaries*. She gave her material the full benefit of her large intelligence, her powers of observation, her humane
wit, and her wide reading. Her books are delightful, in the original
sense of the word: they are full of delights.

She understood the life of the obscure and the overlooked partly
because she had lived it: her study of Jane Austen reveals a deep
sympathy with the plight of the woman novelist toiling incognito, appreciated only by an immediate circle but longing for her
due. Born in 1935 in the United States, Shields was at the tail end of
the postwar generation of North American college-educated
women who were convinced by the mores of their time that their
destiny was to get married and have five children. This Carol did;
she remained a devoted mother and a constant wife throughout
her life. Her husband Don was a civil engineer; they moved to
Canada, beginning with Toronto in the sixties, a time of poetic ferment in that city. Carol, who was already writing then and
attended some readings, said of that time, 'I knew no writers.'
Undoubtedly she felt relegated to that nebulous category, 'just a
housewife', like Daisy in *The Stone Diaries* and like Mary Swann, the
eponymous poet who is murdered by her husband when her talent
begins to show. (Canadian readers would understand the allusion,
but British ones who might consider this plot far-fetched will be
interested to know that there was a Canadian woman poet murdered in this way: Pat Lowther, whose best-known collection is *The
Stone Diary*.)

After obtaining an MA at the University of Ottawa, Shields
taught for years at the University of Manitoba, in Winnipeg, where
she began publishing in the seventies. But this was the decade of
rampant feminism, in the arts at least. Her early books, including
Others Intersect, *Small Ceremonies*, and *The Box Garden*, which examined

the vagaries of domestic life without torpedoing it, did not make a large stir, although some of their early readers found them both highly accomplished and hilarious. She had her first literary break-through – not in terms of quality of writing, but in terms of audience size – in Britain rather than in North America, with her 1992 novel *The Republic of Love*.

Her glory book was *The Stone Diaries*, which was shortlisted for the Booker Prize and won the Canadian Governor General's Award, and then, in 1995, the American Pulitzer Prize, a feat her dual citizenship made possible. Her next novel, *Larry's Party*, won the Orange Prize in 1998. To say that she was not thrilled by success would be to do her an injustice. She knew what it was worth. She'd waited a long time for it. She wore her new-found prominence with graciousness and used it with largesse. One of the last instances of her enormous generosity of spirit may not be well-known: she supplied a jacket quotation for Valerie Martin's fine but challenging novel, *Property* – a book which went on to win the 2003 Orange Prize. It takes place in the American South during slavery, and none of the characters are 'nice', but as Carol remarked in a letter she wrote me, that was the point.

Unless, her last novel, was written in the small space of time she spent in England, after beating cancer the first time and before it came back. It's a hymn to the provisional: the sense of happiness and security as temporary and fragile is stronger than ever. *Unless* was published in 2002; although it was shortlisted for just about every major English-language prize, the Munro Doctrine, informally named after Alice Munro, had set in by then – after a certain number of prizes you are shot into the stratosphere, where you circulate in radiant mists, far beyond the ken of juries.

Several months before her death, Carol published – with co-editor Marjorie Anderson – *Dropped Threads 2*, the sequel to the spectacularly successful 2001 anthology *Dropped Threads*. This was a frankly feminist collection, taking 'feminist' in its broadest sense: contributors were asked to write about subjects of concern to women that had been excluded from the conversation so far. Those who had heard Carol Shields interviewed were probably surprised by this strain in her character, and by the angry letters addressed to male pundits dismissive of woman writers in *Unless*, because in conversation she was discreet and allusive. The little frown, the shake of the head, said it all.

Possibly feminism was something she worked into, as she published more widely and came up against more commentators who thought excellent pastry was a facile creation compared with raw meat on skewers, and who in any case could not recognize the thread of blood in her work, though it was always there. The problem of the luminous is that their very luminosity obscures the shadows it depends on for its brilliance.

I last saw Carol Shields at the end of April. Her new house was spacious, filled with light, outside the windows the tulips in her much-loved garden were in bloom. Typically for her, she claimed she couldn't quite believe she deserved to live in such a big and beautiful house. She felt so lucky, she said.

Although she was very ill, she didn't seem it. She was as alert, as interested in books of all kinds, and as curious as ever. She'd recently been reading non-fiction works on biology, she told me: something new for her, a new source of amazement and wonder. We did not speak of her illness. She preferred to be treated as a person who was living, not one who was dying.

And live she did, and live she does for as John Keats remarked, every writer has two souls, an earthly one and one that lives on in the world of writing as a voice in the writing itself. It's this voice, astute, compassionate, observant, and deeply human, that will continue to speak to her readers everywhere.

43

He Springs Eternal

If Studs Terkel were Japanese, he'd be a Sacred Treasure. As John Kenneth Gaibraith has said of him, 'Studs Terkel is more than a writer, he is a national resource.' *Hope Dies Last* is the latest in the series of American oral histories he's been publishing since *Division Street, America* appeared in 1967. In the thirty-six years between then and now, he's covered, in separate books, the Great Depression, World War Two, race relations, working, the American Dream, and ageing. For each book, he interviewed an amazing variety of people – where does he meet some of these folks, anyway? – and the entire oeuvre has an exhaustiveness and monumentality that will make it necessary reading for future social historians of the American twentieth century.

The arrangement of subjects begins to look less serendipitous than schematic. Books about youth and middle age – initiation, ordeal, and daily life in action – were followed by books about contemplation and stock-taking. The second-to-last was entitled *Death: Will the Circle Be Unbroken?* (2001), which carried us into the unknown: Will there be an afterlife? (The general consensus: maybe, maybe not.) The series now resembles a planned cycle, like the cycles of mystery plays put on in medieval towns. You'd think *Death* would have ended it, but with the addition of *Hope Dies Last*, the pattern is now similar to that of Armistice Day ceremonies, where taps, the sundown signal, is followed by reveille, the wakeup call, symbolizing the Resurrection. Death and hope are paired as well on many Christian tombstones, which hear the words *In Spe*. No coincidence then that Terkel kicks off his book with an upward-tending sentiment: 'Hope has never trickled down. It has always sprung up.' First the dead body, then the young green leaves of grass.

It's very Terkelesque – by now, the man requires an adjective of his own – that after death should come hope, for Terkel's optimism has seldom failed him. His lifetime of ninety-one years has spanned the boom times of the twenties, the Depression, World War Two, the McCarthy red-hunting era, the Civil Rights Movement, the hippie activists of the late sixties, and on into present times. He grew up in Chicago in the 1920s, eavesdropping on the arguments that went on in the lobby of the workingmen's hotel run by his widowed mother – arguments that pitted old Wobblies from the International Workers of the World against anti-unionists, with ordinary working stiffs who 'didn't give a hoot one way or the other' putting their oars in too. This was the perfect education for a man who was to become the American interviewer *par excellence*: Terkel became a practised listener. He learned how to take the measure of what he was hearing, and to assess who was saying it.

He spent three dispiriting years at the University of Chicago Law School, then took up acting in radio soap operas to avoid being a lawyer – 'I was always typecast as a Chicago gangster,' he says. Then he became a disc jockey – classical, jazz, and folk – and, with the advent of television, an unorthodox talk show host. On *Studs's Place*, he ran a version of the entertaining hotel lobby debates of his youth – improvised, filmed live, scrappy, unpredictable. His kind of TV was known as 'TV, Chicago style'; it had its own manner, a rough-and-tumble ambience with a whiff of Carl Sandburg's famous Chicago poem about it: 'City of the Big Shoulders', 'with lifted head singing so proud to be alive and coarse and strong and cunning', not to mention the fearless, defiant, brawling, dusty-faced, white-teethed laughter to which Sandburg gives pride of place.

Terkel was always a laugher in this sense, though of the puckish kind rather than the brawling, white-teethed variety; and he was never afraid of putting himself on the line. Naturally, he got involved with picket lines and petitions – 'I never met a picket line or a petition I didn't like,' he says, with daunting Pickwickian geniality. Needless to say, he found himself an object of repeated scrutiny during the McCarthy era. FBI agents used to visit him in solemn twosomes, and though his wife was cool toward them, he himself was 'always hospitable. Remember, I was an innkeeper's boy.' When an emissary from NBC showed up, demanding that he say he was 'duped by the communists', he refused. 'Suppose communists come out against cancer. Do we have to come out *for* cancer?' he asked. 'That is *not* very funny,' said the NBC official, like many a schoolmarm before him.

Terkel was then blacklisted for several years, during which he made a living lecturing to women's clubs about jazz. (He's proud of these women's clubs, for they too were fearless Chicago-style laughers: though warned off him, not one club ever cancelled an engagement.) In the mid-fifties he was finally rescued by Mahalia Jackson, who insisted he be the host of her weekly CBS radio show. When an emissary from the network turned up with a loyalty oath, insisting Studs sign it or else, Mahalia said, 'If they fire Studs . . . go find another Mahalia.' 'In saying no,' says Terkel, Mahalia Jackson 'revealed more self-esteem, let alone what our country is all about, than . . . all the sponsors and agencies rolled into one.'

Those who have had the pleasurable workout of being interviewed by Studs Terkel during his long-running book program on NPR will agree that it was an interview experience like no other. Unlike some, Studs would always read the book. Then he'd reread it. When you arrived for the interview, there would be Studs, hugging your book, which would look as if he'd been rolling around on the floor with it. It would be underlined in different pens and pencils, cross-referenced, with little bits of coloured paper sticking out all over it. Then he'd start in – 'I stayed up all night reading this, I couldn't put it down' – and you'd realize that he knew more about your book than you did yourself. This knowledge was not used to make you look like an idiot, but to prop you up. The enthusiasm, the energy, the excitement, were put across with a verve that had you reeling out of the place feeling you'd just participated in a rafter-raising musical comedy, in which Studs had given you the role of star tap-dancer without your having auditioned for it.

While conducting the interviews for his oral history series, Terkel evidently drew on many of the same skills, though he concerned himself not with books but with people. He has made himself into a conduit through which voices have flowed – familiar voices, powerful voices, but also obscure voices, ordinary voices, voices that otherwise might not have been heard. It's been a huge amount of work, in aid of which he's travelled all over the country. In his later years it can't have been physically easy for him – he recounts with appreciation his trip, while visiting a Chicago tycoon, up a flight of stairs in an electric armchair – and it must also have been hard in other ways: the stories he's recorded have not been without their conflicts and defeats, the lives celebrated have often been tough, and not all of them have had happy endings. Some of those he interviewed for this book were old and ill. Their wives had died, or they'd had a stroke, or they were using a walker, or they were in a wheelchair. The two people to whom the book is dedicated are the lawyer Clifford Durr and his Southern belle wife, Virginia Durr, of Montgomery, Alabama, who spearheaded the Civil Rights Movement there in the fifties, against fearful odds. Both are dead.

What drove Terkel on? Partly it was the same kind of alert and open curiosity that led him to interviewing in the first place. 'I've always wondered what made Virginia and Clifford Durr tick,' he muses, without coming up with a definitive theory. But it's more than simple wondering. The answers to such questions, he implies, are in the stories, and he lets his subjects tell these stories for themselves.

It's perhaps helpful to think of Studs Terkel as the inheritor of the same strain of American idealistic romanticism that produced Walt Whitman, and Mark Twain's Huckleberry Finn, and John Dos Passos, and John Steinbeck, and many more. According to this tradition, 'democracy' is a serious idea, indeed an article of belief, rather than a snippet of election-year rhetoric or Oscar Wilde's wisecrack about the bludgeoning of the people, by the people, for the people. For those who still keep faith with the early, bright-eyed concept of American democracy, all men really are created equal, and to treat any human being as less than human is a heresy. No coincidence that Terkel quotes Tom Paine, that eighteenth-century gadfly and apologist for the rights of man, and finds his words appropriate in the America of 2003:

> Freedom had been hunted round the globe; reason was considered as rebellion; and the slavery of fear had made men afraid to think. But such is the irresistible nature of truth that all it asks, and all it wants, is the liberty of appearing . . . In such a situation, man becomes what he ought. He sees his species, not with the inhuman eye of a natural enemy, but as a kindred.

'One's-Self I sing, a simple separate person, / Yet utter the word Democratic, the word En-masse,' says Whitman . . .

> One of the Nation of many
>   nations, the smallest the same
>   and the largest the same . . .
> Of every hue and caste am I, of
>   every rank and religion,
> A farmer, mechanic, artist,
>   gentleman, sailor, quaker,
> Prisoner, fancy-man, rowdy,
>   lawyer, physician, priest.

This could almost be a prospectus for Terkel's life's work: the bringing together of diverse voices until they join in harmony and
counterpoint, the goal being a unified whole in which every individual nevertheless remains distinct. 'It's . . . like a legion of Davids,
with all sorts of slingshots. It's not one slingshot that will do it,' says
Terkel.

But there are problems with a legion of Davids. An aroused and
rightfully annoyed society is not the same thing as a mob on the
rampage, but how do you keep the one from turning into the
other? And if the Davids win, won't some of them become Goliaths
in their turn, as witness the histories of some unions? *E pluribus
unum*, says the Great Seal of the United States, but it doesn't say
what kind of one is to be made out of the many, or how you keep
the country from becoming a *de facto* dictatorship, ruled by fear,
with everybody snooping on everybody else. These are the difficulties faced by a pluralistic, individualistic, market-driven, yet
officially democratic society like that of the United States. 'The
price of liberty is eternal vigilance,' said Thomas Jefferson. Terkel
might amend this to, 'The price of liberty is eternal slingshots.'
But does liberty mean you can do whatever you like as long as you
don't get caught? At what point does the liberty of one depend on
the serfdom of another? And what Goliaths, exactly, ought the
Davids to shoot at with their slingshots? Any Goliaths who forget
that liberty entails responsibility. Terkel would probably reply: walk
on people and you're fair game.

The subject of *Hope Dies Last* isn't just any kind of hope, such as
'Hope you're feeling better', 'Hope for the best', or even 'I hope you
die'. Lots of things have been said about hope; nor has it always had
a good press. For some, hope is a phantom, a deluding will-o'-the-
wisp, luring men away from reality – presupposed to be grim – and
into attractive but deadly swamps. For some, Camus included, it's
the dirty trick at the bottom of Pandora's box, the deceptive gizmo
that keeps Sisyphus rolling the stone up the hill. 'Hope sustains us,
to be replaced sooner or later by a walking stick,' said the Bulgarian

epigrammatist Kouncho Grosev. 'There is an abundance of hope, but none for us,' said Franz Kafka. 'I can't go on, I have to go on, I'll go on,' says Beckett in *The Unnameable*.

Terkel knows his Camus and his Beckett and the Greek myths, but does not change course for them. Two of his subjects refer to Emily Dickinson's poem:

> 'Hope' is the thing with
>   feathers –
> That perches in the soul –
> And sings the tune without the
>   words –
> And never stops – at all –
>
> And sweetest – in the Gale – is
>   heard –
> And sore must be the storm –
> That could abash the little Bird –
> That kept so many warm . . .

This is the kind of hope Terkel means, the hope that persists in the face of discouragement. All but a few of the people he interviews in his book have been chosen because they did not cease from mental fight, or let their swords sleep in their hands: they took up their bows of burning gold and their arrows of desire, and let fly.

If there are biblical echoes here it's not by accident. 'Studs . . . you have such a big mouth, you should have been a preacher,' Terkel quotes a pal as saying. But he is a sort of preacher. One branch of Christianity has always led to activism: according to it, all souls are equal before God, the first shall be last and the last shall be first, and you must love your neighbours as yourself and visit them when they are sick and in prison, and if you do bad things unto the least of these, you do them unto God. (There's another branch of Christianity that rests on the verse about those who have getting

more, and those who have not being deprived even of what they
have, which these folks interpret financially; but that's another
story.) A number of the subjects in this book started out along the
path of religion: among them are priests, seminarians, Quakers,
Methodists, Baptists.

As for hope, it goes hand in hand – biblically – with faith and
charity: you might say faith is the belief, hope is the emotion made
possible by it, and charity is the action required. Terkel's hope is not
vain hope, but is one with the kindly light that leads amid the
encircling gloom: it's hope for something better. The book's title
comes from a saying that was current among the Spanish-speaking
farm workers organized by Cesar Chavez – '*La esperanza muere
última*' – but is cited by others in the book as well. Terkel comments, 'It was a metaphor for much of the twentieth century.' He
quotes Kathy Kelly of the Voices in the Wilderness project: 'I'm
working toward a world in which it would be easier for people to
behave decently.'

It's possible to get swept away by what at times resembles an inspi-
rational revival meeting. The spirit moves you; Good Samaritan
kindly feelings suffuse you; you feel like rushing out and joining
something. Perhaps a caveat is in order: one person's hope-inspired
activism is another's pain in the neck. Who's to choose what 'a
better world' is, and how to best bring it about? There's a point of
view that might characterize various well-intentioned activities as
misguided obstructionism, illegal interference, subversive under-
mining of the social order, godless communism, and so on. Should
actions be judged by the sincerity of their intentions? Yes, say the
Romantics; no, say the historians, they should instead be judged,
like wars, by their outcomes. As for good intentions, we know
what Hell's paved with. Were the Resistance fighters behind the
German lines in World War Two brave heroes striking a blow for
freedom, or were they criminal thugs? Depends on who's doing the
labelling.

Hope respects no national boundaries, and it crosses ideological lines at will. Terkel's book dodges this issue, though his inclusion of General Paul Tibbetts – pilot of the *Enola Gay*, the plane that dropped the bomb that wiped out Hiroshima – makes us sit up and blink. To be sure, Tibbetts says he was motivated by hope of a kind – he hoped his action would end the war and 'save a lot of lives'. American lives, it's understood, for his attitude toward the Japanese civilians who were snuffed out is cavalier: 'That's their tough luck for being there.' As Lenin famously remarked, you can't make an omelette without breaking eggs, but what kind of omelette is needed will always be a matter of dispute, and there's no long line of candidates anywhere for the position of egg.

That said, *Hope Dies Last* captures the reader, though the choices will not be to everyone's taste. Terkel's main emphasis is on people from the parts of society familiar to him: old lefties, workers in housing projects and among the poor, students who fought on behalf of custodial staff during the sit-in at Harvard in 2001, union activists as well as activists against corruption in unions, civil rights workers, peace workers, teachers in difficult neighbourhoods. No surprise that quite a few of these are from Chicago.

But there are surprises of other kinds. In one section – 'Easy Riders' – the interviewees share only the fact that they ride around on bicycles. One is a courier, living in the moment. Another is a doctor who goes: 'a half day every week out into Golden Gate Park on my bicycle with medicines. . . . Usually, if you work in a clinic, people come to you. Whereas if you're doing outreach in the park, you go up and offer your services. It's a different kind of playing field.'

Another section, 'Immigrants', contains a sound engineer of Iraqi origin, two undocumented Guatemalans whose hope consists in the hope of not being found out, and a man of Japanese descent who describes how, as a high-school senior, he was put in a detention camp with his family after Pearl Harbor and has since worked with the movement to redress the harm done to the Japanese. Will American Iraqis one day have their own redress movement? After September 11, Mr Usama Alshaibi told Terkel, 'I was very worried

because the government took three thousand men and put them
in detention centers. They weren't officially charged . . . I wouldn't
be surprised right now if they grabbed me and just started asking
me a bunch of questions.'

The unpleasant surprises include many horror stories – jailings,
beatings, murders. Among them are the account of wheelchair-
ridden Dierdre Merriman, a recovering alcoholic whose neck was
broken by an ex-boyfriend and who now lives in a single room in a
large Chicago apartment building and works as a rape-victim advocate, and that of Leroy Orange, tortured with electrodes to obtain
a confession of murder during a police-department reign of terror
in Chicago, wrongfully convicted, and finally pardoned by
Governor George Ryan in 2003 after a courageous legal campaign.

By no means all of Terkel's subjects are from the bottom crust of
the social pie. John Kenneth Galbraith contributes a pithy statement to the section called 'Concerning Enronism':

> As things now stand, we allow enormous incompetence and enor-
> mous compensation to those who have power. I see that as a great
> unsolved problem of our time. And since it is all quite legal, I call
> it the likelihood of innocent fraud. I entered the world of politics at
> a time when there were Fifth Amendment communists, and I've
> reached the age of ninety-four, when there are Fifth Amendment
> capitalists.

He's followed by Wallace Rasmusson, who worked his way up
through the Depression to become the president and CEO of
Beatrice Foods, a company worth $7.8 billion when he retired in 1975.
'What's happened at Enron and WorldCom – cooking books – is
criminal. A great country lasts about four hundred years. We're in
the declining-morality period. That is what ruined Rome . . .
Greed . . . I always said, "In God we trust, everything else we audit."'

There are several kinds of activism that might seem obvious to
some readers, but that are not much represented in *Hope Dies*

Last. The Women's Movement marks one of the most noteworthy
social shifts of the last two centuries, but it is barely present here.
There are women interviewed, yes – seventeen out of fifty-eight –
and intrepid women at that. One of those mentioned is anonymous – an old white woman who kept a sit-in at a Woolworth's
lunch counter in Nashville from becoming a massacre, purely
through force of character and through believing that some ways
are no way to behave – a case of Miss Manners to the rescue. 'I
just came in to buy an egg poacher,' was her story. She walked

> up and down between the students seated and the mob that would
> come up and put out a cigarette on them, spit on a young woman's
> neck and all. The students just sat, they didn't protest. This old
> woman . . . [would] go up and talk to these young white thugs.
> 'How would you feel if that was your sister?' And they would kind
> of, 'Oh, I didn't mean nothing.' Then they'd go back in the mob
> and someone else would take over.

Some of the women are among Terkel's bravest subjects –
women like Kathy Kelly, jailed for planting corn on missile silos,
and Mollie McGrath, who worked to reform sweatshops and took
part in protests against the World Trade Organization – but they
are included because they were involved in movements of other
kinds. Why is that? Terkel has nothing against women; in fact, so
non-discriminatory is he toward them that he doesn't appear to
view them as a special category, or not one needing a movement of
their own. Maybe he has the somewhat bashful attitude – so
common among men once – of not wanting to butt in on a hen
party. Maybe he can't quite believe in oppression by a gender, of a
gender, because of gender. There are no gay activists here, either.

With Mollie McGrath the anti-globalization movement gets a
look-in, but no more than that. The green movement is touched
on through Pete Seeger, folk singer to a generation, now busily
trying to clean up the Hudson River; also through Frances Moore
Lappé. Many will remember Lappé fondly as the author of *Diet for*

a Small Planet. How would we ever have known about soy flour without her? *Hope Dies Last* is so filled with quotable quotes you sometimes think you're reading Bartlett's, and Lappé has some ringers. 'Hunger is not caused by a lack of food, it's caused by a lack of democracy,' she says.

> My daughter, Anna, loves to say, 'I used to think that hope was for wimps.' Hope is not for wimps; it's for the strong-hearted who can recognize how bad things are and yet not be deterred, not be paralyzed.

> Hope is not something we find, hope is something we become.

> This is the first generation to know that the choices we're making have ultimate consequences. It's a time when you either choose life or you choose death . . . Going along with the current order means that you're choosing death.

> We're just a drop in the bucket . . . If you have a bucket, those raindrops fill it up very fast . . . Our work is helping people see that there is a bucket. There are all these people all over the world who are creating this bucket of hope.

If we were picking teams – the Hopes vs the Despairs – Lappé would be my first choice for captain of the Hopes. Her outlook is global, she knows where we stand as a species, she's tough as a week-old soy flour biscuit, and she's looking ahead, not back.

And Studs Terkel would be the umpire. No, I'll rethink that: he'd be too biased on the side of the Hope team. He'd have to be the coach. He'd bring to the task many decades of experience, the ability to galvanize, lots of anecdotal lore, and a store of energy to help out during the hard parts. That's what *Hope Dies Last* is, in essence: not just a social document, not just fascinating American history, but a coach's manual, complete with a number of model pep talks that may get you out of your armchair and propel you right into Blake's mental fight. It's all the more impressive that Terkel was putting this book together in the days after September 11 and before the invasion of Iraq, when it might have looked as if he'd be preaching to the sea. Now many will find the words he's collected both inspiring and timely: Representative Dennis Kucinich speaks for many in *Hope Dies Last* when he says, 'We're challenged to insist even more strongly on the basic freedoms that we have, because it is through those freedoms that we're vindicated. If we lose those freedoms, we're not America any more.'

44

To Beechey Island

The tourist is part of the landscape of our times, as the pilgrim
was in the Middle Ages.

— V. S. Pritchett, *The Spanish Temper*

A week before my pilgrimage began, my partner Graeme Gibson
and I found a dead crow in the backyard. 'West Nile Virus,' we
thought. We put it in the freezer and called the Humane Society.
They took the frozen crow away, but said they would not be inform-
ing us of the diagnosis as they did not want panic to spread. About
this time it occurred to me that I ought to have put on some DEET
before pruning the rose bushes: there had been a few mosquitoes.

The day before my departure, I noticed some pink blotches
around my waist. I put them down to a Thai spring roll I'd eaten.
Perhaps I had an allergy.

Soon the blotches were more numerous, and spreading out-
wards. I checked my tongue for furriness, my brain for
light-headedness, my neck for stiffness. I did feel peculiar, although
no one else seemed to be noticing. By this time I was on a plane bound
for Greenland, and, then, suddenly – time passes quickly when you're
infested with microbes – I found myself on a Russian Arctic-research
vessel called the *Akademic Ioffe*. I was a temporary staff member of an
outfit called Adventure Canada, which sublet the Russian research
ship from Peregrine, an Australian tour company that leased the
boat for Antarctic cruises. On board with me were a mixed bunch:
the Russian crew, the Australian folks who ran the 'hotel' aspects
of the trip, and the Canadians who planned and executed the daily
programmes for the sake of the hundred or so eager adventurers

who had booked passage. My job was to give a couple of talks on northern exploration as shaped by literary and artistic concepts – a job that, in my virus-addled state, I felt ill-equipped to perform.

Soon we were sailing down the long, long Sonderström Fiord – a fiord being, as our on-board geologist explained, a valley originally scooped out by glaciers and subsequently filled by the sea. Then we turned north and skirted the western coast of Greenland, cruising among huge and spectacular icebergs. The sea was blue, the sky was blue, the icebergs were blue as well, or their recently sheared surfaces were: an unearthly blue, ink-like, artificial. As we cruised among them in our rubber Zodiacs, thousand-year-old ice fizzed in the water as its compressed air escaped.

We were bound – eventually – for Baffin Bay, then Lancaster Sound, and finally for Beechey Island, where the first three members of the doomed 1847 Franklin Expedition were buried. Was I fated to join them? I wondered, as the mountains rose to the right, and the dazzling ice-filled sea stretched out to the left, and the sunsets went on for hours. Was my head about to explode, for reasons that would appear mysterious to those observing? Was history poised to repeat itself, and would I perish of unknown causes, to be followed shortly by the entire passenger list and crew, just as in the Franklin Expedition? I shared these thoughts with no one, although I felt it might be fitting to make a few illegible but poignant notes, to be discovered later, in a tin can or plastic pill container, like the garbled scrap that survived the Franklin debacle: *Oh, the dire sad.*

But the subject is pilgrimages, or a pilgrimage. I was supposed to be writing about one – this one, the one I was on. But in my blotchy state – the blotches had now reached my wrists, and possibly my brain – I couldn't quite focus on the general idea. What was a pilgrimage? Had I ever made one before? Could what I was doing now be considered one? And if so, in what sense?

I'd made some literary pilgrimages in my youth, of a sort. I'd thrown up beside the road in Wordsworth country; I'd inspected the Brontë manse and marvelled at the tiny size of its famous inhabitants; I'd been to Dr Johnson's house in London, and to the House of the Seven Gables, in Salem, Massachusetts; but did such visits count? All of them had been accidents: I happened to be passing by. How much of the essence of a pilgrimage resides in the intention, rather than in the journey as such?

The dictionary provides some flexibility: a pilgrim can mean simply a wanderer, a sojourner; or it can mean one who travels to a sacred place as an act of religious devotion. Motion is involved, relics not necessarily. But the motion has to be protracted – a stroll to the corner store for a loaf of bread wouldn't qualify. It also has to be – surely – non-commercial in nature. Marco Polo, although a magnificent traveller, was not a pilgrim. Also, a pilgrimage was supposed to be good for you: good for your health (Temples of Asclepius, Lourdes, the heart of Brother André, with its trail of abandoned crutches), or good for the state of your soul (purchase an indulgence, get time off in Purgatory; become a Pilgrim Father, found the righteous New Jerusalem, somewhere in the Boston area).

Needless to say, not all pilgrimages work out as advertised. Consider the Crusades.

When I thought of pilgrims, however, I thought first of literature. Most of the pilgrims I'd known had been encountered there.

There's Chaucer, of course: his Canterbury pilgrims are a sociable batch, making their trip together because it's spring, and they've got wanderlust, and they want to have fun. Whatever religious gloss they may put upon it, what they really enjoy is travelling in a merry company, and observing one another's wardrobes and foibles, and telling tales.

There's the seventeenth-century variety of pilgrim, exemplified by those in Bunyan's *Pilgrim's Progress*. For these hardy Protestants, the pilgrim's journey took him, not to a shrine, but through this mortal vale of tears and spiritual battles towards his goal, the heavenly home to be gained after his death.

The eighteenth century went on grand tours and sentimental journeys rather than pilgrimages, but with the Romantic age the pilgrimage was back. Consider Lord Byron's long poem, *Childe Harold's Pilgrimage*. Its hero is a wastrel, though filled with restless longing for he knows not what. But the sacred places he visits are not churches; they are sublime landscapes, with many a cliff and chasm, and the poem ends with a panegyric to the immensity of the sea, which contains the frequently-quoted stanza,

> Roll on, thou deep and dark blue ocean – roll!
> Ten thousand fleets sweep over thee in vain;
> Man marks the earth with ruin – his control
> Stops with the shore; – upon the watery plain
> The wrecks are all thy deed, nor doth remain
> A shadow of man's ravage, save his own,
> When for a moment, like a drop of rain
> He sinks into thy depths with bubbling groan,
> Without a grave, unknell'd, uncoffin'd and unknown.

Putting all these varieties of pilgrimages together, what do we get? At first glance, nothing very consistent. However, there are a few links. For instance, a pilgrim – it seems – is never first on the ground. Someone else has always been there before him, and has come to an unfortunate (though heroic or saintly) end. It is in honour of these forerunners that the pilgrim takes up his staff. Chaucer's jolly company is headed to Canterbury, scene of the murder of Thomas à Becket. Bunyan's pilgrims are following in the footsteps of the crucified Christ; and even Byron's *Childe Harold* ends with the contemplation of a myriad tragic shipwrecks and drownings. A dead body, it seems, usually precedes the live pilgrim.

*

The journey I undertook had elements of all three sorts of pilgrimages. I sojourned with a merry company, and told tales, and listened to them as well. I observed sublime landscapes, and sublime seascapes too, and meditated on dead sailors and drowned vessels.

As for spiritual battles, although I myself did not engage in any, those who'd given the route its haunted notoriety had most certainly engaged in them. We were taking the same sea-road travelled by Franklin and his crew when they set out to discover the Northwest Passage in 1847 and were never seen again; between their hopeful departure and the discovery of their silverware and gnawed bones, much anguish must have occurred.

But Franklin himself was not the direct object of my pilgrimage. My immediate agenda concerned a friend of mine, fellow poet Gwendolyn MacEwen. In the early 1960s, when she was in her early twenties, she'd written a remarkable verse drama for radio about the Franklin expedition, named after Franklin's two ships: the *Terror*, the *Erebus*. I'd heard this play when it was first broadcast, and had been very impressed by it – all the more so because Gwen had never been to the Arctic, and had never visited the Franklin expedition's three poignant graves. She had sailed these seas in imagination only, and had died in her mid-forties, without ever seeing an iceberg.

My pilgrimage – if it can be called that – was undertaken for her. I would go where she'd been unable to go, stand where she had never stood, see what she had seen only with the mind's eye.

A sentimental gesture, but then, pilgrimages are sentimental by nature.

The voyage proceeded. Elements of the Chaucerian pilgrimage manifested themselves at mealtimes, with merry tales, and jests involving Viking outfits and kilts and false beards, and, on one memorable occasion, fur sunglasses and fur jockstraps. The Protestant-style soul-searching spiritual journey was an individual matter, as such things are: there was a lot of journal-keeping aboard ship. Ruminations of the human state and the state of nature were frequent: anxiety, not over the life to come, but over the near future, for it was evident even to an untrained eye that the glaciers are receding at a rapid pace.

The Byronic version of the pilgrimage was experienced on the bridge, or – with mittens – out on deck, as the – where are the adjectives? 'spectacular', 'grand' and 'sublime' hardly do it – as the indescribable scenery drifted past. 'Look at that iceberg/cliff/rock-face,' people would say, entranced. 'It looks just like a Lawren Harris painting.' And yes, it did, only better, and so did that one, and the amazing one over there, purple and green and pink in the sunset, and then indigo and an unearthly yellow colour . . . You found yourself just standing, with eyes and mouth open, for hours.

By the time of my first talk on board ship, the original pink blotches were fading, but more had appeared. (Considerately, they stopped at the neckline.) The disorganization of my discourse was probably set down to the scrambled state in which 'creative' people are thought to exist on a daily basis. I considered explaining about my curious disease, but then people might have thought they were on a plague ship and jumped overboard, or got themselves air-lifted. Anyway, I was still walking and talking. It's just that I didn't appear to myself to be entirely responsible for what was coming out of my mouth. 'Was that all right?' I asked Graeme. But he had been up on the bridge, watching fulmars.

What did I say? I think I began by remarking to my audience that Voltaire would have considered them all mad. To pay money for a voyage, not to some centre of civilization where the proper study of mankind would be – as it ought to be – man, or even to some well-tended chateau with symmetrical plantings surrounding it, but to an icy waste with very large amounts of rock, water, and sand in it – this would have seemed to Voltaire the height of folly. Men did not risk their lives in such places unless there was a reason – money to be made, for instance. What changed between Voltaire and us – or between Voltaire and, for instance, Hillary uselessly climbing Mount Everest, Scott uselessly freezing himself in the Antarctic? A changed world view. Burke's idea of the Sublime became a Romantic yardstick, and the sublime could not be the Sublime without danger. The history of Arctic exploration in the nineteenth century was seen through this glass, and those who went north and described and painted these landscapes did so with the Romantic hero looking over their shoulders.

Franklin's expedition – I think I said – occurred at a sort of hinge in time – the moment when such risky explorations ceased to be undertaken in hope of gain – no one deeply believed, by 1847, that the Northwest Passage would be the key to China and would make Britain very, very rich – and began to be undertaken in the spirit of heroic enterprise, as a sort of barrel trip over Niagara Falls. What was being defied by derring-do explorers and potential martyrs was not pagans, but Nature herself. 'They forged the last link with their lives,' reads the inscription on Franklin's memorial in Westminster Abbey – an inscription for which Lady Jane Franklin, the widow, worked long and hard, as she worked to ensure that Franklin was seen as a hero in the Christian Romantic mode. But the last link of what? Of an idea. For as Ken McGoogan so ably demonstrates in his book, *Fatal Passage* – a book I was reading as I was ferried blotchily across Baffin Bay – Franklin didn't really find the Northwest Passage. He found a body of water that was always choked with ice, instead; which ought not to have counted.

After he died, and after his ships had been locked in the ice for three years, his men set out overland, cooking and eating one another as they went. When the first news of these culinary activities reached England, brought by the intrepid explorer John Rae, Lady Franklin was most distressed: for if Franklin had indulged in cannibalism, he would not be a hero, but only a sort of chef. (John Rae, we now know, was right about the cannibalism, though Franklin himself had undoubtedly died before it got under way.)

Some time during this admittedly rambling talk, I read from Gwendolyn's verse drama, in which she suggests that Franklin created the Northwest Passage by an act of imagination and will:

Ah, Franklin!
To follow you, one does not need geography.
At least not totally, but more of that
Instrumental knowledge the bones have,
Their limits, their measurings.

The eye creates the horizon,
The ear invents the wind,
The hand reaching out from a parka sleeve
By touch demands that the touched thing be.

A fitting motif for pilgrimages: for what inspires them if not a purely imaginative link between place and spirit?

Having crossed Baffin Bay, we travelled through Lancaster Sound, and finally along the wild, and — again, adjectives fail — oddly Egyptian-looking sandstone cliffs of Devon Island. Devon is the largest uninhabited island in the world. Was it here we saw two polar bears eating a dead walrus, while groups of seal swam in the little harbour? I find I have recorded the event and the date — September 1 — but not the exact location. There were several sites from the Thule people — those who preceded the present Inuit — and our on-ship archeologist explained them to us. The huge whale ribs that once acted as roof beams were still there.

The sun shone, the breezes blew. Although it was autumn, several small arctic flowers were still in bloom. Pakak Inuksuk and Akoo Peters, Inuit culture resource people, drum-danced and sang. At such moments the Arctic is intensely alive. It seems a benign landscape, mild and hazy and welcoming, a place of many delights.

The next day it was colder and the wind was up. We reached the westernmost end of Devon Island and dropped anchor in the harbour of Beechey Island, a small knob at the western end of Devon. Franklin's two ships, the *Terror* and the *Erebus*, spent their first winter there, protected from the crush of ice. The shore, once the edge of a warmer sea where marine life thrived, is now fossil-strewn, barren, windswept. Many have visited since Franklin's day; many have posed for the camera beside the three graves there; many have pondered.

Some years ago the three bodies were disinterred, in an attempt to learn more about the expedition. The scientists engaged in this venture — as recorded in John Geiger's book, *Frozen in Time* —

discovered that high levels of lead poisoning from tinned food must have made a substantial contribution to the disaster. The tin cans themselves can still be seen on the beach: lead as thick as candle drippings closes their seams. The dangers of eating lead were not well understood then, and the symptoms mimicked scurvy. Lead attacks the immune system, and causes disorientation and lapses in judgement. The supplies that were supposed to keep the expedition members alive were in fact killing them.

We disembarked from the Akademic Ioffe in Zodiacs and walked along the beach. I was blotch-free by this time; nevertheless I felt quite weightless. After visiting the graves – the markets are replicas now, as the originals suffered from the pilgrim's urge to chip off a piece of the action – Graeme and I sat on the shingle near an old coal depot where ships used to leave supplies for other ships until polar bears tore the storage building apart. We ate a piece of chocolate, hoarded by me for this occasion, and toasted Gwen in water from our water bottles, and Graeme sang 'The Ballad of Lord Franklin,' the words swallowed up by the wind. Farther along the beach, some bag-piping was underway, so faint we could scarcely hear it.

Inchoate thoughts about spaces, emptiness, gaps; jumping crevasses, I wrote in my notebook. *Words travelling across.*

The next day we were beset by drifting pack ice, just like Franklin. It was astonishing how quickly the ice moved, and with what strength. We had to go seventy miles around to get away from it.

Pilgrims have traditionally brought something back with them from their journeys. Sometimes it was a cockleshell to show they'd been to Jerusalem, or an expensive splinter claiming to be a piece of the true cross, or the alleged finger-bone of a saint. Modern-day pilgrims, disguised as tourists, bring photos of themselves sticking out their tongues in front of the Eiffel Tower, or postcards, or purchased mementoes – coffee spoons with the crests of cities on them, baseball caps, ashtrays.

There was no stand selling bits of explorer's finger or T-shirts with *Souvenir of Beechey Island* on them, so I brought back a pebble. It was identical with the millions of other pebbles on the beech – dun-coloured sandstone, no distinguishing features. This pebble travelled with me to Toronto in a make-up kit.

I called my doctor as soon as I arrived, and described my symptoms. 'I think I've had West Nile Virus,' I said. 'Hard to tell,' was his reply. Worst come to worst, at least I wouldn't have been buried in the permafrost. I'd have been popped into the ship's freezer kept specially for that one purpose, so as not to get the bodies mixed up with the beef stroganoff.

On a hot, dry day in mid-September, I put the Beechey Island pebble into my pocket, took a serving spoon from the kitchen, and walked over to Gwendolyn MacEwen Park, imagining to myself the rather sardonic poem Gwen might have made, both out of the park and out of the pebble event in which I was about to indulge. Accompanying me was David Young, one of whose plays – *Unimaginable Island* – deals with the unsung heroes of the Scott Antarctic expedition – unsung because they'd had the dubious taste to survive. In order to be a hero – at least in the nineteenth and early twentieth centuries – it was almost mandatory to be dead.

When we got to the park, David looked the other way while I dug a dusty hole with my spoon and inserted the pebble. So now, somewhere in the heart of darkest Toronto, its exact location known only to me, there's a tiny piece of geology brought all the way from Beechey Island. The only link between the two places is an act of the imagination, or perhaps two acts – Franklin's imagining of the Northwest Passage, and the twenty-two-year-old Gwendolyn MacEwen's imagining of Franklin.

> So I've followed you here
> Like a dozen others, looking for relics
>   of your ships, your men.
> Here to this awful monastery,
>   where you, where Crozier died,
>   and all the men with you died,
> Seeking a passage from imagination to reality . . .

45

Uncovered: An American *Iliad*

Suppose you grow up in a culturally rich and economically stable society. All around you are the vividly carved symbols of the invisible spirits that inform your dealings with the natural and human worlds. Living inside your village is like living inside a Norman cathedral, crossed with a mediaeval castle, crossed with a network of Stonehenge ley lines. Your ancestry in all its intricate twists and turns and its relation to the spirit world is posted – literally – outside your home, like a wooden, vertical coat of arms. This is an oral society: it has a highly developed system of signs, but it does not have writing as such.

As in any culture, children are gifted in different ways. You yourself have a talent for remembering stories, and for combining them in surprising patterns that yield novel meanings. You become a mythteller. You perform the stories to an appreciative audience, one that holds its breath during the scary parts and identifies the allusions, laughs at the jokes. These performances are yours in the same way as, say, Olivier's *Hamlet* was his – so much in a performance is carried by tone of voice, by expression, by the spaces left in speech – but more so, since you have put the performances together in unique ways.

Then catastrophe strikes. A mysterious disease sweeps through

your community. The mortality rate is 95 per cent. The houses
and their decorations crumble away. At the same time, an influx of
strangers with nasty weapons and odd convictions appears, ready
to destroy the ceremonial objects and to suppress the ancient customs, and to tell you that your stories are obsolete or evil.

You yourself survive the disease. You remember your performances, but you have no apprentice: you can't hand your work on.
And even if you could, is there anyone left who can understand it?

This was the plight of two remarkable poets, Skaay and the
younger Ghandl, who had been blinded by the disease. Both were
from the Haida, one of the many cultures that flourished along the
northwest coast of North America before the arrival of the
smallpox-carrying, Gospel-bearing Europeans in the nineteenth
century. Their land was – and is – an island cluster some five hundred miles north of Vancouver. At the beginning of the nineteenth
century the population was twelve thousand. At its end, some
eight hundred were left.

A last-ditch possibility presented itself to Skaay and Ghandl.
When Skaay was seventy-three and Ghandl was about fifty, they
encountered an ethnographer/linguist. His name was John Reed
Swanton. Unwittingly, he acted as a messenger to the future: he
was collecting stories, as a way into learning a language. Skaay and
Ghandl performed their creations, not for Swanton – he couldn't
speak Haida – but through a Haida-speaking intermediary, who
wrote them down phonetically.

To the poets themselves this must have seemed as desperate an
act as putting a jewel into a bottle and flinging it into the sea. It's
the sort of despairing gamble taken by those who wrote down the
Mayan *Popol Vuh* when the Spaniards were at their doorstep. Hope
against hope; and yet, in both cases, something did survive.

Skaay and Ghandl died in the early years of the twentieth century. Their stories gathered dust in libraries for almost a hundred
years. Then along came Robert Bringhurst, American-turned-
Canadian, poet-in-his-own-right, expert on typography, and easy
to confuse with the sort of obsessive-compulsive nit-picking

polymath that turns up in post-Romantic fiction. Think of Sherlock Holmes as a self-taught reader of Haida phonetic transliterations, crossed with someone like Shelley or Chopin to supply the large dollop of passionate enthusiasm, and you'll have some idea.

For twelve years Bringhurst – with the aid of many helpers – hacked his way through the brambles of the staggeringly difficult language, rubbed the tarnished old lamp, pried the cork out of the bottle. Count the metaphors here, figure out how many of them would mean nothing to you if you hadn't read any European/Arabian fairy tales, then estimate your chances of understanding very much about Haida symbol-systems without help. In any case, Bringhurst laboured. Finally, as in the tale of Sleeping Beauty, those who seemed dead awoke. As in a story by Ghandl or Skaay, bones rubbed with medicine plants came back to life. As in the tale of Aladdin, out came the genie. And one humdinger of a genie it is.

Like a lot of genies, it's a book. Actually it's three of them. You can get them singly, or in a boxed set called *A Story as Sharp as a Knife: Masterworks of the Classical Haida Mythtellers.* Volume One is *A Story as Sharp as a Knife: The Classical Haida Mythtellers and Their World.* This is the one you need to start with, or you'll be like someone looking at the aforesaid Norman cathedral and its Creation-to-Last-Judgement picture sequences without any knowledge of the Bible or of Christian symbolism. Volume Two – *Nine Visits to the Mythworld* – is devoted to the works of Ghandl, and *Being in Being*, Volume Three, to the works of Skaay. Each includes biographical and historical material that locates the poets in time and space and aids in an evaluation of their achievements. Each volume is also illustrated – happily, since the visual art of the culture was an extension of the stories, and vice versa.

An astonishing fact: this is the first time the name of any North American oral poet has ever appeared on the front of a book as the author of what's between the covers. It's the same with most of the oral material that's come to us. As soon as it got written down – as

soon as the tale became separable from the telling – the names of
the individual creators had a habit of vanishing, to be subsumed by
the well-known Anonymous or treated as the collective creation of
a tribe. As Bringhurst says,

> . . . others have written at great length on the nature of oral cul-
> ture, but rarely in such works do we encounter an actual oral text.
> Still less often do we meet an actual speaker. The result is that the
> real human beings who inhabit oral cultures disappear, and stereo-
> types replace them. Native American oral poets have so often been
> mistreated in this way that their namelessness has come to seem
> routine. (p. 16, Vol. 1.)

Bringhurst is the editor and translator of these two poets, but
he's a good deal more than that. He has thought long and carefully
about the many issues involved in his task, and he has an agenda.
On it is a long list of things I can't begin to summarize, but here are
a few of them.

Oral poetry is poetry, and the people who made it are poets. The
Iliad and the *Odyssey* are oral poetry written down, and so is much
of the Bible, and so are the poem cycles of Skaay and Ghandl. Oral
poetry is different in nature from the poetry produced by a society
in which writing is the norm. It depends on individual performance, and therefore on audience. It is heard, in the way that music
is heard, and it employs many of the same devices. It is embedded
in land-forms and bears witness to a close interaction with what we
call Nature. It is profoundly local.

This doesn't mean that the work of these two poets is provincial,
or limited in interest. No, it can stand with the best, because it
goes beyond its culture of origin to stand side by side with the great
myth-based artistic creations of the world. Thus the anger of certain factions who claim that Bringhurst, being white, has no
business messing with stories that are 'owned' by the Haida –
though in some ways understandable, considering the havoc
wreaked and the thefts committed in the past by strangers – is

misplaced. As well to say nobody should translate Tolstoy because
he is 'owned' by the Russians. Tolstoy could not have existed without the Russians, true, but should nobody else be permitted to
read him?

To continue with the Bringhurst fiats: for North Americans,
these poems and others like them should be part of the great stack
of building blocks in what we call our 'identity', our 'history', our
'story'. Why should our groundworks come from Greece and
Rome and the Bible and European sagas, and not also from the
places where we actually live? These are questions not without
interest for the inhabitants of – for instance – the United States and
Australia and New Zealand and South America and Mexico. As
Bringhurst says, 'Isn't it just possible that if we listened to the stories and the voices native to the place, we'd be a bit less eager to
stripmine it, clearcut it, pave it and pollute it in the name of
making money?'

Furthermore, these are not 'just poems'. They are – especially in
the case of Skaay – works of philosophy. So claims Bringhurst.

Hang on a minute, you say. You mean to tell me that a story
about Raven eating the cranberries in his own excrement is part of
a philosophical meditation on the nature of Being? Well, actually,
yes. But this is an argument that must be followed closely by those
more skilled at such arguments than I. I'll merely add that, though
philosophy in our own time is far removed from religion, the two
used to be joined at the hip, and both were inseparable from narrative. 'Being' is what it does, and what it does is embodied in the
often violent and upsetting stories about it, not in a set of abstract
propositions. Nor can you depend on Being to act the way you
think it should. (This set of concepts is a lot more modern than the
hierarchies and certainties and pieties of the Victorians, which were
what Skaay and Ghandl were up against.) If we can deal with the 'I
am that I am' of *Exodus* as a legitimate comment on the mystery of
Being, we ought to be able to grasp Voicehandler, whose face
cannot be seen, and who behaves towards men much as God did to
Job.

Why has Canada produced so many thinkers concerned with the same matters that have caught Bringhurst's attention – with such spectacular, and, at times, such peculiar results? Why Edmund Carpenter and the 1950s magazine *Explorations*, which went hand in hand with Marshall McLuhan and his great book on the effects of literacy, *The Gutenberg Galaxy*? ('The Medium is the Message' = 'Oral is not the same as written'.) Why was Leonard Cohen's first poetry collection called *Let Us Compare Mythologies*? Why Northrop Frye and his exhaustive studies of myth and literature? Why – more recently – Sean Kane and his widely-praised book, *The Wisdom of the Mythtellers*, which deals with Haida myths, among others?

Anyone who came of age reading Canadian poetry will remember the title 'A Country Without a Mythology' – a challenge if there ever was one. We so dislike being told that there's a desirable cultural goodie we haven't got. Either we do have it, and it's been overlooked – the Bringhurst response – or we have to make it ourselves, which was the task undertaken by the Canadian poets and writers of the generations just before his. But in making it – anytime, anywhere – how much of other people's 'we' should we include in our 'we'?

There's a brawl going on over the word 'we', of course. Shall 'we' become bigger, or smaller? Shall 'we' include all of humanity, or would that be to share 'our' secrets with a lot of dunderheads who will degrade and rob us? Who gets into our magic circle, and by what tokens? Do poems belong to those who compose them, or to those who appreciate them? It's one of the features of such battles that each side often wounds its own champions.

You can follow the back-and-forth in a small pamphlet that comes with the three-volume *magnum opus*, and in which Bringhurst gives his thorny answers to the thorny questions that have been thrust upon him. But such territorial squabbling cannot obscure the fact that Bringhurst's achievement is gigantic, as well as heroic. It's one of those works that rearranges the inside of your head – a profound meditation on the nature of oral poetry and myth, and on the habits of thought and feeling that inform them. It restores to life two exceptional poets we ought to know. It gives us some insight into their world – in Bringhurst's words, 'the old-growth forest of the human mind' – and, by comparison, into our own. In our march towards the secular, the orderly, the urban, the mechanized, what have we lost?

46

Headscarves to Die For

Snow, the seventh novel by the Turkish writer Orhan Pamuk, is not only an engrossing feat of tale-spinning, but essential reading for our times.

In Turkey, Pamuk is the equivalent of rock star, guru, diagnostic specialist, and public-affairs pundit: the Turkish public reads his novels as if taking its own pulse. He is also highly esteemed in Europe: his sixth novel, the lush and intriguing *My Name is Red*, carried off the 2003 Dublin IMPAC Award, adding to his long list of literary prizes.

He deserves to be better known in North America, and no doubt he will be, as his fictions turn on the conflict between the forces of 'Westernization' and those of the Islamists. Although it's set in the 1990s and written before September 11, 2001, *Snow* is eerily prescient, both in its analyses of fundamentalist attitudes and in the nature of the repression and rage and conspiracies and violence it depicts.

Like Pamuk's other novels, *Snow* is an in-depth tour of the divided, hopeful, desolate, mystifying Turkish soul. It's the story of Ka, a gloomy but appealing poet who hasn't written anything in years. But Ka is not his own narrator: by the time of the telling he has been assassinated, and his tale is pieced together by an 'old friend' of his who just happens to be named Orhan Pamuk.

As the novel opens, Ka has been in political exile in Berlin, but has returned to Istanbul for his mother's funeral. He's making his way to Kars, an impoverished city in Anatolia, just as a severe snowstorm begins. ('Kar' is 'snow' in Turkish, so we have already been given an envelope inside an envelope inside an envelope.) Ka claims to be a journalist interested in the recent murder of the city's mayor and the suicides of a number of young girls forced by their schools to remove their headscarves, but this is only one of his motives. He also wants to see Ipek, a beautiful woman he'd known as a student. Divorced from a one-time friend of Ka's turned Islamist politician, she lives in the shabby Snow Palace Hotel, where Ka is staying.

Cut off from escape by the snow, Ka wanders through a decaying city haunted by its glorious former selves – architectural remnants of the once-vast Ottoman empire; the grand Armenian church standing empty, testifying to the massacre of its worshippers; ghosts of Russian rulers and their lavish celebrations; pictures of Ataturk, founder of the Turkish Republic and instigator of a ruthless 'modernization' campaign, which included – not incidentally – a ban on headscarves.

Ka's pose as a journalist allows Pamuk to put on display a wide variety of opinions. Those not living in the shrunken remains of former empires may find it hard to imagine the mix of resentful entitlement (We ought to be powerful!), shame (What did we do wrong?), blame (Whose fault is it?), and anxiety about identity (Who are we really?) that takes up a great deal of head-room in such places, and thus in *Snow*.

Ka tries to find out more about the dead girls, but encounters resistance: he's from a bourgeois background in cosmopolitan Istanbul, he's been in exile in the West, he has a snazzy overcoat. Believers accuse him of atheism; the secular government doesn't want him writing about the suicides – a blot on its reputation – so he's dogged by police spies; common people are suspicious of him. He's present in a pastry shop when a tiny fundamentalist gunman murders the director of the Institute that has expelled the headscarf girls. He gets mixed up with his beloved's former husband, the two of them are arrested, and he witnesses the brutality of the secularist regime. He manages to duck his shadowers long enough to meet with an Islamist extremist in hiding, the persuasive Blue, said to be behind the director's murder. And so he goes, floundering from encounter to encounter.

In *Snow*, the line between playful farce and gruesome tragedy is very fine. For instance, the town's newspaper publisher, Serder Bey, prints an article describing Ka's public performance of his poem, 'Snow'. When Ka protests that he hasn't written a poem called 'Snow' and is not going to perform it in the theatre, Serder Bey replies, 'Don't be so sure. There are those who despise us for writing the news before it happens . . . Quite a few things happen only because we've written them up first. This is what modern journalism is all about.' And sure enough, inspired by the love affair he begins with Ipek and happier than he's been in years, Ka begins to write poems, the first of them being 'Snow'. Before you know it, there he is in the theatre, but the evening also includes a ridiculous performance of an Ataturk-era play, *My Fatherland or My Headscarf*. As the Religious School teenagers jeer, the secularists decide to enforce their rule by shooting the audience.

The twists of fate, the plots that double back on themselves, the trickiness, the mysteries that recede as they're approached, the bleak cities, the night prowling, the sense of identity-loss, the protagonist in exile – these are vintage Pamuk, but they're also part of the modern literary landscape. A case could be made for a genre called 'The Male Labyrinth Novel', which would trace its ancestry through De Quincy and Dostoevsky and Conrad, and would include Kafka, Borges, Marquez, Don DeLillo, and Paul Auster, with the Hammett-and-Chandler *noir* thriller thrown in for good measure. It's mostly men that write such novels and feature as their rootless heroes, and there's probably a simple reason for this: send a woman out alone on a rambling nocturnal quest and she's likely to end up a lot deader a lot sooner than a man would.

Women – except as idealized objects-of-desire – have not been of notably central importance in Pamuk's previous novels, but *Snow* is a departure. There are two strong female characters, the emotionally battered Ipek and her sister, the stubborn actress Kadife. In addition, there's a chorus: the headscarf girls. Those scrapping for power on both sides use these dead girls as symbols, having put unbearable pressure on them while they were alive. Ka, however, sees them as suffering human beings.

It wasn't poverty or helplessness that Ka found shocking in these stories. Neither was it the constant beatings to which these girls were subjected, or the insensitivity of fathers who wouldn't even let them go outside, or the constant surveillance of jealous husbands . . . [it] was the way these girls had killed themselves: abruptly, without ritual or warning, in the midst of their everyday routines . . .

Their suicides are like the other violent events in the novel: sudden eruptions of violence thrown up by relentless underlying forces.

The attitudes of men towards women drive the plot in *Snow*, but even more important are the attitudes of men towards one another. Ka is always worrying about whether or not other men respect or despise him, and that respect hinges, not on material wealth, but on what he is thought to believe. Since he himself isn't sure, he vacillates from one side to another. Shall he stick with the Western enlightenment? But he was miserable in Berlin. Shall he return to the Muslim fold? But, despite his drunken hand-kissing of a local religious leader, he can't fit in.

If Ka were to run true to the form of Pamuk's previous novels he might take refuge in stories. Stories, Pamuk has hinted, create the world we perceive: instead of 'I think, therefore I am', a Pamuk character might say, 'I am because I narrate'. It's the Scheherazade position, in spades. But poor murdered Ka is no novelist: it's up to 'Orhan Pamuk' to act as his Horatio.

Snow is the latest entry in Pamuk's long-time project: narrating his country into being. It's also the closest to realism. Kars is finely drawn, in all its touching squalor, but its inhabitants resist

'Pamuk's' novelizing of them. One of them asks him to tell the reader not to believe anything he says about them, because 'No one could understand us from so far away.' This is a challenge to Pamuk and his considerable art, but it is also a challenge to us.

47

Ten Ways of Looking at *The Island of Doctor Moreau*

H. G. Wells's *The Island of Doctor Moreau* is one of those books that, once read, is rarely forgotten. Jorge Luis Borges called it an 'atrocious miracle', and made large claims for it. Speaking of Wells's early tales – *The Island of Doctor Moreau* among them – he said, 'I think they will be incorporated, like the fables of Theseus or Ahasuerus, into the general memory of the species and even transcend the fame of their creator or the extinction of the language in which they were written.'[1]

This has proved true, if film may be considered a language unto itself. *The Island of Doctor Moreau* has inspired three films – two of them quite bad – and doubtless few who saw them remembered that it was Wells who authored the book. The story has taken on a life of its own, and, like the offspring of Mary Shelley's *Frankenstein*, has acquired attributes and meanings not present in the original. Moreau himself, in his filmic incarnations, has drifted towards the type of the Mad Scientist, or the Peculiar Genetic Engineer, or the Tyrant-in-Training, bent on taking over the world; whereas Wells's Moreau is certainly not mad, and is a mere vivisectionist, and has no ambitions to take over anything whatsoever.

Borges's use of the word 'fable' is suggestive, for – despite the realistically-rendered details of its surface – the book is certainly not a novel, if by that we mean a prose narrative dealing with observable social life. 'Fable' points to a certain folkloric quality that lurks in the pattern of this curious work, as animal faces may lurk in the fronds and flowers of an Aubrey Beardsley design. The term may also indicate a lie – something fabulous or invented, as opposed to that which demonstrably exists – and employed this way it is quite apt, as no man ever did or ever will turn animals into human beings by cutting them up and sewing them together again. In its commonest sense, a fable is a tale – like those of Aesop – meant to convey some useful lesson. But what is that useful lesson? It is certainly not spelled out by Wells.

'Work that endures is always capable of an infinite and plastic ambiguity; it is all things for all men,' says Borges, '. . . and it must be ambiguous in an evanescent and modest way, almost in spite of the author; he must appear to be ignorant of all symbolism. Wells displayed that lucid innocence in his first fantastic exercises, which are to me the most admirable part of his admirable work.'[2] Borges carefully did not say that Wells employed no symbolism: only that he appeared to be ignorant of doing so.

Here follows what I hope will be an equally modest attempt to probe beneath the appearance, to examine the infinite and plastic ambiguity, to touch on the symbolism that Wells may or may not have employed deliberately, and to try to discover what the useful lesson – if there is one – might be.

Ten Ways of Looking at *The Island of Doctor Moreau*

I. ELOIS AND MORLOCKS

The Island of Doctor Moreau was published in 1896, when H. G. Wells was only thirty years old. It followed *The Time Machine*, which had appeared the year before, and was to be followed two years later by *The War of the Worlds*, this being the book that established Wells as a force to be reckoned with at a mere thirty-two years of age.

To some of literature's more gentlemanly practitioners – those, for instance, who had inherited money, and didn't have to make it by scribbling — Wells must have seemed like a puffed-up little counter-jumper, and a challenging one at that, because he was bright. He'd come up the hard way. In the stratified English social world of the time, he was neither working class nor top crust. His father was an unsuccessful tradesman; he himself apprenticed with a draper for two years before wending his way, via school-teaching and a scholarship, to the Normal School of Science. Here he studied under Darwin's famous apologist, Thomas Henry Huxley. He graduated with a first-class degree, but he'd been seriously injured by one of the students while teaching, an event that put him off school-mastering. It was after this that he turned to writing.

The Time Traveller in *The Time Machine* — written just before *The Island of Doctor Moreau* — finds that human beings in the future have split into two distinct races. The Eloi are pretty as butterflies, but useless; the grim and ugly Morlocks live underground, make everything, and come out at night to devour the Eloi, whose needs they also supply. The upper classes, in other words, have become a bevy of Upper Class Twitterers and have lost the ability to fend for themselves, and the working classes have become vicious and cannibalistic.

Wells was neither an Eloi nor a Morlock. He must have felt he represented a third way, a rational being who had climbed up the ladder through ability alone, without partaking of the foolishness and impracticality of the social strata above his nor of the brutish crudeness of those below.

But what about Prendick, the narrator of *The Island of Doctor Moreau*? He's been pootling idly about the world, for his own diversion we assume, when he's shipwrecked. The ship is called the *Lady Vain*, surely a comment on the snooty aristocracy. Prendick himself is a 'private gentleman' who doesn't have to work for a living, and, though he — like Wells — has studied with Huxley, he has done so not out of necessity but out of dilettantish boredom — 'as a relief from the dulness of (his) comfortable independence'. Prendick, though not quite as helpless as a full-fledged Eloi, is well on the path to becoming one. Thus his hysteria, his lassitude, his moping, his ineffectual attempts at fair play, and his lack of common sense —

he can't figure out how to make a raft because he's never done 'any carpentry or suchlike work' in his life, and when he does manage to patch something together, he's situated it too far from the sea and it falls apart when he's dragging it. Although Prendick is not a complete waste of time – if he were, he wouldn't be able to hold our attention while he tells his story – he's nonetheless in the same general league as the weak-chinned curate in the later *War of the Worlds*, that helpless and drivelling 'spoiled child of life'.[3]

His name – Prendick – is suggestive of 'thick' coupled with 'prig', this last a thing he is explicitly called. To those versed in legal lore, it could suggest 'prender', a term for something you are empowered to take without it having been offered. But it more nearly suggests 'prentice', a word that would have been floating close to the top of Wells's semi-consciousness, due to his own stint as an apprentice. Now it's the upper-class turn at apprenticeship! Time for one of them to undergo a little degradation and learn a thing or two. But what?

2. SIGNS OF THE TIMES

The Island of Doctor Moreau comes not only midway in Wells's most fertile period of fantastic inventiveness; it also comes during such a period in English literary history. Adventure romance had taken off with Robert Louis Stevenson's *Treasure Island* in 1882, and Rider Haggard had done him one better with *She* in 1887. This latter coupled straight adventure – shipwreck, tramps through dangerous swamps and nasty shrubbery, encounters with bloody-minded savages, fun in steep ravines and dim grottos – with a big dollop of weirdness carried over from earlier Gothic traditions, done up this time in a package labelled 'Not Supernatural'. The excessive powers of 'She' are ascribed, not to a close encounter with a vampire or god, but to a dip in a revolving pillar of fire, no more supernatural than lightning. 'She' gets her powers from Nature.

It's from this blend – the grotesque and the 'natural' – that Wells took his cue. An adventure story that would once have featured battles with fantastic monsters – dragons, gorgons, hydras –

keeps the exotic scenery, but the monsters have been produced by the very agency that was seen by many in late Victorian England as the bright, new, shiny salvation of mankind: Science.

The other blend that proved so irresistible to readers was one that was developed much earlier, and to singular advantage, by Jonathan Swift: a plain, forthright style in the service of incredible events. Poe, that master of the uncanny, piles on the adjectives to create 'atmosphere'; Wells, on the other hand, follows R.L. Stevenson and anticipates Hemingway in his terse, almost journalistic approach, usually the hallmark of the ultra-realists. *The War of the Worlds* shows Wells employing this combination to best effect – we think we're reading a series of news reports and eyewitness accounts – but he's already honing it in *The Island of Doctor Moreau*. A tale told so matter-of-factly and with such an eye to solid detail surely cannot be – we feel – either an invention or an hallucination.

3. SCIENTIFIC

Wells is acknowledged to be one of the foremost inventors in the genre we now know as 'science fiction'. As Robert Silverberg has said, 'Every time-travel tale written since *The Time Machine* is fundamentally indebted to Wells . . . In this theme, as in most of science fiction's great themes, Wells was there first.'[4]

'Science fiction' as a term was unknown to Wells; it did not make its appearance until the 1930s, in America, during the golden age of bug-eyed monsters and girls in brass brassières.[5] Wells himself referred to his science-oriented fictions as 'scientific romances' – a term that did not originate with him, but with a lesser-known writer called Charles Howard Hinton.

There are several interpretations of the term 'science'. If it implies the known and the possible, then Wells's scientific romances are by no means scientific: he paid little attention to those boundaries. As Jules Verne remarked with displeasure, '*Il invente!*' The 'science' part of these tales is embedded instead in a world-view that derived from Wells's study of Darwinian principles under Huxley, and has to do with the grand study that engrossed him throughout his career: the nature of man. This too may account for his veering, throughout his career, between extreme Utopianism (if man is the result of evolution, not of Divine creation, surely he can evolve yet further?) and the deepest pessimism (if man came from the animals and is akin to them, rather than to the angels, surely he might slide back the way he came?). *The Island of Doctor Moreau* belongs to the debit side of the Wellsian account book.

Darwin's *The Origin of Species* and *The Descent of Man* were a profound shock to the Victorian system. Gone was the God who spoke the world into being in seven days and made man out of clay; in its place stood millions of years of evolutionary change, and a family tree that included primates. Gone too was the kindly Wordsworthian version of Mother Nature that had presided over the first years of the century; in her place was Tennyson's 'Nature, red in tooth and claw/ With ravine'. The devouring *femme fatale* that became so iconic in the 1880s and 1890s owes a lot to Darwin. So does the imagery and cosmogony of *The Island of Doctor Moreau*.

4. ROMANCE

So much for the 'scientific' in 'scientific romance'. What about the 'romance'?

In both 'scientific romance' and 'science fiction', the scientific element is merely an adjective; the nouns are 'romance' and 'fiction'. In respect to Wells, 'romance' is more helpful than 'fiction'.

'Romance', in today's general usage, is what happens on Valentine's Day. As a literary term it has slipped in rank somewhat – being now applied to such things as Harlequin Romances – but it was otherwise understood in the nineteenth century, when it was used in opposition to the term 'novel'. The novel dealt with known social life, but a romance could deal with the long ago and the far away. It also allowed much more latitude in terms of plot. In a romance, event follows exciting event at breakneck pace. As a rule, this has caused the romance to be viewed by the high literati – those bent more on instruction than on delight – as escapist and vulgar, a judgement that goes back at least two thousand years.

In *The Secular Scripture*, Northrop Frye provides an exhaustive analysis of the structure and elements of the romance as a form. Typically a romance begins with a break in ordinary consciousness, often – traditionally – signalled by a shipwreck, frequently linked with a kidnapping by pirates. Exotic climes are a feature, especially exotic desert islands; so are strange creatures.

In the sinister portions of a romance, the protagonist is often imprisoned or trapped, or lost in a labyrinth or maze, or a forest that serves the same purpose. Boundaries between the normal levels of life dissolve: vegetable becomes animal, animal becomes quasi-human, human descends to animal. If the lead character is female, an attempt will be made on her virtue, which she manages miraculously to preserve. A rescue, however improbable, restores the protagonist to his or her previous life and reunites him or her with loved ones. *Pericles, Prince of Tyre*, is a romance. It's got everything but talking dogs.

The Island of Doctor Moreau is also a romance, though a dark one. Consider the shipwreck. Consider the break in the protagonist's consciousness – the multiple breaks, in fact. Consider the pirates, here supplied by the vile captain and crew of the *Ipecacuanha*. Consider the name *Ipecacuanha*, signifying an emetic and purgative: the break in consciousness is going to have a nastily physical side to it, of a possibly medicinal kind. Consider the fluid boundaries between animal and human. Consider the island.

5. THE ENCHANTED ISLAND

The name given to the island by Wells is Noble's Island, a patent irony as well as another poke at the class system. Say it quickly and slur a little, and it's *no blessed island*.

This island has many literary antecedents, and several descendants. Foremost among the latter is William Golding's island in *Lord of the Flies* – a book that owes something to *The Island of Doctor Moreau*, as well as to those adventure books, *Coral Island* and *The Swiss Family Robinson*, and of course to the great original shipwreck-on-an-island classic, *Robinson Crusoe*. *Moreau* could be thought of as one in a long line of island-castaway books.

All those just mentioned, however, keep within the boundaries set by the possible. *The Island of Doctor Moreau* is, on the contrary, a work of fantasy, and its more immediate grandparents are to be found elsewhere. *The Tempest* springs immediately to mind: here is a beautiful island, belonging at first to a witch, then taken over by a magician who lays down the law, particularly to the malignant animal-like Caliban, who will obey only when pain is inflicted on him. Doctor Moreau could be seen as a sinister version of Prospero, surrounded by a hundred or so Calibans of his own creation.

But Wells himself points us towards another enchanted island. When Prendick mistakenly believes that the beast-men he's seen were once men, he says: '(Moreau) had merely intended . . . to fall upon me with a fate more horrible than death, with torture, and after torture the most hideous degradation it was possible to conceive – to send me off, a lost soul, a beast, to the rest of (the) Comus rout.'

Comus, in the masque of that name by Milton, is a powerful sorcerer who rules a labyrinthine forest. He's the son of the enchantress Circe, who in Greek myth was the daughter of the Sun and lived on the island of Aeaea. Odysseus landed there during his wanderings, and Circe transformed his crew into pigs. She has a whole menagerie of other kinds of animals – wolves, lions – that were also once men. Her island is an island of transformation: man to beast (and then to man again, once Odysseus gets the upper hand).

As for Comus, he leads a band of creatures, once men, who have drunk from his enchanted cup and have turned into hybrid monsters – they retain their human bodies, but their heads are those of beasts of all kinds. Thus changed, they indulge in sensual revels. Christina Rossetti's *Goblin Market,* with its animal-form goblins who tempt chastity and use luscious edibles as bait is surely a late offshoot of Comus.

As befits an enchanted island, Moreau's island is both semi-alive and female, but not in a pleasant way. It's volcanic, and emits from time to time a sulphurous reek. It comes equipped with flowers, and also with clefts and ravines, fronded on either side. Moreau's beast-men live in one of these, and since they do not have very good table manners it has rotting food in it and it smells bad. When the beast-men start to lose their humanity and revert to their beast-natures, this locale becomes the site of a moral breakdown that is specifically sexual.

What is it that leads us to believe that Prendick will never have a girlfriend?

6. THE UNHOLY TRINITY

Nor will Doctor Moreau. There is no Mrs Moreau on the island. There are no female human beings at all.

Similarly, the God of the Old Testament has no wife. Wells called *The Island of Doctor Moreau* 'a youthful piece of blasphemy', and it's obvious that he intended Moreau – that strong solitary gentleman with the white hair and beard – to resemble traditional paintings of God. He surrounds Moreau with semi-biblical language, as well: Moreau is the lawgiver of the island; those of his creatures who go against his will are punished and tortured; he is a god of whim and pain. But he isn't a real god, because he cannot really create; he can only imitate, and his imitations are poor.

What drives him on? His sin is the sin of pride, combined with a cold 'intellectual passion'. He wants to know everything. He wishes to discover the secrets of life. His ambition is to be as God the Creator. As such, he follows in the wake of several other aspirants, including Doctor Frankenstein and Hawthorne's various alchemists. Doctor Faustus hovers in the background, but he wanted youth and wealth and sex in return for his soul, and Moreau has no interest in such things: he despises what he calls 'materialism', which includes pleasure and pain. He dabbles in bodies, but wishes to detach himself from his own. (He has some literary brothers: Sherlock Holmes would understand his bloodless intellectual passion. So would Oscar Wilde's Lord Henry Wooton, of that earlier *fin de siècle* transformation novel, *The Picture of Dorian Gray*.)

But in Christianity, God is a trinity, and on Moreau's island there are three beings whose names begin with M. *Moreau* as a name combines the syllable 'mor' – from *mors, mortis*, no doubt – with the French for 'water', suitable in one who aims at exploring the limits of plasticity. The whole word means 'moor' in French. So the very white Moreau is also the Black Man of witchcraft tales, a sort of anti-God.

Montgomery, his alcoholic assistant, has the face of a sheep. He acts as the intercessor between the beast-folk and Moreau, and in this function stands in for Christ the Son. He's first seen offering Prendick a red drink that tastes like blood, and some boiled mutton. Is there a hint of an ironic Communion Service here – blood drink, flesh of the Lamb? The communion Prendick enters into by drinking the red drink is the communion of carnivores, that human communion forbidden to the beast-folk. But it's a communion he was part of anyway.

The third person of the Trinity is the Holy Spirit, usually portrayed as a dove – God in living but non-human form. The third M-creature on the island is M'Ling, the beast creature who serves as Montgomery's attendant. He too enters into the communion of blood: he licks his fingers while preparing a rabbit for the human beings to eat. The Holy Spirit as a deformed and idiotic man-animal? As a piece of youthful blasphemy, *The Island of Doctor Moreau* was even more blasphemous than most commentators have realized.

Just so we don't miss it, Wells puts a serpent-beast into his dubious garden: a creature that was completely evil and very strong, and that bent a gun-barrel into the letter S. Can Satan, too, be created by man? If so, blasphemous indeed.

7. THE NEW WOMAN AS CATWOMAN

There are no female human beings on Moreau's island, but Moreau is busily making one. The experiment on which he's engaged for most of the book concerns his attempt to turn a female puma into the semblance of a woman.

Wells was more than interested in members of the cat family, as Brian Aldiss has pointed out. During his affair with Rebecca West, she was 'Panther', he was 'Jaguar'. But 'cat' has another connotation: in slang, it meant 'prostitute'. This is Montgomery's allusion when he says – while the puma is yelling under the knife – 'I'm damned . . . if this place is not as bad as Gower Steet – with its cats.' Prendick himself makes the connection explicit on his return to London when he shies away from the 'prowling women (who) would mew after me'.

'I have some hope of her head and brain,' says Moreau of the puma. '. . . I will make a rational creature of my own.' But the puma resists. She's almost a woman – she weeps like one – but when Moreau begins torturing her again, she utters a 'shriek almost like that of an angry virago'. Then she tears her fetter out of the wall and runs away, a great bleeding scarred suffering female monster. It is she who kills Moreau.

Like many men of his time, Wells was obsessed with the New Woman. On the surface of it he was all in favour of sexual emancipation, including free love, but the freeing of Woman evidently had its frightening aspects. Rider Haggard's *She* can be seen as a reaction to the feminist movement of his day – if women are granted power, men are doomed – and so can Wells's deformed puma. Once the powerful monstrous sexual cat tears her fetter out of the wall and gets loose, minus the improved brain she ought to have courtesy of Man the Scientist, look out.

8. THE WHITENESS OF MOREAU, THE BLACKNESS OF M'LING

Wells was not the only nineteenth-century English writer who used furry creatures to act out English socio-dramas. Lewis Carroll had done it in a whimsical way in the *Alice* books, Kipling in a more militaristic fashion in *The Jungle Books*.

Kipling made the Law sound kind of noble, in *The Jungle Books*. Not so Wells. The Law mumbled by the animal-men in Moreau is a horrible parody of Christian and Jewish liturgy; it vanishes completely when the language of the beasts dissolves, indicating that it was a product of language, not some eternal God-given creed.

Wells was writing at a time when the British Empire still held sway, but the cracks were already beginning to show. Moreau's island is a little colonial enclave of the most hellish sort. It's no accident that most (although not all) of the beast-folk are black or brown, that they are at first thought by Prendick to be 'savages' or 'natives', and they speak in a kind of mangled English. They are employed as servants and slaves – a regime that's kept in place with whip and gun – they secretly hate the real 'men' as much as they fear them, and they disobey the Law as much as possible, and kick over the traces as soon as they can. They kill Moreau and they kill Montgomery and they kill M'Ling, and, unless Prendick can get away, they will kill him too, although at first he 'goes native' and lives among them, and does things that fill him with disgust, and that he would rather not mention.

White man's burden, indeed.

9. THE MODERN ANCIENT MARINER

The way in which Prendick escapes from the island is noteworthy. He sees a small boat with a sail, and lights a fire to hail it. It approaches, but strangely: it doesn't sail with the wind, but yaws and veers. There are two figures in it, one with red hair. As the boat enters the bay, 'Suddenly a great white bird flew up out of the boat, and neither of the men stirred nor noticed it. It circled round, and then came sweeping overhead with its strong wings outspread.' This bird cannot be a gull: it's too big and solitary. The only white seabird usually described as 'great' is the albatross.

The two figures in the boat are dead. But it is this death-boat, this life-in-death coffin-boat, that proves the salvation of Prendick.

In what other work of English literature do we find a lone man reduced to a pitiable state, a boat that sails without a wind, two death-figures, one with unusual hair, and a great white bird? The work is of course *The Ancient Mariner*, which revolves around man's proper relation to Nature, and concludes that this proper relation is one of love. It is when he manages to bless the sea-serpents that the Mariner is freed from the curse he has brought upon himself by shooting the albatross.

The Island of Doctor Moreau also revolves around man's proper relation to Nature, but its conclusions are quite different, because Nature itself is seen differently. It is no longer the Nature eulogized by Wordsworth, that benevolent motherly entity who never did betray the heart that loved her, for between Coleridge and Wells came Darwin.

The lesson learned by the albatross-shooting Mariner is summed up by him at the end of the poem:

> He prayeth well, who loveth well
> Both man and bird and beast.
>
> He prayeth best, who loveth best
> All things both great and small;
> For the dear God who loveth us,
> He made and loveth all.

In the Ancient-Mariner-like pattern at the end of *The Island of Doctor Moreau*, the 'albatross' is still alive. It has suffered no harm at the hands of Prendick. But he lives in the shadow of a curse anyway. His curse is that he can't love or bless anything living: not bird, not beast, and most certainly not man. He has another curse, too: the Ancient Mariner is doomed to tell his tale, and those who are chosen to hear it are convinced by it. But Prendick chooses not to tell, because, when he tries, no one will believe him.

10. FEAR AND TREMBLING

What then is the lesson learned by the unfortunate Prendick? It can perhaps best be understood in reference to *The Ancient Mariner*. The God of Moreau's island can scarcely be described as a dear God, who makes and loves all creatures. If Moreau is seen to stand for a version of God the Creator who 'makes' living things, he has done – in Prendick's final view – a very bad job. Similarly, if God can be considered as a sort of Moreau, and if the equation 'Moreau is to his animals as God is to man' may stand, then God himself is accused of cruelty and indifference – making man for fun and to satisfy his own curiosity and pride, laying laws on him he cannot understand or obey, then abandoning him to a life of torment.

Prendick cannot love the distorted and violent furry folk on the island, and it's just as hard for him to love the human beings he encounters on his return to 'civilization'. Like Swift's Gulliver, he can barely stand the sight of his fellow-men. He lives in a state of queasy fear, inspired by his continued experience of dissolving boundaries: as the beasts on the island have at times appeared human, the human beings he encounters in England appear bestial. He displays his modernity by going to a 'mental specialist', but this provides only a partial remedy. He feels himself to be 'an animal tormented . . . sent to wander alone . . .'

Prendick forsakes his earlier dabblings in biology, and turns instead to chemistry and astronomy. He finds 'hope' – 'a sense of infinite peace and protection' in 'the glittering hosts of heaven'. As if to squash even this faint hope, Wells almost immediately wrote *The War of the Worlds*, in which not peace and protection, but malice and destruction, come down from the heavens in the form of the monstrous but superior Martians.

The War of the Worlds can be read as a further gloss on Darwin. Is this where evolution will lead – to the abandonment of the body, to giant sexless bloodsucking heads with huge brains and tentacle-like fingers? But it can also be read as a thoroughly chilling coda to *The Island of Doctor Moreau*.

NOTES
1. Borges, *Other Inquisitions*, p. 87.
2. Ibid.
3. *War of the Worlds*, p. 117.
4. *Voyages in Time*
5. The 'brass brassière' is from an oral history of science fiction prepared by Richard Wolinsky for Berkeley's KPFA-FM.

Bibliography

PART ONE: 1970–1989

1. Travels Back. *Maclean's*, Vol. 86 (January 1973), pp. 28, 31, 48.
2. Review of *Diving into the Wreck*. Review of *Poems 1971–1972* by Adrienne Rich. *New York Times Book Review*, 30 December 1973, pp. 1–2. © 1973 by The New York Times Company.
3. Review of *Anne Sexton: A Self-Portrait in Letters*, eds. Linda Gray Sexton and Lois Ames. *New York Times Book Review*, 6 November 1977, p. 15. © 1977 by The New York Times Company.
4. The Curse of Eve – Or, What I Learned in School. From *Women on Women*, ed. Ann B. Shteir. (Toronto: York University, Gerstein Lecture Series, 1978), pp. 13–26.
5. Northrop Frye Observed. From *Second Words: Selected Critical Prose 1960–1982* by Margaret Atwood. (Toronto: Anansi, 1982), pp. 398–406.
6. Writing the Male Character. A somewhat different version of this paper was delivered as a Hagey Lecture at Waterloo University, February 1982. This version printed in *This Magazine*, Vol. 16, No. 4 (September 1982), pp. 4–10.
7. Wondering What It's Like to be a Woman. Review of *The Witches of Eastwick* by John Updike. *New York Times Book Review*, 13 May 1984, pp. 1, 40.
8. Introduction to *Roughing It in the Bush, Or, Life in Canada* by Susanna Moodie. (London: Virago, 1986), pp. vii–xiv.
9. Haunted by Their Nightmares. Review of *Beloved* by Toni Morrison. *New York Times Book Review*, 13 September 1987, pp. 1, 49–50.
10. Writing Utopia. Unpublished speech, 1989.
11. Great Aunts. From *Family Portraits: Remembrances by Twenty Distinguished Writers*, ed. Carolyn Anthony. (New York: Doubleday, 1989).

12. Introduction: Reading Blind. Introduction to *The Best American Short Stories, 1989*, eds. Margaret Atwood and Shannon Ravenel. (New York: Houghton, 1989), pp. xi–xxiii.

13. The Public Woman as Honorary Man. Review of *The Warrior Queens* by Antonia Fraser. *Los Angeles Times Book Review*, 2 April 1989, p. 3.

PART TWO: 1990–1999

14. A Double-Bladed Knife: Subversive Laughter in Two Stories by Thomas King. From *Native Writers and Canadian Writing*, ed. W. H. New. (Vancouver: UBC Press, 1990), pp. 243–250.

15. Nine Beginnings. From *The Writer on Her Work, Volume 1*, ed. Janet Sternburg. (New York: Norton, 1990, 2000), pp. 150–56.

16. A Slave to His Own Liberation. Review of *The General in His Labyrinth* by Gabriel García Márquez. *New York Times Book Review*, 16 September 1990, pp. 1, 30.

17. Angela Carter: 1940–1992.

18. Afterword to *Anne of Green Gables* by Lucy Maud Montgomery. (Toronto: M&S, 1992), pp. 331–336.

19. Introduction: *The Early Years*. Introduction to *The Poetry of Gwendolyn MacEwen: The Early Years*, eds. Margaret Atwood and Barry Callaghan. (Toronto: Exile Editions, 1993), pp. vii–xii.

20. Spotty-Handed Villainesses: Problems of Female Bad Behaviour in the Creation of Literature. An address delivered in the Cheltenham Lecture Series, University of Gloucester, 8 October 1993.

21. The Grunge Look. *Writing Away: The PEN Canada Travel Anthology*, ed. Constance Rooke. (Toronto: M&S, 1994), pp. 1–11.

22. Not So Grimm: The Staying Power of Fairy Tales. Review of *From the Beast to the Blonde: On Fairy Tales and Their Tellers* by Marina Warner. *Los Angeles Times Book Review*, 29 October 1995, p. 1.

23. 'Little Chappies With Breasts'. Review of *An Experiment in Love* by Hilary Mantel. *New York Times Book Review*, 2 June 1996, p. 11.

24. In Search of *Alias Grace*: On Writing Canadian Historical Fiction. An address given at Bronfman Lecture Series (Ottawa: November 1996), Smithsonian Institute (Washington: 11 December 1996), Chicago Library Foundations (6 January 1997), Oberlin College Friends of the Library (8 February 1997), City Arts & Lectures (San Francisco: 5 March 1997). Reprinted in *American Historical Review*, Vol. 103, No. 5 (December 1998), p. 1503 (1).

25. Why I Love *Night of the Hunter*. Review of *The Night of the Hunter*, dir. Charles Laughton (1955). *Guardian*, 19 March 1999, p. 12.

PART THREE: 2000–2005

26. Pinteresque. *The Pinter Review*, Fall 2000.
27. Mordecai Richler: 1931–2001: Diogenes of Montreal. *Globe and Mail*, 4 July 2001, pp. R1, R7.
28. When Afghanistan Was at Peace. *New York Times Magazine*, 28 October 2001, p. 82.
29. Introduction to *She* by H. Rider Haggard. (New York: Random House, 2002), pp. xii–xxiv.
30. Introduction to *Doctor Glas* by Hjalmar Söderberg, trans. Paul Britten Austin. (New York: Anchor, 2002), pp. 5–10.
31. Mystery Man. Review of *The Selected Letters of Dashiell Hammett, 1921–1960*, eds. Richard Layman and Julie Rivett; *Dashiell Hammett: A Daughter Remembers* by Jo Hammett; and *Dashiell Hammett: Crime Stories & Other Writings*, ed. Steven Marcus. *New York Review of Books*, Vol. 49, No. 2 (14 February 2002), pp. 19–21.
32. Of Myths and Men. Review of *Atanarjuat: The Fast Runner*, dir. Zacharias Kunuk (2001). *Globe and Mail*, 13 April 2002, p. R10.
33. Cops and Robbers. Review of *Tishomingo Blues* by Elmore Leonard. *New York Review of Books*, Vol. 49, No. 9 (23 May 2002), pp. 21–23.
34. The Indelible Woman. *Guardian*, 7 September 2002.
35. The Queen of Quinkdom. Review of *The Birthday of the World and Other Stories* by Ursula K. Le Guin. *New York Review of Books*, Vol. 49, No. 14 (26 September 2002).
36. Victory Gardens. Foreword to *A Breath of Fresh Air: Celebrating Nature and School Gardens* by Elise Houghton. (Toronto: Sumach Press, 2003), pp. 13–19.
37. Mortification. From *Mortifications: Writers' Stories of Their Public Shame*, ed. Robin Robertson. (London: Fourth Estate, 2003), pp. 1–4.
38. Writing *Oryx and Crake*. Book of the Month Club/Bookspan (January 2003).
39. Letter to America. *The Nation*, 14 April 2003, pp. 22–23.
40. Edinburgh and Its Festival. *Edinburgh Festival Magazine*, May 2003.
41. George Orwell: Some Personal Connections. An address broadcast on the BBC Radio 3 on 13 June 2003. Reprinted as 'Orwell and Me', *Guardian*, 16 June 2003.

42. Carol Shields, Who Died Last Week, Wrote Books That Were Full of Delights. From 'Lives & Letters: Carol Shields'. *Guardian*, 26 July 2003, p. 28.

43. He Springs Eternal. Review of *Hope Dies Last: Keeping the Faith in Difficult Times* by Studs Terkel. *New York Review of Books*, 6 November 2003, pp. 78–80.

44. To Beechey Island. From *Solo: Writers on Pilgrimage*, ed. Katherine Govier. (Toronto: M&S, 2004), pp. 201–16.

45. Uncovered: an American *Iliad*. Review of *A Story as Sharp as a Knife: The Classical Haida Mythtellers and Their World* by Robert Bringhurst. *The Times Weekend Review*, 28 February 2004, pp. 10–11.

46. Headscarves to Die For. Review of *Snow* by Orhan Pamuk, trans. Maureen Freely. *New York Times Book Review*, 15 August 2004, pp. 1, 8–9.

47. Ten Ways of Looking at *The Island of Doctor Moreau*. Introduction to *The Island of Doctor Moreau* (London: Penguin, 2005).

Acknowledgements

My thanks to all who have contributed to this book. To Lennie Goodings of Virago, who did the pestering; to Vivienne Schuster, Diana McKay, and Phoebe Larmore, my agents; to Adrienne Leahey, for helping to pull the book together; to Jen Osti, my assistant, and to Surya Bhattacharya, who helped to track things down; and to Coleen Quinn, who kept me in working order. There are many, many newspaper and magazine editors with whom I've worked over the years: thank you to all.

And to Graeme Gibson, who has so often and so wisely said, 'I wouldn't write that if I were you'; and to Jess Gibson, constant reader, who is sometimes able to correct my slang.

Lastly, to the four Irish women on the train from Galway to Dublin, overheard by me while discussing my books. 'The last ones have been rather long,' they said. Right after this I became violently ill and spent the rest of the trip locked in the washroom — some of us are sensitive to criticism, or maybe it was the injudicious carrot juice — but I would like these commentators to know that I took their comments to heart. Some of the pieces in this book are quite short. So I've tried.

Index

Achebe, Chinua
    Anthills of the Savannah, 111
Adventure Canada, 360
Afghanistan, 4, 245–7
Agee, James, 232
agriculture, 311
Alias Grace (Atwood), 130, 223–8
Alphabet (magazine), 168
American Revolution, 73, 222
Ancient Mariner, The, 394, 395
Anderson, Marjorie, 343
Anderson, Sherwood, 269–70
Anderson-Dargatz, Gail
    The Cure for Death by Lightning, 220
Animal Farm (Orwell), 333–6, 338
Anne of Green Gables (Montgomery),
    159–64
Anne Sexton - A Self-Portrait in Letters,
    19–21
Anthology (radio programme), 167
Atanarjuat: The Fast Runner (film), 277–80
Atwood, Margaret
    ambition to become a writer, 37,
        104
    aunts of, 95–107
    birth, 210
    childhood and upbringing, 49, 71,
        98, 102

    first writers' conference attended,
        95, 96–8
    grandparents, 10, 99–100, 102, 105
    mortifications, 317–20
    mother of, 95, 99, 100–1
    poetry readings, 9–11
    schooling, 8–9, 37–8
    trip to Afghanistan (1978), 245–7
    trip to England and France (1964),
        187–96
    at Victoria College, 23, 38
Aunt J., 95–8, 99, 100, 101, 103, 104–5,
    106
Aunt K., 99, 100, 101, 102, 104–5, 106
'Aunt Moon's Young Man' (Hogan),
    120
Aunt Winnie, 101–2
Austen, Jane, 26, 32
    Pride and Prejudice, 174
autobiography, 211
Avison, Margaret, 166

Beauty and the Beast, 199
Beckett, Samuel
    Krapp's Last Tape, 213–14
Becky Sharpe character, 185
Beecher Stowe, Harriet, 33
Beechey Island, 360, 366–7

Bellamy, Edward
  Looking Backward, 87, 299
  Beloved (Morrison), 79–84, 183
Benjamin, Walter, 301
Berlin Wall
  fall of (1989), 4–5, 6
Berton, Pierre, 58–9
Bettelheim, Bruno
  The Uses of Enchantment, 198
Bible, 87
Billings, Miss, 37–8
Birney, Earle, 217
Birthday of the World, The (Le Guin), 297–308
bissett, bill, 167
'Black Hand Girl, The' (Boyd), 120
Blais, Marie-Claire, 166
Blind Assassin, The (Atwood), 237, 238
Boadicea, 123–4
Bodily Harm (Atwood), 58, 59
Bolívar, Simón, 151–4
book reviews
  Anne Sexton – A Self-Portrait in Letters, 19–21
  Beloved (Morrison), 79–84
  The Birthday of the World (Le Guin), 297–308
  Dashiell Hammett books, 263–74
  Diving into the Wreck (Rich), 15–18
  An Experiment in Love (Mantel), 203–7
  From the Beast to the Blonde (Warner), 197–201
  The General in His Labyrinth (Márquez), 151–4
  Hope Dies Last (Terkel), 345–57
  Snow (Pamuk), 377–81
  A Story as Sharp as a Knife (Bringhurst), 369–75
  Tishomingo Blues (Leonard), 281–91
  The Warrior Queens (Fraser), 123–5
  The Witches of Eastwick (Updike), 65–70
Borges, Jorge Luis, 383
Bowering, George
  Burning Waters, 219
'Boy on the Train, The' (Robinson), 119
Boyd, Blanche McCrary
  'The Black Hand Girl', 120
Bradbury, Ray, 299–300
Bradstreet, Ann, 77
Brave New World (Huxley), 87, 88, 335, 338, 339
Breath of Fresh Air:
  Celebrating Nature and School Gardens
  Foreword to, 309–16
Bringhurst, Robert
  A Story as Sharp as a Knife, 369–75
Britain
  emigration to Canada, 73–4
Brontë, Charlotte, 32, 192
Brontë, Emily, 32, 111, 192
Brooke, Dorothea, 26
Brown, Larry
  'Kubuku Rides (This Is It)', 119–20
Browning, Elizabeth Barrett, 32
Buckler, Ernest, 103–5
  The Mountain and the Valley, 103–4
Bunyan, John
  Pilgrim's Progress, 362
Butler, Samuel
  Erewhon, 87, 299
Byron, Lord
  Childe Harold's Pilgrimage, 362

Calasso, Roberto, 129
Camus, 293
Canada, 12
  emigration from Britain to, 73–4
  preponderance of women writers in, 78

Canada House, 188, 189
Canadian Authors' Association, 96–7
Canadian Forum, The, 43, 165
Canadian historical fiction writing, 209–29
Canadian literature, 40–1, 42–3, 77–8, 216
Canadian poets, 166–7, 168
Capek, Karel, 299
Carroll, Lewis, 393
Carter, Angela, 155–7
Catherine the Great, 124, 125
Cat's Eye (Atwood), 5, 6
Chandler, Raymond, 264, 270
    The Simple Art of Murder, 114
characters, fictional 209–10
    see also female characters; male characters
Chaucer, Geoffrey122, 361
Cohen, Leonard, 166, 374
    Let Us Compare Mythologies, 168
Coleridge, Samuel, 40
'Concert Party, The' (Gallant), 120–1
Conrad, Joseph
    Heart of Darkness, 255
Cooper, Fennimore, 269
Corey, Giles, 274
Crystal Age, A (Hudson), 87, 88, 305
Cunningham, Alison, 191, 192–4
Cunningham, Michael
    'White Angel', 117

Dali, Salvador
    The Persistence of Memory, 213
Darkness at Noon (Koestler), 89, 335
Darwin, Charles, 388, 396
    Dashiell Hammett: A Daughter Remembers (Jo Hammett), 265
Dashiell Hammett: Crime Stories & Other Writings, 265, 268–9, 270–1
Davies, Robertson, 210

Murther and Walking Spirits, 219
Defoe, Daniel, 53
Delilah, 184
DeMarinis, Rick
    'The Flowers of Boredom', 117–18
detective stories, 177
Devon Island, 366
Dickens, Charles, 30, 53, 55
Dickinson, Emily, 7, 32, 40, 174, 325, 351
dictatorships, 91–2
'Disneyland' (Gowdy), 118
'Displacement' (Louie), 120
Diviners, The (Laurence), 33, 219
Diving into the Wreck (Rich), 15–18
Doctor Glas (Söderberg), 257–61
Doerr, Harriet
    'Eddie: A Life', 119
Dolan, Josephine, 268
Don Giovanni, 30
Dreyer, Benjamin, 238
Durr, Clifford, 348
Durr, Virginia, 348
Dystopia, 86–9

'Eddie: A Life' (Doerr), 119
Edel, Leon, 213
Edible Woman, The (Atwood), 3, 318
Edinburgh, 4, 329–32
Edinburgh Festival, 311, 312
editors, 239
Eliot, George, 26, 32, 111
    Middlemarch, 57, 58
Eliot, T.S., 78, 95
Elizabeth I, Queen, 124, 125
Engel, Marian
    Bear, 219
    The Honeymoon Festival, 25–6
England
    trip to (1964), 188–91
Erewhon (Butler), 87, 299
Experiment in Love, An (Mantel), 203–7

Fabre, Henri, 50
fairy tales, 113, 181–2, 197–201
Farmers' Rebellion, The (play), 219
Faulkner, William, 53, 111,
270, 293
female characters, 25–6, 27–31, 34–5
bad behaviour of, 171–6
and heroes, 29–30
list of stereotypes, 27–8
supernatural aura given to
powerful women, 30
Fiedler, Leslie
Love and Death in the American Novel, 53
film reviews
Atanarjuat: The Fast Runner, 277–80
The Night of the Hunter, 231–4
Findley, Timothy
The Piano Man's Daughter, 220
The Wars, 219
You Went Away, 220
'Flowers of Boredom, The'
(DeMarinis), 117–18
food, 309–12
during Second World War, 309–11
forgetting, 213–14
Fowles, John
A Maggot, 152
France
trip to, 192–4
Franklin Expedition (1847), 218, 360, 363,
365, 366–7, 368
Franklin, Lady Jane, 365
Fraser, Antonia
The Warrior Queens, 123–5
From the Beast to the Blonde (Warner),
197–201
Frye, Northrop, 37–45, 374
Anatomy of Criticism, 38, 168
influence of, 39, 40
The Secular Scripture, 254, 389
teaching style, 38

Fuentes, Carlos, 154

Galbraith, John Kenneth, 344, 354
Gallant, Mavis
'The Concert Party', 120–1
gardens, 312–13, 314–15
during Second World War, 309–10
and schools, 316
Gaskell, Mrs, 33
Geiger, John
Frozen in Time, 367
General in His Labyrinth, The (Márquez),
151–4
Ghandl, 370, 371, 372
Gibson, Graeme, 4, 245, 329–30
Perpetual Motion, 219, 220
Gide, André, 174
Gilbert, Sandra and Gubar, Susan
No Man's Land, 253, 255
Gilman, Charlotte Perkins *Herland*, 87,
305
Gish, Lillian, 232
Glover, Douglas
'Why I Decide to Kill Myself and
Other Jokes', 120
Golding, William
Lord of the Flies, 389
Gone with the Wind, 58
Good Bones (Atwood), 130
'good man/woman', 61
Govier, Katherine
Angel Walk, 220
Gowdy, Barbara
'Disneyland', 118
Graves, Robert
The White Goddess, 31–2, 40
Greene, Graham, 281
The Lawless Roads, 118
The Ministry of Fear, 213
Greenland, 360
Gregory, Philip, 321

Grendel/Grendel's mother, 27, 30
Grimm's Fairy Tales, 181–2
Grosev, Kouncho, 351
Grossman, Edith, 152
Grubb, Davis, 232
The Night of the Hunter, 232, 283

Haggard, Rider
    She, 27, 238, 249–56, 386, 393
Haida, 370, 372
Hamlet, 55
Hammett, Dashiell, 263–74
Hammett, Jo, 263, 265–6, 267, 273
Handmaid's Tale, The (Atwood), 5–6, 247,
        337, 338
    writing of, 85–94
Hardy, Thomas
    Tess of the D'Urbervilles, 55, 183
Hartley, L.P
    The Go-Between, 220
Harvard Graduate School, 90
Hawthorne, Nathaniel
    The Scarlet Letter, 184, 222–3
Heart of Darkness (Conrad), 56, 255
Hébert, Anne
    Kamouraska, 219
Hellman, Lillian, 264, 265, 266, 267, 268,
        274
Hemingway, Ernest, 270, 293
Herland (Gilman), 87, 305
heroes, 29–30
Hiassen, Carl, 270
Highway 17, 7, 8
Hilton, James, 255
Hine, Daryl, 166
Hinton, Charles Howard, 387
historical fiction
    writing Canadian, 209–29
history, 211, 212, 225
Hoban, Russell
    Riddley Walker, 299

Hogan, Linda
    'Aunt Moon's Young Man', 120
Honeymoon Festival, The (Engel), 25–6
Hope Dies Last (Terkel), 345–57
horticulture, 311
House of Anansi Press, 3
Hudson, W.H.
    A Crystal Age, 87, 88, 305
Hutchinson, Anne, 65
Huxley, Aldous
    Brave New World, 87, 88, 335, 338, 339
    Point Counter Point, 185–6

Il Postino (film), 229
Iliad (Homer), 372
Innuksuk, Pakak, 280
Island of Doctor Moreau (Wells), 283–96

Jackson, Mahalia, 347
James, Henry
    Portrait of a Lady, 55
    The Turn of the Screw, 177
Jameson, Anna
    *Winter Studies and Summer Rambles in
        Canada*, 77
Jezebel character, 183
'Joe the Painter and the
        Deer Island Massacre' (King), 133–6
Johnson, Pauline, 131
Jonas, George, 224
Jones, Doug, 219
Jong, Erica
    Fear of Flying, 30
Journals of Susanna Moodie, The (Atwood),
        72, 218, 223
Joyce, James, 111
Judith, 184

Kafka, Franz, 351
Kane, Sean, 374
Keats, John, 175, 344

Kelly, Kathy, 352, 355
King, Mackenzie, 218
King, Thomas, 133–41
   'Joe the Painter and the Deer Island
      Massacre' (King), 133–6, 140–1
   'One Good Story, That One'
      (King), 136–41
Kipling, Rudyard, 253
   The Jungle Books, 393
Klein, A.M., 43
Koestler, Arthur
   Darkness at Noon, 89, 335
Kroetsch, Robert
   The Studhorse Man, 30
'Kubuku Rides (This Is It) (Brown),
   119–20
Kucinich, Dennis, 357
Kundera, Milan
   The Book of Laughter and Forgetting, 214

Lady MacBeth character, 183
Langton, Anne
   Gentlewoman in Upper Canada, 77
Lappé, Frances Moore, 355–6
Laughton, Charles, 231–2
Laurence, Margaret
   The Diviners, 33, 219
   The Stone Angel, 209
Lawrence, D.H.
   'The Virgin and the Gypsy', 29
Layman, Richard, 263, 265
Le Carré, John, 282
Le Guin, Ursula K.
   The Birthday of the World, 297–308
   The Left Hand of Darkness, 301, 303–4
Leacock, Stephen, 216
Leaside High School, 37
LeFanu, Sheridan
   Carmilla, 254
Left Hand of Darkness, The (Le Guin), 301,
   303–4

Leonard, Elmore, 270
   Tishomingo Blues, 281–91
Lethem, Jonathan
   Motherless Brooklyn, 270
'Letter to America', 239, 325–8
'Letter Writer, The' (Sharif), 119
Lewis, C.S., 255, 298
Lewis, Sinclair, 325
Life Before Man (Atwood), 56
Life in the Clearings (Moodie), 72, 73,
   223–4, 226
literary critics, 175, 176
Lochhead, Liz, 330
Longfellow, Henry
   Giles Corey of the Salem Farms, 274
Looking Backward (Bellamy), 87, 299
Lord of the Rings, The (Tolkein), 255
Louie, David Wong
   'Displacement', 120
Lowther, Pat, 342

Macbeth, 29, 55, 183
Macbeth (character), 29
Macdonald, Anne Marie
   Fall on Your Knees, 220
MacDonald, George
   Curdie fantasies, 252
Macdonald, Wilson, 97
MacEwen, Gwendolyn, 165–9, 367
   Terror and Erebus, 218, 363, 365–6, 368
McGoogan, Ken
   Fatal Passage, 365
McGrath, Mollie, 355
Mackenzie, William Lyon, 211, 226
MacLeod, Alistair, 323
McLuhan, Marshall, 168, 176
   The Gutenberg Galaxy, 374
Macphail, Agues, 35
Macpherson, Jay, 166–7
Madame Bovary, 184
Maggot, A (Fowles), 152

male characters, writing of, 47–63
'Management of Grief, The' (Mukherjee), 120
Manguel, Alberto, 298
Mantel, Hilary
  An Experiment in Love, 203–7
Marcus, Steven, 263
Marias, Javier
  All Souls, 214
Marks, Grace, 223–8
Marlatt, Daphne
  Ana Historic, 219
Marlowe, Philip, 270
Márquez, Gabriel García
  The General in His Labyrinth, 151–4
Martin, Valerie
  Property, 343
Marxism, 87
Medea, 183
Melville, Herman
  Moby Dick, 52, 55–6
memory, 212, 213
'Meneseteung' (Munro), 121, 219
Meredith, George, 55, 323
Merriman, Dierdre, 354
metonymy, 44, 47
Michaels, Anne
  Fugitive Pieces, 220
Middlemarch (Eliot), 57, 58
Miller, Arthur, 325
  The Crucible, 274
Miller, Perry, 90
Millett, Kate
  Sexual Politics, 53
Mitchum, Robert, 232
Moby Dick (Melville), 52, 55–6
Montgomery, Lucy Maud
  Anne of Green Gables, 159–64
Moodie, Susanna, 71–8
  emigration to Canada and settler's life in, 74–6

Life in the Clearings, 72, 73, 223–4, 226
Roughing It in the Bush, 71–2, 76–7, 78, 223
Moore, Brian
  Blackrobe, 219
More, Sir Thomas
  Utopia, 86, 87, 298
Morning in the Burned House (Atwood), 130
Morris, William, 253
  News From Nowhere, 87, 299
Morrison, Toni
  Beloved, 79–84, 183
  The Bluest Eye, 111
Mother Goose, 198–9
Mountain and the Valley, The (Buckler), 103–4
Mukherjee, Bharati
  'The Management of Grief', 120
Munro, Alice, 33, 341, 343
  'A Wilderness Station', 219
  'Meneseteung', 121, 219

Navasky, Victor, 239
Negotiating with the Dead (Atwood), 238
New York, 11
New York Review of Books, 239
Newby, Eric
  A Short Walk in the Hindu Kush, 76
Night and Fog (film), 214
Night of the Hunter, The (book), 232, 283
Night of the Hunter, The (film), 231–4
9/11, 238, 322, 339, 353–4
Nineteen Eighty-Four (Orwell), 87, 89, 214, 335–7, 339
North Bay, 10–11
Nova Scotia, 98, 102
novels, 50, 52, 174–6
  female bias of, 57
  function of, 24–5
  what they are not, 174–5

obituaries
  Angela Carter, 155–7
Odyssey (Homer), 372
Ondaatje, Michael, 167
  The English Patient, 219
  In the Skin of a Lion, 219, 220
'One Good Story, That One' (King),
    136–41
oral poetry, 371–2
Orange, Leroy, 354
Orwell, George, 57, 333–40
  Animal Farm, 333–6, 338
  Nineteen Eighty-Four, 87, 89, 214, 335–7,
    339
Oryx and Crake (Atwood), 238
  writing, 321–3
Ottawa, 210–11
*Oxford Book of Canadian
  Poetry in English*, 5

Page, P.K., 166
Paine, Tom, 349
Pamuk, Orhan
  My Name is Red, 377
  Snow, 377–81
Paris, 194
Pater, Walter, 253
Pérez-Reverte, 270
Phillips, Dale Ray
  'What Men Love For', 118
Piercey, Marge
  Woman on the Edge of Time, 87, 88, 305
pilgrims/pilgrimages, 361–2
Pinter, Harold, 6, 241–2
Plath, Sylvia, 21, 33, 169
Plato, 298
  Republic, 87
poetry
  and historic events, 218, 219
  oral, 371–2
Point Counter Point (Huxley), 185–6

population explosion, 315
Power Politics (Atwood), 3
Pratt, E.J., 43, 218
Pride and Prejudice (Austen), 174
Purdy, Al, 219
Puritans, 90
Pynchon, Thomas, *V*, 270

Quebec, 73, 78, 217

Rae, John, 365
Rasmusson, Wallace, 354
Ravenel, Shannon, 109–10
reading blind, 109–22
Reaney, James, 166, 168, 219
  'The Canadian Poet's
    Predicament', 131
Rebellion (1837), 211, 226
Red Shoes, The (film), 31
resources
  exhaustion of natural, 315
reviews *see* book reviews;
  film reviews
Rich, Adrienne
  Diving into the Wreck, 15–18
Richard, Mark
  'Strays', 118
Richardson, Major
  Wacousta, 215
Richardson, Samuel, 54–5
  Sir Charles Grandison, 55
Richardson, Tony, 3
Richler, Mordecai, 238, 243–4
Rivett, Julie M., 263, 265
Robber Bride, The (Atwood), 130
Robinson, Arthur
  'The Boy on the Train', 119
'role model', 25
'romance', 388–9
Rosenblatt, Joe, 167
Rossetti, Christina, 32

Goblin Market, 390

Rossetti, Dante Gabriel, 253

Roughing It in the Bush (Moodie), 71–2, 76–7, 78, 223

Rousseau, Jean-Jacques, 334

Rushdie, Salman, 6

Salutin, Rick

    The Farmers' Rebellion, 219

Sansom, William, 261

Scarlett Letter, The (Hawthorne), 184, 222–3

Schlorndorff, Volker, 6

school gardening movement, 316

science fiction, 297–300, 302, 387

Scott, F.R., 96–7

Scott, Robert, 367

Scott, Walter, 60

Scrooge, 215

sea's resources, 315

Second World War

    Victory Gardens and food during, 309–10

Seeger, Pete, 355

Selected Letters of Dashiell Hammett, 265–6, 267–8

September 11th *see* 9/11

Service, Robert

    'The Cremation of Dan McGrew', 130

Sexton, Anne, 33

    A Self-Portrait in Letters, 19–21

Shakespeare, William, 178

Sharif, M.T.

    'The Letter Writer', 119

She (Haggard), 27, 238, 249–56, 386, 393

Shearer, Moira, 31

Shelley, Mary

    Frankenstein, 298

Shields, Carol, 341–4

    Dropped Threads, 343

    The Stone Diaries, 219, 342, 343

Unless, 343

short stories, judging of, 109–22

Short Walk in the Hindu Kush, A (Newby), 76

Silverberg, Robert, 387

Silvers, Robert, 239

Sir Charles Grandison (Richardson), 55

Skaay, 370, 371, 372, 373

Snow (Pamuk), 377–81

'Snow White and the Seven Dwarfs', 181, 183

Söderberg, Hjalmar

    Doctor Glas, 257–61

Solitary Weeper, 28–9, 30

Spade, Sam, 270, 272

Stevenson, Robert Louis, 61

    Treasure Island, 386

Stoker, Bram

    Dracula, 177, 254

Stone Diaries, The (Shields), 219, 342, 343

Stonehenge, 196

story, voice of the, 111–14

Story as Sharp as a Knife, A (Bringhurst), 369–75

'Strays' (Richard), 118

Strickland, Samuel, 74

suicide, 21

Surfacing (Atwood), 3

Survival (Atwood), 3–4, 131–2

Swanton, John Reed, 370

Swift, Jonathan, 299, 387

    Gulliver's Travels, 87, 298

Swinburne, Algernon, 253

synecdoche, 44, 47

Tempest, The, 390

Tennyson, Alfred, 388

    The Idylls of the King, 252

Terkel, Studs

    Hope Dies Last, 345–57

Tess of the D'Urbervilles (Hardy), 55, 183

Thackeray, William
   Vanity Fair, 185
Thatcher, Margaret, 124, 125
Time Machine, The (Wells), 87, 384, 385
Times, The, 239
Tishomingo Blues (Leonard), 281–91
To the Lighthouse (Woolf), 293–5
Tolkein, J.R
   The Lord of the Rings, 255
Toronto, 40, 166
Traill, Catherine Parr, 74, 77, 219
   *The Young Emigrants: or, Pictures of
      Canada*, 74
Tulliver, Maggie, 26
Twain, Mark, 269
   Huckleberry Finn, 269

uncertainty principle, 115–17
Updike, John
   The Witches of Eastwick, 65–70
Urquhart, Jane
   Away, 219
   The Whirlpool, 219
Utopia (More), 86, 87, 298
Utopian writing, 86–94

vampire/werewolf stories, 177
Vanderhaeghe, Guy
   The Englishman's Boy, 220
Vanity Fair (Thackeray), 185
Verne, Jules, 298, 387
Victoria College (University of
   Toronto), 23, 38
Victory Gardens, 309–11, 313, 316
villains, 30
   and heroes, 29
voice of the story, 111–14
Vonnegut, Kurt
   Slaughterhouse Five, 299

Wagner, Erica, 239, 253

Walker, Alice
   The Color Purple, 82
War of the Worlds, The (Wells), 384, 385,
   387, 396
Warner, Marine, 197
   From the Beast to the Blonde, 197–201
Warrior Queens, The (Fraser), 123–5
Webb, Phyllis, 166
Webster, Mary, 90
Webster, Noah, 269
Wells, H.G., 299
   background, 385
   The Island of Doctor Moreau, 283–96
   The Time Machine, 87, 384, 385
   The War of the Worlds, 384, 386, 387,
      396
West, Dame Rebecca, 186
West, Nathanael, 270
Wharton, Edith
   The Custom of the Country, 185
'What Men Love For' (Phillips), 118
'White Angel' (Cunningham), 117
White Goddess, The (Graves), 31–2, 40
Whitman, Walt, 325, 349
'Why I Decide to Kill Myself and
   Other Jokes' (Glover), 120
Wiebe, Rudy, 220
   The Scorched Wood People, 219
   The Temptations of Big Bear, 219
Wilde, Oscar
   The Picture of Dorian Gray, 391
Wilderness Tips (Atwood), 129
Wilkinson, Anne, 166
Winters, Shelley, 232
Wiseman, Adele, 33
Wister, Owen, 269
witchcraft, 68–9
Witches of Eastwick, The (Updike), 65–70
Wizard of Oz, The, 68–9
Woman on the Edge of Time (Piercey), 87,
   88, 305

women writers, 26–7
  in Canada, 78
  lives of, 32–3
  obstacles to, 33, 144–5
women's movement, 178, 179, 317, 355
'women's novels', 58
Wonder Woman, 31, 351
Woolf, Virginia
  To the Lighthouse, 293–5
Wordsworth, William, 75, 253
writing, 143–9

Wuthering Heights, 60
Wyndham, John, 299, 305

Young, David, 367–8
Young Emigrants; or, Pictures of Canada
  (Traill), 74

Zamyatin, Yvgeny
  We, 338
Zola, Émile 52